WHY NOT JAIL?

Federal and state laws make it a crime for corporations and their employees to jeopardize workers, consumers, the public at large, or the environment by acting recklessly. When the Upper Big Branch mine collapsed, killing 29; the isom tower at the Texas City refinery exploded, killing 15; the *Deepwater Horizon* oil rig blew out, killing 11; peanut processors shipped nuts laced with salmonella, killing 9; and a small pharmacy shipped 17,000 vials of steroid medications contaminated by meningitis, killing 64, the responsible corporate officials acted recklessly, focused on profits not safety. To their credit, federal prosecutors have indicted a handful of corporations and mid-level managers in three of these cases, but it's too soon to have any confidence that these modest efforts will change years of neglect. This book, the first of its kind, analyzes these five catastrophes, uncovering their root causes that encompass crimes of commission and omission. Written in plain English, the book argues that far more aggressive prosecution is both appropriate and possible under the law, and as a matter of sound policy and achieving justice.

Rena Steinzor is a professor of law at the University of Maryland's Francis King Carey School of Law. She is the president of the Center for Progressive Reform (www.progressivereform.org), a think tank composed of sixty working academics from universities across the country that is a nationally recognized source of research and opinion on public health, worker and consumer safety, and the environment. Steinzor's publications include *Mother Earth and Uncle Sam: How Pollution and Hollow Government Hurt Our Kids* (2007); *The People's Agents and the Battle to Protect the American Public: Special Interests, Government, and Threats to Health, Safety, and the Environment* (with Sidney Shapiro, 2010); and *Rescuing Science from Politics: Regulation and the Distortion of Scientific Research* (coedited with Wendy Wagner, 2006.)

D0838744

Why Not Jail?

INDUSTRIAL CATASTROPHES, CORPORATE
MALFEASANCE, AND GOVERNMENT INACTION

RENA STEINZOR

University of Maryland, Francis King Carey School of Law

CAMBRIDGE
UNIVERSITY PRESS

CAMBRIDGE
UNIVERSITY PRESS

32 Avenue of the Americas, New York, NY 10013–2473, USA

Cambridge University Press is part of the University of Cambridge.

It furthers the University's mission by disseminating knowledge in the pursuit of education, learning, and research at the highest international levels of excellence.

www.cambridge.org
Information on this title: www.cambridge.org/9781107633940

First published 2015

Printed in the United States of America

A catalog record for this publication is available from the British Library.

Library of Congress Cataloging in Publication Data
Steinzor, Rena, author.
Why not jail? : industrial catastrophes, corporate malfeasance, and government inaction / Rena Steinzor.
    pages   cm
ISBN 978-1-107-05340-3 (hardback) – ISBN 978-1-107-63394-0
1. Commercial crimes – Law and legislation – United States.   2. Offenses against the environment – Law and legislation – United States.   3. Banking law – United States – Criminal provisions.   4. Punishment – United States – Philosophy.   I. Title.
KF9350.S74   2014
364.1′40973–dc23   2014026904

ISBN 978-1-107-05340-3 Hardback
ISBN 978-1-107-63394-0 Paperback

Contents

Acknowledgments

I am grateful to several friends and colleagues for encouraging me to write this book: Anne Havemann, Lisa Heinzerling, Shana Jones, Tom McGarity, Celeste Monforton, Michael Patoka, Sid Shapiro, Matt Shudtz, and Ronald Wright. Special thanks to Shana, Celeste, Michael, and Matt for providing insightful comments on the text although, as the tradition holds, I am solely responsible for any mistakes in this volume. I appreciated the opportunity to confer with John Paterson, Emre Usenme, and Greg Gordon, Scottish colleagues at the University of Aberdeen where I was fortunate enough to spend several weeks during the *Deepwater Horizon* spill in the Gulf of Mexico, comparing our approach to deepwater drilling with the one taken in the North Sea. I also thank Itzchak Kornfeld, a professor of law at the Hebrew University of Jerusalem, who is also a geologist and has worked in the oil fields offshore. His astute sense of how the industry really operates was invaluable to me.

I could not have completed the volume without the able assistance of the University of Maryland Carey School of Law library staff, especially Sue McCarty who edited all my footnotes, a lengthy and important process. Four generations of law students provided invaluable research assistance, including Brian Auchincloss, Joshua Dhyani, Kay Fallon, Christine Gentry, Fernando Guerra, Melissa Heitt, Laura Koman, Jessica Kyle, Jessica Laws, Mollie Rosenzweig, Gabriel Rubinstein, Ameet Sarpatwari, James Sheehan, and Allan Thorson.

The book is dedicated to the people, too numerous to name here, who died or were injured in the industrial catastrophes explained in Chapters 4, 5, and 6. May they not have died or suffered in vain.

Introduction

On April 5, 2010, an enormous explosion tore through Massey Energy's Upper Big Branch mine in Montcoal, West Virginia, propelling flames at a speed of one thousand feet per second in all directions from the point of ignition as far as two miles underground. Twenty-nine men were killed instantly in the worst mine disaster in four decades.[1] Numerous blatant and well-known violations of mine safety laws caused the explosion, from the chronic buildup of highly combustible methane to the malfunctioning equipment that produced the igniting spark.[2] In the weeks leading up to the accident, Mine Safety and Health Administration (MSHA) officials had ordered the evacuation of Upper Big Branch on three separate occasions because excessive methane made the mine too dangerous to work.[3] Despite these efforts to nudge Massey back into line with safety requirements, 13,000 citations for illegal conduct throughout the industry were pending before MSHA at the time, including several hundred involving the Upper Big Branch mine, because the agency was paralyzed by its own dysfunctional system for enforcing these requirements.[4]

To his great credit, Booth Goodwin, West Virginia's top federal prosecutor, filed criminal charges against four Massey employees, including three relatively low-level supervisors and the senior manager of the subsidiary responsible for

---

[1] Erik Reece, *The End of Illth: In Search of an Economy That Won't Kill Us*, HARPER'S MAG., Oct. 4, 2013, *available at* http://harpers.org/print/?pid=242893 (subscription required).

[2] MINE SAFETY & HEALTH ADMIN., U.S. DEP'T OF LABOR, REPORT OF INVESTIGATION – FATAL UNDERGROUND MINE EXPLOSION 2 (Dec. 6, 2011), *available at* http://www.msha.gov/Fatals/2010/UBB/FTL10c0331noappx.pdf.

[3] Ian Urbina & Michael Cooper, *Deaths at West Virginia Mine Raise Issues About Safety*, N.Y. TIMES, Apr. 6, 2010, http://www.nytimes.com/2010/04/07/us/07westvirginia.html?_r=0.

[4] Rawan Jabaji, *The Upper Big Branch Explosion: One Year Later*, THE DAILY NEED (Apr. 5, 2011), http://www.pbs.org/wnet/need-to-know/the-daily-need/the-upper-big-branch-explosion-one-year-later/8409/. ("[B]etween January 2009 and the April 2010 blast, Massey mines had been cited for almost 13,000 violations.")

the Upper Big Branch mine.[5] The senior manager, David C. Hughart, is cooperating with Goodwin, and hopeful rumors circulate in neighboring communities that Don Blankenship, Massey's notorious chief executive officer, is the ultimate target of the investigation.[6] If Blankenship is indicted and either pleads guilty or is tried, the case will be the first in decades to travel up the chain of command to the person who was ultimately responsible for the catastrophe.

Why prosecutors duck opportunities to indict corporations and their executives for violations that cost lives, cause grievous injuries, and threaten environmental viability is the central, puzzling reality tackled in this volume. Criminal cases involving pollution had their heyday during the period from 1987 to 2002 but have since slowed to a trickle. Criminal prosecutors have never paid sustained attention to crimes involving workplace hazards and the sale of dangerous products, especially food and drugs, leaving erratic civil enforcement as the only deterrent. (The word "prosecutors" is used to refer to officials that bring criminal charges. In this book, the words "regulators" or "inspectors" refer to officials who focus on civil cases.)

Federal and state laws cover crimes committed both by individuals at work and the corporations that employ them. The choice of which category of defendant to indict is difficult and complicated, depending on the nature and scope of the crime, the quality and quantity of available evidence, and the remedial goals of the prosecution. Individuals can go to jail, of course, and corporations cannot. On the other hand, government criminal settlements with corporations can exact very large fines, while individual prosecutions may motivate corporate executives to establish even more effective prevention on their own. In too many cases, though, individuals escape scrutiny and corporations pay modest fines that are an expected cost of doing business and have little effect on the serious problems that plague their internal management of health, safety, and environmental risks. As illustrated by the Upper Big Branch explosion, routine regulatory civil enforcement has faded into the background, lacking the power to deter reckless behavior that has become increasingly common.

These unfortunate realities are obscured at the moment by the reemergence of a shrill campaign against regulation in any form. Spearheaded by regulated industries and conservatives, and tolerated by centrists, few days go by when a member of Congress fails to finger excessive regulation as the root cause of

---

[5] *See* Ken Ward, Jr., *Former Massey Official Sentenced to 42 Months in Prison*, CHARLESTON GAZETTE, Sept. 10, 2013, http://www.wvgazette.com/News/201309100025?display=print (discussing Goodwin's prosecutions against Thomas Harrah, Hughie Elbert Stover, Gary May, and David C. Hughart).

[6] *Id.*

America's most profound economic problems.[7] Requirements that protect public health, worker and consumer safety, and the environment are not the sole target of these relentless attacks. Efforts to implement the Dodd-Frank Act's tighter controls on the financial services industry, as well as health care reform, inspire resistance that is at least as passionate.

This deregulatory narrative has overshadowed a series of deeply troubling incidents that have imposed cumulative death and injury tolls in the thousands. These events are the inevitable result of "hollow government" – a term used here to encompass outmoded and weak legal authority, funding shortfalls that prevent the effective implementation of regulatory requirements, and the relentless bashing of the civil service. From the blowout of the Macondo well in the Gulf of Mexico – death toll 11 – to a Massachusetts pharmacy's shipment of tainted steroid injections that caused fungal meningitis – death toll 64 – the rote response is to excoriate federal officials for failing to prevent the incident without considering why they are having such difficulties.

In the aftermath of the Macondo blowout, for example, an estimated 205 million gallons of crude oil coursed into the Gulf over a period of two and a half months as BP engineers tried frantically to plug the leak. Yet Congress never upgraded the legal authority of Department of Interior regulators in the Gulf and appropriations for enhanced enforcement remain pitifully inadequate. At last reporting, some 79 inspectors police 3,500 deepwater drilling rigs and platforms. In a similar vein, remedial legislation to strengthen the Food and Drug Administration's (FDA) capacity to supervise compounding pharmacies was weakened after that industry's trade association swarmed Capitol Hill. Without aggressive FDA intervention, which will require statutory changes and money, such facilities will remain virtually unregulated by state pharmacy boards.

The phrase "too big to jail" had its genesis in *Too Big to Fail*, Andrew Sorkin's disturbing account of the 2008 worldwide financial crisis.[8] Both phrases have a sardonic undercurrent, gently mocking the expectation that institutions or individuals will be held accountable for causing a global recession of unprecedented proportions. But on March 6, 2013, Sorkin's clever catchphrase was adopted as truth by the nation's top prosecutor and in that instant ceased to be remotely funny. Attorney General Eric Holder said:

> I am concerned that the size of some of these institutions becomes so large that it does become difficult for us to prosecute them when we are hit with

7   For a trenchant analysis of this phenomenon, *see* Brian Domitrovic, Econoclasts: The Rebels Who Sparked the Supply-Side Revolution and Restored American Prosperity (2012).
8   Andrew Ross Sorkin, Too Big to Fail: The Inside Story of How Wall Street and Washington Fought to Save the Financial System – and Themselves (2009).

indications that if you do prosecute, if you do bring a criminal charge, it will have a negative impact on the national economy, perhaps even the world economy. And I think that is a function of the fact that some of these institutions have become too large.[9]

Or, as the situation was characterized in a more direct fashion by a former Senate investigator in an interview with *Rolling Stone*'s Matt Taibbi: "Everything's fucked up, and nobody goes to jail. That's your whole story right there. Hell, you don't even have to write the rest of it. Just write that."[10] Taibbi proceeded to document in copious detail the political connections that trumped investigations of insider trading and other blatantly illegal behavior by some of the leading players in Sorkin's book.

In grand Washington tradition, Holder has tried to "walk back" his statement, promising to get tough on corporate crime.[11] Yet, as we shall see, his Department of Justice (DOJ) has not changed the underlying policies that motivated his statement. Half the cases brought by its criminal section were settled without guilty pleas, under a strange legal hybrid called "deferred prosecution agreements" (DPAs).[12] Prosecutors and media commentators constantly refer to the 2005 collapse of Arthur Andersen, which served as Enron's accounting firm, as the reason why the DOJ hesitates to charge corporations with crimes that could put them out of business. This rationale is misplaced. Arthur Andersen's clients began to desert the firm when news of Enron's collapse hit Wall Street. The DOJ indictment was issued months later. The indictment charged that Andersen partners ordered the shredding of tons of documents revealing the massive fraud it had helped Enron to perpetrate. No major publicly traded corporation wanted to be tainted by continued association with Arthur Andersen in the wake of the scandal. At best, the indictment played a minor role in the rapid demise of the firm.

---

[9] *Oversight of the U.S. Department of Justice: Hearing Before the S. Comm. on the Judiciary*, 113th Cong. (Mar. 6, 2013) (transcript of testimony of Att'y Gen. Eric Holder), http://www. americanbanker.com/issues/178_45/transcript-attorney-general-eric-holder-on-too-big-to-jail-1057295-1.html.

[10] Matt Taibbi, *Why Isn't Wall Street in Jail?*, ROLLING STONE, Feb. 16, 2011, http://www. rollingstone.com/politics/news/why-isnt-wall-street-in-jail-20110216.

[11] Mark Gongkoff, *Eric Holder: Actually, I Meant to Say No Banks Are Too Big to Jail*, HUFFINGTON POST, May 15, 2013, http://www.huffingtonpost.com/2013/05/15/eric-holder-too-big-to-jail_n_3280694.html.

[12] In a "deferred prosecution agreement," the Justice Department agrees to drop the criminal charges after a set period of time if the company in question abides by the terms of the settlement. SORKIN, *supra* note 8, at 155. Sorkin explains that "[a]fter the indictment of … Arthur Anderson … led to its collapse, the government preferred the softer cudgel of deferred prosecution agreements as a kind of probation … " *Id.*

In any event, the DOJ persists with its "too big to jail" policy in financial cases, most memorably invoking it in the case of HSBC, the world's third-largest publicly held bank, which stood accused of laundering money for Mexican drug cartels and opening bank accounts for possible terrorists in Sudan and Libya. HSBC signed a deferred prosecution agreement, escaping any admission that it had committed multiple felonies.[13]

As tempting as it is to get sidetracked by the twisted logic of DOJ's anxiety about prosecuting big banks, my focus here is on crimes that harm public health, worker and consumer safety, and the environment. Where the two areas intersect, I will explore those synergies. For example, the DOJ's obvious inability to hold Wall Street players accountable for the meltdown continues to infuriate the public. The parallel failure to hold senior executives liable for crimes involving public health, safety, and the environment deserves a similarly high profile.

The two areas are comparable in another important way: a critical mass of traditional regulatory programs designed to prevent the worst abuses have crossed the line from workable to dysfunctional. Given the harsh rhetoric of deregulation that dominates national policy debates, the resources and political commitment necessary to accomplish their resurrection is unlikely to materialize anytime soon. Instead, ultimately more aggressive, targeted, and less expensive criminal prosecutions offer a more effective and viable solution. If handled well, such prosecutions could create robust incentives for top managers to create their own internal system of incentives and punishment.

This book illustrates these problems and searches for potential solutions by examining the root causes of five recent incidents, all of which involve substantial loss of life, billions of dollars in damage, the shocking dearth of internal corporate safety cultures, and dysfunctional regulatory systems. They include: the Massey Energy Upper Big Branch mine collapse, the Macondo well blowout oil rig and Texas City refinery explosions, the Peanut Corporation of America's shipment of peanut paste contaminated with salmonella, and the New England Compounding Center's sale of tainted steroid injections that caused fungal meningitis. All five involve circumstances where top management must have been aware of serious operational risk but did not pause long enough to consider the intolerable consequences at stake, instead

---

[13] Press Release, Dep't of Justice, Office of Public Affairs, HSBC Holdings Plc. and HSBC Bank USA N.A. Admit to Anti-Money Laundering and Sanctions Violations, Forfeit $1.256 Billion in Deferred Prosecution Agreement (Dec. 11, 2012), *available at* http://www.justice.gov/opa/pr/2012/December/12-crm-1478.html. For the actual agreement, see Deferred Prosecution Agreement, United States v. HSBC Bank USA NA and HSBC Holdings PLC, Crim. No. 12-763 (E.D.N.Y. filed Dec. 11, 2012), *available at* http://www.justice.gov/opa/documents/hsbc/dpa-executed.pdf.

focusing on profitability at the expense of safety. Because each episode involves a major industry that has great importance to American social welfare, these are not traditional case studies but rather rise to the level of historical events that had major effects on the economy, social attitudes, and industry behavior. Groundbreaking journalism and extensive investigation by public and private sector entities document these failures in meticulous detail, providing a rich context for evaluating the deterrent effects of self-regulation, government regulation, and criminal prosecution.

In addition to regulatory failure, the most significant challenge to criminal prosecutions is the deeply engrained tendency among investigators and prosecutors to take the route of least resistance, bringing civil cases against corporations and settling for amounts less than the compliance costs the company avoided by breaking the law. Of course, the legal burden for criminal cases – "beyond a reasonable doubt" – is far more difficult to meet than the "preponderance of the evidence" standard generally applicable to civil cases. The first connotes the conclusion that there is no other reasonable explanation for what happened while the second means only that the evidence shows it is more likely than not that the defendant was at fault. Three additional factors deter prosecutors: the risk of losing, limited resources, and apprehension about the intensity of the potential defense. An attitudinal pivot will be the hardest to accomplish, not least because prosecutors are awash in misleading legal commentary asserting that they cannot win criminal cases under current law.[14]

I argue here that criminal prosecution should be considered by federal and state authorities whenever industrial activities cause grave harm to public health, consumer or worker safety, or the environment. Existing law, including the judicial "responsible corporate officer" doctrine, provides ample authority to support such indictments. The potential for prosecutions under state manslaughter rules is especially encouraging.

In many cases, "accidents" cause the harm, with that term defined as an admittedly unintended consequence that was nevertheless the inevitable outcome of a series of acts or omissions by managers who should and did know better. Unfortunately, legal scholars' preoccupation with the *mens rea* of crimes – the knowing state that justifies the harsh penalty of imprisonment – has undermined the development of criminal law in the health, safety, and environmental arenas. Unless and until *mens rea* is conceived more broadly to

---

[14] *See, e.g.,* Sara Sun Beale, *Is Corporate Criminal Liability Unique?*, 44 AM. CRIM. L. REV. 1503 (2007) (warning against weakening corporate criminal liability laws because of the difficulty of prosecuting).

include systematic and prolonged acts or omissions that magnify risk, the criminal option will be drastically underused.

Criminal prosecutions should target the highest level of official against whom adequate evidence can be developed, avoiding cases against line supervisors who acted or failed to act because they feared reprisal. Once executives and their corporations are charged criminally, settlements should require defendants to acknowledge their crimes and, where the corporation is the defendant, take every feasible step toward establishing enduring safety protocols that pervade their operations top-to-bottom and side-to-side.

Scholars have long identified criminal prosecutions as the expression of a society's moral revulsion regarding specific conduct. In this sense, the criminal justice system is as important to the ultimate embodiment of a society's values as it is in keeping public peace. The great legal historian Lawrence M. Friedman has written:

> [C]riminal justice tells us where the moral boundaries are; where the line lies between good and bad. It patrols those boundary lines, day and night, rain or shine. It shows the rules directly, dramatically, visually, through asserting and enforcing them. (There are lessons from nonenforcement, too: from situations where the boundaries are indistinct, or the patrol corrupt or asleep; and society is quick to learn these lessons, too.) ...
>
> ... [T]he history of criminal justice is not only the history of the forms of rewards and punishment; it is also a story about the dominant *morality*, and hence a history of power.[15]

Viewed from this perspective, the criminal justice system is a sad commentary on the values our society claims to hold dear. America's 5,000 prisons hold about 2.3 million inmates, more than in any other country that records such statistics, including Russia.[16] An additional 4.1 million people live under the supervision of correctional institutions, primarily on probation, for a total of 6.4 million, or one in thirty-four Americans. African Americans are eight times more likely to be incarcerated than whites. A young black man has a 32 percent

---

[15] LAWRENCE M. FRIEDMAN, CRIME AND PUNISHMENT IN AMERICAN HISTORY 10 (1993).

[16] Comprehensive statistics on prison populations can be found at the Bureau of Justice Statistics website. LAUREN E. GLAZE & ERIKA PARKS, U.S. DEP'T OF JUSTICE, No. NCJ 239972, CORRECTIONAL POPULATIONS IN THE UNITED STATES (2011), *available at* http://www.bjs. gov/content/pub/pdf/cpus11.pdf. The comparative rates were calculated in the mid-2000s. BECKY PETTIT, INVISIBLE MEN 11–12 (2012). For more extensive discussion of the acute social problems and injustice caused by mass incarceration, in addition to the Pettit book, see PAUL BUTLER, LET'S GET FREE: A HIP-HOP THEORY OF CRIMINAL JUSTICE (2009), TODD R. CLEAR, IMPRISONING COMMUNITIES: HOW MASS INCARCERATION MAKES DISADVANTAGED NEIGHBORHOODS WORSE (2007), and MICHAEL TONRY, PUNISHING RACE: A CONTINUING AMERICAN DILEMMA (2011).

chance of going to prison; his white counterpart has a six percent chance. Prisons cost the nation about $60 billion annually.[17]

Until the 1970s, the number of Americans in prison was roughly comparable to other developed countries. Over the next three decades, the nation pulled out ahead of that norm. A large private sector prison industry was established, and contractors became at least as powerful as the criminologists, sociologists, policymakers, wardens, prison guards, and elected officials with an interest in the system. A conservative political movement demanded zero tolerance for the most minor crimes; in fact, these are the same interest groups that now demand deregulation of the industrial sector. Apparently, government has an essential role to play in incarcerating its citizens but not in protecting them from the worst threats of industrialization.

Some might imagine that escalating crime rates justified this laser focus on so-called "street crime." But crime rates have fallen in most cities, in some cases quite precipitously, at the same time that prison populations continued to grow. Over the decade beginning in 2001, eight million people were arrested for marijuana; simple possession charges accounted for 88 percent of this total and marijuana was the target of 52 percent of all drug arrests.[18] African Americans were 3.73 times more likely to be arrested than whites. Recently and to his credit, Attorney General Holder announced that federal prosecutors would stop charging minor drug offenders with crimes that trigger mandatory minimum sentences, a step that could begin to turn this powerful tide.[19]

Holder was motivated by the common view among criminologists that, as the rate of incarceration increased, a tipping point was reached and prison became a counterproductive, off-target response to perceptions of social threat, as opposed to the actual incidence of violent street crime. Nowhere is this cruel irony illustrated more plainly than in the extension of the zero tolerance movement into the public schools, where children as young as twelve are fed into the juvenile branch of the criminal system for misbehavior such as shouting, wearing the wrong color clothing, leaving class without

---

[17] PETTIT, *supra* note 16, at 1; *see also* JOHN J. GIBBONS & NICHOLAS DE B. KATZENBACH, CONFRONTING CONFINEMENT: A REPORT OF THE COMMISSION ON SAFETY AND ABUSE IN AMERICA'S PRISONS 11 (2006), *available at* http://www.vera.org/sites/default/files/resources/downloads/Confronting_Confinement.pdf.

[18] This and the following statistics on racially discriminatory marijuana arrests were reported by the AMERICAN CIVIL LIBERTIES UNION, THE WAR ON MARIJUANA IN BLACK AND WHITE (2013), *available at* https://www.aclu.org/sites/default/files/assets/090613-mj-report-rfs-rel1.pdf.

[19] Eric Holder, Att'y Gen., Remarks at the Annual Meeting of the American Bar Association's House of Delegates, San Francisco, CA (Aug. 12, 2013), *transcript available at* http://www.justice.gov/iso/opa/ag/speeches/2013/ag-speech-130812.html.

permission, or shoving a classmate.[20] The disruption caused by the time off from school, stigmatization, and economic hardship imposed on low-income parents by these poorly supervised programs has significantly increased the chances that teenagers will drop out of school and end up in prison themselves.

The most troubling manifestation of discord in American politics is the skyrocketing rate of the public's distrust of government.[21] These concerns parallel an unprecedented concentration of wealth: according to economist Joseph Stiglitz, the amount of money that goes to the upper one percent of the American people has doubled since 1980, and the amount that goes to the top 0.1 percent has tripled.[22] Perceptions that the middle class is having a harder time earning a dwindling living and that its children may well not be better off than their parents are deeply troubling to many Americans. When the vicious cycle of racially discriminatory mass incarceration of poor people is juxtaposed against the vivid descriptions of the crimes committed by well-heeled corporate executives, it is hard to imagine the contrast does not have a corrosive effect on people's confidence in government institutions. Quite apart from the intrinsic unfairness of the failure to prosecute white collar crime far more aggressively, we sacrifice the benefits of deterring events that harm ordinary people.

Silver Spring, Maryland

August 4, 2014

---

[20] TEXAS APPLESEED, TEXAS' SCHOOL-TO-PRISON PIPELINE: TICKETING, ARREST & USE OF FORCE IN SCHOOLS 84, 91, 5, 55 (2010), *available at* http://www.texasappleseed.net/images/stories/reports/Ticketing_Booklet_web.pdf (describing incidents where students were ticketed for disrupting classrooms, wearing gang-related colors, leaving without permission, or pushing another student down).

[21] In November 1958, when Eisenhower was president, 73 percent of the public said they trusted government. That number steadily eroded, rising sharply and only temporarily in response to events like the terrorist attacks on September 11, 2001. Nineteen percent said they trusted government in October 2013. *Public Trust in Government: 1958–2013*, PEW RESEARCH CENTER FOR THE PEOPLE AND THE PRESS (Oct. 18, 2013), http://www.people-press.org/2013/01/31/trust-in-government-interactive/. Public attitudes toward state and local government are generally significantly more positive, with 57 percent having a favorable view of state government and 63 percent having a favorable view of local government in April 2013. *State Governments Viewed Favorably as Federal Government Hits New Low*, PEW RESEARCH CENTER FOR THE PEOPLE AND THE PRESS (Apr. 15, 2013), http://www.people-press.org/2013/04/15/state-govermnents-viewed-favorably-as-federal-rating-hits-new-low/.

[22] JOSEPH E. STIGLITZ, THE PRICE OF INEQUALITY: HOW TODAY'S DIVIDED SOCIETY ENDANGERS OUR FUTURE (2012).

Part One

The Status Quo

The arduous transition to an industrial economy in Europe and North America brought with it considerable improvement in overall social welfare. Populations increased by orders of magnitude, life expectancy was extended, and a middle class emerged as an alternative to landed gentry, introducing the powerful idea that hard work could improve social status and quality of life. Nevertheless, the harsh underbelly of this remarkable transformation included grave and avoidable suffering. Worker fatalities in hazardous industries such as mining were common, children labored under unspeakably bad conditions, and consumers were prey to hawkers of bad medicine and worse food. Government intervention to control the hazards to health and safety lagged several decades behind the Industrial Revolution, a pattern that persists to this day with respect to the innovations and emerging threats of industrialization in a global economy.

The spread of the Industrial Revolution across America began in earnest right after the Civil War when steam-powered manufacturing replaced horsepower. The government focused on encouraging these developments by building roads and railroads and helping to stabilize currency and the banking system. In the early 1900s, scandals involving dangerous patent remedies and tainted meat motivated passage of the Pure Food and Drug Act, which prohibited mislabeling and deceptive advertising claims, and the Meat Inspection Act, which banned the sale of tainted or adulterated meat. These authorities were expanded through repeated cycles of media exposés and congressional reaction, slowly but surely bringing mining, child labor, and other troubling facets of industrialization under government control.

During the late 1960s and the early 1970s, the kinetic forces of Vietnam War protests, an incipient environmental movement motivated by Rachel Carson's *Silent Spring*,[1] and a growing consumer movement spearheaded by Ralph Nader produced a burst of congressional activity comparable to the New Deal. Four new agencies were born: the Consumer Product Safety Commission (CPSC), the Environmental Protection Agency (EPA), the Occupational Safety and Health Administration (OSHA), and the National Highway Traffic Safety Administration (NHTSA). Congress gave them unprecedented power to inspect, permit, shut down, recall, and assess civil and criminal penalties with respect to a large universe of industrial activities.

American industry executives were disturbed by these developments, which created the potential for massive government interference with their daily operations. But the popular movements that dominated the media made outright opposition seem dangerous, and a shrewd consensus emerged that business groups would not risk public opposition to the legislation as it proceeded through Congress. Instead, groups such as the Chamber of Commerce (founded in 1912) and the Business Roundtable (founded in 1972) took their concerns about an overreaching regulatory state to the White House, where they found a sympathetic audience. Or, in other words, while environmentalists, organized labor, and consumer advocates played an "outside game" that relied on public sentiment and the media to amplify pressure on Congress, regulated industries responded with an "inside game," leveraging presidential perceptions about the electoral advantages of having business support. Over the long run, as we shall see, the inside game has proved a more effective strategy because it has allowed presidents and members of Congress to have their political cake and eat it, too, expressing verbal support for popular initiatives in areas like environmental protection but placating business interests behind the scenes.

The conflicts between outside and inside strategies and tactics have haunted policymaking in the area ever since. The heyday of liberal social movements in the early 1970s was followed with surprising quickness by the election of Ronald Reagan, who once declared that trees cause more pollution than automobiles, prompting a humorist to post a sign reading "Cut me down before I kill again!" on a tree near the airport where his campaign jet was to land.[2] As Reagan did his best to cut the budget of the young agencies and install overseers hostile to their

[1]   RACHEL CARSON, SILENT SPRING (1962).
[2]   Francis X. Clines, *Candidates Also Appeal to Those Basic Virtues*, N.Y. TIMES, Oct. 26, 1980, at E2 ("Mr. Reagan, of course, put an even finer point on his faith in the people's virtue this year

missions to keep them in check, the Watergate class of Democrats in Congress rebelled, strengthening the agencies' authority and enlarging their mandates. Much of this power struggle was centered on the EPA. The agency had emerged as the focus of strong popular support, spawning the creation of a public interest movement second only to organized labor in funding, and political power that was countered by equally determined industry opposition. The reach and stringency of the new statutes prompted business interests to fight far more openly against these legislative initiatives and to slow or cripple the EPA's programs through funding reductions and more restrictive White House controls.

The last major reauthorization of an environmental statute was the 1990 Clean Air Act Amendments. Close to a quarter century later, industry and environmentalists are still locked in a struggle to the death over implementation of its provisions. All of the agencies have fallen on desperate times from a funding perspective, with appropriations that are significantly less in real dollars than they had available in the early 1980s. Although Congress has occasionally responded to major crises by once again strengthening and expanding agency authority – an ambitious statute to modernize the FDA's approach to food safety enacted in 2010 is the most recent example – it is now overcome by an intense backlash to all such regulatory efforts. Centered in the House among conservative Republicans, this intense and persistent reaction has pulled the debate far to the right, muffling voices that counsel moderation.

If history is to be believed, the pendulum will swing back eventually as the economy eases, depriving the opposition of the potent argument that regulations cost jobs. A series of new crises akin to those highlighted here will persuade a large majority that regulatory infrastructure must be rebuilt. For the time being, however, the grim reality is that the agencies lack the legal tools and political support they need to address many of these problems in a *preventive* manner. The efficacy of civil penalties is attenuated, and the fatal accidents that reach the front pages are the tip of far more chronic lawbreaking. To bridge the growing gap between prevention and reality, a far stronger deterrent is necessary.

Chapter 1 documents the dysfunction of the existing regulatory system. Chapter 2 explains the laws that govern crimes against public health, safety, and the environment. Chapter 3 analyzes the arguments against white collar prosecution, in general and as applied to those crimes.

when he took the approach on the air pollution issue of heaping blame on trees and plants. Even some of his campaign aides have had to smile at reports that someone in California responded by placing a sign on a tree, by which the tree is left pleading: 'Cut me down before I kill again!'").

1

Regulatory Dysfunction

When a jury last week found a former suburban Chicago water department chief guilty of 11 charges related to mixing contaminated well water into a town's drinking water supply, the verdict represented an important victory for the U.S. EPA's criminal enforcement efforts.

EPA officials hope the potential five-year terms that could accompany each of the 11 counts will send a strong message to penny-pinching authorities who put their own interests ahead of the people they are supposed to serve. But the victory is also bigger than that.

Two months into sequestration – when across-the-board budget cuts and staffing reductions are taking a toll on EPA's criminal enforcement efforts – reminding environmental wrongdoers that the agency can still pack a punch may be more important than ever.

Doug Parker, the director of the agency's Criminal Investigation Division (CID), acknowledged last week that limitations on new hiring and furloughs mandated by sequestration are making the thin green line of EPA special agents even thinner.

"There are areas where there were boots on the ground where there are no longer boots on the ground," Parker said.

He declined to be more specific about where the holes in coverage have developed for fear of alerting the bad guys.

John McArdle, Greenwire[1]

A GLASS HALF FULL

Although regulation has fallen on hard times, its historic accomplishments are unimpeachable. Especially when compared to the dire straits of countries that have industrialized helter-skelter without such controls – China comes first to

John McArdle, *EPA: "There Are Significant Geographic Regions We Can No Longer Cover" – Agency's Top Cop*, GREENWIRE (May 6, 2013), http://www.eenews.net/special_reports/seques tration/stories/1059980622.

mind[2] – the United States has achieved minor miracles in ameliorating the worst outcomes of economic development. In fact, until the implications of worldwide climate change became manifest a decade ago, modest self-satisfaction was appropriate. Without any question, traditional pollution problems persist, including ground level ozone (smog) in most major U.S. cities, dead zones in great waters from the Chesapeake Bay to the Gulf of Mexico, toxic chemical exposure in the workplace, endocrine disrupters in the food supply, and hazardous imports from countries that do not have regulatory controls. But grit is gone from the air, workplace and foodborne illness deaths are down dramatically, and consumer products, from cars to lawn mowers, are much safer. Each aspect of this progress is attributable directly to regulation or to the efforts made by regulated parties to get out ahead of it.[3]

The National Institute of Occupational Safety and Health (NIOSH) estimates that workplace fatalities declined by 43 percent between 1980 and 1995, from 7.5 to 4.3 deaths per 100,000 workers.[4] Between 1994 and 2011, workplace fatalities recorded by the Bureau of Labor Statistics (BLS) dropped by another one-third, from 6,588 to 4,609, to a low of 3.5 deaths per 100,000 workers.[5] In the early 1900s, more than 1,000 coal miners died on the job annually.[6] That number decreased to an average of some 450 annual

---

[2] Researchers have estimated that pollution and environmental degradation in China cause 2.4 million deaths annually; adjusted for population size, the American equivalent would be 558,000 deaths per year. Junfeng Zhang et al., *Environmental Health in China: Progress Towards Clean Air and Safe Water*, 375 Lancet 1110 (2010).

[3] For further information about successful rules, see James Lardner, Demos, Good Rules: 10 Stories of Successful Regulation (2011), *available at* http://www.demos.org/sites/default/files/publications/goodrules_1_11.pdf.

[4] National Institute of Occupational Safety & Health, Worker Health Chartbook, 2000, at v (Sept. 2000), *available at* http://www.cdc.gov/niosh/docs/2000-127/pdfs/2000-127.pdf. For a description of the report's findings, see http://www.cdc.gov/niosh/updates/chartup.html.

[5] These figures are hedged by both obvious and hidden caveats. As just one example, the 3.5/100,000 figure involves "full-time equivalent" workers. *See Commonly Used Statistics*, OSHA, http://www.osha.gov/oshstats/commonstats.html (last visited Feb. 19, 2014). An exploration of the fatality rate of increasingly common "temporary" workers is well worth undertaking but beyond my scope here. Numbers for nonfatal injuries are so notoriously unreliable that they are omitted here. For further information, see Kenneth D. Rosenman et al., *How Much Work-Related Injury and Illness Is Missed by the Current National Surveillance System?*, 48 J. Occupational & Envtl. Med. 357 (2006); J. Paul Leigh et al., *An Estimate of the U.S. Government's Undercount of Nonfatal Occupational Injuries*, 46 J. Occupational & Envtl. Med. 10 (2004); Leslie I. Boden & David Ozonoff, *Capture-Recapture Estimates of Nonfatal Workplace Injuries and Illnesses*, 18 Annals Epidemiology 500 (2008).

[6] *Online Fact Sheet: Injury Trends in Mining*, Mine Safety & Health Administration, http://www.msha.gov/MSHAINFO/FactSheets/MSHAFCT2.HTM#.Utf_NLT9ywI (last visited Feb. 19, 2014) ("[A]nnual coal mining deaths numbered more than 1,000 a year in the early part of the 20th century … ").

fatalities in the 1950s.[7] By the 1970s, the annual average decreased to 140.[8] Between 2006 and 2010, fatalities were down to 35/year.[9]

The Centers for Disease Control (CDC) estimate that 3,000 people die each year from foodborne illness, down from 5,000 in 1999.[10] Quantifying the number of deaths avoided as a result of safer drugs is impossible, and the challenges of teasing apart the reasons for deaths caused by adverse drug reactions are similarly daunting (wrong dosage, medical error in prescribing, or unsafe product?). Nevertheless, incidents involving the sale of tainted drugs are relatively rare and, when they do occur, often involve imports. For example, heparin imported from China in 2008 was contaminated by a toxic chemical that mimicked some characteristics of the real drug but caused dozens of deaths in this country and abroad.[11]

Air pollution, the greatest remaining environmental threat to public health, decreases lung function and aggravates respiratory and cardiovascular disease, causing death in the most severe cases. Children are especially vulnerable to ozone and fine particulate matter pollution, which trigger asthma attacks and other respiratory diseases, and can cause cancer. Lead pollution in the air and the soil (what goes up must come down, after all) has devastating effects on developing nervous systems, causing IQ loss and diminished ability to learn, remember, and control hyperactive behavior. Air pollution also damages the environment, diminishing the growth of plants and trees and indirectly threatening entire ecosystems. The Clean Air Act has produced a 59 percent aggregate reduction in the emissions of six major air pollutants, including particulate matter, carbon monoxide, volatile organic compounds, sulfur dioxide, and nitrogen oxide from 1990 to 2005.[12] Emissions of toxic air pollutants are down by approximately 42 percent during the same period.[13] Lead pollution, so dangerous to children, dropped by 83 percent, largely because the EPA fought successfully to eliminate lead from gas.[14] Strict controls on

---

[7] *Id.*

[8] *Id.*

[9] *Id.*

[10] *Online Fact Sheet:* 2011 *Estimates of Foodborne Illness,* CENTERS FOR DISEASE CONTROL & PREVENTION, http://www.cdc.gov/foodborneburden/2011-foodborne-estimates.html (last visited Mar. 7, 2014).

[11] Gardiner Harris, *U.S. Identified Tainted Heparin in* 11 *Countries,* N.Y. TIMES, Apr. 22, 2008, http://www.nytimes.com/2008/04/22/health/policy/22fda.html?pagewanted=all&_r=0; Walt Bogdanich, *The Drug Scare that Exposed a World of Hurt,* N.Y. TIMES, Mar. 30, 2008, http://www.nytimes.com/2008/03/30/weekinreview/30bogdanich.html.

[12] U.S. ENVIRONMENTAL PROTECTION AGENCY, OUR NATION'S AIR: STATUS AND TRENDS THROUGH 2010, at 5 (2011), *available at* http://www.epa.gov/airtrends/2011/report/fullreport.pdf.

[13] *Id.* at 1.

[14] *Id.*

power plants, chemical and other manufacturing facilities, coke ovens, and motor vehicles account for these improvements.[15] They have meant that hundreds of thousands of deaths were avoided, along with tens of millions of days off work and school.

The Clean Water Act marked its fortieth anniversary in 2012. Born out of intense conflict – an unusually unified Congress overrode a presidential veto to make it law – the Act took the traditional approach of requiring major "point" sources (sewage treatment plants, factories, etc.) to install state-of-the-art pollution control equipment. Before its passage, fully two-thirds of America's lakes, streams, ponds, and creeks were unsafe for fishing and swimming because they were contaminated by sewage, pesticides, oil, and toxic chemicals.[16] Today, that number is down by 50 percent, with 65 percent of surface waters fit for all uses, and 35 percent still categorized as impaired. Before the Act, some 500,000 acres of wetlands were destroyed each year by excessive development; today wetland losses are down to 60,000 acres annually.[17]

Americans drive three times as much as they did when the National Highway Traffic Safety Administration (NHTSA) was created in 1970. But the number of fatalities has fallen from 54,000 in 1972 to under 34,000 in 2009. Taking miles traveled into account, this progress is even more impressive: the nation has gone from 4.2 deaths per million miles in 1972 to about 1.16 deaths per million miles today.[18]

What is especially noteworthy about all these accomplishments is that regulatory agencies achieved them despite strong resistance by regulated industries. Battalions of lawyers and technical experts were deployed to the agencies to negotiate more favorable terms with the regulators. Among other outcomes, these negotiations produced rules that were complex and lengthy as technical experts battled for small advantages over their competitors with different technologies. Unfortunately, the complexity of the rules provided fodder to contemporary critics who say that the rules are unintelligible, ignoring their genesis and the role of regulated industries in writing them that way. If industry representatives were still dissatisfied with a rulemaking after wringing the best deal they could out of career agency experts, they appealed for White House intervention or dragged the agencies off to court. Yet the agencies persevered, holding their own until relatively recently.

[15]   *Id.*

[16]   William K. Reilly, *Keep the Clean Water Act Strong*, N.Y. TIMES, Nov. 28, 2011, http://www. nytimes.com/2011/11/29/opinion/keep-the-clean-water-act-strong.html.

[17]   *Feature: Forty Years of the Clean Water Act*, CLEAN WATER FUND, http://www.cleanwater fund.org/feature/forty-years-clean-water-act (last visited Mar. 19, 2014).

[18]   JAMES LARDNER, DĒMOS, GOOD RULES: 10 STORIES OF SUCCESSFUL REGULATION 15 (2011), *available at* http://www.demos.org/sites/default/files/publications/goodrules_1_11.pdf.

By the turn of the twenty-first century, agencies such as the EPA, the FDA and the MSHA had internalized the implications of every challenge to their statutory missions. This anxiety – a kind of "muscle memory" for anticipated attacks – led regulators to study problems extensively, spending inordinate amounts of time worrying about the costs of their proposals and – most significantly for our purposes – hesitating to write new rules.

Sensing this insecurity, and encouraged by conservatives in the House of Representatives, the agencies' opponents grew ever more aggressive. Industry representatives soon learned to appeal to congressional allies during their campaigns to slow or derail rules. When the economic recession hit in 2008, these challenges intensified, giving deregulators the opportunity to argue that the nation could no longer afford to expand health, safety, and environmental regulations that cost jobs. Agencies deteriorated, verging into dysfunction and even paralysis.

The result was that in too many cases, specific statutory provisions and their implementing regulations are little more than "symbolic law," a phrase that Professor John Dwyer coined to describe requirements that remain on the books but are not enforced.[19] Backsliding has begun, and solutions to pressing new problems, including climate change, seem out of reach. Four accelerating trends now account for the regulatory failures that were a leading cause of the high-profile incidents featured in Part II: (1) acute funding shortfalls or hollow government; (2) outmoded statutory authority; (3) the politicization of the rule-making process; and (4) constant attacks on the integrity of the civil service.

HOLLOW GOVERNMENT

The two parties' stalemate over the budget has become the most serious manifestation of the polarized politics that produce gridlock on almost all issues, domestic and international. Even sophisticated Congress-watchers such as Thomas Mann and Norman Ornstein, who exist in a state of cynical bemusement after decades of experience, were alarmed by the crisis over the extension of the debt limit in 2011, when recalcitrant House Republicans embracing Tea Party views came close to destroying the federal government's credit rating. They write:

---

[19] John P. Dwyer, *The Pathology of Symbolic Legislation*, 17 ECOLOGY L.Q. 233 (1990). Dwyer meant laws that set such impractically high standards for protecting public health that they cannot be carried out until their "symbolic" goals are moderated. I would expand this definition of "symbolic" to include laws and rules that are perfectly practical but have been left to molder on the books by regulators who no longer have the political support, personal will, or resources to enforce them.

Watching the debt limit debacle unfold led us to our title for this book: *It's Even Worse Than It Looks*. As bad as the atmospherics were, the new and enhanced politics of hostage taking, of putting political expedience above the national interest and tribal hubris above cooperative problem solving, suggested something more dangerous, especially at a time of profound economic peril.[20]

In the aftermath of this crisis, a stalemate between Congress and President Obama triggered a "sequester" – Washington-speak for a five percent across-the-board budget cut applied to discretionary spending, including support of regulatory agencies. These cuts were triggered automatically by Congress' failure to reach a budget deal. The shortfalls in social safety nets and regulatory programs ended up distressing liberal Democrats and delighting conservative Republicans. More showdowns are inevitable as Democrats try to restore the cuts by raising taxes and Republicans refuse to entertain such proposals, instead demanding greater reductions in the discretionary portion of the budget that includes regulatory agencies.

The central reason for conservative success is the framing of deficit reduction in terms that inspire deep passion among sympathetic grassroots activists, many of whom re-emerged under the Tea Party banner following President Obama's first electoral victory. This group is interested in reducing the staggering amount of government debt, to be sure, but they are even more committed to the overarching goal of shrinking government. As Grover Norquist, head of the conservative group Americans for Tax Reform and the chief architect of this strategy, has explained, this movement seeks to shrink government "down to the size where we can drown it in the bathtub."[21]

Overall, the deficit remains an intractable problem. Decisions to combine deep tax cuts with expensive wars in Iraq and Afghanistan have left both federal spending and deficits at record highs, and the global financial recession made this bad situation much worse. Congress and the president are well aware that record deficits cannot be tamed by cutting the discretionary portion of the budget, and instead will require significant cuts to popular entitlement programs such as Social Security. Yet neither party wants to take the first step off a political cliff by proposing such changes. In fact, the Tea Party does not support curtailing popular programs like Social Security.[22] But because their ultimate

---

[20] THOMAS E. MANN & NORMAN J. ORNSTEIN, IT'S EVEN WORSE THAN IT LOOKS 4 (2012).

[21] Robert Dreyfuss, *Grover Norquist: "Field Marshall" of the Bush Plan*, THE NATION, May 14, 2001, at 11, 12.

[22] The movement is widespread and not monolithic, but a website operated by "Tea Party Patriots" (www.teapartypatriots.org) reports that "older citizens have earned Social Security" and that "Think Tanks support privatization; grassroots does not." *On the Issues*, TEA PARTY PATRIOTS, http://www.ontheissues.org/Tea_Party.htm#Social_Security (last visited Feb. 19, 2014).

objective is drastic reductions in the size of government, grassroots activists embrace with enthusiasm even incremental progress in eliminating or curtailing government programs funded by the discretionary portion of the budget. The goal of reducing spending for regulatory programs is also deeply appealing to business interests. The companies most directly affected by these programs have sharply skewed their contributions to Republicans, giving conservative legislators powerful incentives to pursue ever more punishing budget cuts.[23]

For the health, safety, and environmental agencies considered here, the latest rounds of budget cuts come on top of two decades of underfunding.[24] Long-term orphans of the federal budgeting process, they first felt the sting of cuts in the Reagan Administration, and matters have not significantly improved from there. On a bipartisan basis, all of the last four presidential administrations were preoccupied with other priorities and low-balled the five agencies' budgets. Unlike the Department of Defense, none of the agencies have enjoyed the support of congressional appropriators. The lack of communication between authorizing committees, which write the legislation that assigns the agencies new statutory mandates, and appropriating committees, which allocate the sums to pay for the implementation of those programs, has exacerbated the problem.[25] Because these two realms are jealous of their prerogatives, missions and funding are never reconciled. In sum, low funding for regulatory programs became an acceptable, bipartisan outcome even before the bitter contemporary battles over deficits and debt ceilings.

The results are devastating. Measured in constant dollars to account for inflation, neither the EPA nor the OSHA has had a significant budget increase

---

[23] For an overview of contributions during the election cycle 2012, by party, *see* Center for Responsive Politics, *Top Overall Donors*, OPENSECRETS.ORG, http://www.opensecrets.org/overview/topcontribs.php (last visited Feb. 19, 2014). For example, the Edison Electric Institute (EEI) is a trade association representing coal-fired power plants that has played a major role in opposing EPA regulatory proposals under the Clean Air Act. *See, e.g.,* JAMES E. MCCARTHY & CLAUDIA COPELAND, CONG. RESEARCH SERV., R 41914, EPA's REGULATION OF COAL-FIRED POWER: IS A "TRAIN WRECK" COMING? (2011), *available at* http://new.nationalaglawcenter.org/wp-content/uploads/assets/crs/R41914.pdf. In 2012, EEI ranked 20th out of 4,368 entities for lobbying expenditures, according to the Center for Responsive Politics. During the 2012 election cycle, it contributed twice as much to Republican politicians as it did to Democrats. For additional information, see Center for Responsive Politics, *Edison Electric Institute: Profile for 2012 Election Cycle*, OPENSECRETS. ORG, http://www.opensecrets.org/orgs/summary.php?cycle=2012&type=P&id=D000000297 (last visited Mar. 19, 2014).

[24] For more extensive discussion of these issues, see RENA STEINZOR & SIDNEY SHAPIRO, THE PEOPLE'S AGENTS AND THE BATTLE TO PROTECT THE AMERICAN PUBLIC: SPECIAL INTERESTS, GOVERNMENT, AND THREATS TO HEALTH, SAFETY, AND THE ENVIRONMENT (2010).

[25] Again, for a more extensive discussion of these issues, see *id.* at 56.

since the mid-1980s, when their workloads were considerably lighter. (As just one simplistic indicator, the American population was 236 million in 1984 and is 317 million today.[26]) The FDA has had modest budgetary increases primarily because it relies on drug industry fees to fund new drug approvals, but it remains painfully underfunded in such critical areas as food safety.

From a fiscal perspective, such frugality makes little sense. In fiscal year 2012, Congress appropriated $13.3 billion, or 0.35 percent of the $3.6 trillion in U.S. government expenditures that year, for the agencies with jurisdiction over the incidents described in Part II: the EPA (at $8.4 billion), the FDA (at $3.8 billion), the OSHA (at $565 million), the MSHA (at $374 million), and the Department of Interior's Bureau of Safety and Environmental Enforcement (BSEE) (deepwater drilling) (at $182 million). Increasing agency budgets to levels that would allow them to carry out all of their statutory mandates in a timely way would not affect the federal deficit in any meaningful manner. Alternatively, Congress could eliminate some of those mandates, bringing the workload within reach of the resources it is willing to make available. Either approach would improve the agencies' long-term credibility by allowing them to do what the lawmakers mandate without perpetuating the destructive cycle of excoriating senior agency officials when regulatory failure emerges in life-threatening ways.

Just how bad are the shortfalls from an operational perspective? A comprehensive recitation of all the problems they cause is beyond my scope here. The following statistics are representative, however, and they are offered to give the reader some sense of how far the agencies have fallen behind.

Inspectors are the frontline of effective enforcement, discovering violations and referring them for further action. In 1975, 2,405 OSHA inspectors were responsible for policing workplaces employing 67.8 million workers, or one for every 28,000 workers.[27] By 2012, the worker population had grown to 127.8 million, and the number of OSHA inspectors had fallen to 2,178, or one for every 58,687 workers.[28]

The nonpartisan and highly respected Government Accountability Office (GAO) keeps a running list of thirty government programs that pose "high"

---

[26] *See U.S. Population by Year*, Multpl, http://www.multpl.com/united-states-population/table (last visited Feb. 19, 2014).

[27] AFL-CIO, Death on the Job: The Toll of Neglect – A National and State-by-State Profile of Worker Safety and Health in the United States (2007), *available at* http://digitalcommons.ilr.cornell.edu/cgi/viewcontent.cgi?article=1016&context=laborunions.

[28] AFL-CIO, Death on the Job: The Toll of Neglect – A National and State-by-State Profile of Worker Safety and Health in the United States (2012), *available at* http://www.aflcio.org/content/download/22781/259751/DOTJ2012nobugFINAL.pdf.

risks to the public because they are poorly managed; susceptible to waste, fraud, or other abuse; or have the potential to cause grave harm to health and well-being.[29] Given the GAO's excellent reputation, inclusion on such a short list should motivate both alarm and reform. The FDA's program to inspect foreign drug manufacturers is listed, as is the EPA's program to regulate toxic chemicals.

Most Americans probably do not realize that manufacturers of drugs sold here depend on imports for about 80 percent of the active pharmaceutical ingredients and 40 percent of finished drugs.[30] The FDA is legally required to inspect domestic drug manufacturing at least once every two years; no comparable requirement dictates the frequency of international inspections. In 2009, the agency managed to inspect about 11 percent of these facilities, concentrating most of its attention on developed countries, as opposed to China and India where most of these imports originate and the worst episodes of tainted products have originated.[31]

In a similar vein, the GAO added the EPA's program to regulate exposures to toxic chemicals in 2009 because the agency had not yet developed sufficient information to assess "many chemicals that may pose substantial health risks."[32] Most of the 80,000 chemicals now circulating in commerce – including those produced and sold at the highest volumes every year – lack a full suite of toxicity tests, making the agency's task of limiting use and exposure virtually impossible. The EPA's Integrated Risk Information System (IRIS), a crucial program aimed at developing risk thresholds for common chemicals on the basis of already published data operates at the snail's pace of two to four chemicals annually.

Last but not least, even after the Macondo catastrophe revealed the dangers of drilling for oil miles underwater, as well as the extraordinary weakness of regulatory efforts to oversee this high hazard industry, significant increases in funding to support adequate federal inspections did not materialize. As of June 2011, seventy-nine inspectors were trying to cover all of the site visits to some

---

[29] U.S. GOV'T ACCOUNTABILITY OFFICE, GAO-13-283, HIGH-RISK SERIES: AN UPDATE (2013), *available at* http://www.gao.gov/assets/660/652133.pdf.

[30] U.S. FOOD & DRUG ADMINISTRATION, GLOBAL ENGAGEMENT 3, 6 (2012), *available at* http://www.fda.gov/downloads/AboutFDA/ReportsManualsForms/Reports/UCM298578.pdf.

[31] U.S. GOV'T ACCOUNTABILITY OFFICE, GAO-10-961, REPORT TO THE COMMITTEE ON OVERSIGHT AND GOVERNMENT REFORM, HOUSE OF REPRESENTATIVES – DRUG SAFETY: FDA HAS CONDUCTED MORE FOREIGN INSPECTIONS AND BEGUN TO IMPROVE ITS INFORMATION ON FOREIGN ESTABLISHMENTS, BUT MORE PROGRESS IS NEEDED 15 (Sept. 2010), *available at* http://www.gao.gov/assets/320/310544.pdf.

[32] U.S. GOV'T ACCOUNTABILITY OFFICE, GAO-10-292, CHEMICAL REGULATION: OBSERVATIONS ON IMPROVING THE TOXIC SUBSTANCES CONTROL ACT 2 (2009), *available at* http://www.gao.gov/new.items/d10292t.pdf.

3,500 rigs and platforms. Most are located miles offshore, are only accessible by helicopter, and employ complex technology that only well-trained, multi-disciplinary teams can understand. Investigative reporting by the *Wall Street Journal* noted that a "small cadre" of inspectors armed with "checklists and pencils" had failed to make much of a dent in overseeing offshore operations throughout the Gulf: "[T]hese inspectors have been overruled by industry, undermined by their own managers, and outmatched by the sheer number of offshore installations they oversee. Inspectors come into the job with little or no hands-on experience in deep-water drilling, learning as they go."[33]

INADEQUATE LEGAL AUTHORITY

Compounding the agencies' funding problems are their struggles to make do with laws passed so long ago that they no longer provide adequate legal authority to combat modern problems. Unfortunately, although stakeholders across the political spectrum agree that the statutes should be updated, their disagreements on the content of such changes are intensely polarized. They also harbor disparate levels of self-interest in making reforms happen, which further complicates the project. For companies that have invested heavily in pollution control or consumer safety, for example, a compromise that brought unregulated competitors into the regulatory tent could inspire negotiations with environmentalists or consumer groups. For those left largely unaffected, though, including retailers who buy goods from manufacturers in Southeast Asia, stalemate is preferable. These factors combine to make the crafting of legislative compromises all but impossible.

A leading example of an urgent problem that is not addressed adequately by existing law is climate change. The last update of a major environmental statute occurred a quarter century ago when Congress passed the 1990 Clean Air Act Amendments. Despite its ambitious coverage and the detailed nature of most of its mandates, this landmark law does not give the EPA guidance on how to combat the most urgent and intractable problem the global population must face: namely, climate change.[34] In 2007, a landmark Supreme

[33] Leslie Eaton et al., *Inspectors Adrift in Rig-Safety Push*, WALL ST. J., Dec. 3, 2010, at A1. For reporting on the BSEE budget, see Ben Geman, *Interior Beefs Up Offshore Inspections with Multiperson Teams*, E2 WIRE: THE HILL'S ENERGY & ENVIRONMENTAL BLOG (June 13, 2011, 3:18 PM), http://thehill.com/blogs/e2-wire/e2-wire/166105-interior-beefs-up-offshore-inspections-with-multi-person-teams.

[34] For example, scientists who participate in the Intergovernmental Panel on Climate Change (IPCC), by far the most comprehensive effort worldwide to analyze and interpret existing data in every relevant field of research, estimate that 40–70 percent of the world's animal species could become extinct if temperatures rise by more than 3.5 degrees. INTERGOVERNMENTAL

Court decision decreed that the existing Clean Air Act could be read to cover the anthropogenic greenhouse gases (GHGs).[35] The Court directed the EPA to decide whether climate change endangered the environment and, if so, to start writing rules to combat it. The EPA under President Obama decided that the dangers posed by climate change were real and required government action, and the agency began to craft rules requiring reductions in GHGs. Those efforts took on more significance when Congress was unable to pass climate change legislation in 2010.

But the agency soon found itself in a statutory trap: existing law says the EPA can only regulate sources that produce more than 100 tons of a given pollutant annually (tons per year or TPY). Because sources emit GHGs in amounts far larger than they emit more conventional pollutants, the 100 TPY cutoff was impractical – far too many sources would be covered by the demanding new climate change rules if that threshold was imposed. So the EPA wrote a "tailoring" rule raising the statutory threshold to facilities emitting at least 75,000 TPY, thereby reducing the universe of regulated facilities to a workable number. Following the typical calculation that delaying rules through litigation saves more money than it costs, the electric utility industry challenged this interpretation of the statute in court and the case traveled all the way up to the Supreme Court. In an opinion authored by conservative Justice Antonin Scalia, the Supreme Court upheld the EPA's decision on the basis of reasoning so convoluted and limited that it casts the agency's future authority to write climate change rules into doubt.[36] "We are not willing to stand on the dock and wave goodbye as EPA embarks on this multiyear voyage of discovery. We reaffirm the core administrative-law principle that an agency may not rewrite clear statutory terms to suit its own sense of how the statute should operate."[37] Or, in other words, without congressional action to update the act, the EPA will be forced to fight every step of the way as it tries to bring GHGs into alignment for the continuation of sustainable life on earth, consuming scarce resources and further weakening the effort the agency can expend on curbing other pollution.

A second example of the problems caused by outmoded laws is the EPA's lack of legal authority under the Clean Water Act to deal with "nonpoint" water pollution caused by rain-induced runoff from agricultural fields and parking lots. This water carries large quantities of nutrient pollution (nitrogen,

PANEL ON CLIMATE CHANGE, CLIMATE CHANGE 2007: SYNTHESIS REPORT 54 (2007), *available at* http://www.ipcc.ch//assessment-report/ar4/syr/ar4_syr.pdf.

[35] Massachusetts v. EPA, 559 U.S. 497 (2007).

[36] Utility Air Regulatory Group v. EPA, 134 S. Ct. 2427, 573 U. S. ____ (2014).

[37] *Id.* at 2446.

phosphorus, and sediment) into lakes, rivers, and streams and from there into great water bodies like the Chesapeake Bay and the Gulf of Mexico. Nutrient loading causes algal blooms that result in fish kills and have reached menacing proportions in recent years. As just one prominent example, scientists say that the Gulf of Mexico will soon have a dead zone the size of the state of New Jersey due largely to spring flooding of farm fields throughout the Midwest.[38]

Last but not least, consider the case of the OSHA's painfully outdated penalty provisions. Under the statute, employers whose willful disregard of safety standards contributes to a workplace fatality face half as much jail time (no more than six months) as a person who "harasses" a wild burro or horse in a national park (up to one year in prison).[39] The specific provisions are cited in the footnotes for the convenience of anyone who doubts the veracity of this sentence. As troubling, the statute allows employers cited for clear violations of safety and health rules to obtain a "stay" on any requirement that they abate those violations simply by filing an appeal of the citation. This catch-22 provision means that if OSHA enforcers want a company to fix dangerous conditions immediately and the company remains intransigent with respect to the civil penalties it will pay, the agency's enforcement staff must bargain away civil penalties to achieve corrective action.[40] No comparable provision exists in the statutes authorizing protection of public health and consumer safety.

POLITICIZATION OF THE RULEMAKING PROCESS

Decrying the "politicization" of any process in a democracy could seem naïve and wrong-headed. Politics, after all, are nothing more than the methods that politicians use to win elections. Once they have won, politics become the elaborate series of events (fundraisers, town halls, etc.) intended to compel politicians to anticipate the next election, using those perceptions to inform the votes they cast as members of Congress or the high-profile decisions presidents make in an executive capacity. In perpetual response to the ebb and flow of election cycles, Congress and the president have muddled along

---

[38] News Release, Univ. of Michigan, U-M Researcher and Colleagues Predict Possible Record-Setting Gulf of Mexico "Dead Zone" (June 18, 2013), http://ns.umich.edu/new/releases/21538-u-m-researcher-and-colleagues-predict-possible-record-setting-gulf-of-mexico-dead-zone-modest-chesapeake-bay-oxygen-starved-zone.

[39] *Compare* the Wild Free-Roaming Horses and Burros Act of 1971, 16 U.S.C. §§ 1331–1340 (2012) (imposing up to one year imprisonment on any person who "maliciously causes the death or harassment of any wild free-roaming horse or burro" because "Congress finds and declares that wild free-roaming horses and burros are living symbols of the historic and pioneer spirit of the West"), *with* Occupational Safety & Health Act, 29 U.S.C. § 666(e) (2006) (imposing a term not to exceed six months imprisonment for a "willful violation causing death to an employee").

[40] 29 U.S.C. § 659 (2006).

for more than two hundred years, filling the law books and raising or spending the public fisc. Having decision makers who are directly accountable to the people, with all the messy politics that come along with that approach, is a badge of pride for the country.

Of course, money has always played a major role in politics, however idealistic the self-congratulatory statements about direct democracy i will not be the only one reading this and saying, no the United States has a representative democracy; there's a difference that politicians haul out on Independence Day. From Boss Tweed to the rumors that John F. Kennedy Sr. bought the election for his son, the history of American democracy is not pretty, but – to mangle Winston Churchill – it is clearly better than anything else. But as resigned as we may be to taking the bitter (the corruption of politics by wealthy special interests) with the sweet (the exercise of direct democracy), the Supreme Court's decision in *Citizens United v. Federal Election Commission*[41] accelerated the trend toward making elections prohibitively expensive and elevating fund-raising to become the central preoccupation of office holders.[42] Because American business benefits so greatly from deregulatory campaigns, these developments make undermining federal regulatory agencies like shooting fish in a barrel.

Ironically, the fear that regulated industries would capture and immobilize administrative agencies was the original motivation for creating and expanding the size of the civil service, with the idealistic goal of insulating certain decisions from the rough and tumble of campaign politics.[43] The theory was that by assigning the difficult job of regulating harmful conduct to technocrats of many disciplines, who would do their best to reach solutions that are informed by science and economics, we would prevent capture and all the damage that comes with it. However much commentators have fretted about the inordinate power awarded to bureaucrats and the economic ills of regulatory excess, the administrative system has achieved independent credibility and it is difficult to imagine any workable coalition for abandoning it, however dysfunctional it becomes.[44]

Rulemaking is the threshold function of the modern regulatory state established four decades ago to protect public health, worker and consumer safety,

[41] 558 U.S. 310 (2010).
[42] *See, e.g.,* Center for Responsive Politics, *The Money Behind the Elections: Total Cost of US Elections* (1998–2012), OPENSECRETS.org, http://www.opensecrets.org/bigpicture/ (last visited Mar. 6, 2014) (showing the combined costs for congressional and presidential elections to be $6.3b in 2012, $5.3b in 2008, $4.1b in 2004, and $3.1b in 2000).
[43] *See generally* JOANNA L. GRISINGER, THE UNWIELDY AMERICAN STATE: ADMINSTRATIVE POLITICS SINCE THE NEW DEAL (2012); JAMES M. LANDIS, THE ADMINISTRATIVE PROCESS (1938); RONALD J. PESTRITTO, WOODROW WILSON AND THE ROOTS OF MODERN LIBERALISM (2005).
[44] *See generally* WILLIAM A. NISKANEN, BUREAUCRACY: SERVANT OR MASTER? (1973).

and the environment. Without it, regulated industries might not know what they are required to do to prevent harm or, even if they do know, economic constraints could make them ignore these options, especially in highly competitive markets. If all we wanted to do was compensate people who are injured by dangerous products, tainted drugs, or contaminated water, we could leave them to gain access to the court system through private lawsuits to recover the damages they suffer. If the goal is to prevent harm, prescriptive rules are the best alternative.

Strongly influenced by fears that money would come to dominate the regulatory process as it often has dominated politics, liberals in Congress wrote requirements into the new health, safety, and environmental laws passed in the early 1970s that guaranteed public interest groups a seat at the table when rules are written but, inevitably, agencies cut deals with regulated industries. Called the "pluralist" model,[45] this system has eroded to the point that it barely functions at agencies like the OSHA and is under siege at agencies like the EPA. Four aspects of these circumstances prove the case: (1) extraordinary delays in developing and promulgating final rules; (2) industry domination of the formal rulemaking process; (3) White House control of agency decision making and the introduction of crassly political considerations into those deliberations; and (4) extensive, successful, and equally politicized interference by Congress to kill or drastically modify rules that regulated industry does not like.

Ossification

Rulemaking, never the most nimble of processes, has slowed to a crawl and even to a halt at many agencies. Unless their authorizing statutes set deadlines for specific rules, agencies have become nearly paralyzed, eking out new regulation at an extraordinarily slow pace. Even in cases where statutes impose specific deadlines for action, agencies like the EPA, the most prominent entity of the group considered here that is governed by deadlines, almost always fail to begin a rulemaking until a public interest group drags it to court.[46] Agencies typically spend several years formulating their proposals, generally in consultation with special interest groups and the White House.[47] This aspect of the

---

[45] For an explanation of the model, see JAMES Q. WILSON, THE POLITICS OF REGULATION 385 (James Q. Wilson ed., 1980). *See also* GEORGE HOBERG, PLURALISM BY DESIGN: ENVIRONMENTAL POLICY AND THE AMERICAN REGULATORY STATE 8 (1992).

[46] The result of such "deadline suits" is a court order negotiated with the agency for when it will propose for comment and then finish the rulemaking. *See, e.g.,* 42 U.S.C. § 7604(a)(2) (2006).

[47] For an overview of the rulemaking process, see CORNELIUS M. KERWIN, RULEMAKING: HOW GOVERNMENT AGENCIES WRITE LAW AND MAKE POLICY (3d ed. 2003).

process is conducted behind closed doors, although the EPA, to its credit, posts notifications that it has had contact with an outside party. To run the gauntlet of further review, especially by the White House, and win approval to publish an actual rulemaking proposal, agencies must undertake elaborate analysis of the scientific and technological foundations of the proposal, as well as the uncertain economics of its costs and benefits.[48]

After a second round of White House review, the formal proposal is put out for public comment through publication in the *Federal Register*, the federal government's vehicle for informing the public about what it is doing. Controversial rules generate – quite literally – thousands of comments. These comments, the most important of which are each hundreds of pages long, must be read, analyzed, and summarized. Agencies must also prepare analyses of how the proposed rule will affect small business, communities of color, and state and local governments. Once an agency head makes a decision on the content of the final rule, it is forwarded to the White House for yet another round of review. Several years after the process begins, the rule is promulgated in final form.

The cumulative delays are known as "ossification" in the legal literature, a problem that was the motivation for Congress to write deadlines into the statutes in the first place.[49] For an accurate, albeit discouraging map of the process, visit the Public Citizen website and search for the "Flowchart of the Federal Rulemaking Process."[50] This complicated set of procedural and substantive hurdles is sufficiently daunting that agencies without statutory directives have strong incentives to avoid rulemaking, even though they may continue to go through the motions of slowly pursuing a few proposals. For example, the OSHA did not produce a single new rule during the first four years of the Obama administration and, at the rate it is going, may well not finish one during the second four years.

Time, Money, and Dominion

Obviously, this elaborate, highly technical, yet heavily politicized process is not for the faint of heart or the poorly financed. The empirical studies of rulemaking participants and outcomes show that such proceedings are overwhelmingly dominated by regulated industries.

---

[48] For a more detailed discussion of these issues, see STEINZOR & SHAPIRO, *supra* note 24.

[49] For a full discussion of the problem, see Thomas O. McGarity, *Some Thoughts on "Deossifying" the Rulemaking Process*, 41 DUKE L.J. 1385 (1992).

[50] *The Federal Rulemaking Process*, PUBLIC CITIZEN, http://www.citizen.org/documents/Regulations-Flowchart.pdf.

Jason and Susan Webb Yackee studied forty rules produced by four agencies from 1994 to 2001.[51] They found that business interests submitted 57 percent of the comments filed, governmental interests (e.g., states, cities, and towns) submitted 19 percent, and nonbusiness, nongovernmental interests filed 22 percent. A more recent study by Wendy Wagner, Katherine Barnes, and Lisa Peters suggests that this trend has accelerated significantly.[52] The Wagner study considered 90 EPA rules mandated by the 1990 Clean Air Act amendments to control emissions into the ambient air of toxic chemicals – "air toxics" for short. It found that even before a rule is proposed for official public comment, 178 "formal" (in writing) and "informal" (verbal communication) contacts per rule occurred. On average, industry representatives accounted for 170 of these contacts, while public interest groups were involved in approximately 0.7 per rule. Imbalance continued once the formal comment period began. Over 81 percent of the comments submitted on the 90 rules came from industry. Public interest groups participated in only 48 percent of the rulemakings, while industry representatives participated in all of them. Wagner and her colleagues went one crucial step further than simply counting noses, however, concluding that 83 percent of the changes made to final rules made them substantively weaker.

Centralized Review

In the arena of health, safety, and environmental policymaking, the Obama Administration began auspiciously enough when the president appointed qualified people to head the five agencies featured here: Lisa Jackson at the EPA, Margaret Hamburg at the FDA, David Michaels at the OSHA, Joe Main at the MSHA, and Michael Bromwich at the Department of Interior's Bureau of Ocean Energy Management, Regulation, and Enforcement. But by the end of his first year in office, it had become clear that Cass Sunstein, the White House "regulatory czar," had significantly more power than any of these presidential appointees.

The Obama administration has become well known for making virtually all significant policy decisions at the White House, sharply diminishing the influence and authority of the Cabinet. The president's historical legacy is out of focus at this close juncture, but historians are likely to take note of this drive toward centralized decision making because it has meant that issues and

---

[51] Jason Webb Yackee & Susan Webb Yackee, *A Bias Towards Business? Assessing Interest Group Influence on the U.S. Bureaucracy*, 68 J. POL. 128 (2006).

[52] Wendy Wagner et al., *Rulemaking in the Shade: An Empirical Study of EPA's Air Toxic Emission Standards*, 63 ADMIN. L. REV. 99 (2011).

initiatives considered by the White House staff to be unimportant or, even worse, harmful to the president's political fortunes are suppressed.

Sunstein, formerly a professor at the University of Chicago Law School and a personal friend of the president, directed the Office of Information and Regulatory Affairs (OIRA) within the Office of Management and Budget (OMB) during the president's first term. The OIRA is a surprisingly small institution with a staff of approximately thirty desk officers (mostly economists) who are responsible for reviewing five hundred to seven hundred agency regulations each year. A series of executive orders going back to President Ronald Reagan's time commanded every Executive Branch agency and department to obtain the OIRA's review before releasing a "significant" proposed or final rule, with the term defined as requirements that would impose $100 million or more in costs. In theory, agency heads could send rulemaking documents to the *Federal Register* for publication even if OIRA disapproved of their content, but in the four decades of White House review of such proposals, no presidential appointee has ever defied the White House.

Despite its small size, the OIRA has a firmly established track record as a one-way ratchet toward weakening health, safety, and environmental rules.[53] It employs a methodology known as "cost-benefit analysis," which is well known for overestimating regulatory costs and underestimating benefits that will be achieved by regulation, setting the stage for revamping rules that the OIRA thinks are too costly for industry.[54] These strong biases are exacerbated by the fact that, regardless of the time and energy that the originating agency spends on meeting with interested parties as it formulates a proposal, collecting and analyzing public comment, and drafting the voluminous analyses required to justify its final decision, the OIRA habitually runs its own version of a rule-making process. It has adopted the remarkable policy of meeting with anyone who asks. As a practical matter, once again, this policy means it is inundated with aggrieved industry representatives who have failed to badger the agency to produce the outcomes they desire.

A study I conducted with colleagues at the Center for Progressive Reform (CPR) examined 6,194 separate OIRA "reviews" of regulatory proposals and

---

[53] To read more about the OIRA's track record and history, see Rena Steinzor, *The Case for Abolishing Centralized White House Regulatory Review*, 1 MICH. J. ENVTL. & ADMIN. L. 209 (2012).

[54] For a more detailed discussion of these issues, see FRANK ACKERMAN & LISA HEINZERLING, PRICELESS: ON KNOWING THE PRICE OF EVERYTHING AND THE VALUE OF NOTHING (2004); David M. Driesen, *Is Cost-Benefit Analysis Neutral?*, 77 U. COLO. L. REV. 335 (2006); Thomas O. McGarity & Ruth Ruttenberg, *Counting the Cost of Health, Safety, and Environmental Regulation*, 80 TEX. L. REV. 1997 (2002); Richard W. Parker, *Grading the Government*, 70 U. CHI. L. REV. 1345 (2003).

final rules between October 16, 2001, when the OIRA first began to post notices of meetings held with outside parties on the Internet, and June 1, 2011, when the research period ended.[55] The study covered 1,080 meetings with 5,759 participants. Some 65 percent of the attendees at these meetings represented industry, about five times the number of people who appeared on behalf of public interest groups. Many of these participants were smart enough to approach the OIRA before an agency's rulemaking proposal was even released to the public: 452 (43 percent) of the meetings occurred at this early stage. This percentage was actually higher during the Obama administration (47 percent) than it was during the George W. Bush administration (39 percent). Such early interference means that the public sees the agency's proposal only after it has been reshaped by lobbyists and OIRA economists.

The CPR study also showed that the OIRA is preoccupied, you could even say obsessed, with the EPA. The agency sent 11 percent of the total number of matters reviewed by the OIRA during the study period, but was the subject of 41 percent of the 1,080 meetings. The OIRA reported that it changed 84 percent of these EPA rules, in comparison to a 65 percent change rate for other agencies. The CPR study did not attempt to determine the nature of such changes. Conceivably, they may have consisted primarily of the correction of typographical or grammatical mistakes, although that outcome suggests industry behavior that is irrational in the extreme.

As these results suggest, the early promise of the Obama administration for progress on health, safety, and environmental initiatives withered, and public interest advocates soon found themselves fighting the same battles they had undertaken during previous administrations. But the president remained officially supportive of an active rulemaking agenda. Following the 2010 midterm elections, however, with conservatives firmly in charge of the House of Representatives and already mounting a spirited attack on regulations, President Obama pivoted from benign neglect to repudiation, publishing an opinion piece in the *Wall Street Journal* promising to create a "twenty-first-century" system that eliminates "dumb" rules and avoids "excessive, inconsistent, and redundant regulation."[56] In two high-profile incidents involving the suspension of controversial rules, the president demonstrated that his message was neither rhetorical nor casual.

---

[55] Rena Steinzor et al., Ctr. for Progressive Reform, Behind Closed Doors at the White House: How Politics Trump Protection of Public Health, Worker Safety, and the Environment (2011), *available at* http://www.progressivereform.org/articles/OIRA_Meetings_1111.pdf.

[56] Barack Obama, Op-Ed., *Toward a 21st-Century Regulatory System*, Wall St. J., Jan. 18, 2011, at A17. For a progress report, see Cass Sunstein, Op-Ed., *21st-Century Regulation: An Update on the President's Reforms*, Wall St. J., May 26, 2011, at A17.

The first and most notorious involved the EPA's obligation under the Clean Air Act to periodically consider and, if necessary, upgrade standards for when levels of the air pollutant ozone (commonly called smog) are harmful to public health.[57] Excessive ozone triggers asthma and other respiratory problems; it also exacerbates heart disease. But because so many sources are implicated for more stringent controls when the EPA tightens the standard – motor vehicles, factories, power plants, even oil-based paints and other coatings – each five-year review is accompanied by intense lobbying on both sides of the issue.

In 2009, shortly after President Obama took office, Jackson promised environmentalists and public health groups that she would act as quickly as possible to tighten the 75 parts per billion standard established by President George W. Bush, whose reputation on environmental issues was poor. The Bush standard was harshly criticized by the EPA's highly regarded Clean Air Science Advisory Committee (CASAC) because it was not consistent with persuasive scientific evidence showing that a more stringent number – somewhere between 60–70 parts per billion – was necessary to accomplish the statute's goal of providing protection with an "adequate margin of safety."[58] In fact, the EPA calculated that by lowering the standard to 70 parts per billion, 2,200 heart attacks and 4,300 deaths could be avoided annually. On the basis of Jackson's promises, public interest groups put their lawsuit challenging the Bush standard on hold, an unusual demonstration of good will and faith in the new president. EPA staff got back to work on a new standard.

In September 2011, with the 2012 presidential election looming, President Obama ordered Jackson to stand down because of the bad economy: "I have continued to underscore the importance of reducing regulatory burdens and regulatory uncertainty, particularly as our economy continues to recover. With that in mind, and after careful consideration, I have requested that Administrator Jackson withdraw the draft Ozone National Ambient Air Quality Standards at this time."[59] This statement was quickly supplemented by a letter from Sunstein explaining that the White House was concerned about "minimiz[ing] regulatory costs and burdens, especially in this economically challenging time."[60] Jackson was blind-sided and for a few days the

---

[57] For basic information about ozone and its health effects, see *Ozone*, Am. Lung Ass'n, http://www.lung.org/healthy-air/outdoor/resources/ozone.html (last visited Mar. 19, 2014). The statutory provisions of the Clean Air Act dealing with the EPA's obligation to set National Ambient Air Quality Standards (NAAQS), of which ozone is one, appear at 40 C.F.R. § 50 (2013).

[58] 42 U.S.C. § 7409 (2006).

[59] 2011 Daily Comp. Pres. Doc. 1 (Sept. 2, 2011).

[60] Letter from Cass A. Sunstein, Administrator, OIRA, to Lisa Jackson, Administrator, EPA (Sept. 2, 2011), *available at* http://www.whitehouse.gov/sites/default/files/ozone_national_ambient_air_standards_letter.pdf.

media speculated that she might resign.[61] She did not, although she departed government soon after the 2012 election.

In the aftermath of the ozone decision, skillful investigative reporting by John Broder of the *New York Times* revealed that business executives at the highest levels had swarmed the White House, meeting with Richard Daley, then the president's chief of staff. Jack Gerard, the "pugnacious" head of the American Petroleum Institute brought maps showing the states where metropolitan areas would be out of compliance with the new standard – ones along the East Coast and in the Midwest were colored red and were central to the president's reelection strategy:

> "The maps were on the table," said Khary Cauthen, director of federal relations for the petroleum group and a White House environmental adviser in the Bush administration. "One of the CEOs had a whole spiel he was going to do, 'This is so bad here, so bad there,' but Daley shut him up. He was like, 'I got that.'"[62]

The truly remarkable implication of this exchange is not that the lobbyists would make such a blatant appeal if given the chance, but rather that the political opportunity to brag about cleaning up Chicago's air was swept off the table so easily. Fully understanding the repercussions of the decision, Gene Karpinski, president of the influential League of Conservation Voters, said it was "the worst thing a Democratic president had ever done on our issues."[63]

The second episode signaling that President Obama is not only running regulatory policy from the White House, but wants his political appointees to back off new rules, involved the Department of Labor's (DOL) Wage and Hour Division, and the ticklish problem of child labor on the farm. A series of gruesome accidents involving teenagers as young as fourteen who were smothered in grain elevators while "walking on the corn" to break up clotted chunks or who lost legs to giant augers used to remove such crops from elevators and silos prompted the DOL to propose tightening prohibitions on children engaging in "hazardous occupations" in agriculture.[64] Existing rules are shamefully outdated; they were written four decades ago and have never been updated. The fatality rate for young agricultural workers is *four times* greater than for peers in other workplaces.

---

[61] Gabriel Nelson, Greenwire, *Greens Urge Jackson Not to Quit EPA over Obama's Ozone Standard*, N.Y. TIMES, Sept. 9, 2011, http://www.nytimes.com/gwire/2011/09/09/09greenwire-greens-urge-lisa-jackson-not-to-quit-epa-over-15509.html.

[62] John M. Broder, *Re-Election Strategy Is Tied to a Shift on Smog*, N.Y. TIMES, Nov. 16, 2012, at A1.

[63] *Id.*

[64] For detailed information about the proposal and its fate, see Rena Steinzor, *The Age of Greed and the Sabotage of Regulation*, 47 WAKE FOREST L. REV. 503 (2012).

Issued under the Fair Labor Standards Act (FLSA), the DOL's proposed rule would have prohibited children under eighteen years old from working for hire to: (1) operate motorized farm machinery; (2) feed, herd, or otherwise handle farm animals (4-H activities were exempt); (3) manage crops stored in grain elevators or silos; or (4) pick tobacco. The proposal continued to exempt children who work for their parents or a relative or friend standing in the place of a parent, no matter what the children's age or the activity. The DOL received more than 10,000 comments on the proposal and was considering revisions through the normal rulemaking process. But in late January 2012, the House Small Business Committee's Subcommittee on Agriculture, Energy, and Trade held a hearing on the rule. Witnesses were stacked four to one against the proposal, and they spent the session explaining how the proposal would end "family farming" as we know it. Two represented the Farm Bureau, the large trade association that represents agricultural interests and primarily supports Republican candidates.

Rep. Denny Rehberg (R-Mont.), who was trying to unseat Democratic Senator Jon Tester, threatened to attach a rider to DOL's appropriations bill to stop the rulemaking. The justification? The proposal might prohibit the congressman from hiring his ten-year-old neighbor to herd his cashmere goats by riding a Kawasaki "youth" motorcycle after the undoubtedly startled critters: "I think you're sitting around watching reruns of 'Blazing Saddles' and that's your interpretation of what goes on in the West," he informed DOL deputy wage and hour administrator Nancy Leppink.[65]

On April 26, 2012, when press coverage had ebbed for the day, DOL issued a short, four-paragraph press release announcing it was withdrawing the entire proposal and would instead develop an "educational program" to reduce accidents among younger workers. This highly unusual action was taken before the DOL even had a chance to read public comments. Jon Tester won his race against Rehberg, although of course we will never know whether the Obama administration's effort to placate the Farm Bureau by killing the child labor rule made any difference. But the death of the proposal is likely to mean that the DOL will not return to the updating project for years to come and that it will take even longer for it to reach the abysmal working conditions confronted by migrant children as young as twelve, who work with the full knowledge of their parents in fields laced with pesticides and bereft of shade, in temperatures as high as 110 degrees.

---

[65] Dave Jamieson, *Denny Rehberg, GOP Congressman and Senate Hopeful, Blasts Child Labor Regulations*, HUFFINGTON POST, Feb. 2, 2012, http://www.huffingtonpost.com/2012/02/02/denny-rehberg-child-labor_n_1250207.html.

Blood Sport Rulemaking

As these incidents suggest, in lieu of decision making based on the best available science, technology, and economics, the process of writing most important regulations has degenerated into what Professor Thomas McGarity has memorably dubbed "blood sport."[66] The courts, the White House, and the Congress all provide opportunities to slow or derail regulatory initiatives, and no expense is spared by special interests with a financial stake in the outcome of such proceedings. The result is a disorganized, extraordinarily costly process during which affected industries spend millions of dollars to delay or derail regulatory proposals that will prove even more expensive if implemented. In the meantime, the possibility of winning even more valuable benefits for society as a whole by, for example, preventing another Wall Street meltdown or reducing air pollution, falls by the wayside, scarcely mentioned by the combatants or their politician targets. McGarity attributes this development to the polarized politics caused by deep rifts over the appropriate role of government: protector and intervenor versus facilitator of a "free" marketplace.

Multiple tools are available to blood sport combatants. In addition to meeting early and often with agency regulators, submitting public comments, running to the White House and the courts of appeal, they may request that appropriators attach to must-pass budget bills "riders" barring agencies from spending available funds to engage in any activity, including finishing or implementing a rule. In especially controversial proceedings, freestanding legislation proposing alternative solutions can be introduced. Although these bills may not go anywhere, they consume valuable and increasingly scarce time. Indeed, their most promising use is to chill agency officials from taking on such big fights again, especially given shrinking resources and growing problems.

Once again, empirical research helps to gauge the nature and scope of blood sport rulemaking. The Lobbying Disclosure Act requires individuals who represent clients before Congress to file registrations making their activities transparent.[67] A 2005 study showed that business or trade associations constituted over 94 percent of such reports and only three percent of registrants were public interest groups.[68] A 2009 study by the Center for Public Integrity

---

[66] Thomas O. McGarity, *Administrative Law as Blood Sport: Policy Erosion in a Highly Partisan Age*, 61 Duke L.J. 1671, 1671 (2012).

[67] 2 U.S.C. § 1603 (2012).

[68] Scott R. Furlong, *Businesses and the Environment: Influencing Agency Policymaking*, in Business and Environmental Policy 155, 175 (Michael E. Kraft & Sheldon Kamieniecki eds., 2007).

reported that industry groups worried about climate change legislation hired four lobbyists for each individual member of Congress, as compared with the approximately 170 lobbyists who work for environmental and health groups.[69] It is reasonable to assume that when the legislation died, many of this cadre shifted their lobbying efforts to the EPA, which is writing rules to accomplish greenhouse gas reductions.

Major corporations do not seem to hesitate to engage in blood sport rule-making. Yet their experience of this newly virulent process must seem like a cross between a war of attrition and a nuclear arms race. With hundreds of millions, even billions, at stake and multiple opportunities to wreak havoc, they must believe that they cannot afford to spend a dollar less than their opponents, nor can they stint on the human effort: dragging their chief executive officers (CEOs) to the Capitol for hearings and to lobby, analyzing an endless flood of opposition research and argumentation, wearing out shoe leather visiting twenty-something legislative aides in both houses, and choosing and supervising battalions of consultants. If they win, these extraordinary exertions may well seem worthwhile in retrospect. If they lose, the missed opportunity costs of more profitable endeavors must loom larger. From that perspective, a return to the days when regulatory decisions were made more or less on the merits in a process that was time-limited and predictable, by people who understand the full implications of the options from scientific, technical, economic, and legal points of view could seem like the good old days.

BUREAUCRACY BASHING

Long-serving and invariably astute *Washington Post* columnist Jim Hoagland once wrote: "Americans distrust government's powers and motives. They immediately get the joke that has a federal inspector or a state administrator fatuously saying, 'We're from the government and here to help.' Such suspicion is a healthy instinct – but one that is being carried to destructive and demagogic lengths."[70] Demagogic lengths? Really? Should we care about the

---

[69] Marianne Lavelle, *The Climate Change Lobby Explosion: Will Thousands of Lobbyists Imperil Action on Global Warming?*, CTR. FOR PUB. INTEGRITY (Feb. 25, 2009), http://www.public. org/node/4593 ("[M]ore than 770 companies and interest groups hired an estimated 2,340 lobbyists to influence federal policy on climate change in the past year, as the issue gathered momentum and came to a vote on Capitol Hill. ... [That] means that Washington can now boast more than four climate lobbyists for every member of Congress."); Marianne Lavelle, *The Climate Lobby from Soup to Nuts*, CTR. FOR PUB. INTEGRITY (Dec. 27, 2009), http://www. publicintegrity.org/2009/12/27/5479/climate-lobby-soup-nuts (reporting 160 environmental lobbyists).

[70] Jim Hoagland, *Dissing Government*, WASH. POST, Nov. 30, 2003, at B7.

time-honored tradition of beating up on political appointees and the civil service? This staple of American politics has reached new heights of bitterness and rage, subjecting administrators to punishing abuse at congressional hearings and delaying Senate confirmation of controversial nominations for months and even years, prompting many to withdraw.

Political scientists and public administration experts call the practice of demeaning government employees in public "bureaucracy bashing." In 2006, a team of such scholars assembled focus groups of Senior Executive Service managers to discuss the effects of the practice.[71] Participants characterized the effects of such criticism as destructive, even devastating, and said they hesitated to acknowledge they were civil servants in some social situations: "[Y]ou really felt uneasy about being federal employees. People would look at you as if you had cancer."[72] The authors of the study concluded that "[s]enior managers repeatedly said that bashing creates permanent and overwhelming negative mental frames and political symbols for career bureaucrats, which affects morale, recruitment, training, and overall work environment."[73]

It may be hard to imagine that the practice of what political scientists and public administration experts call "bureaucracy bashing" could have deteriorated from the days in 1995 when then-House majority leader Tom Delay (R-TX) compared the EPA to the Gestapo in a rant on the floor[74] and former House speaker Newt Gingrich (R-GA) called FDA head David Kessler a "thug and a bully."[75] But it has. When Gina McCarthy, President Obama's nominee for EPA administrator, was undergoing confirmation, she was handed 1,100 questions to answer before Republicans would vote on her nomination. After answers were submitted, Sen. David Vitter (R-LA) put her nomination on hold until the agency agreed to submit some version of the underlying data used in 1997 to write clean air rules. At her nomination hearing, McCarthy was grilled not about her thoughts on the work done by the agency, but rather about her use of personal email to conduct EPA business. She was compelled to admit that she sometimes used a personal account to email documents to herself that she needed to review while she was staying at a family home in Boston. McCarthy's nomination was ultimately upheld, but she continues to bear

---

[71] R. Sam Garrett et al., *Assessing the Impact of Bureaucracy Bashing by Electoral Campaigns*, 66 PUB. ADMIN. REV. 228 (2006).

[72] *Id.* at 232.

[73] *Id.* at 234.

[74] Bruce Burkhard, *Year in Review: Congress vs. Environment; Environmental Laws Suffer under GOP-Controlled Congress*, CABLE NEWS NETWORK, Dec. 29, 1995, http://edition.cnn.com/EARTH/9512/congress_enviro/.

[75] John Schwartz, *Conservative Foes of Government Regulation Focus on the FDA*, WASH. POST, Jan. 21, 1995, at A7.

the brunt of bitter browbeating at numerous oversight hearings, when she is constantly interrupted, frequently scolded, and sometimes ridiculed. Her ordeal cannot have encouraged potential future candidates for the position.[76]

CONCLUSION

Traditional regulation to protect public health, worker and consumer safety, and the environment is a hit-or-miss proposition these days and the costs of this dysfunction are increasingly obvious and unbearable. So much is wrong, both with the regulatory systems and with the institutions that must play a central role in reforming them, that it seemed quite obvious to me about two years ago that it was time to think far outside the box. The result is the first book-length justification I have seen to the effect that we use the criminal justice system to throw the book at the worst cases, thereby shoring up the regulatory system until something far closer to real reform can be achieved. We should have paid more attention to criminal enforcement twenty, thirty, or forty years ago. Expanding its application now is justified not only by the gravity of the crimes but by the weakness of the alternative approach.

---

[76] *See, e.g.*, *Rep. Gardner Questions Gina McCarthy on Expansion of EPA's Red Tape*, COMM. ON SPACE, SCIENCE & TECH. YOUTUBE CHANNEL (June 29, 2012), http://www.youtube. com/watch?v=EOwBL_Z9aj8; *Senator Barrasso Questions EPA Nominee Gina McCarthy at EPW Hearing*, COMM. ON ENERGY & COMMERCE YOUTUBE CHANNEL (Apr. 11, 2013), http://www.youtube.com/watch?v=CW-Ho9KnptI; *Congressman Harris Questions EPA*, COMM. ON SPACE, SCIENCE & TECH. YOUTUBE CHANNEL (Sept. 23, 2011), http://www. youtube.com/watch?v=OS5ovprREAA; *Congressman Morgan Griffith Questions EPA Official on Farm Dust*, REP. MORGAN GIFFITH YOUTUBE CHANNEL (Oct. 25, 2011), http://www. youtube.com/watch?v=1H8vu3NXoXw; *10-25-11 E&P Hearing on "Farm Dust Regulation Prevention Act of 2011" (H.R. 1633)*, CONGRESSMAN GARDNER YOUTUBE CHANNEL (Oct. 26, 2011), http://www.youtube.com/watch?v=CNpriQvAdyY.

2

White Collar Crime Today

Thus criminal justice tells us where the moral boundaries are, where the line lies between good and bad. It patrols those boundary lines, day and night, rain or shine. It shows the rules directly, dramatically, visually through asserting and enforcing them. (There are lessons from non-enforcement, too: from situations where the boundaries are indistinct, or the patrol corrupt or asleep; and society is quick to learn these lessons, too.)

Lawrence M. Friedman, *Crime and Punishment in American History*[1]

WHITE COLLAR NEGLECT

American law provides federal and state prosecutors with powerful authority to charge individuals and corporations with crimes and to win, but they rarely pursue such cases. This paradox is especially poignant with respect to criminality that kills or injures workers or consumers, or that causes irretrievable damage to natural resources. Prosecutors have largely turned a blind eye to such violations, depending instead on a broken regulatory system to deter illegal behavior. To be sure, some of the criminal statutes that apply to health and safety offenses treat them lightly: purveyors of tainted food or grossly negligent employers face misdemeanor charges providing for prison terms of a year or less. Rather than working to develop cases that overcome these weaknesses by, for example, charging multiple violations that add up to significant jail time, prosecutors have largely abandoned those fields.

One conundrum running throughout the field of neglected criminal enforcement is whether to charge corporations or their employees. The decision is admittedly complex, but forgoing enforcement altogether should not be a third and favored option. As a matter of principle, corporations should be subject to prosecution when the violations were endemic to the corporate

---

[1] Lawrence M. Friedman, Crime and Punishment in American History 10 (1993).

structure, as opposed to the brainchild of isolated, rogue employees. Individuals can and should be charged alongside their corporate employers, providing a different kind of deterrent to future malfeasance.

In recent years, criminal fines in the hundreds of millions, and even billions, of dollars have been collected from corporations. When BP pled guilty in December 2012 to charges of manslaughter, environmental crimes, and lying to Congress, for example, it paid $4 billion in fines.[2] The deterrent effect of such very large fines, which hopefully will prove to be trendsetters, remains to be seen. For large and profitable companies they could easily be absorbed as a cost of doing business. Indeed, America's traumatic experiences with BP indicate that forcing a company to plead guilty to criminal charges does not necessarily motivate changes that prevent eerily similar disasters. In the years leading up to the Macondo fiasco, the corporation had entered into multiple criminal plea agreements relating to the Texas City refinery explosion and spills of oil on Alaska's North Slope. None had enough of an effect.[3]

Of course, prosecutors do not face an "either/or" choice between corporations and their employees. As explored in greater detail in the third part of this volume, charges against individuals can and should be brought in tandem with prosecutions against their corporate employers. To return again to BP, criminal charges have been brought against two supervisors who were in charge of the drilling crews aboard the ill-fated rig. Neither man had adequate technical training and both were left virtually unsupervised under a fundamentally flawed management system that took engineers out of the chain of command responsible for verifying due care during the delicate and extraordinarily dangerous job of closing down the well.[4]

---

[2]   Azmat Khan, *BP to Pay Record $4.5 Billion for 2010 Gulf Oil Spill*, FRONTLINE (Nov. 15, 2012), http://www.pbs.org/wgbh/pages/frontline/business-economy-financial-crisis/the-spill/bp-to-pay-record-4-5-billion-for-2010-gulf-oil-spill/.

[3]   United States v. BP Prods. N. Am. Inc., 610 F. Supp. 2d 655, 670 (S.D. Tex. 2009) (accepting the proposed guilty plea agreement by BP for felony violation of the Clean Air Act in the Texas City explosion); Consent Decree, United States v. BP Exploration (Alaska) Inc., No. 3:09–00064-JWS (D. Alaska May 3, 2011), *available at* http://www.epa.gov/compliance/resources/decrees//cwa/bpn orthslope-cd.pdf (setting forth the details of the criminal plea agreement in the North Slope spill); *see also* Jane F. Barrett, *When Business Conduct Turns Violent: Bringing BP, Massey, and Other Scofflaws to Justice*, 48 AM. CRIM. L. REV. 287, 297, 302 (2011) (discussing how the North Slope spill and the Texas City explosion both occurred a few short years before the Deepwater Horizon accident, and failed to make necessary changes to BP's corporate decision making).

[4]   Robert M. Kaluza and Donald J. Vidrine, the two highest ranking supervisors on the Deepwater Horizon rig, were the "well site leaders" employed by BP. *See* Superseding Indictment at 9–14, United States v. Kaluza, No. 2:12-cr-00265-ILRL-ALC, 2012 WL 5520720 (E.D. La. Nov. 14, 2012), *available at* http://www.justice.gov/iso/opa/resources/2520121115143638743323.pdf. Kaluza and Vidrine were charged with eleven counts of involuntary manslaughter, eleven counts of seaman's

Prosecutors are rarely asked why they failed to pursue white collar criminal enforcement in the health, safety, and environmental arenas and these motivations have never been studied empirically at the federal level. But their reluctance to prosecute members of the financial services industry in the wake of the 2008 market crash has generated undulating waves of criticism that have proven quite revealing. When confronted by members of Congress with questions about the Department of Justice's (DOJ) poor track record, Attorney General Eric Holder has cited concern about the stability of the U.S. and global economies as a central factor. The history of how this career federal prosecutor and the people who work for him convinced themselves that their mission included the responsibility of ignoring blatant wrongdoing because criminal charges could push companies out of business is well known among criminal law *cognoscenti* but quite obscure to the general public.

ACTUS REUS AND MENS REA

American law defines a crime as consisting of two elements: an illegal act, or *actus reus*, and a guilty state of mind, or *mens rea*.[5] Bad acts are identified as criminal under statutes that are written and approved by legislatures and signed by chief executives. For the purposes of the crimes discussed here – behavior that harms or threatens to harm the public health, worker or consumer safety, and the environment – a bad act can include a failure to take action that could have prevented the crime.

Actus reus is in turn divided into the legal categories of *mala in se* – crimes that are unanimously recognized as evil in and of themselves, such as murder, robbery, or assault – and *mala prohibita* – crimes that breach standards that may change, such as requirements that workers be provided with certain types of protective gear if they are asked to undertake dangerous activities. "Regulatory violations" are assigned to the *mala prohibita* category and, to the disadvantage of their human victims, are viewed by legal experts as less serious than overtly violent crimes deemed *mala in se*. Sociologists have added two more pragmatic labels to the mix: "street crime," always the

---

manslaughter, and one count for a CWA violation of negligently discharging oil or causing oil to be discharged in connection with the Macondo well blowout. *Id.*

[5]   This chapter is designed to give lay people a basic understanding of existing criminal law as a foundation for the investigation of industrial catastrophes contained in Part II of this volume. It is not intended to be either a comprehensive or a sophisticated discussion of the criminal law, as written or applied. For thorough information about criminal law in the U.S., see JOSHUA DRESSLER, UNDERSTANDING CRIMINAL LAW (6th ed. 2012).

overriding priority for federal, state, and local prosecutors, and "white collar crime," which they pursue erratically.[6]

Prosecutors prove state of mind through circumstantial, as opposed to direct, evidence because the U.S. Constitution protects defendants from any demand that they admit culpability.[7] The challenges of amassing such evidence against senior executives have emerged as the most important hurdle to mounting white collar criminal cases against individuals as well as corporations.

Mens rea doctrine remains a crucial component of criminal prosecutions because it enabled the evolution from old English law, which embraced a potent brew of feudal values, to enlightenment, when moral norms became determinative. In his seminal 1931 article *Mens Rea*,[8] Harvard Professor Francis Bowes Sayre describes English law as based on blood feuds and vengeance, when society expected a senior member of the victim's family to avenge a violent death by killing the murderer. He explains the law's later evolution and its reflection of the more humane idea that people can only be condemned if they know what they did and intended a bad outcome. Or, in other words, the development of *mens rea* marked the rejection of an "eye for an eye" system of citizen-administered justice in favor of the infinitely more sophisticated government-sponsored examination of whether the defendant should be culpable.

Until the turn of the twentieth century, almost all crimes were categorized as *mala in se* – against the laws of nature – and were prosecuted at the local level. District attorneys and the police worked to catch murderers, rapists, arsonists, and armed robbers, bringing them to trial in state courts and locking them away in prison. The federal government played at most a minor role, concentrating on crimes such as counterfeiting that undermined the national economy. The Federal Bureau of Investigation (FBI) did not exist until 1908 and the predecessor of the Bureau of Alcohol, Tobacco, Firearms, and Explosives (BATF) was established at the beginning of Prohibition (1920–33). Legal historian Lawrence Friedman describes the federal role in policing crime during the country's first 130 years as akin to "brain of a dinosaur: a tiny ganglion, in Washington, D.C., inside a huge and extensive body."[9]

The Industrial Revolution profoundly changed the relationship between the federal government and its state and local counterparts. Burgeoning

---

[6] The phrase "white collar crime" was coined by sociologist Edwin Sutherland in 1949. His book, WHITE COLLAR CRIME: THE UNCUT VERSION (1983), is a classic in the field and has been reprinted and read by generations of criminologists.

[7] U.S. CONST. amend. V.

[8] Francis Bowes Sayre, *Mens Rea*, 45 HARV. L. REV. 974 (1932). Legal scholarship seems to have been sufficiently sparse in those days to allow the great minds of the time to assign broad and grandiose titles to their most important work product.

[9] FRIEDMAN, *supra* note 1, at 113.

population, the great migrations from the East to the West and from South to North, and the gradual evolution from rural agriculture to urban manufacturing prompted Congress and a series of willing presidents to move in on areas traditionally occupied by state and local governments with remarkable force and rapidity. At the turn of the twentieth century, when exposés by muckraking journalists regarding the safety of the food supply and the sale of dangerous home remedies alarmed the public, Congress began, slowly but surely, not only to create a new kind of crime but to wrest control over the prosecution of people who ran afoul of the new laws from state and local prosecutors to the federal agencies they created to police the marketplace.

This sweeping federal expansion made no effort to take over the enforcement of traditional criminal laws, unless the crime crossed state lines (for example, kidnapping), involved certain federally related institutions (for example, insured banks), or took place in federally controlled places (for example, army bases or Native American reservations). Instead, federal police and prosecutors were assigned to enforce a torrent of what legal scholars call "economic regulation," a broad term that encompassed everything from the banking industry in the aftermath of the Great Depression to the FDA's supervision of drugs, food, and medical devices. This trend toward federal hegemony and the creation of new regulatory programs waxed again in the 1970s, when Congress created a new roster of federal agencies, including the EPA, writing criminal liability provisions into each new authorizing statute. The upshot was the establishment of an estimated three thousand federal crimes, most focused on particular types of behavior covered by regulatory requirements.[10]

Although white collar health and safety cases were firmly lodged conceptually within the newly powerful federal criminal enforcement establishment, they were soon eclipsed by crimes like interstate and international drug dealing and, more recently, terrorism. The media, prosecutors, and politicians consistently portrayed those offenses as urgent problems that are more elemental, more threatening, and more injurious.

This stark reality is well illustrated by the U.S. Bureau of Justice Statistics website, which is the central repository that captures data about prosecutorial and criminal trends at all levels of government. The site displays reports and statistics galore on street crime, from violent offenses like murder or assault to property theft to trends in the marauding activities of urban gangs.[11] The last comprehensive study of white collar crime was conducted in 1988, coinciding with a period of about fifteen years when flamboyant behavior on Wall Street,

[10] W. John Moore, *The High Price of Good Intentions*, NAT'L J., May 8, 1993, at 1140 ("Once upon a time, all crime was local. At last count, though, there were more than 3,000 federal crimes.").
[11] U.S. BUREAU OF JUSTICE STATISTICS, http://www.bjs.gov/.

a wave of high-profile corporate bankruptcies, and popular support for environmental protection briefly put white collar prosecutions back on the map.[12]

Despite this long and discouraging period of neglect, recent indictments of responsible corporate officers involved in the Macondo blowout, the Big Branch mine collapse, and the Peanut Corporation of America shipment of peanut paste laced with salmonella suggest that prosecutors may resuscitate criminal prosecutions as a weapon to combat the scofflaws that now pervade regulated industries.

CORPORATE CRIMINALS

Consistent with the media's obsessive preoccupation with street crime, most people assume that defendants in criminal cases are always human beings. Yet the country has convicted corporations and other institutions of white collar crimes for over a century. The Supreme Court first decided in 1909 that corporations could be convicted of crimes committed by their human agents because to immunize them would deprive the government of one of its most potent tools for preventing illegal behavior.[13] Congress followed suit, and under the vast majority of white collar criminal statutes, the companies that own or operate the facilities where problems originate are liable under the same standards and with the benefit of the same defenses as their individual employees.

When it established corporate criminal liability, the 1909 Supreme Court drew a direct analogy to tort law, which has long allowed injured parties to recover monetary damages from corporations when employee negligence caused the harm. Of course, corporations, which are created on paper and directed by groups of people, do not have separate minds that are capable of harboring evil intent. Instead, prosecutors must argue that their employees' *mens rea* should be imputed to the company. A company has a valid defense if its employees act outside the scope of their employment or act in a manner that harms the company. The most obvious example is a financial officer who embezzles from corporate accounts.

Obviously, corporations cannot go to prison. Instead, they are punished through the collection of monetary fines and judicial orders requiring them to take action to correct the underlying violations. In the pungent words of Edward, First Baron Thurlow, an English Chancellor of court in the late eighteenth century, "Did you ever expect a corporation to have a conscience, when it has no soul to be damned, and no body to be

---

[12]   Stanton Wheeler et al., *White Collar Crimes and Criminals*, 25 AM. CRIM. L. REV. 331 (1988).

[13]   N.Y. Cent. R.R. Co. v. United States, 212 U.S. 481 (1909).

kicked?"[14] The corrective action available today can be quite elaborate, including the overhaul of the facilities and managerial systems that caused the violation. These charges can cost more than the criminal fines assessed against a company, although their price tags may remain undisclosed. Nevertheless, except in cases involving small, closely held companies, where the owners are likely to have been directly involved in the crime, corporate fines and other costs are absorbed as a cost of doing business and, as a result, may have little impact on senior management.

Academics have consumed an astounding amount of ink and gigabytes wringing their hands about the logic and fairness of imputing morality, much less bad intent, to an inanimate entity.[15] For the most part, the courts and practicing lawyers are uninterested in these abstractions. In any event, the fundamental nature of corporate criminal liability is unlikely to change any time soon, a reality that begs the difficult question of when to prosecute a firm, when to target its officers, and when to include both in an indictment.

The threshold argument pursued by opponents of corporate criminal liability is that pursuing the corporation has the potential to drive customers away, lowering the company's stock price, with the result that stockholders, presumed to be innocent bystanders, lose money. On the other hand, stockholders arguably benefited from the corporation's corner-cutting on regulatory requirements. Forcing the company to disgorge these ill-gotten gains and fix the root causes of the violations seems fair, not least from the perspective of competitors who complied with the letter and spirit of the law. Prosecutors may also be tempted to charge corporations precisely because they have the

[14] Professor John C. Coffee Jr., in his well-known article *"No Soul to Damn: No Body to Kick": An Unscandalized Inquiry into the Problem of Corporate Punishment*, 79 MICH. L. REV. 386 (1981) (giving Edward, First Baron Thurlow, as the source of the quote, as quoted in M. KING, PUBLIC POLICY AND THE CORPORATION 1 (1977)).

[15] *See, e.g.*, Patricia S. Abril & Ann Morales Olazábal, *The Locus of Corporate Scienter*, 2006 COLUM. BUS. L. REV. 81; M. Diane Barber, *Fair Warning: The Deterioration of Scienter Under Environmental Criminal Statutes*, 26 LOY. L.A. L. REV. 105 (1992); Andrea M. Fike, *A Mens Rea Analysis for the Criminal Provisions of the Resource Conservation and Recovery Act*, 6 STAN. ENVTL. L.J. 174 (1986–1987); V. S. Khanna, *Is the Notion of Corporate Fault A Faulty Notion?: The Case of Corporate Mens Rea*, 79 B.U. L. REV. 355 (1999); William S. Laufer, *Corporate Bodies and Guilty Minds*, 43 EMORY L.J. 647 (1994) (critiquing some methods of finding corporate *mens rea* and proposing a constructive model of corporate culpability); David Luban et al., *Moral Responsibility in the Age of Bureaucracy*, 90 MICH. L. REV. 2348 (1992); Susan F. Mandiberg, *The Dilemma of Mental State in Federal Regulatory Crimes: The Environmental Example*, 25 ENVTL. L. 1165 (1995); Lawrence E. Mitchell & Theresa A. Gabaldon, *If I Only Had a Heart: Or, How Can We Identify a Corporate Morality*, 76 TUL. L. REV. 1645 (2002); Lawrence E. Mitchell, *Cooperation and Constraint in the Modern Corporation: An Inquiry into the Clauses of Corporate Immorality*, 73 TEX. L. REV. 477 (1995); Raymond Paternoster & Sally Simpson, *Sanction Threats and Appeals to Morality: Testing a Rational Choice Model of Corporate Crime*, 30 LAW & SOC'Y REV. 549 (1996).

resources to take remedial action, a goal that may be far more important than the potential risk of stigma.

Indicting employees in lieu of the corporation has the advantage of punishing those who are directly responsible for the crime. It can also have a more potent deterrent effect than assessing fines that seem like a routine cost of doing business. Yet convicting line supervisors who have little choice but to make do with the training and other resources upper management has provided is unjust in many circumstances and is likely to have far less deterrent effect on future misconduct than charging upper level decision makers. Proving intent on the part of managers two, three, or more levels removed from the activity that gave rise to the crime can be difficult, even if it is clear that the policies they imposed – for example, cutting maintenance or requiring abusive amounts of overtime – set the stage for the violations. But such prosecutions are well worth the extra effort.

In his excellent book, *Just Culture*, Sidney Dekker examines cases in which nurses and paramedics were prosecuted criminally when patients died.[16] Prosecutors generally did not charge the doctors and hospital administrators who were responsible for creating the circumstances that led to the death. Dekker argues that this approach defeats the establishment of a safety culture within an institution because it deters frontline workers from talking candidly with supervisors or outsiders about dangerous practices. In addition, only charging low-level employees reduces the deterrence value of prosecutions from the perspective of corporate executives, who are then free to rationalize the crime as the product of individual human error.

Dekker's objections are important on both fairness and deterrence grounds. In general, prosecutors should think twice about pursuing low-level employees when a firm's culture is really to blame. But low-level employees sometimes engage in behavior so egregious that prosecutors cannot possibly ignore it. Pursuing such behavior can also produce evidence that allows prosecutors to climb the corporate ladder, building cases against more senior executives. With the growing dysfunction of traditional regulation, the deterrence potential of expanded criminal prosecution has become an overridingly important goal. I will argue here for a case-based approach to the choice of defendant. I suggest criteria for determining how prosecutors might balance these conflicting values in the final section of the book.

The crimes described in this chapter run along a continuum from manslaughter under state law to "reckless endangerment" under federal law to regulatory violations considered sufficiently egregious that they warrant criminal prosecution. Manslaughter and reckless endangerment charges are felonies.

---

[16] SIDNEY DEKKER, JUST CULTURE: Balancing Safety and Accountability (2d ed. 2012).

Federal regulatory violations can be classified as misdemeanors or felonies, depending on the statute at issue.

STATE CRIMES

The Ford Pinto Fiasco

A county prosecutor in Elkhart, Indiana, brought the first prosecution of a major U.S. corporation for reckless homicide. In 1978, Michael Cosentino and his small staff obtained an indictment against the Ford Motor Company over the Pinto, the company's first subcompact car. The Pinto's gas tank was installed in the rear without sufficient protection, a flaw that turned it into a fireball in the event of even a slow-moving rear-end collision. Three young women who lived in Elkhart burned to death when their Pinto was struck by a beer delivery truck.

The case was a fiasco for the prosecutor. Ford outspent Cosentino's office by a factor of 100 to 1 ($2 million to $20,000). The Indiana statute defining reckless homicide as a crime was passed in 1977, meaning that prosecutors could not introduce the most compelling evidence against the company: memos written years earlier that revealed Ford's decision not to install safety measures that would have cost a few dollars and prevented most fatalities. Cosentino, his staff, and volunteer attorneys were instead compelled to argue that it was Ford's contemporary failure to recall the car that constituted the crime.[17] Even though the jury ultimately acquitted Ford, the case is still studied in business schools as an example of the worst that can happen if corporate ethics are corrupted.[18]

---

[17] LEE PATRICK STROBEL, RECKLESS HOMICIDE: FORD'S PINTO TRIAL 58 (1980) ("[Judge] Jones ruled that the indictment was constitutional only when read to charge that Ford acted recklessly by failing to repair or warn about the Pinto during the 41-day time period before the [crash at issue]. The elements of the indictment concerning the car's defective and dangerous design were relevant only to establish the reason why Ford should have warned the public or fixed the car during that 41-day period."); Gary T. Schwartz, *The Myth of the Ford Pinto Case*, 43 RUTGERS L. REV. 1013, 1017–18 (1991) ("In August 1978 – half a year after the verdict in the [*Grimshaw*] tort case – a 1973 Pinto was involved in a fatal crash in Ulrich, Indiana. Indiana public officials decided to prosecute Ford for the crime of reckless homicide. Because the reckless homicide statute had been enacted only in 1977, Ford could not be prosecuted for the reckless design of the Pinto; rather, *the prosecution needed to show a reckless post-1977 failure by Ford to repair or warn*. Largely because of the narrowness of the resulting issue, at trial the prosecution was not able to secure the admission of internal Ford documents on which it had hoped to build its case. ... In March 1980 the Indiana jury found Ford not guilty. The jury ... concluded that Ford had avoided recklessness in the conduct of its recall program.") (emphasis added).

[18] For an idea of the reading assigned in such courses, see Dennis A. Gioia, *Pinto Fires and Personal Ethics: A Script Analysis of Missed Opportunities*, 11 J. BUS. ETHICS 379 (1992). Mr. Gioia was a senior manager at Ford who was responsible for responding to reports of defects

Murder vs. Manslaughter

State criminal prosecutions today are governed by statutes patterned on the *Model Penal Code* in two-thirds of the states. The *Code* was written after years of deliberation by a group of distinguished academics, judges, and practitioners with the goal of modernizing rules that had evolved in fits and starts since colonists brought English precedents to the American continent. I will use the *Code* as my only source for how states handle these matters because that approach simplifies the discussion, which is intended as enough of a general overview to permit readers to evaluate the policy questions at the heart of this volume.

The *Code* distinguishes between murder – a killing committed with forethought and deliberation – and manslaughter – a killing committed in the heat of passion (voluntary manslaughter) or "without due caution and circumspection" (involuntary manslaughter).[19] In the health, safety, or environmental arena, any act or omission that resulted in death would be considered involuntary manslaughter because white collar employees engaged in industrial activity do not intend to kill their fellow workers, themselves, or innocent bystanders. When their acts or omissions cause an explosion, a mine collapse, or the manufacture of a drug tainted by fungus, the subsequent trouble can cripple careers and cost hundreds of millions – even billions, drive down stock prices, and can even put companies out of business. People involved in the chain of command must hire lawyers, sometimes compensated by the company and sometimes not. Trying to make a case that such employees, especially those in more senior positions, have murdered their employees or members of the public would be fruitless and inappropriate. Yet people who operate industrial facilities can be so inured to unacceptable risk, so focused on profit, or so careless about the way they operate that they deserve the harsh punishment of a manslaughter conviction when their behavior contributes to the killing of others. If managers are not punished for turning a blind eye to great and foreseeable risk, the government loses the opportunity to deter others who function in the same way.

In a manslaughter case, the defendant must have been more than just careless but instead must exhibit gross negligence or recklessness. Professor Joshua Dressler, who has written an influential treatise on American criminal law, dubs this category "criminal negligence."[20] Because manslaughter,

at the time the Pinto problem arose. He then became an academic, teaching and writing about organizational behavior.

[19] DRESSLER, *supra* note 5, § 31.08, at 535 (quoting 4 WILLIAM BLACKSTONE, COMMENTARIES *192).

[20] *Id.* at 535.

especially when it is involuntary, is viewed as less serious than murdering a person in cold blood, the sentence for such a crime is lighter, involving prison terms of a few years, as opposed to life terms or the death penalty.

The *Code* defines the *mens rea* for manslaughter as acting either "negligently" or "recklessly," and these terms are often used interchangeably, although they have distinctly different meanings.[21] A person acts *negligently* if he should be aware of a substantial risk, but continues to act or fail to act without regard to it. A person acts *recklessly* if he both anticipates and consciously disregards a substantial and unjustified risk.

At this point, a short detour into the law of torts (the recovery of private damages for an injury caused by another's acts or omissions) is necessary. Most lawsuits allege that the defendant – or tortfeasor – was negligent. To win her case, the plaintiff must show that the defendant owed her a duty of care and breached that duty in a way that directly caused the plaintiff's injury. Duties of care are established by reference to industry standards – what typical firms do to avoid hazards. Breaches are judged from the perspective of the hypothetical "reasonable person" – what the average or typical person would do under the circumstances, not what the defendant says he did. These concepts also apply in the criminal context. So, in sum, to be culpable in a criminal case, a defendant must have been extraordinarily careless, with disastrous results, as judged by a reasonable person standard.

A Guilty Mind

Determining the nature and degree of *mens rea* that triggers culpability is a complicated endeavor because the process for applying such rules is neither centralized nor uniform. State standards vary depending on how they are applied to the facts of a given case. Depending on the state and the specific court involved, decisions in criminal trials are made either by juries or by judges after so-called bench trials, further complicating the applications of *mens rea* rules.[22] When judges preside over trials where a jury will make the decision, they give the jury instructions that attempt to explain the law in plain English and are often the subject of bitter disputes between prosecutors and defense attorneys. The defense may continue fighting over jury

---

[21] *Id.* § 10.07[B][3], at 142.

[22] Many people probably assume that criminal trial by jury is a requirement in America, but this right has eroded substantially. For further information, see T. Ward Frampton, *The Uneven Bulwark: How (and Why) Criminal Jury Trials Vary by State*, 100 CALIF. L. REV. 183 (2012).

instructions on appeal. Indeed, among the most common grounds for an appeal is that the judge "charged" the jury erroneously.

The *Code* imposes additional conditions for proving *mens rea* against a corporate defendant on the theory that because liability is based on imputing the bad behavior of its employees, it should not be held liable for bad behavior it made every effort to avoid. First, the statute defining the crime must evince a clear intention to impose liability on corporations, and not just individuals. Second, senior managers or the board of directors must have "authorized, requested, commanded, performed or recklessly tolerated," the "commission of the offense."[23] From a prosecutorial perspective, these rules are considered quite burdensome. Professor Kathleen Brickey, a leading national expert on white collar crime, has written that the *Code* provision reflects the view that "if we must tolerate [the idea of] corporate criminal liability at all, we should tolerate precious little of it."[24] Among the states that have adopted the *Code*, most have made their provisions regarding corporate culpability more stringent or, in other words, made such cases easier for prosecutors to prove.

Willful Blindness

Once the prosecutor starts to climb the corporate ladder in search of culpable parties, evidence demonstrating actual knowledge of bad acts can be quite hard to obtain. Unless they left an explicit paper trail or made unambiguous verbal admissions to codefendants, defendants are free to argue that, as the old adage goes, they saw no evil, heard no evil, and spoke no evil. Unwilling to allow such an easy escape, federal and state courts have developed jury instructions intended to block this kind of defense when the defendants' denials amount to "willful blindness," defined by the *Model Penal Code* as situations where "a person is aware of a *high probability* of [a fact's] existence, unless he actually believes it does not exist."[25] The jury instructions that are based on this concept are known, appropriately enough, as an "ostrich" charge.[26]

---

[23] MODEL PENAL CODE § 2.07(1)(c) (2001).

[24] Kathleen F. Brickey, *Rethinking Corporate Liability under the Model Penal Code*, 19 RUTGERS L.J. 593, 629 (1988).

[25] MODEL PENAL CODE § 2.02(7) (2001). For a discussion of these issues, see Ira P. Robbins, *The Ostrich Instruction: Deliberate Ignorance as a Criminal Mens Rea*, 81 J. CRIM. L. & CRIMINOLOGY 191 (1990).

[26] United States v. Ramsey, 785 F.2d 184, 189 (7th Cir. 1986) (stating, inter alia, that "[a]n ostrich instruction informs the jury that actual knowledge and deliberate avoidance of knowledge are the same thing").

FEDERAL CRIMES

The Prosecutors

Federal criminal law is enforced either by prosecutors assigned to specialized units within the DOJ headquarters in Washington, D.C. or Assistant U.S. Attorneys (AUSAs) working under the ninety-three U.S. Attorneys assigned to each federal court district, in a manner roughly aligned with the sizes of the geographical areas covered and their populations. For example, California, New York, and Texas have four U.S. Attorneys each, while the smaller states of Arizona, Maryland, and Nevada have only one. Prosecutors file their cases before federal district courts, which either accept pleas or conduct trials in response to those indictments. District court decisions are reviewed by one of eleven circuit courts of appeal. All of these attorneys and their support personnel work under the overall supervision of the Attorney General, the top law enforcement officer in the country. However, U.S. Attorneys operate with significant autonomy from "main Justice," as DOJ's headquarters in Washington, D.C., is commonly known, and generally do not ask permission of DOJ unit chiefs in Washington, D.C., whether they can pursue criminal cases. This reality has led some defense attorneys to claim that the inconsistencies in prosecutorial policy disadvantage their clients.[27]

The Health, Safety, and Environmental Statutes

All of the agencies mentioned in Chapter 1 – the EPA, the OSHA, the MSHA, the FDA, and the BSEE – have criminal provisions in their authorizing statutes. The criminal provisions in environmental statutes administered by the EPA are significantly more stringent than laws to protect consumers and workers, perhaps because Congress has updated them more recently and because environmental protection is popular with the public. The disparities between these provisions make little sense from a public policy perspective, producing troubling anomalies in the penalties available for employers who kill scores of workers and get off lightly versus conduct that does not cause immediate, visible harm but is punished quite harshly.

---

[27] Kevin A. Gaynor et al., *Environmental Criminal Prosecutions: Simple Fixes for a Flawed System*, 3 Vill. Envtl. L.J. 1 (1992). They write: "Indeed, whether a violation is treated criminally, civilly or administratively is more a function of what type of investigator learns of the violation first and in what judicial district the violation occurs, not the nature or environmental severity of the violation." *Id.* at 4.

One additional threshold concept is quite important. State manslaughter laws look holistically at the circumstances in determining whether behavior that caused fatalities constitutes manslaughter. In contrast, federal prosecutors depend on the identification of a "regulatory violation" – a specific act *or* omission that runs afoul of a prohibition *or* requirement contained either in the statute or in its implementing regulations. This approach means that if the regulations have gaps, and the conduct that causes an accident is not explicitly covered, federal prosecutors will have difficulty mounting a criminal case. Because no one gets to review the records of potential cases that are never brought, it is impossible to tell how significant this problem is in real life. But in the hands of inexperienced or poorly prepared prosecutors, the need to prove regulatory violations can have the effect of fragmenting the theory of the case the prosecutor is trying to advance, forcing judges and juries to pick their way through technical requirements and subtly undermining the description of overall culpability that is essential to conviction. The case can degenerate into a laundry list of very specific misdeeds, as opposed to a narrative that explains the managerial malpractice that caused the accident.

Pollution Crimes

The most stringent provisions in the major federal environmental statutes involve crimes that result in the "knowing endangerment" of "another person" by putting that person "in imminent danger of death or serious bodily injury."[28] Under the Clean Water Act (CWA), for example, such behavior is subject to a fine up to $250,000 and a fifteen year prison term. The fine for a corporate defendant goes up to $1,000,000. Repeat offenders face double fines and prison terms. Less serious criminal penalties apply when the defendant commits a "knowing violation" ($50,000/day/violation and imprisonment up to three years). If a defendant is merely "negligent" (careless), the government may seek misdemeanor-level penalties ($25,000/day/violation and imprisonment for up to one year). Once again, penalties double for repeat offenders.

In essence, the CWA prohibits the discharge of contaminated wastewater into a body of surface water (lakes, rivers, creeks, or streams) without a permit or in excess of permit limits. If a violation is ongoing – for example, discharges that are not subject to a permit continue for many days – the penalty amount is assessed for each single twenty-four-hour period that it continues. So, for example, if a factory had an accident that spilled an acutely toxic chemical

---

[28] This language is drawn from the Clean Water Act. Its criminal provisions appear at 33 U.S.C. § 1319(c) (2006).

into an adjacent river used for drinking water by a downstream town, and the contamination reached water taps, killing or injuring dozens or hundreds of people, the person or company responsible would confront a large number of violations produced by a single incident.

The Resource Conservation and Recovery Act (RCRA) governs the disposal of "solid waste" – basically every material that is discarded and is not in gaseous form. The most toxic types of waste are designated as "hazardous" and must be transported under a stringent regulatory regime requiring manifests with hazard warnings, labeling, and secured containers. Hazardous waste must be disposed of in special landfills that are engineered to prevent seepage from the bottom of what is most often a large hole in the ground. These facilities must be secured against illegal dumping, and monitored to make sure they do not start to leak.

Once again, under RCRA, a person who illegally places another person in imminent danger faces a fine up to $250,000 and imprisonment up to fifteen years.[29] Knowing violations trigger $50,000/day/violation and up to three years imprisonment, but handling hazardous waste without requisite permits jumps the prison term to five years. Repeat offenders face double these fines and terms. An example of a worst case scenario would be illegal dumping of toxic chemical waste in a marshland where children play, with the result that they suffer nervous system damage.

The Clean Air Act follows the same structure. Releasing a hazardous air pollutant that puts another person in imminent danger carries a prison term of up to fifteen years and a fine up to $1,000,000 per violation; in the event of repeat violations, the penalty doubles.[30] If the release of the hazardous air pollutant is negligent, the term is reduced to one year and fines are set pursuant to the general criminal provision contained in Title 18 of the U.S. Code.[31] Knowing violations of the Act (for example, operating without a permit, violating the terms of a permit, failing to monitor air emissions) carry a prison term up to five years.

The EPA has focused its criminal enforcement efforts primarily on the provisions of the Clean Air Act, the Clean Water Act, and the Resource Conservation and Recovery Act. On occasion, when the facts demand, the agency and the DOJ may turn to several other environmental laws governing the safety of drinking water,[32] the handling of pesticides,[33] and the introduction

---

[29] The Resource Conservation and Recovery Act's criminal provisions appear at 42 U.S.C. § 6928(d) (2006).

[30] The Clean Air Act's criminal provisions appear at 42 U.S.C. § 7413(c) (2006).

[31] Those provisions set fine amounts based on seriousness of the crime. So, for example, a felony or a misdemeanor that results in death carries a fine up to $250,000. 18 U.S.C. § 3571 (2006).

[32] The Safe Drinking Water Act's criminal provisions appear at 42 U.S.C. § 300h-2(b) (2006).

[33] The Federal Insecticide, Fungicide, and Rodenticide Act's criminal provisions appear at 7 U.S. C. § 136l(b) (2006).

of new chemicals into the marketplace.[34] All contain criminal provisions similar to the ones described above.

To prove *mens rea* in any of these cases, prosecutors must show that defendants know what they did and know that their activities were potentially harmful, whether or not the defendant is aware of the specific legal requirements that control such behavior. This approach is grounded in the overall criminal law principle that "ignorance of the law is no defense."[35]

Again, because protecting the environment is so popular with the public, the EPA is fortunate enough to have a dedicated section of prosecutors at the DOJ assigned to pursue charges under the various statutes, and their work overall is a bright beacon in an otherwise dim landscape. But even there, with dedicated resources and a high level of motivation to develop such cases, sharp declines have occurred since the heyday of environmental enforcement in the late 1990s.

Worker Safety Laws

In comparison to these stringent penalties, the criminal provisions of the Occupational Safety and Health Act (OSH Act) are shockingly weak. An employer who commits a "willful" violation that results in the death of a worker faces a fine up to $10,000 (yes, no missing zeros there) and imprisonment up to six months.[36] These scant penalties make the crime a misdemeanor under the statute.[37] Repeat violations double to the grand total of not more than $20,000 and one year in prison. The Mine Safety and Health Act is marginally more advanced than the OSH Act: any mine operator who willfully violates a mandatory health or safety standard or knowingly fails to follow an MSHA order may be punished by a fine up to $250,000 and imprisonment up to one year.[38] Despite the higher fine, the crime itself remains a misdemeanor. Congressional decisions to require proof that violations were willful and to limit such crimes to misdemeanors have undermined OSHA's criminal enforcement program. Agency staff has internalized the unfortunate message that developing criminal charges is a waste of their increasingly limited time, in large measure because overworked federal prosecutors have scant interest in pursuing misdemeanor – as opposed to felony – cases.

One clear indication that OSHA criminal enforcement efforts are extraordinarily modest is the fact that only one federal court of appeals has ever

---

[34] The Toxic Substances Control Act's criminal provisions appear at 15 U.S.C. § 2615(b) (2006).

[35] DRESSLER, *supra* note 5, § 13.01–02, 170–78.

[36] 29 U.S.C. § 666(e) (2006).

[37] The classifications appear at 18 U.S.C. § 3559(a) (2012).

[38] 30 U.S.C. § 820(d) (2006).

considered the meaning of the willful standard in the context of the agency's authorizing statute. *United States v. Dye Construction Co.*, brought by OSHA shortly after it was created in 1971, involved a gruesome, common, and entirely avoidable trench cave-in at a construction site owned by the defendant.[39] Workers dug a trench nine to twelve feet deep to enable them to lay pipes along its bottom. The soil they excavated was considered unstable, meaning that they should not have expected it to remain in place without "shoring," as required by OSHA regulations. Shoring is the placement of braced walls made of wood or metal along the sides of the trench to prevent cave-ins. The practice was developed during the Roman Empire. This obvious step was omitted, undoubtedly to save time, and the trench collapsed, killing a worker who stood on the trench bottom. The court held that the prosecutor either must show that (1) the defendant "intentionally disregarded" the statute or its implementing regulations or (2) the defendant was "plainly indifferent" to its requirements.[40]

In 2011, 4,609 workers were killed on the job and some 50,000 died from occupational illnesses; millions more suffered serious injury.[41] Many of these deaths and injuries arose from workplace conditions that were shockingly out of compliance with fundamental OSHA rules that have been in effect for decades, including requirements to provide readily accessible off/on switches for heavy machinery, to protect workers from electrocution, and, as explained earlier, to shore trenches properly. Yet in a good year, the OSHA refers only ten to twelve cases to the DOJ for potential criminal prosecution.[42]

In 2003, veteran *New York Times* reporter David Barstow[43] reported that in the previous two decades, OSHA investigated 1,242 deaths on the job. Agency officials described these incidents as "horror stories" caused by "willful" violations of the law.[44] "Workers [were] decapitated on assembly lines, shredded in machinery, burned beyond recognition, electrocuted, buried alive,"

---

[39] United States v. Dye Constr. Co., 510 F.2d 78 (10th Cir. 1975). The case was brought four years after the agency was created.

[40] *Id.* at 81.

[41] The AFL-CIO produces an excellent annual report on these casualties. *See, e.g.*, AFL-CIO, Death on the Job, The Toll of Neglect (22d ed. 2013), *available at* http://www.aflcio.org//download/79181/1933131/DOTJ2013.pdf.

[42] *OSHA Enforcement: Committed to Safe and Healthful Workplaces*, OSHA, https://www.osha.gov/dep/2010_enforcement_summary.html (last visited Mar. 19, 2014) (showing number of criminal referrals ranging annually from 10 to 14 for the years 2007 to 2010).

[43] Barstow has been an investigative reporter for the *New York Times* since 2002 and has won the Pulitzer Prize for his reporting three times, including once for the series on workplace deaths cited here.

[44] David Barstow, *U.S. Rarely Seeks Charges for Deaths in Workplace*, N.Y. Times, Dec. 22, 2003, at A1.

Barstow reported.[45] But the agency declined to pursue criminal prosecution in 93 percent of these cases. The agency's recalcitrance "persisted even when employers had been cited before for the very same safety violation. It persisted even when the violations caused multiple deaths, or when the victims were teenagers. And it persisted even where reviews by administrative judges found abundant proof of willful wrongdoing."[46] When pressed for an explanation, one retired inspector said: "I personally didn't think, 'Oh, it's fatal, it's willful, it should go criminal. ... You just don't need that grief. The honest to God truth is that it's just going to slow you down. They want numbers, lots of inspections, and it will hurt you to do one of these cases.'"[47] The habit of emphasizing inspections and deemphasizing enforcement persists to this day.

Consumer Law

Congress has updated the FDA's statutory authority in recent years, most notably expanding its mandate to ensure food safety.[48] Defendants who "knowingly" sell, purchase, distribute, trade, or import a drug in violation of FDA regulations may face felony convictions punishable by imprisonment up to ten years and a fine up to $250,000. The FDA may seek up to one year in prison and a $1,000 fine against defendants who manufacture, introduce into interstate commerce, or accept delivery of any food, drug, device, tobacco product, or cosmetic that is adulterated. When Congress considered amendments strengthening the FDA's regulatory authority over food in the waning hours of the lame duck session of 2010, it decided to leave food violations as misdemeanors. That outcome is mystifying, especially given the disturbing cases that motivated the legislation, including the deliberate shipping of peanut paste that tested positive for salmonella, killed nine, and sickened hundreds.

On the other hand, beginning in 2004, the FDA and the DOJ have grown remarkably aggressive about prosecuting large drug companies for the off-label marketing of drugs. They have brought twenty-seven criminal cases against corporations and ten cases against individual drug company executives. Twenty-two resulted in guilty pleas and five – all involving individuals – went to court. A total of $5.9 billion in criminal fines and forfeitures was recovered. The theory of these cases is that if the FDA has not approved a

---

[45] *Id.*
[46] *Id.*
[47] *Id.*
[48] The FDA's criminal enforcement authority appears at 21 U.S.C. § 333 (2012). Also relevant is 21 U.S.C. § 331 (2012) (defining prohibited acts).

specific use of a brand name drug – for example, Synthroid for thyroid problems – then promoting the drug for uses not covered by the approval – called "off-label marketing" – constitutes the sale of a "misbranded" or "unapproved" drug under the statute.[49]

In some of these prosecutions, companies sent their sales teams out to promote drugs for specific uses despite clinical trials indicating that the drug could be harmful for such patients.[50] For example, the giant pharmaceutical firm Eli Lilly & Company was prosecuted for marketing Zyprexa as a treatment for dementia even though five clinical trials indicated that such patients died at twice the rate of a control group that received a placebo.[51] In other cases, companies market drugs for a use despite research showing it is ineffective. An example is the drug Actimmune, marketed by InterMune for treatment of lethal lung conditions even though it was useless in that context; the drug caused side effects, including headaches and irregular heartbeat and cost $50,000/patient.[52]

The drug industry as a whole argues that such prosecutions are unfair because they punish companies and their executives for providing useful information to physicians, who make the final decisions about what medications to prescribe their patients. Other commentators say the companies are so aggressive that overworked doctors, who do not have time to do original research, succumb too easily to such pressure, as well as other blandishments like free dinners, memorabilia, and expensive tickets to sports events. Whatever your view of the merits of such cases, the off-label marketing enforcement program is far more robust than efforts in other areas that have caused more immediate and obvious harm to public health, worker and consumer safety, and the environment. The disparities are puzzling and do not enhance the credibility of the DOJ.

Deepwater Drilling

Finally, the Bureau of Safety and Environmental Enforcement (BSEE), the office at the Department of the Interior that oversees deepwater drilling for oil

---

[49] *See generally* Allison D. Burroughs et al., *Off-Label Promotion: Government Theories of Prosecution and Facts that Drive Them*, 65 FOOD & DRUG L.J. 555 (2010).

[50] An excellent analysis of these cases is David Evans, *Big Pharma's Crime Spree*, BLOOMBERG MARKETS, Dec. 2009, at 74.

[51] *See* Margaret Cronin Fisk et al., *Lilly Sold Drug for Dementia Knowing It Didn't Help, Files Show*, BLOOMBERG (June 12, 2009), http://www.bloomberg.com/apps/news?pid=newsarch ive&sid=aTLcF3zT1Pdo.

[52] Press Release, U.S. Department of Justice, Biopharmaceutical Firm InterMune to Pay U.S. over $36 Million for Illegal Promotion and Marketing of Drug Actimmune (Oct. 26, 2006), http://www.justice.gov/opa/pr/2006/October/06_civ_728.html.

in the Gulf of Mexico and off the country's northwestern coast, is authorized to seek criminal penalties for "knowing and willful" violations by the Outer Continental Shelf Lands Act; such offenses are felonies and can be punished by up to $100,000 in fines and up to ten years in prison.[53] In addition, a 200-year-old statute entitled the Seaman's Manslaughter Act[54] imposes criminal liability for "misconduct" that results in a death at sea. The DOJ has invoked this authority to pursue criminal charges against supervisors involved in the Macondo well disaster, although a district court judge subsequently dismissed those charges. The Seaman's Act is notable because its criminal provisions allow prosecutors to secure a felony conviction punishable by up to ten years in prison by showing that the death was caused by negligence or some other misconduct on the part of a "captain, engineer, pilot, or other person employed" on a seagoing "vessel."[55] This burden of proof is significantly lighter than the higher standard of gross negligence that typically applies to criminal provisions. In fact, the law is sometimes described as a "strict liability" statute because it allows prosecutors to sidestep the need to prove either *mens rea* or a specific regulatory violation. Most strict liability statutes are considered so harsh that they are limited to misdemeanor-level fines and prison terms. In this respect, though, the Seaman's Manslaughter Act is again an exception: those convicted face felony-level punishment, including prison terms up to ten years.

Public Welfare Offenses

The Supreme Court first discussed public welfare offenses in a landmark 1943 case, *United States v. Dotterweich*, with an opinion written by the renowned Justice Felix Frankfurter.[56] The defendants (company and president) were charged with shipping misbranded and adulterated drugs in violation of what was then known as the Food and Drugs Act. "The purposes of this legislation thus touch phases of the lives and health of people which, in the circumstances of modern industrialism, are largely beyond self-protection," Frankfurter wrote.[57] The doctrine created by the opinion – known as the "responsible corporate officer" or "responsible relation" rule – expands the scope of potentially culpable defendants to managers who had oversight responsibility for the activities that generated the hazard and could have

---

[53] The criminal provisions of the Outer Continental Shelf Lands Act appear at 43 U.S.C. § 1350 (c) (2006).

[54] The Act appears at 18 U.S.C. § 1115 (2012).

[55] *Id.*

[56] United States v. Dotterweich, 320 U.S. 277, 280–81 (1943). The doctrine was reiterated in *United States v.*, 421 U.S. 658, 675 (1975).

[57] *Dotterweich*, 320 U.S. at 280.

prevented those illegal acts. The Court reaffirmed the doctrine in 1975, when it upheld the jury instructions given in a case involving a national grocery chain called Acme Markets.[58] The FDA prosecuted the company and its president, a man named John Park, for failure to clean up a food storage warehouse overrun by rodents. Park was the only witness called by the defense. He testified that the company was so large, with 36,000 employees and 874 retail outlets, that he delegated certain functions, including the maintenance of sanitary conditions at its facilities, to a series of upper- and middle-level managers. The Court was unimpressed, upholding instructions that told the jury it could convict the defendant if he "had a responsible relation to the situation, even though he may not have participated personally."[59] It wrote that the sanctions provided by the statute:

> reach and touch the individuals who execute the corporate mission ... [imposing] not only a positive duty to seek out and remedy violations when they occur but also, and primarily, a duty to implement measures that will insure that violations will not occur. The requirements of foresight and vigilance imposed on responsible corporate agents are beyond question demanding, and perhaps onerous, but they are no more stringent than the public has a right to expect of those who voluntarily assume positions of authority in business enterprises whose services and products affect the health and well-being of the public that supports them.[60]

Defense counsel and conservative commentators contend that the responsible corporate officer doctrine is an unprecedented dilution of *mens rea* because it allows convictions of individuals far removed from the criminal activity.[61] Of course, this interpretation of the doctrine does not fit the facts of either *Dotterweich* or *Park* because in those cases the defendants were either directly involved in the illegal activity (Dotterweich supervised misbranded drug shipments) or well informed in advance about the government's demand that the illegal activity cease (Park received the initial FDA letter demanding that the warehouse be remediated and delegated the job of responding to it to his employees). Prosecution-oriented advocates for stringent criminal liability

---

[58] United States v. Park, 421 U.S. 658.

[59] *Park*, 421 U.S. at 665 n. 9.

[60] *Park*, 421 U.S. at 672.

[61] See, e.g., WASHINGTON LEGAL FOUNDATION, FEDERAL EROSION OF BUSINESS CIVIL LIBERTIES 1–5 (2010), *available at* http://www.wlf.org/Upload/WLF_Spcl_Rprt_2010_Ed.pdf ("[T]he level of mens rea or intent required to be proven has been greatly watered down by the courts and Congress over the years."); *id.* at 1–14 ("Although many federal statutes require a conviction based on a 'knowing' violation of the law, prosecutors have tried to dilute the mens rea requirement further and make their jobs easier by requesting a 'conscious avoidance' jury instruction.").

have also pointed out that the responsible corporate officer doctrine is more correctly viewed as a modification of *actus reus* because it establishes categories of conduct – managerial supervision or lack of supervision – that can be deemed a component of the behavior that triggers criminal culpability.[62]

OBSTRUCTION OF JUSTICE CHARGES

Federal and state laws protect the integrity of the criminal justice system by imposing criminal penalties for lying to the government, destroying evidence, or interfering with witnesses or juries. These types of violations can be easier to prove than regulatory violations because they depend on dual choice – either one lied or did not, destroyed evidence or did not – allowing prosecutors to avoid explaining a relatively complex rule and how the defendant's behavior ran afoul of its nuanced requirements or prohibitions. Especially at the federal level, considering the application of provisions punishing "false statements" is a crucial part of scoping cases.

Obstruction provisions are spread throughout the federal code, tied to statutes regulating conduct in specific industries. Perhaps the most prominent generic version is § 1001 of U.S. Code Title 18, which provides for imprisonment for up to five years (a felony) for any person who "knowingly and willfully" (again, a higher standard than simply knowing) commits any one of three offenses: (1) "falsifies, conceals or covers up … a *material* fact"; (2) makes any *materially* false, fictitious, or fraudulent statement or representation"; or (3) makes *or uses* any false writing or document knowing [that it contains "any *materially* false, fictitious, or fraudulent statement or entry."[63] Verbal statements count as much as written ones and the bar for what is a "material" falsehood is set relatively low: if a statement has the capacity to influence what the government does in response to it, whether or not it actually has the effect, it is deemed material.[64]

Commentators have criticized the federal government for entrapping defendants by taking routine and understandable denials of culpability and prosecuting them as false statements that can rack up considerable prison time.[65] They say

---

[62] Todd S. Aagard, *A Fresh Look at the Responsible Relation Doctrine*, 96 J. Crim. L. & Criminology 1245 (2006).

[63] 18 U.S.C. § 1001 (2012). The term "corruptly" is defined at 18 U.S.C. § 1515(b) (2012).

[64] United States v. Gaudin, 515 U.S. 506, 509 (1995).

[65] For a discussion of these issues, see Lisa Kern Goodwin, *Criminal Lying, Prosecutorial Power, and Social Meaning*, 97 Calif. L. Rev. 1515 (2009); Alexandra Bak-Boychuk, Comment, *Liar Laws: How MPC §241.3 and State Unsworn Falsification Statutes Fix the Flaws in the False Statements Act (18 U.S.C. §1001)*, 78 Temp. L. Rev. 453 (2005). The statute proved a favorite with independent counsels who investigated politicians for lying to the FBI during background checks. Paul Glastris, *"False Statements": The Flubber of All Laws*, U.S. News & World Report, Mar. 30, 1998, at 25.

that prosecutors lean on their false statement authority to shore up cases that they could not support under the substantive law that applies to the behavior at issue. And they point to cases where the federal government has prosecuted defendants who claimed innocence when confronted by a federal agent. After all, these critics reason, if accused of a crime, what should the potential defendant do: admit guilt in order to avoid a charge of making a felonious false statement to the government? The Supreme Court rejected the argument that a defendant has the right to falsely deny wrongdoing in 1997[66] and the law is that there is no such thing as a justified, albeit false, "exculpatory no." In any event, few argue that the government should be deprived of the ability to prosecute obstruction of justice through false statements in appropriate cases, and the federal government continues to bring such cases, most recently in the context of the Macondo blowout.

Despite Supreme Court validation of the application of federal false statement laws to verbal admissions, drafters of the *Model Penal Code* rejected this approach, instead defining the crime of obstructing a public official in the performance of her duty as a misdemeanor, not a felony, and excluding verbal statements from culpability.[67] The *Code* further requires prosecutors to prove that the defendant's purpose was to mislead.

HURDLES AND EXCUSES

Why federal prosecutors are so reluctant to bring white collar criminal cases in response to regulatory violations, even during the administration of a president regarded as a liberal by a large minority of the population, is an urgent question only rarely addressed in the scholarly literature. Criminologists, sociologists, and legal academics overlook this threshold problem both in their models of how the world may work and their empirical research regarding how it does work. Despite extensive searching, I was unable to find any empirical survey of federal prosecutors and their perceptions of how case selection decisions are made. In the only two empirical studies of why state and local prosecutors avoid white collar cases, scarce resources and the availability of other remedies (for example, enforcement actions seeking civil penalties) were the two most common reasons why the Pinto case remains an exception, not the rule.[68]

---

[66] Brogan v. United States, 522 U.S. 398 (1998).

[67] MODEL PENAL CODE § 241.3 (2001).

[68] Kenneth A. Ayers Jr. & James Frank, *Deciding to Prosecute White-Collar Crime: A National Survey of State Attorneys General*, 4 JUST. Q. 425 (1987); Michael L. Benson et al., *District Attorneys and Corporate Crime: Surveying the Prosecutorial Gatekeepers*, 26 CRIMINOLOGY 505 (1988).

Of course, prosecutors have long been preoccupied with street crime at the state level and terrorism and drug offenses at the federal level. Prosecutors may perceive that the public is more concerned about street than white collar crime. They are always short of resources and white collar criminal cases are admittedly expensive to investigate.

But the perception that the public cares more about street than white collar crime is undermined by an unusually robust 2005 study conducted under the auspices of the National White Collar Crime Center, an association of federal, state, and local enforcement officials.[69] In a telephone survey, researchers asked 1,605 U.S. adults to rank the seriousness of twelve brief scenarios – eight involving white collar and four involving street crimes. Ranking ran along a numerical scale running from one (not serious) to seven (very serious). Respondents were asked to assume that the scenario "a person steals a car worth $10,000 parked on the street" ranks as four – a number "in the middle" of the range.[70] Overall, the researchers reported, scenarios involving white collar and street crime were evenly dispersed with respect to mean seriousness ratings.

A scenario involving a man carjacking a teenager's car and shooting and killing one of the car's passengers was ranked most serious, while a burglary of $500 in jewelry from an elderly couple's home while they were vacationing was ranked least serious. Yet a scenario involving a small factory disposing of toxic waste that pollutes the community's water supply "in order to cut costs and sustain the town's job market" achieved the second highest – most serious – mean score after the carjacking, and a scenario involving a pharmaceutical company that "hides information revealing important health and safety issues for consumers" when releasing a new drug received the third highest rating.[71] These decidedly white collar scenarios ranked so high even though they were arrayed against other scenarios in which a person is seriously injured during a barroom fight and people steal money through a variety of unsavory techniques, including computer hacking, false insurance claims, and online sales fraud.

In fairness, prosecutors are heavily dependent on regulators to discover and investigate cases, and regulators routinely deemphasize criminal prosecutions. Without agency support in discovering potential criminal cases and

---

[69] John Kane & April D. Wall, Nat'l White Collar Crime Center, The 2005 National Public Survey on White Collar Crime (2006), *available at* http://www. nw3c.org/docs/ations/national_public_household_survey116858C367CA.pdf?sfvrsn=8.

[70] *Id.* at 14–15, 28–29.

[71] *Id.*

developing supporting evidence rapidly, the DOJ could not change its policies. Regulators have grown far more accustomed to assessing civil penalties. They are also prone – for understandable but increasingly quixotic reasons – to believe that the elaborate rules they have spent four decades crafting work with most of the people most of the time and in an era of tight budgets have deemphasized enforcement. But this neglect is a two-way street: the DOJ's disinterest in such cases clearly discourages the agencies from pursuing criminal cases even in egregious circumstances. More to the point, regardless of agency neglect and prosecutorial disinterest, presidents are certainly capable of changing everyone's priorities.

Weak laws like the OSH Act are partly to blame for the dearth of prosecutions. Still, the average middle-class manager is unlikely to shrug off the prospect of becoming the target of a draining and expensive criminal investigation, even if prison terms and fines are set at the misdemeanor level. The prosecution of a handful of individuals and companies in particularly hazardous industries (meat packing, agriculture, construction, to name just the worst) would have significant deterrence potential to stop sloppy, illegal practices that violate the law. Laws cannot deter unless they are enforced and OSHA's refusal to devote resources to criminal prosecutions cannot be justified by its employees' frustration with its statutory authority.

CONCLUSION

Federal and state criminal laws, at least in theory, give prosecutors the tools they need to prosecute white collar crime in the health, safety, and environmental area. The development of such cases remains stunted, in line with the overall neglect of white collar abuses. State prosecutors, who have the powerful charge of manslaughter available, largely ignore such cases. Federal prosecutors are deterred by the difficulty of first proving a regulatory violation and by the fact that too many offenses, regardless of their effects, are misdemeanors. To overcome these problems, prosecutors will need resources, imagination, and determination because they can expect corporate defendants to field well-informed and effective defense teams.

Of all things, why would a prospective white collar prosecutor need imagination? Traditional doctrines regarding, for example, reckless endangerment have been developed in a street crime context. The criminal law is heavily fact-specific and the published cases do not address the difficult problems of institutional displacement of accountability and management dysfunction that so often cause fatal incidents. Because charging and litigating white collar crimes will mean trying to persuade the courts to apply long-standing principles to new circumstances, prosecutors may run a higher risk of losing, an outcome they do not like to risk. I return to these problems in Chapter 7.

3

Cons and Pros

What a community chooses to punish and how severely tells us what (or whom) it values and how much. That members of the public understand punishment to have this signification is confirmed by the familiar complaint that an insufficiently severe punishment endorses the criminal's behavior and devalues his victim. ...

... A theory of criminal-law policy that abstracts from social meaning – by, say, reducing the value of all policies solely to their cost effectiveness in deterring crime – will generate morally uncompelling, and hence politically naïve, prescriptions.

Dan M. Kahan, *Social Meaning and the Economic Analysis of Crime*[1]

LEGAL COMMENTATOR OPPOSITION AND SOCIAL SCIENTIST SUPPORT

Two discrete groups of commentators – the first from the legal academy and the second from the closely connected disciplines of sociology and criminology – have dominated the policy debate over the merits of prosecuting corporations and individuals for white collar crimes. Surprisingly, after extensive research I have not uncovered much collaboration between the two groups and I believe this book is the first to juxtapose their insights.

A prolific group of business-oriented legal academics argues that white collar criminal prosecutions are unfair and ineffective, especially with respect to corporations. The gist of their position is that corporations are paper entities that lack minds capable of formulating the guilty intent (*mens rea*) considered as an indispensable element of criminal culpability. Because the largest corporations have complex management structures and depend on the activities of many employees, no single executive – or even a committee of executives – is able to police everyone's conduct. Individuals may well violate

[1] Dan M. Kahan, *Social Meaning and the Economic Analysis of Crime*, 27 J. LEGAL STUD. 609, 615–16 (1998).

the criminal law, but most often they engage in such behavior contrary to official corporate policy. Criminal prosecutions impose considerable stigma and can result in grave and disproportionate damage to the corporation's profitability. Therefore, such charges are both unfair to innocent bystanders such as the company's stockholders and unwise in all but the most egregious circumstances. Instead, the government and the public at large should rely on civil actions to recoup any damages caused by rogue agents.

In strong contrast to this mixture of abstract and pragmatic reasoning, mainstream criminologists and sociologists enthusiastically support the prosecution of white collar crime, including indictment of the corporate entity when it has fostered or failed to prevent a crime. These scholars believe that there should be a bull market for white collar prosecutions fueled by public disillusionment with large institutions. They acknowledge that public outrage over business wrongdoing has ebbed and flowed, but they remain generally optimistic about its potential to inspire pathbreaking cases that will appropriately punish and deter white collar crime. Some sociologists fret that the deterrence value of such prosecutions remains unproven, and they are certainly right that empirical data on the subject is sparse. Yet none express fundamental misgivings about the fairness of white collar prosecutions of either variety – corporate or individual. A few prominent scholars would wait longer to pull the trigger on indictments. Professor John Braithwaite, clearly the most prolific and well-known of their number, advocates that the benefits of "cooperative" approaches be exhausted before the legal system is invoked as a last resort.[2] But all are disturbed by the inequity of deemphasizing white collar crime while punishing street crime harshly.

Folded into this analytical tradition is a smaller group of highly skilled and specialized sociologists who have done groundbreaking investigations to determine the cause of fatal and destructive industrial disasters. This work is exemplified by Professor Diane Vaughan's examination of the "normalization of deviance" at the National Aeronautics and Space Administration (NASA) and Morton Thiokol, NASA's main contractor for the space shuttle *Challenger*. The *Challenger* was one of several shuttles launched despite well-known problems with an essential piece of equipment known as an "O-ring." These aircraft were viewed as NASA's best hope of commercializing

---

[2] Ian Ayres & John Braithwaite, Responsive Regulation: Transcending the Deregulation Debate 33, 50 (1995) (arguing that regulators should "be cooperative at first to give others a chance to put their cooperative self forward; we should be tough with cheaters to give them reason to favor their cooperative selves; and we should extend forgiveness to those who show sign of abandoning cheating in favor of cooperation" in an ideal system where "escalating to punishment is a last resort").

space exploration and it was heavily invested in their success, to the point of papering over serious problems in an effort to meet an inordinately ambitious launch schedule. Space exploration and NASA as an institution were dealt a crippling blow when the *Challenger* exploded within two minutes of its launch from Cape Canaveral, Florida, in January 1986, killing its seven-member crew on live television as millions of Americans watched.[3] Professor Andrew Hopkins, a similarly talented and indefatigable investigator based at the Australian National University, has analyzed the 2005 Texas City refinery and the 2010 Macondo well blowout explosions, as well as other major industrial accidents in his own country and abroad, developing an equally robust literature on why corporations "fail to learn."[4] Vaughan and Hopkins do not believe that such catastrophes are attributable primarily to last-minute human error, but instead dig more deeply into the history of the technology and institutional practices that caused such disasters.

So far, prosecutors and other legal policymakers seem to have paid scant attention to the analyses conducted by Vaughan and Hopkins, as well as parallel work done by public and private investigative bodies such as the U.S. Chemical Safety Board,[5] the President's Commission on the Macondo well blowout,[6] and a variety of blue ribbon panels chaired by well-known public figures such as James Baker, the former Secretary of State in the George H. W. Bush Administration,[7] that were appointed to investigate the disasters discussed in Part II. I suspect that prosecutors ignore such investigations because they think they have little relevance to their ability to win criminal cases against corporate and individual defendants. This attitude is as short-sighted as it is self-defeating. Only by embracing the reality that institutional failure is a crucial context for individual behavior will prosecutors be able to

---

[3] Diane Vaughan, The Challenger Launch Decision: Risky Technology, Culture, and Deviance at NASA (1996).

[4] Andrew Hopkins, Failure to Learn: The BP Texas City Refinery Disaster (2008); Andrew Hopkins, Disastrous Decisions: The Human and Organisational Causes of the Gulf of Mexico Blowout (2012).

[5] U.S. Chemical Safety & Hazard Investigation Board, Investigation Report: Refinery Explosion and Fire (2007), *available at* http://www.csb.gov/assets/1/19/ CSBFinalReportBP.pdf.

[6] Exec. Ord. No. 13,543, 75 Fed. Reg. 29,397 (May 26, 2010) (establishing the commission); *see also* National Commission on the BP Deepwater Horizon Oil Spill and Offshore Drilling, Report to the President: Deep Water – The Gulf Oil Disaster and the Future of Offshore Drilling (Jan. 2011), *available at* http://www. gpo.gov/fdsys/pkg/GPO-OILCOMMISSION/pdf/GPO-OILCOMMISSION.pdf.

[7] James A. Baker et al., Report of the BP U.S. Refineries Independent Safety Review Panel (2007), *available at* http://www.bp.com/liveassets/bp_internet/globalbp/glob albp_uk_english/SP/STAGING/local_assets/assets/pdfs/Baker_panel_report.pdf.

understand the root causes of crime in an industrial setting and structure enforcement to deter it effectively.

THE LEGAL CRITIQUE

Hilton Hotels and Imputed Liability

Professors Daniel Fischel and Alan Sykes are among the most articulate and opinionated members of the group of legal academics opposing corporate criminal liability.[8] They use a 1972 decision by the Ninth Circuit federal Court of Appeals as the centerpiece of their argument that corporate criminal prosecutions have run amok, arguing that the case ratified the criminal liability of a corporation for the illegal activities of a handful of rogue employees.[9] The decision upheld the jury's conviction of Hilton Hotels Corporation for blatant violations of the Sherman Act, an antitrust statute enacted in 1890.[10] Federal prosecutors alleged that Hilton sanctioned its employees' participation in an ad hoc trade association composed of local hotels, restaurants, and their suppliers that was organized to attract conventions to Portland, Oregon. The association was supported by member financial contributions. Specifically, supplier members were expected to donate one percent of their sales. Hotel and restaurant members pledged to boycott suppliers if they did not pay up.

The government alleged that the arrangement was a textbook case of restraint of trade made a crime under the Act. Hilton's lawyers responded that the company itself did not sanction such conduct, pointing to an explicit company policy that prohibited such conduct. One of Hilton's purchasing agents testified that he "violated his instructions" when he threatened to boycott a supplier because of "anger and personal pique."[11] The trial judge refused Hilton's request that he instruct the jury to exonerate the huge company if it found the purchasing agents' activities to be unauthorized, at

---

[8] Daniel Fischel & Alan Sykes, *Corporate Crime*, 25 J. LEGAL STUD. 319 (1996).

[9] *Id.*; the case Fischel and Sykes use to bolster their argument is United States v. Hilton Hotels Corp., 467 F.2d 1000 (9th Cir. 1972). They report that corporations can be prosecuted and held liable for the criminal acts of their agents "even if the corporate employee acts alone and even if the employee's acts are contrary to corporate policy." Fischel & Sykes, *supra* note 8, at 319. However, the only case cited by Fischel and Sykes in support of this sweeping statement is *Hilton Hotels*. The two professors declare not only that "corporate criminal liability is a relatively modern innovation in American law" but that it is a most unfortunate one. The Supreme Court decision clearing the way for criminal prosecutions of corporations was handed down in 1909, more than a century ago. *See* N.Y. Cent. & Hudson River R.R. Co. v. United States, 212 U.S. 481 (1909).

[10] Sherman Act, ch. 647, 26 Stat. 209 (1890) (codified as amended at 15 U.S.C. §§ 1–7 (2012)).

[11] *Hilton Hotels*, 467 F.2d at 1004.

least on paper. Instead, he told the jury that the corporation was responsible for the "acts and statements of its agents" that occur "within the scope of their employment," with that term defined as "in the corporation's behalf in performance of the agent's general line of work."[12] The jury convicted and Hilton appealed, arguing that the judge's instructions to the jury were illegal and that the convictions must therefore be overturned. It contended that instead of merely proving that the corporate employees acted within the scope of employment, prosecutors should have been required to show that the corporation officially authorized such activities.

The Ninth Circuit upheld the judge's instructions and the jury's verdict:

> Congress may constitutionally impose criminal liability upon a business entity for the acts or omissions of its agents within the scope of their employment. Such liability may attach without proof that the conduct was within the agent's actual authority, and even though it may have been contrary to express instructions. ... Legal commentators have argued forcefully that it is inappropriate and ineffective to impose criminal liability upon a corporation, as distinguished from the human agents who actually perform the unlawful acts. ... But it is the legislative judgment that controls. ... Moreover, the strenuous efforts of corporate defendants to avoid conviction, particularly under the Sherman Act, strongly suggests that Congress is justified in its judgment that exposure of the corporate entity to potential conviction may provide a substantial spur to corporate action to prevent violations by employees.[13]

The case remains good law today, standing for the proposition that a company cannot disclaim liability for any employee's actions if he appears to be acting within his authority as a representative of the company. Regardless, Fischel and Sykes argue that the doctrine of imputing criminal liability to a corporation on the basis of the activities of its individual employees has "developed ... without any theoretical justification,"[14] claiming that the United States has "seen an explosion of corporate criminal liability, as is evident from the recent criminal prosecutions of firms like Archer Daniels Midland, Exxon, Drexel Burnham, General Electric, Unisys, Caremark, and many others. Concern about corporate criminal liability has now entered the boardroom of every major corporation in America."[15]

Prosecutorial policies at the federal and state levels do not support Fischel and Sykes's extreme reading of the Hilton precedent. Department of Justice

[12] *Id.*
[13] *Id.*
[14] Fischel & Sykes, *supra* note 8, at 320.
[15] *Id.*

(DOJ) guidance, for example, requires that the criminal activity be sufficiently widespread within the corporation to suggest that it was not an anomaly, but instead was either known or readily discoverable by senior managers who could have put an end to it.[16] The *Model Penal Code* goes further, requiring that the bad behavior be endorsed by top management – either at the chief executive officer or board level,[17] although several states have refused to take such a restrictive view, instead adopting more expansive coverage of potential corporate culpability.

The Rights and Responsibilities of Corporate Personhood

When deciding whether to prosecute a corporate entity – as opposed to or in addition to an individual corporate employee – prosecutors consider whether (1) the patterns of behavior that gave rise to the crime were widespread within the company; (2) relevant employees were acting within the ambit of their job descriptions; and (3) those employees, deemed corporate "agents" by the law, were acting for the benefit of the corporation. (If employees act against the interests of the corporation by, for example, embezzling funds, prosecutors of course will not consider indicting the company that was the victim of the crime.) These restrictions were designed to eliminate corporate prosecutions when a discrete group of rogue employees acts recklessly for their own benefit. Conservative legal scholars argue that such prosecutions undermine the central purpose of creating the corporation as a fundamental institution in American life. As Fischel and Sykes have written:

> Corporations are legal fictions, and legal fictions cannot commit criminal acts. Nor can they possess *mens rea*, a guilty state of mind. Only people can act and only people can have a guilty state of mind. ... Our argument focuses on the obvious fact that corporations cannot be imprisoned; they can only be forced to pay money damages. The essential question, then, is whether the criminal law has any useful role to play in setting the damages that firms must pay for the wrongful acts of their agents. This in turn is really two questions: (1) when should the government rather than private parties sue for damages, and (2) in those cases where the government is the preferred plaintiff, when should the action be criminal rather than civil?[18]

The two are certainly right that the corporate form began as a purely legal construct. But their analysis of the purpose of this "construct" is unfaithful to

---

[16] *See generally* U.S. ATTORNEY'S MANUAL, Title 9, Chapter 9–28.000, *available at* www.justice.gov/opa/documents/corp-charging-guidelines.pdf.

[17] MODEL PENAL CODE § 2.07 (1962).

[18] Fischel & Sykes, *supra* note 8, at 320–21.

history. Among other goals, the corporate form was intended to shield individual employees and the board from liability, instead requiring the firm to pay often costly civil (noncriminal) damages caused by negligent employee behavior. In 1909, the Supreme Court extended this doctrine to criminal fines in *New York Central & Hudson River Railroad Co. v. United States.*[19] Over time, of course, what came to be called the corporate "veil" – a weirdly inappropriate label that suggests a blushing bride or grieving widow – was "pierced" by an increasing number of legal liability doctrines, and the system still struggles to find a balance between firmwide and individual employee liability. The clash between those working to preserve the impenetrability of the veil and those fighting to pierce it has become the central function of many corporate lawyers.

Given this history, Fischel and Sykes's support of civil liability for the legal fiction that is a corporation seems inconsistent with their opposition to criminal sanctions for the same entity. If all that is at stake is the payment of money, either in the form of civil damages or criminal fines, how big a difference does the imputation of liability make as a practical matter? Fischel and Sykes would say that because profound stigma, with its own daunting financial consequences, arises from conviction of a crime, a Rubicon is crossed when the law travels from the imposition of civil penalties to criminal fines. But in both the civil and the criminal contexts, the acts of human employees are imputed to the corporate "fiction." When widespread employee behavior causes death and injury to workers and the public, why shouldn't the corporation pay criminal fines when the bad act arises from behavior sanctioned by the institution as a whole?

Fischel and Sykes's real objection seems to be what they perceive as a violation of the fundamental social contract, which demands that people rather than institutions remain privy to, and therefore accountable for, the most important elements of citizenship. Viewed from this perspective, the more appropriate rejoinder to Fischel and Sykes is the implications of a strong judicial trend toward conceptualizing corporations as "people" for the purposes of such vital constitutional protections as free speech. As long as corporations receive benefits that were intended originally for individual citizens, why shouldn't they also accept culpability for the bad acts done in their name?

Over the last four decades, conservative judges have blocked a series of regulations they view as inordinately intrusive on corporate speech. The changes are as profound a departure from the original conception of an entity licensed or chartered by the state to facilitate commerce as the *Central Hudson*

---

[19] N.Y. Cent. & Hudson River R.R. Co. v. United States, 212 U.S. 481 (1909).

decision that deemed corporations punishable under the criminal law. These rulings granting companies First Amendment rights have gained a secure footing and apparently irreversible momentum. They depend on a conception of the corporation as anthropomorphic – as more of a person than a legal abstraction or fiction. As a result, corporations have been excused from regulations that would have curtailed a broad range of activities, from compiling and selling data profiles of people who buy prescription drugs[20] to unrestricted corporate contributions to political campaigns.[21] Professor Tim Wu, an opponent of these changes who sounds remarkably like Fischel and Sykes despite his obviously liberal stance, has written:

> The idea that "speech is speech" is persuasive, but also wrong. Contrary to [Justice] Powell's assertion, the First Amendment does actually care who is speaking. Children get fewer free speech rights than adults, for example (and a talking chimp would get none). The minority opinion in [one of the first cases to uphold corporate first amendment rights in the political speech arena] strenuously made these points: "A corporation is an artificial being, invisible, intangible, and existing only in contemplation of law," Justice Rehnquist wrote, quoting John Marshall. He added that "liberties of political expression are not at all necessary to effectuate the purposes for which States permit commercial corporations to exist." But the precedent had been established.[22]

Corporate criminal liability and corporate personhood under the Constitution are likely here to stay, regardless of these warnings that our conception of corporations as akin to people has gone too far. The two doctrinal trends have a certain symmetry that is worth recognizing. If the abstraction of the corporate form deserves constitutional protections as vaunted as free speech, corporations should remain exposed to the opprobrium of criminal liability when the people who run them misbehave.

Other critics of corporate criminal liability do not tarry on the theoretical, advancing a series of pragmatic arguments for limiting the scope of existing corporate liability rules.

---

[20] Sorrell v. IMS Health Inc., 131 S. Ct. 2653 (2011).

[21] The seminal case is *First Nat'l Bank of Boston v. Bellotti*, 435 U.S. 765 (1978), in which the Court invalidated a Massachusetts law limiting corporate contributions to referendum campaigns because the state statute abridged corporate rights under the First and Fourteenth Amendments.

[22] Tim Wu, *How Corporations Hijacked the First Amendment*, NEW REPUBLIC, June 3, 2013, http://www.newrepublic.com/article/113294/how-corporations-hijacked-first-amendment-evade-regulation. The case discussed by Wu is First National Bank of Boston v. Bellotti, 435 U.S. 765 (1978). The dissent by Justice Rehnquist appears at 435 U.S. at 822. For another thoughtful discussion of this issue, see Lawrence Friedman, *In Defense of Corporate Criminal Liability*, 23 HARV. J.L. & PUB. POL'Y 833, 844–49 (2000).

Collateral Damage

Legal academics argue that such prosecutions cause collateral damage (sometimes referred to as "overspill") to innocent parties. Professor John Coffee offered the aphorism in a seminal 1981 article that "when the corporation catches a cold, someone else sneezes," identifying a range of bystanders of varying degrees of culpability.[23] He began with shareholders as potentially the least sympathetic of such parties because they may have profited from the externalization of costs permitted by a crime. Bondholders and credit holders follow as close seconds and thirds. The most sympathetic bystanders were "lower echelon employees" who lose their jobs if the criminal fine was large enough.[24]

Professor V. S. Khanna updated these observations in a 1996 article in the *Harvard Law Review*, arguing that in addition to the collateral damage imposed by criminal fines, pleading guilty or being found guilty of such charges costs a corporation and its managers dearly in "lost reputation or stigma."[25] He argued that lost reputation is "rarely a socially desirable sanction in the corporate context" because "no one receives a corporation's lost reputation, whereas someone – the government or a private party – receives the cash fine."[26] He justified this broad conclusion with an economic analysis focused on firms that market high quality products or services and therefore are sensitive to the marshaling and protection of their good name with the consuming public. Khanna contended that in the limited universe of firms sensitive to their standing in the marketplace, "[t]he use of reputation is nonetheless problematic because reputational sanctions are inaccurate and affect only firms with good reputations."[27] Because of the problem of over-deterrence, criminal, as opposed to civil, penalties are justified only when a corporation is judgment proof or when the reputational loss can be imposed early, saving both parties the expense of a trial.

If Professor Khanna is right that criminal prosecutions inflict unjustified and damaging blows to corporate reputations, the possibility of becoming a target should motivate top managers to work hard to stay in compliance. Of course, managers must perceive that prosecutions are a serious risk either because they are likely or because penalties and collateral damage will be unacceptably severe even if the chances of being targeted are small. Unacceptable risk will inspire risk

---

[23] These observations are included in Coffee's classic 1981 article, still cited by contemporary scholars: John C. Coffee, *"No Soul to Damn: No Body to Kick": An Unscandalized Inquiry into the Problem of Corporate Punishment,* 79 MICH. L. REV. 386, 401 (1981).

[24] *Id.*

[25] V. S. Khanna, *Corporate Criminal Liability: What Purpose Does It Serve?,* 109 HARV. L. REV. 1477, 1499 (1996).

[26] *Id.* at 1499, 1503.

[27] *Id.* at 1505.

avoidance in the form of compliance programs designed to find and eliminate significant violations. In fact, these assumptions underlie the entire U.S. system of justice, from speed traps on the highway to the most sophisticated prosecutions of corporate malfeasance. Or, in other words, deterrence-based enforcement that depends on the punishment of the few to motivate the many is the foundation of every set of legal requirements we have adopted, however unpopular some of them may be from the perspective of regulated industries. Criminal charges are the most extreme alternative in the continuum of potential sanctions.

Opponents of corporate prosecutions have two responses to the assertion that deterrence-based enforcement has great value when applied to corporations in the criminal context. The first is that corporate managers are likely to avoid establishing internal audits because they fear the results will be obtained by the government and used to prosecute them. And, they say, self-auditing has greater potential to achieve compliance across-the-board than a deterrence-based approach. I agree with this second statement, although no empirical evidence supports the assumption that criminal prosecutions will chill – as opposed to encourage – self-auditing. In seeming recognition of this possibility, critics argue that robust enforcement will prompt companies to *over*compensate, spending far more money on internal audits than is justified by the economic repercussions of being caught. This obviously contradictory proposition is similarly bereft of empirical support. Moreover, the critics make no effort to quantify – or even to recognize – the other benefits of compliance prompted by self-auditing (for example, cleaner water, safer workers, better consumer products).

In an article published in the *Stanford Law Review*, Israeli professors Assaf Hamdani and Alon Klement open with the proposition that criminal prosecutions are often a "corporate death penalty," offering the Arthur Andersen case as their evidence in chief: "Yet, the prevailing view is that prosecutors should balance the need to deter corporate crime against a conviction's dire consequences for employees and other innocent stakeholders."[28] From this premise, they predict both that companies will – and will not – have increased incentives to monitor their own compliance:

> Most modern firms, however, cannot realistically expect to eliminate wrongdoing, even when they implement adequate compliance measures. Under the prevailing entity-liability regime, a firm might unravel even for an isolated violation that took place notwithstanding the firm's compliance effort.[29]
>
> Again, we do not argue that threatening firms with harsh penalties will always distort monitoring incentives. In some cases, the threat of going out of

---

[28] Assaf Hamdani & Alon Klement, *Corporate Crime and Deterrence*, 61 STAN. L. REV. 271, 274 (2008).
[29] *Id.* at 275.

business can compel firms to make an effort – perhaps even an excessive one – to prevent their agents from breaking the law.[30]

Unfortunately, legal scholars have undertaken little empirical research regarding the deterrent function of the criminal law. Admittedly, such research would be quite difficult to accomplish, not least because the universe of firms that have undergone prosecution is small and their senior managers are likely to be reticent about disclosing the salient details of such experiences.

A few studies regarding the deterrent effect of civil sanctions have been done in the environmental arena, although they were limited for idiosyncratic reasons involving the availability of government data to oil spills and the pulp and paper industries.[31] They generally conclude that frequent monitoring through individual facility inspections is at least as important as the size of any penalty that is assessed. The studies found modest downward trends in prohibited conduct during the same period as routine enforcement actions. The wisdom of the inspection observation is worth underscoring. I spent seven years in private practice counseling a variety of publicly owned utilities regarding the requirements of federal pollution control laws. A visit from federal, state, or local regulators was a momentous event that often prompted a systemwide compliance review regardless of the penalties that resulted. Unfortunately, such visits have become increasingly unlikely due to federal and state budget cuts..[32]

Regulatory Unreasonableness

Opponents of corporate criminal liability are no great fans of the regulatory state. Fischel and Sykes argue that the authorizing statutes used to prosecute Drexel Burnham Lambert, the Wall Street investment banking firm, and its

---

[30] *Id.* at 290.

[31] The EPA itself focused on pulp and paper, making data available to researchers interested in the area. The Coast Guard happens to provide detailed information on oil spills. For an overview of this research, see Mark A. Cohen, *Empirical Research on the Deterrent Effect of Environmental Monitoring and Enforcement*, 30 Envtl. L. Rep. (Envtl. L. Inst.) 10,245 (2000). Other notable studies include Wesley A. Magat & W. Kip Viscusi, *Effectiveness of the EPA's Regulatory Enforcement: The Case of Industrial Effluent Standards*, 33 J.L. & Econ. 331 (1990), and Dennis Epple & Michael Visscher, *Environmental Pollution: Modeling Occurrence, Detection and Deterrence*, 27 J.L. & Econ. 29 (1984). For an interesting discussion of these studies, and the importance of establishing positive social norms to reinforce the fear of prosecution, see Michael P. Vandenbergh, *Beyond Elegance: A Testable Typology of Social Norms in Corporate Environmental Compliance*, 22 Stan. Envtl. L.J. 55 (2003).

[32] *See, e.g.*, U.S. Envtl. Prot. Agency, Fiscal Year 2013 EPA Enforcement and Compliance Results, at 6 (2013), *available at* http://www2.epa.gov/sites/production/files/2014-02/documents/fy-2013-enforcement-annual-results-charts-2-6-14_0.pdf#page=6.

"star employee" Michael Milken are examples of laws that impose "stiff criminal penalties" for "conduct that causes no harm."[33] They cite with approval an article published in 1994 by Professor Richard Lazarus, a prominent environmental law scholar who raised a menu of objections to the potential unfairness of what he characterized as inappropriately low burdens of proof for environmental crimes.[34] Lazarus argued that:

> Environmental law is riddled with paradox. Seemingly nonsensical twists of policy abound in the double helix of statutory enactments and corresponding regulatory schemes . ... Conflict and contradiction are the rule rather than the exception for those hardy enough to go beyond the symbolic rhetoric and promise of environmental policy in an effort to discover the actual terms of environmental law itself.[35]

Given the overwhelming complexity of the law, "the delegation of sweeping prosecutorial discretion in the politically charged area of environmental law is ultimately unworkable."[36] Lazarus was especially troubled by judicial application of the long-standing maxim that ignorance of the law is no defense. He argued that prosecutors should shoulder the burden of proving that the miscreant clearly understood each of the detailed regulatory provisions he stood accused of violating. Given the inherent complexity of the rules, he reasoned, a defendant might know that he had dumped toxic chemicals in an unlined pit, but he might not know that this practice was in fact illegal.

The Lazarus objections were elaborate and intricately reasoned, and he insisted that he sought reform, not elimination, of criminal enforcement. At the time his critique was a noteworthy example of an academic who had a reputation as an environmentalist drawing the line against government overreach.

Regardless, the courts have rejected his concerns. The truth is that prosecutors do not bring cases that appear to pluck an innocent and unsophisticated

---

[33] Fischel & Sykes, *supra* note 8, at 342 ("The case focused on an alleged 'stock parking agreement' between Milken and Ivan Boesky. ... The purpose of the scheme was supposedly to allow both Drexel and Boesky to evade certain regulatory filing requirements.... Assuming the scheme existed (there is substantial doubt whether it did), there were still no obvious victims. Drexel and Milken's exposure under tort law was for all practical purposes zero.").

[34] *See* Richard J. Lazarus, *Assimilating Environmental Protection into Legal Rules and the Problem with Environmental Crime*, 27 LOY. L.A. L. REV. 867, 881–82 (1994). The Lazarus pieces are repetitive, and a reader wishing to get the best handle on his arguments while expending minimal reading time should consult Richard J. Lazarus, *Meeting the Demands of Integration in the Evolution of Environmental Law: Reforming Environmental Criminal Law*, 83 GEO. L.J. 2407 (1995).

[35] Lazarus, *Meeting the Demands, supra* note 34, at 2407.

[36] *Id.* at 2508.

fellow off the factory floor who is incapable of fathoming an impenetrable regulation but has managed to commit an act so objectionable that prosecutors undertake a criminal prosecution. Real-life cases involve conduct that is obviously harmful, whether or not the relatively sophisticated defendants acknowledge that they were well aware of the precise regulatory subsection they disregarded.

THE SOCIOLOGICAL DEFENSE

The Pinto Fiasco

In the popular sociology text *Corporate Crime Under Attack: The Fight to Criminalize Business Violence,*[37] the authors celebrate the 1980 Pinto criminal case, which was the first time that a major American company – the Ford Motor Company – was charged with reckless homicide by a local prosecutor. The indictment involved the deaths of three young women burned to death when their Pinto subcompact was struck from behind by a beer delivery truck and the rear-end gas tank exploded into flames. The case was a *cause célèbre* because it exemplified the worst suspicions of a disillusioned Vietnam War–era public about the raw economic calculations large companies use to decide whether to install safety equipment in consumer products, protect workers on the job, and prevent pollution.

Ford economists had prepared a cost-benefit analysis documenting the costs and benefits of preventing fuel-tank fires precipitated by vehicle roll-overs. The document estimated that the costs of such rules would be substantially more ($137 million) than the monetary value of lives saved ($49.5 million). The economists incorporated into their calculations a value of $200,000 for a lost life and $67,000 for injuries likely to be caused in such accidents. The public and the media were horrified, taking the number-crunching as a revelation of heartless corporate greed. A widely read magazine article by Mark Dowie entitled *Pinto Madness* was published in *Mother Jones* and won the Pulitzer Prize.[38] Ultimately, Ford recalled Pintos and settled private lawsuits for hundreds of millions of dollars, a great deal of money in those days.

The criminal case against Ford was brought by Michael Consentino, a local prosecutor in Elkhart County, Indiana. Unfortunately, Indiana had only recently adopted the reckless homicide provision that was the foundation of

---

[37] FRANCIS T. CULLEN ET AL., CORPORATE CRIME UNDER ATTACK: THE FIGHT TO CRIMINALIZE BUSINESS VIOLENCE (2d ed. 2006).

[38] Mark Dowie, *Pinto Madness*, MOTHER JONES, Sept./Oct. 1977, at 18, 20.

Consentino's case. Claims by a nursing supervisor that the eighteen-year-old driver had admitted on her deathbed that she had stopped the car in the middle of the road to recover a lost gas cap further undermined the prosecution's credibility, resulting in a jury verdict of acquittal. Nevertheless, the case broke an unspoken taboo and has sporadically inspired similar prosecutions. These cases, including the well-publicized case involving the death of a worker killed when he was sent to clean a tank containing cyanide wastes without protective equipment, are discussed in greater detail in Chapter 7.[39]

Ford's attorneys billed the company $2 million in fees and costs in comparison to prosecution expenditures of $20,000, and managed to get the cost-benefit analysis excluded from the trial on the grounds that it was written before the statute passed. Consentino ended up digging into his own pocket to rent cabins at a state park for his team, which was outmatched in every respect including expert testimony by its corporate opponent. Unfortunately, the lesson of the case that is intuited by state and local prosecutors whether or not they have heard about it is that criminal prosecutions against large companies require the commitment of serious resources. Given these constraints, the rewards a prosecutor can achieve by bringing such cases, such as favorable publicity, must be significant.

White Collar Taxonomy

The concept of distinguishing between crimes committed on the street and those that take place in the boardroom predates the Ford Pinto by three decades. Sociologist Edwin Sutherland is widely credited with coining the phrase "white collar crime" in a 1939 address to the American Sociological Association.[40] His subsequent book with the same title was a pathbreaking mixture of social theory and empirical research.[41] Originally published in 1949, just a year before his death, it remains a classic. The impact of Sutherland's theories on criminology theory and practice cannot be overstated. Before he introduced a rationale for elevating the profile of white collar crime, the discipline was preoccupied with street crimes committed by people of low social status who were thought to be preordained to react to their unpleasant circumstances by robbing, murdering, and assaulting each other.

---

[39] People v. O'Neil, 550 N.E.2d 1090 (Ill. App. Ct. 1990) (reversing and remanding the convictions of Film Recovery Systems' agents for murder and the corporation for involuntary manslaughter because of inconsistent mental states, implicitly recognizing that the corporation could be convicted of murder); see, e.g., Ameet Sachdev, *Local Case Influenced BP Criminal Liability*, CHI. TRIB., Nov. 18, 2012, at C1 (discussing and comparing Film Recovery Systems with BP).

[40] Edwin H. Sutherland, *White Collar Criminality*, 5 AM. SOC. REV. 1 (1940).

[41] EDWIN H. SUTHERLAND, WHITE COLLAR CRIME (1949).

These ideas allowed middle- and upper-class people to remain complacent about the white collar versions of criminal activities – embezzlement rather than armed robbery or fatal industrial incidents rather than murder. Sutherland wrote:

> The personal pathologies which have been suggested as explanations of criminal behavior were, at first, biological abnormalities; when research studies threw doubt on the validity of these biological explanations, the next explanation was intellectual inferiority, and more recently emotional instability. ... The thesis of this book is that these social and personal pathologies are not an adequate explanation of criminal behavior.[42]

Sutherland argued that because white collar crime is committed by individuals of middle- and upper-class socioeconomic status in a business context, the behavior is perceived as inoffensive by prosecutors who are hesitant to jail people they view as social counterparts. Too often, white collar crimes are rationalized as an inevitable by-product of doing business. Undertaken within the shrouded boundaries of large corporations, such activities are largely invisible to the public. Social opprobrium, the critical *quid pro quo* for the condemnation and, ultimately, the aggressive prosecution of criminal behavior, therefore fails to materialize.

Sutherland argued that the research confirming the genetic inferiority of street criminals was infected by deep bias within the legal system. He believed that street criminals were targeted by the courts and jailed not because they committed more offenses than members of the upper socioeconomic classes but rather because prosecutors either had little conception of white collar crime or feared to approach white collar criminals:

> The thesis of this book, stated positively, is that persons of the upper socioeconomic class engage in much criminal behavior; that this criminal behavior differs from the criminal behavior of the lower socioeconomic class principally in the administrative procedures which are used in dealing with the offenders; and that variations in administrative procedures are not significant from the point of view of causation of crime. The causes of tuberculosis were not different when it was treated by poultices and bloodletting than when treated by streptomycin.[43]

Sutherland posited that white collar crime was far more likely to be caused by what he labeled "differential association" than by the inherent mental or emotional deficiencies of people who inhabited the lower class:

---

[42] EDWIN H. SUTHERLAND, WHITE COLLAR CRIME: THE UNCUT VERSION 5 (1981).
[43] SUTHERLAND, *supra* note 42, at 7.

The hypothesis of differential association is that criminal behavior is learned in association with those who define it favorably, ... and that a person in an appropriate situation engages in such criminal behavior if, and only if, the weight of the favorable definitions exceeds the weight of the unfavorable definitions. This hypothesis is certainly not a complete or universal explanation of white collar crime or of other crime, but it perhaps fits the data of both types of crimes better than any other general hypothesis.[44]

To document the "problem of white collar crime," Sutherland compiled a list of the seventy largest (and, in his view, most significant) U.S. corporations and researched their interactions with the legal system through court and administrative agency records. This research was affected by the central events of his time, encompassing the economic opportunities presented by World War II, fierce battles between organized labor and management, and the emergence of government efforts to curtail *laissez faire* economic policies. Sutherland discovered evidence of widespread corporate restraints of trade; the employment of labor spies and strike-breaking through violent intervention; and "war crimes" involving opportunistic marketing of valuable technology to future enemies. In fact, his work was considered so inflammatory that the version published in 1949 was heavily redacted to eliminate the identities of the companies he criticized so harshly. Decades after his death, in 1983, the book was republished by Yale University Press as *White Collar Crime: The Uncut Version*, with an introduction by sociologists Gilbert Geis and Colin Goff, and that version is the one referenced here.

Sutherland's emphatic warnings that the shared affluence and respectability of corporate executives and prosecutors often undermine white collar criminal prosecutions remain as relevant today as they were in postwar America. White collar crime has unquestionably moved into the mainstream of the law. But prosecutions, especially of individual, high-ranking corporate executives, seem susceptible to the same interference as they were in Sutherland's time.

Sutherland not only named white collar crime, he put it on the map academically. The sociology of white collar crime became a staple in graduate schools and spawned its own literature, curricula, and doctoral candidates. In 1980, Marshall Clinard and Peter Yeager published a study much like Sutherland's, which was dedicated to him and bore the stark title *Corporate Crime*.[45] Other scholars researched the development of illegality within specific industries. *Wayward Capitalists*,[46] Susan Shapiro's study

---

[44] *Id.* at 240.

[45] MARSHALL CLINARD & PETER YEAGER, CORPORATE CRIME (1980).

[46] SUSAN P. SHAPIRO, WAYWARD CAPITALISTS: TARGETS OF THE SECURITIES AND EXCHANGE COMMISSION (1987).

of enforcement at the Securities and Exchange Commission, and John Braithwaite's *Corporate Crime in the Pharmaceutical Industry*,[47] both published in 1984, are two good examples of this genre. Still others prepared textbooks on the subject that have come out in second and third editions. All of this literature coincided with and was inspired by the broader social movement for government reform that reacted to Watergate and the Vietnam War. White collar criminal enforcement was one tool envisioned by reformers to restore the effectiveness and integrity of the federal government.

Sutherland's colleagues quickly grew restless with his broad definition of white collar crime. Sutherland cast his net very broadly, defining white collar crime as deplorable behavior by people in higher social classes during the course of their occupations. Although he may have had legitimate reasons for this expansive approach in 1939, fellow sociologists believed that he had inadvertently diverted the focus from corporate malfeasance to include politicians, bureaucrats, or other entitled and authoritative figures who were engaged in unsavory, but not necessarily illegal, acts. They argued that the inevitable result was to confuse the identification and development of a theory of white collar corporate behavior that should be criminalized. As Francis Cullen, Gray Cavender, William Maakestad, and Michael Benson, authors of *Corporate Crime under Attack: The Fight to Criminalize Business Violence*, a popular textbook, wrote in 2006:

> The controversy centered around the reality that many of the actions subsumed under Sutherland's concept of white-collar crime are not often defined by the state as criminal. Although important changes have taken place, criminal sanctions have been employed only sparingly in the social control of the business, political, and professional deviance of the affluent.[48]

Or, as lawyer-sociologist Paul Tappan characterized the problem more sharply: despite its "fruitful beginnings" as a definition intended to differentiate upper-class criminality from well-worn assumptions about street lawbreaking, Sutherland's definition lost its conceptual rigor and "spread into vacuity, wide and handsome."[49]

In lieu of Sutherland's class-based definition, Cullen, Gray, Maakestad, and Benson focused on "illegal acts potentially punishable by criminal sanctions, and committed to advance the interests of the corporate organization."[50]

---

[47] John Braithwaite, Corporate Crime in the Pharmaceutical Industry (1984).
[48] Cullen et al., *supra* note 37, at 7.
[49] Paul Tappan, *Who Is the Criminal?*, 12 Am. Soc. Rev. 96, 98 (1947).
[50] Cullen et al., *supra* note 37, at 9.

Not only does this alternative have the important advantage of capturing law-breaking corporations and not just individuals, it places the focus of both investigation and law reform where it belongs: on the way people work within a corporate culture to advance institutional interests.

The Life of the Corporate Manager

In an effort to probe the dynamics of corporate culture even more deeply, a second group of sociologists undertook delicate empirical research to document the intense psychological and social pressures on managers as they rose through the ranks. The inevitable effect of this competitive and highly uncertain environment was to diffuse individual ethics, as well as any internalized sense of individual accountability. Robert Jackall's 1988 volume, *Moral Mazes: The World of Corporate Managers*, reported on interviews with senior managers from three diverse firms, including a major chemical company that was preoccupied with environmental rules. Jackall found that corporate life was chaotic and extraordinarily stressful. Managers trying to advance within the corporation were subject to a constant series of "probationary crucibles" that require them to satisfy managers above them while also sidestepping blame for setbacks at their level of responsibility.[51] Of course, these challenges did not occur in a vacuum: shifts in the global economy, labor disputes, rising costs of raw material, mistakes in long-term strategic planning, the corruption that is a prevalent challenge for business ventures in the developing world, unexpected developments in regulatory policy, and a wide variety of human errors cause constant reversals of fortune within the firm. Because advancement requires the forging of alliances with more senior executives, these reversals make the work less dependent on managers' abilities and increase the sense of powerlessness over their long-term prospects. In this roiling environment, incentives to "starve" or "milk" the plant – or, in today's terminology, "run to failure" – are quite strong.[52] As Jackall writes:

> One way to hit desired numbers is by squeezing the resources under one's control. …. Usually, managers will do everything they can to hold down capital expenditures, everything from maintenance to innovative investment, as long as possible. Done over a short period, this is called "starving a plant"; done over a longer period, it is called "milking a plant."[53]

---

[51] Robert Jackall, Moral Mazes: The World of Corporate Managers 40 (1988).
[52] *See, e.g.,* Abrahm Lustgarten, Run to Failure: BP and the Making of the Deepwater Horizon Disaster (2012).
[53] Jackall, *supra* note 51, at 91–92.

British sociologist Maurice Punch agrees with Jackall's analysis, and musters other studies documenting

> the discrepancy between the surface solidity of the business organization and the fluctuating and even turbulent reality of managerial "backstage" behavior. ... Behind the apparently coherent and rational front of the formal corporation there is a world of power-struggles, rivalry, factionalism, favouritism, politics, manipulation and short-term problem-solving. Managers ... emerge ... as chameleons, buffeted by moral ambiguity and institutional uncertainty. ... In this view the organization is an intricate, ambiguous, contingent, even contradictory arena where deviance may become an acceptable answer to perceived institutional or elite group dilemmas, and where the organizational context and resources are intrinsic to the development of rule-breaking.[54]

Punch draws into his analysis several factors that make corporations vulnerable to disastrous mistakes, including:

- the state of the market in which accident-prone companies operate – the more competitive the market, the greater the incentive to cut corners and take risks;
- the antiregulatory ideology of the company's top management;
- the tendency of some corporate cultures to demonize outsiders, especially regulators and left-wing activists;
- top managers' resistance to hearing bad news and their concerted efforts to push responsibility for fixing problems down to the bottom of the corporate hierarchy;
- the physical distance between high-level executives and the location of industrial accidents;
- failures of basic technology – for example, no warning lights;
- the cognitive dissonance between written procedures and worker habits on the frontlines; and
- pressure to perform life-threatening operations at full speed.

All of these factors are illustrated in vivid detail by the fatal episodes explored in Part II.

Punch expresses frustration that the criminal law's insistence on linking individual behavior to the proximate cause of a fatal accident disregards these factors and their strong influence on conditions that make people blind to – or, more accurately, unaccountable for – clearly unacceptable risk. Writing about a ferry accident in 1987 that took 197 lives when the crew failed to close the ship's

---

[54] Maurice Punch, *Suite Violence: Why Managers Murder and Corporations Kill*, 33 CRIME, L. & SOC. CHANGE 243, 245 (2004).

front-loading doors, causing the ship to flood and sink and ultimately leading to the unsuccessful prosecution of the owner's chief executive officer and the company itself for corporate manslaughter, he explains:

> Townsend Thorensen was one of the new-style entrepreneurial companies of the eighties (that were fostered by the deregulatory regime of Mrs. Thatcher's Conservative government) which believed in free enterprise ... cost-cutting, no trade unions, and on contributing large funds to the koffers of the Conservative Party. At the time of departure the assistant bosun responsible for closing the doors was asleep in his bunk; the officer who was supposed to oversee the assistant bosun was not at his post because operating instructions required him to be in two places at one time and he was on the bridge; and the captain had no mechanical means of knowing that the bow doors were shut despite several requests from masters for a warning device to be fitted on the bridge. ...
>
> The reason that the judge dismissed the case early on in proceedings was because of the difficulty of tracing culpability from the failure to close the bow doors of the ferry directly to managerial decision-making on safety at the board level. ... The judge expressed his difficulty in defining "the mind and will" of the corporation from the evidence. ... And when the prosecution failed against the company then the charges were also dropped against the individuals who had been implicated in the accident.[55]

Approaching these same issues from an ethical perspective, three philosophers, including David Luban, an internationally known legal ethicist, emphasize the "fragmentation of information" within large institutions that allows individual actors to continue their participation in dangerous behavior because they are accountable for only a slice of the complex welter of causes that lead to the unthinkable. These circumstances create "the risk that an individual will do or contribute to great harm without knowing it."[56] They propose solutions to these dilemmas that neither excuse individual misbehavior nor limit a corporation's culpability. Instead, they propose that upper management embrace five "duties" to guide how they define and implement their jobs. The first is investigation, defined as holding individuals responsible for "discerning the nature of their own projects and for discovering what other employees are doing."[57] The second is communication, which means holding individuals "who possess troublesome knowledge morally responsible for communicating it to others."[58] The third is protection, defined as supervisors'

---

[55] *Id.* at 249.
[56] David Luban et al., *Moral Responsibility in the Age of Bureaucracy*, 90 MICH. L. REV. 2348 (1992).
[57] *Id.* at 2383.
[58] *Id.* at 2384.

"moral obligations to protect their subordinates from adverse consequences of investigation and communication."[59] The fourth is prevention, defined as managers' "moral obligations to forestall wrongdoing."[60] The fifth is precaution, which means holding individuals responsible for avoiding corrupt organizations in the first place.

Institutional Failure

These principles set the stage for the work of a third category of sociologists, who have traced the institutional causes of industrial catastrophes, painstakingly working their way back from the height of these events to their root causes. Investigators such as Diane Vaughan and Andrew Hopkins trace what happened in the days, months, and even years leading up to an incident, working systematically to discover each of the individual actions, normal routines, and documented procedures that preceded it. Their analysis reveals the extent to which managers allow dangerous habits to become engrained in a corporation's routine activities. Eventually, these habits produce chain reactions that may appear idiosyncratic but in fact represent an institution's failure to prevent unacceptable risks. Several discrete manifestations of institutional failure arise repeatedly:

1. Relentless and irrational demands that employees save time and money;
2. Stove pipe management that diffuses accountability for growing hazards by distributing decision-making authority among several independent organizational units;
3. Creation of elaborate paper tigers – written policies that are systematically ignored in the field;
4. Shoot the messenger systems of communication that heavily discourage lower- and mid-level managers from bringing upper-level managers bad news; and
5. The normalization of deviance, meaning the gradual redefinition of acceptable risk to encompass intolerably high hazard outcomes.

Time and Money

Intense and extended pressure from upper management to perform work more quickly and to reduce maintenance costs has played a central role in several industrial catastrophes. This pressure can be reinforced by incentive systems

[59] *Id.*
[60] *Id.*

that offer generous bonuses for speeding up production lines and cutting costs. Managers may demand that line workers neglect safety measures in order to get work done faster. High-hazard operations are undertaken without performing testing that should be routine and that would indicate whether complicated procedures are having their desired effect.

The most notorious example is BP. Sir John Browne, the company's chief executive officer from 1995 to 2007, was determined to transform the already giant corporation into the world's largest oil producer. As he committed most of the company's liquid assets to a series of major acquisitions, he implemented a relentless cost-cutting campaign that sharply reduced maintenance budgets and eliminated supervisory personnel. This relentless, ill-considered campaign provoked a crisis when Don Parus became the plant manager at BP's Texas City refinery in 2002. The plant had already suffered severe degradation in physical infrastructure as a result of round after round of cost-cutting. After several workers were killed in accidents that should not have happened, Parus commissioned a safety inspection that uncovered $235 million in recommended upgrades. He repeatedly asked for more money in the plant's annual budget to implement the most urgent of these recommendations, but was rebuffed just as often. Parus hired the Telos Group, a private consultant, to undertake a confidential assessment of worker morale. Telos reported that several employees said they feared for their lives when they came to work.[61]

At the time, the plant at Texas City was BP's most profitable refinery, earning $900 million annually. But London executives ordered an additional $65 million in cost reductions from a $300 million annual budget because the plant was "NOT delivering on profitability vs. % of capital

---

[61] Telos Group, BP Texas City Site Report of Findings (Jan. 21, 2005), *available at* http://s3.documentcloud.org/documents/5170/the-telos-report.pdf. Selected quotes from that report, completed by the Telos Group, include:

> The heroes around here are the ones working to the production goals and who complete them early. 80 to 90 per cent of what gets recognized is *doing it fast* counts.
> *Telling the manager what they want to hear,* **that** gets rewarded. For example, one person who had cut costs, done a lot of Band-Aids with maintenance and had a quit-your-bellyaching, quit-your-complaining attitude was rewarded in the last reorganization. When his replacement was brought into his previous maintenance position, his replacement found that not a single pump was fit for service; air compressors, not one spare was fit for service.
> Units are 90% of the time run to failure, due to postponing turnarounds [maintenance]. So making money or saving money for that particular year looks good on the books. This is a serious safety concern to operating personnel. We do not walk the talk all the time. Costs and budgets are preached to reduce costs.

Id. at 6, 17 (emphasis in original).

investment."[62] In a move that signaled how desperate Parus had become, he presented a PowerPoint to top BP executives showing pictures of the men who had died.[63] Shortly after he returned from that meeting, a massive explosion caused by stunning neglect of several routine safety protocols killed 15 people at the plant. BP eventually sold the refinery, after paying billions in damages to surviving family members. Despite this horrendous and well-publicized sequence of events, many of the same mistakes were repeated for the same reasons in the months leading up to the Macondo well blowout.

Blurry Decision Making and Stove Pipe Management

The larger a corporation, the more difficult it is to maintain the integrity of the chain of command. Executives have experimented with a series of method-ologies for overcoming neglect of health and safety problems, from risk management departments to company-wide safety protocols, to the award of affirmative incentives for safe operations. But in the absence of these remedies, all of which take substantial time, attention, and resources to implement successfully, the most common default structures is stove pipe management. Isolated organizational units may share jurisdiction over a brewing and poten-tially severe problem but often fail to communicate.

One classic example of ill-considered efforts to overcome organizational silos is the blurring of institutional chains of command, leading to decisions made on the basis of consensus. For example, a team leader overseeing employees in different divisions sends out a long and technical email, with his covering message asking if "anyone has a problem with this?" Few respond because they do not feel individually accountable for double-checking the team leader's work and may not even read the message and its copious attachments. Equally bad, decision-making authority is sometimes assigned to managers who lack the technical background necessary to determine the implications of such corner-cutting. Technical experts who could advise the manager of an obvious hazard are either housed at a different location or report to a supervisor in a different organizational unit. Both problems hobbled the effectiveness of BP engineers who as a result were unable to supervise effectively the temporary closure of the Macondo well, causing the

---

[62] Ryan Knutson, *Blast at BP Texas Refinery in '05 Foreshadowed Gulf Disaster*, PROPUBLICA (July 2, 2010), http://www.propublica.org/article/blast-at-bp-texas-refinery-in-05-foreshadowed-gulf-disaster (emphasis in original).

[63] Don Parus, Texas City Plant Manager, PowerPoint Presentation entitled "Texas City Is Not a Safe Place to Work," *available at* http://s3.documentcloud.org/documents/11343/don-parus-powerpoint-presentation.pdf.

explosion of the Deepwater Horizon, as explained in Chapter 6. Siloed decision making, according to a report prepared by a law firm hired by the Tennessee Valley Authority, contributed to the collapse of a huge, poorly designed and maintained impoundment of waste coal ash slurry spilling 1.1 billion gallons over 300 acres in rural Kingston, Tennessee. Four separate divisions within the giant company had some responsibility for overseeing the impoundment but rarely communicated and, even when they did, did not do it well.

Paper Tigers

The vast majority of companies engaged in industrial manufacturing or the production of energy and fuel have elaborate protocols intended to prevent workplace and consumer fatalities and injuries as well as damage to natural resources. Some of these protocols are generated in compliance with various federal health, safety, and environmental laws. Others are demanded by customers who are intent on ensuring that they receive functional products or services and that they are protected from liability in the event of manufacturing errors. Perhaps the largest number are drafted by corporate compliance officers who study federal and state regulations and then translate their requirements into internal procedures, checklists, decision trees, forms, instructions, codes of conduct, and other documentation. Unfortunately, the postmortem on the vast majority of industrial accidents reveals that compliance with such documentation varies in inverse proportion to its volume and complexity.

For example, the Peanut Corporation of America (PCA) routinely prepared "Certificates of Analysis" (COAs) for such Fortune 500 clients as the Kellogg Company and Nestle Prepared Foods each time it shipped peanut paste for incorporation into products like cereal or desserts. The COAs incorporated the results of testing conducted to ensure that the paste was not contaminated with microbial contaminants such as salmonella or coliforms. Salmonella causes bacterial infections in the intestinal tract. Coliforms, which derive from animal feces, are not necessarily harmful in themselves but provide a strong indication that the originating plant is operated under unsanitary conditions. The DOJ indictment issued against PCA's senior executives, including PCA owner and president Stewart Parnell, alleges that they routinely shipped peanut paste either before they received test results or after they received results indicating that the paste was contaminated with salmonella and coliforms above acceptable levels. COAs were provided in such instances, but were filled in on the basis of testing done with respect to previous shipments. In the end, these practices caused 9 deaths and sickened 714 people.

Killing the Messenger

Jackall explains that a key aspect of corporate internal culture is to show progress in the form of ever-increasing levels of profit and to protect the managers who supervise them from negative perceptions or facts:

> This "management-by-objective" system, as it is usually called, creates a chain of commitments from the CEO down to the lowliest production manager or account executive. In practice, it also shapes a patrimonial authority arrangement that is crucial to defining both the immediate experiences and the long-run career chances of individual managers. In this world, a subordinate owes fealty principally to his immediate boss. This means that a subordinate must not overcommit his boss, lest his boss "get on the hook" for promises that cannot be kept. ... It is characteristic of this authority system that details are pushed down and credit is pulled up.... [T]he pushing down of details creates great pressure on middle managers not only to transmit good news but, precisely because they know details, to act to protect their corporations, their bosses, and themselves in the process.[64]

Jackall's observations are confirmed by Hopkins's analyses of the 2005 Texas City refinery explosion, where he repeatedly emphasizes the unwillingness of upper echelon management to hear bad news from lower-level managers, especially about problems that will cost money to fix. In *Failure to Learn, the BP Texas City Refinery Disaster*, Hopkins writes:

> [T]he view of many observers was that [BP CEO Sir John] Browne was the type of leader who only wanted to hear good news. According to [Rene Carayol, a journalist and management expert] who interviewed various BP managers in preparation for a BBC documentary on Browne, BP had a culture in which many top people knew of problems but few would speak up:
> "Only good news flowed upwards," he said. "No one dared say the wrong things or challenge the boss." ...
> "There were no dissenting voices in the boardroom. He [Browne] was no longer self-aware. Where's his sounding board? Where did he go for feedback?"[65]

Theoretically, the fail-safe for this powerful strain of executive blindness would be the regulatory system and its threat of deterrence-based enforcement. Lax enforcement and the inadequacy of civil penalties have weakened

---

[64] JACKALL, *supra* note 51, at 19–21.

[65] HOPKINS, FAILURE TO LEARN, *supra* note 4, at 108–09 (quoting Loren Steffy, HOUSTON CHRONICLE (Oct. 14, 2007)).

this offsetting force to the point that it cannot counter entrenched corporate culture.

The Normalization of Deviance

The explosion of the space shuttle *Challenger* on January 28, 1986, effectively ended America's love affair with space exploration. At the time, NASA was engaged in a frantic, underfunded effort to commercialize space shuttle flights to the point that the program might become self-supporting. In the aftermath of the disaster, it embarked on a massive effort to circle the wagons, shutting out reporters and investigators who attempted to understand the causes of the accident. Among other crucial information, NASA did not disclose that on the eve of the launch, engineers from the shuttle's main contractor, Morton Thiokol, tried to persuade NASA managers to abort the mission because they feared that unseasonably cold temperatures at the launch site in Cape Canaveral, Florida, could provoke the catastrophic failure of the craft's O-rings. The engineers were overruled by NASA managers. Even without an Internet, thousands of television channels, YouTube, and the 24/7 news cycle they feed, this omission looked like a blatant coverup, eventually resulting in the conclusion that incompetence and a crass disregard for safety caused the explosion.

But in her pathbreaking book *The Challenger Launch Decision, Risky Technology, Culture, and Deviance at NASA*, Diane Vaughan concludes that the popular explanation that individual managers went rogue is both off-the-mark and unhelpful because it distracts attention from a much more serious and common problem within the NASA hierarchy. Vaughan coined the phrase the "normalization of deviance" to explain this phenomenon, by which she means the recognition that a serious engineering (or other technical) problem exists that cannot really be fixed without disrupting a project's forward progress. Therefore, those responsible gradually increase the parameters of the risks they are willing to accept to what should be unacceptable levels. This concept is crucial because it represents an analysis of organization-wide misconduct, rather than attributing failure to a few individual bad apples who exerted sudden power over decision making. Vaughan writes:

> If NASA managers were concerned about meeting the demands of military and civilian customers to keep their payloads aloft, would they knowingly violate rules designed to assure the safety of those precious income-producing payloads? Completing missions was essential to obtaining the resources necessary for continuing the program. To argue that the *Challenger* launch decision was amoral – blatant and intentional disregard of formal safety requirements in the interest of production pressures and

economic necessity – is to argue that decision makers acted in direct opposition to NASA's competitive interests, rather than in concert with them.[66]

Instead of assuming inexplicable bad faith and worse judgment on the part of individual managers, Vaughan documents the development over several years of a far more pervasive "workgroup culture" that gradually accepted increasing levels of risk that the two sets of O-rings on the shuttle would fail catastrophically. So strong was the momentum of this normalization process that engineers from both organizations – Thiokol and NASA's Marshall Space Center – spent endless hours debating, verbally and on paper, the nature, scope, and seriousness of the O-ring problem at the same time that they continued to sign off on shuttle flights. Even when evidence slowly accumulated through nine shuttle launches that the first of a double set of O-rings was heavily damaged during launch and therefore subject to failure, the engineers and the managers who supervised them reasoned that because the situation incorporated redundancy through a second, back-up O-ring, both would not fail. Or, to put what Vaughan describes as the "incremental expansion of the bounds of acceptable risk" another way: the failure of both O-rings, which admittedly would result in catastrophe, was sufficiently unlikely that it became part of what those running the program understood to be a routine operating condition in an enterprise already fraught with risk.

In an eerie refrain of this exact situation, Hopkins documents how the engineers and managers aboard the ill-fated oil rig persuaded themselves that the blowout protector designed to shut down the piping leading to the roiling well was a redundancy that made the taking of other large risks acceptable.[67]

CONCLUSION

In the final part of this book, I argue for an unprecedented expansion of the criminal law to cover the conduct that results from institutional failure when it becomes acute enough to cause death, injury, and severe environmental degradation. Rather than focusing on the workers and lower-level supervisors who were standing by machinery when it failed, the law must authorize prosecutors to climb the managerial ladder to find those responsible for making such incidents inevitable. Broadened liability will deter the extreme

---

[66] VAUGHAN, *supra* note 3, at 48.
[67] ANDREW HOPKINS, DISASTROUS DECISIONS: THE HUMAN AND ORGANIZATION CAUSES OF THE GULF OF MEXICO BLOWOUT (2012).

carelessness that characterizes too much of corporate behavior in the post-modern era, when we have the technology and the money to prevent most fatal accidents. As important, reform would allow the prosecution of white collar crime to deliver the retribution that criminal law was intended to achieve.

Given the legal academy's objections to even the constrained and scant prosecutions that have occurred over the last two decades and the sociologists' preoccupation with their own investigations, reform will be, as the politicians are wont to say, a very heavy lift.

Part Two

The Lessons of Catastrophe

"ACCIDENTS" AND INSTITUTIONAL FAILURE

The gradual demise of the regulatory system has left major manufacturing sectors adrift. Some operate without any meaningful regulatory oversight. Others are blanketed with detailed regulatory requirements but, on the rare occasions when inspectors show up to check compliance, enforcement actions are erratic and unpredictable and penalties are relatively low. These circumstances provide the owners and operators of plants and production sites with strong incentives to avoid substantial investments in upfront compliance costs, especially safety and pollution control equipment. Instead, they consciously take the risk of waiting to see if they will be caught. Admittedly, that outcome would be unpleasant, but it is also one that seems increasingly unlikely. Compounding the challenge of motivating compliance is the reality that the national political environment is dominated by angry allegations that overregulation is killing the nation's economy. The spectacle of Obama administration political appointees appearing before disdainful House Republicans further suggests that companies may self-regulate as they see fit.

Large-scale disasters have been a fixture of the Industrial Revolution since its inception, and all of the events chronicled in the next few dozen pages have precursors, from the Triangle Shirtwaist fire to the Sago mine disaster to the Exxon Valdez oil spill.[1] Overall, safety has improved and death and injury rates have followed a steady downward trajectory. But over the past 15 years or so, backsliding has become more evident. The pace and scope of industrial catastrophes is escalating, with episodes that kill dozens, injure thousands, and cause environmental damage that costs billions of dollars to remediate. It's too soon to say that the regulatory system has collapsed, although the stories told here suggest that government oversight is dysfunctional in sectors that pose great risk to public health, worker safety, and the environment.

This judgment is underscored by congressional reaction to the worst incidents, news of which circulates in the national news for weeks, even months, at a time. As always, committee chairs in both houses, eager to demonstrate their concern to the public, have held hearings in the august high-ceilinged rooms of the Rayburn House and Russell Senate Office Buildings. Grief-stricken families of the gravely injured remain a staple of these events. In the past, the result of such hearings was legislation expanding and strengthening the authority of the agencies featured in these pages. What's different today is that bills drafted to address underlying regulatory failure most often founder or, in a minority of instances, emerge in such weakened form that they are unlikely to do any good. The grief and outrage fade and weak rules are implemented half-heartedly, setting the stage for worse mistakes.

The synergistic forces of government impotence and erratic self-regulation have produced superficially random patterns of causation in industries as disparate as deepwater oil production and small pharmacy production (called "compounding") of small lots of prescription drugs. When these episodes are lined up side-by-side, though, troubling patterns emerge. Unifying them all is the pressure of global competition and the siren call of easy money. The substantial expense of slowing down manufacturing or production to the point that safety protocols can be checked and rechecked falls by the wayside as top level executives push the many levels of managers below them to work faster and more inexpensively. Corners are cut: the huge machines used to cut coal end up with broken water hoses, the peanut roaster breaks, and the chemical

---

[1] On March 25, 1911, fire broke out at New York's Triangle Shirtwaist Factory, resulting in 146 deaths. *Remembering the 1911 Triangle Factory Fire*, CORNELL ILR SCHOOL (2011), http://www. ilr.cornell.edu/trianglefire/. A coal mine explosion occurred on January 2, 2006 in the Sago Mine in Sago, West Virginia, killing 12 of 13 trapped miners. Tamara Jones & Ann Scott Tyson, *After 44 Hours, Hope Showed Its Cruel Side*, WASH. POST, Jan. 6, 2006, http://www.washingtonpost.com/ wp-dyn/content/article/2006/01/04/AR2006010400247.html. On March 24, 1989, the oil tanker *Exxon Valdez* hit a reef and released over 11 million gallons of oil into the waters off Alaska. *Exxon Valdez*, ENVTL. PROTECTION AGENCY, http://www.epa.gov/oem/content/learning/ exxon.htm (last visited Mar. 5, 2014).

production tower is overfilled. The results are nothing less than catastrophic: twenty-nine miners dead after an explosion fueled by dry coal ash pulls down a mountain on top of them, nine consumers die and hundreds are sickened after inadequately heated peanut paste ships with salmonella contamination, and fifteen workers dead as a volatile chemical plume escaping from the overfilled tower is ignited by an idling pickup truck parked in the wrong place.

Postmortems reveal more commonality. Written procedures were ignored. Employees, their supervisors, and upper-level managers recognized the risks well but, under pressure to produce more quickly, either ignored them or rationalized them as normal. Remedies that would have cost small amounts of money were rejected in the cost-cutting fervor. Line supervisors and mid-level managers understood they were being set up as scapegoats, but could not figure out how to escape. Until very recently, the criminal law was irrelevant and, even now, prosecutions move up the chain only rarely, never reaching those with the power to trigger the chain of events that end so badly.

A common reaction to the fatal incidents addressed throughout this volume is that accidents happen because people are imperfect: they make errors at the spur of the moment, killing themselves and others for reasons that were unanticipated. This diagnosis is pushed so aggressively by employers of workers who are killed or badly injured on the job that health and safety specialists who work for organized labor refuse to use the word accident in connection with such incidents.[2] They have an excellent point. In its dictionary definition, the word "accident" means an incident that happens "unexpectedly and unintentionally," "by chance" or "without apparent or deliberate cause."[3] None of the incidents featured here have any of these attributes. All were disasters waiting to happen, clearly foreseeable to those in authority had they been paying attention.

Nevertheless, in its common usage, the word accident has a significantly broader connotation. It encompasses incidents so large and horrific that they

---

[2] *See, e.g.,* ANDREW HOPKINS, LESSONS FROM ESSO'S GAS PLANT EXPLOSION AT LONGFORD (2000), *available at* http://www.sirfrt.com.au/Meetings/IMRt/Southeast/IMRt%20East%2000Nov30/Andrew%20Hopkins%20presentation/Lonford%20talk.PDF ("There is often an attempt to blame major accidents on operator error. This was the position taken by Esso at the Royal Commission. ... The company claimed that operators had been trained to be aware of the problem and Esso even produced the training records of one operator in an attempt to show that he should have known better. However, the Commission took the view that the fact that none of those on duty at the time understood just how dangerous the situation was indicated a systematic training failure. ... The Commission concluded that inadequate training of operators and supervisors was the 'real cause' of the accident. It is clear therefore that operator error does not adequately account for the Longford incident. This is a general finding of all inquiries into major accidents.") (citations omitted).

[3] OXFORD DICTIONARY OF ENGLISH 9 (3d ed. 2010).

deserve to also be called catastrophes or disasters. It also covers preventable deaths on the smaller scale. I use the word accident here to mean any episode that does not involve sabotage or have as its sole cause a last-minute human error. Every episode described in this book was foreseeable, preventable, and, I argue, these anticipated and unacceptable risks were recklessly ignored.

As for the legal treatment of such episodes, if an incident is truly an accident in the narrow, dictionary definition of the word, no one connected with it should be culpable for a crime because they lacked any discernible intent to cause harm and did not have any reasonable expectation regarding such an outcome. But the criminal law prohibits a third kind of behavior that falls along the continuum beyond blamelessness and intentional mayhem. Involuntary manslaughter, a crime in every state and under federal environmental laws, is a felony that occurs when reckless or grossly negligent behavior triggers a chain reaction that results in death, injury, or environmental destruction.

I do not argue here that each and every episode involving a fatality, a severe injury, or significant environmental degradation is caused by institutional failure. That assertion is no more true or convincing than the assertion that every such incident was caused by individual human error. However, the much more pervasive problem is not that we jump to the conclusion that institutional failure caused such incidents. Rather, until very recently, regulators rarely considered the role of institutional failure, least of all in a criminal context. As we learn more about the ramifications of this dysfunction, we must conclude that the thin line between regrettable and criminal is crossed when those failings become systematic and senior executives steadfastly emphasize rapid and lucrative production ahead of the prevention of harm.

Each of the following chapters is organized by the same framework: (1) what happened; (2) why it happened from the tripartite perspectives of individual malfeasance, private institutional failure, and public regulatory failure; and (3) whether the behavior known to the public should or could be considered criminal. That last caveat bears emphasis: obviously, this work is limited by the public record as opposed to the details of an intensive government investigation. When a defendant pleads guilty, these details never emerge. Few of the cases where indictments have been issued and defendants have refused to plead guilty have yet gone to trial. Nevertheless, the extraordinary records amassed by the blue ribbon panels and government agencies that have probed these incidents after the fact make the analysis of publicly available information well worth the effort.

One final admission: because I obviously have a policymaking axe to grind, I have deliberately selected the most shocking episodes of industrial destruction that have occurred over the last decade and a half, and perhaps ever. The reader may fairly ask whether I think my criminal remedy will hold up in more mundane situations. I argue that these theories should be applied because the sources of the mayhem represented by each of these episodes run deep both organizationally and in temporal terms, with unthinkable risks assumed months, even years before they come to fruition.

A BRIEF WORD ABOUT BP

Of the five incidents described here, two involve BP, now the third-largest energy company in the world. British Petroleum or BP, as it renamed itself in 2000, looms large not just in these narratives but in the roster of companies that have caused the most memorable industrial fiascos in the postmodern age. Its most notorious disaster, the Macondo well blowout, killed 11 and deposited 205 million gallons of crude oil along America's southern coast. The explosion occurred aboard the *Deepwater Horizon*, a moveable drilling rig owned by Transocean Ltd., one of the world's largest offshore drilling companies, which BP had leased to develop the Macondo well, which in turn was located 40 miles offshore. I refer to the incident by the well name in order to emphasize that the disaster was caused by the interaction of the two giant companies – BP and Transocean – along with Halliburton Company, one of the world's largest oil field services companies despite the fact that BP has received the lion's share of the blame for what happened when Macondo blew out.

BP assumed and has never lost the spotlight because it has such a bad safety record extending back many years in America. Macondo's precursor was another explosion that killed 15 and injured 180 at the company's Texas City refinery in July 2005. That same month, BP's $5 billion Gulf Coast production platform, which was nicknamed "Thunder Horse," tipped at a sharp angle toward the sea because a valve was installed backwards. A few months later, 200,000 gallons of oil spilled from a BP pipeline on Alaska's North Slope.

Investigations by private and government sources attributed all of these incidents to frenetic growth as the huge corporation's larger-than-life CEO, Lord John Browne, and his handful of top aides, nicknamed the "Turtles," raced through the late 1990s and early 2000s to transform BP into the largest oil company in the world. BP swallowed American competitors such as Amoco and Atlantic Richfield but neglected to knit management of the two companies together effectively. It fired mid-level managers and in the process became more dependent on outside contractors operating beyond its immediate control. It pushed the envelope of technology in its search for oil in the frozen Alaska wilderness and forbiddingly deep waters of the Gulf of Mexico. As top managers in London eyed the accumulation of burdensome debt that accompanies breakneck acquisitions, they decided to cut costs with ruthless intensity. To enforce these strictures, top executives in London retained tight control over expenditures, down to the lowest levels of BP's international operations.

Grim warning signs emerged that better-looking, investor-friendly financials were being produced at the expense of safe and efficient operations at all of BP's facilities. Hundreds of millions in deferred maintenance costs were mounting, turning equipment that was already past its prime dangerous. Frontline supervisory jobs were cut, leaving potentially high-hazard processes unsupervised. Contractors did shoddy work, but BP employees were not around to discover it.

BP lawyers settled three separate criminal cases against the corporation during the period leading up to the Macondo explosion and signed record-breaking civil settlements for violations of worker safety and environmental laws. During each headline-grabbing episode, CEO Browne would rush to the scene and apologize to workers and the public. Regardless, the company did little to change its most destructive practices, including and especially cost-cutting. This pattern of behavior was costing the company money, killing its workers, and attracting highly negative press, yet senior executives persevered.

This high risk existence came to an abrupt halt on April 20, 2010, when the Macondo well blew out. For a while, it looked as if the explosion, loss of life, and uncontrolled spill would be the straw that broke the BP camel's back. The company sold $38 billion in assets to pay for spill cleanup, government penalties, and individual claims. It pled guilty to multiple counts of federal criminal violations, paying a stratospheric $4 billion in fines. The federal government debarred the company, ending any prospect that it would receive new leases to drill for oil in either the Gulf of Mexico or Alaska. For two years after the incident, company executives carefully kept a low profile, waiting for all the negative attention to die down.

But in a startling turnaround that should provide convincing refutation of the Justice Department's fuzzy concerns about pushing companies out of business with criminal prosecutions, the giant company emerged from this period, pivoting 180 degrees from its hangdog public posture and went on the offensive. It placed full-page ads in the *New York Times* asserting that the alleged "victims" of the Deepwater Horizon spill were taking advantage of its great generosity.[4] Senior managers, especially Robert Dudley, its first

---

[4] Paula Forbes, *BP Takes Out a Full Page NYT Ad Against Emeril LaGasse's Oil Spill Claim*, EATER, Dec. 16, 2013, http://eater.com/archives/2013/12/16/bp-takes-out-a-full-page-nyt-ad-over-emeril-lagasses-oil-spill-claim.php; *BP Challenges Settlements in Gulf Oil Spill*, N.Y. TIMES, June 26, 2013, http://www.nytimes.com/2013/06/26/business/energy-environment/bp-challenges-settlements-in-gulf-oil-spill.html; Andrew Callus, *BP's Tough Talk Will Backfire, Gulf Spill*

American CEO, pronounced the company ready to resume business-as-usual: "I think we have done an enormous amount to change the shape of BP and the portfolio and the way it manages risk. After that terrible accident in 2010, we had no choice. But that also allowed us to refocus almost our purpose [*sic*] as a company."[5] The EPA lifted the debarment after signing a consent agreement with BP that required an independent auditor to visit once a year. Within days, BP had purchased twenty-four new "blocks" – underground drilling sites – in the Gulf for exploration. "As the nation's largest energy investor, BP is committed to the deepwater Gulf of Mexico, where we have been an active player for a quarter century and have a multibillion dollar investment program underway," said spokesman Brett Clanton.[6]

Today, BP is the eighteenth largest publicly held company in the United States. Its profit rebounded from a $3.3 billion loss in 2010 to nearly $26 billion in 2012 and, according to CNN Money, it is "well on the way to righting itself."[7] Its stock price is slowly climbing back to where it stood in March 2010, right before the explosion and spill.

BP may have learned its lesson, rejecting its short-sighted focus on the bottom line in favor of an approach that emphasizes public and worker safety and health. People within the ambit of its far-flung operations can only hope this moral-of-an-amazing-story is true. But in January 2013, a contingent of Al Qaeda terrorists attacked an Algerian desert plant that was producing natural gas under a contract with BP, the Norwegian state-owned oil company Statoil, and an Algerian state energy firm, ultimately killing thirty-eight hostages, including four BP employees. Algerian armed forces were responsible for security at the facility and were easily overwhelmed by the well-armed guerrillas, and in the wake of the bloody attack, security experts speculated that had BP and Statoil hired private armed guards, the terrorists might have been repelled. BP dismissed those claims in a statement issued a week after the attack, declaring haughtily that "[a]s with oil and gas installations in many other countries, it is the host government that is responsible for providing security."[8] Three weeks later, the *Wall Street Journal* reported that an internal

Lawyer Says, REUTERS, Aug. 15, 2013, http://uk.reuters.com/article/2013/08/15/uk-bp-spill-rice-idUKBRE97EoK920130815.

[5] Stanley Reed, *At BP, There's Optimism in the Corner Office*, N.Y. TIMES, Jan. 25, 2014, http://www.nytimes.com/2014/01/25/business/energy-environment/bp-still-struggling-to-put-gulf-spill-behind-it.html?ref=bpplc.

[6] Phil Taylor, *Gulf Sales Net $872M, Including Return of BP*, E&E News PM, Mar. 19, 2014, http://www.eenews.net/eenewspm/stories/1059996398/.

[7] J. P. Mangalindan, CNN *Global 500: BP*, CNN MONEY, http://money.cnn.com/magazines/fortune/global500/2012/snapshots/6327.html (last visited Mar. 5, 2014).

[8] Benoit Faucon, *BP Report Warned of Risks in Algeria*, WALL ST. J., Feb. 14, 2013.

BP report written in 2011 warned about the potential for such an attack following the assassination of Osama Bin Laden. Like so many other internal warnings, senior executives ignored the threat.

Meanwhile, the company's competitors have made sustained, blatantly self-serving efforts to leverage its infuriating track record into a public perception that the huge corporation is a "rogue." This narrative contends that although BP deserves whatever punishment the U.S. government can deliver, its destructive misbehavior does not justify more stringent regulation of the other oil industry players. This negative public relations campaign is stoked by subtle reminders that BP is a British company that has misbehaved on American soil. (Cue distant melodies of fife and drum.) The BP-as-rogue story is as convenient as it is reassuring, but the best of the exhaustive investigations of the fatal accidents at Texas City and in the Gulf have refuted it definitively.

In 2007, the OSHA initiated a "national emphasis program" (NEP) for refineries; such initiatives focus inspection resources on industries that have especially poor safety records. Richard Fairfax, the OSHA's director of enforcement, said the effort was "the most depressing program we've ever done," adding that inspectors were "shocked and dismayed" by what they found and that "[t]he state of process management is frankly just horrible."[9] Inspectors were sent to sixty-five plants. Most received multiple citations, with an average penalty of $166,000. Testifying before Congress in June 2010, OSHA's second in command, Jordan Barab, said that the results of the program were "deeply troubling": "Not only are we finding a significant lack of compliance during our inspections, but time and again, our inspectors are finding the same violations in multiple refineries, including those with common ownership, and sometimes even in different units in the same refinery."[10] As an example, Barab pointed out that BP's Husky Refinery in Toledo, Ohio was committing the same violations as BP Texas City, prompting OSHA to assess $3 million in penalties.

Barab's testimony, CSB safety experts, and in-depth reporting by the Center for Public Integrity emphasize that senior managers at refineries frequently ignore so-called "near misses" – seemingly minor accidents that portend far worse to come. "Since the beginning of 2009, at least 80 fires have broken out at 589 refineries," Center reporters Jim Morris and Chris Hamby reported in

---

[9] Patricia Ware, *Process Safety Violations at Refineries "Depressingly" High, OSHA Official Says,* Occupational Safety & Health Daily (BNA) (Aug. 27, 2009).

[10] *Production over Protections: A Review of Process Safety Management in the Oil and Gas Industry: Hearing Before the Subcomm. on Employment and Workplace Safety of the S. Comm. on Health, Education, Labor, and Pensions,* 111th Cong. 8 (June 10, 2010) (testimony of Jordan Barab, Deputy Assistant Secretary, OSHA).

2011.[11] They add that, according to the American Petroleum Institute, the industry's main trade association, even a fire that causes damage as little as $2,500 may flag a weakness that could cause a major accident. Morris and Hamby explain further that "regulators have little sway over refineries," noting that 53 percent of the citations issued by federal and state regulators are appealed in a blatant effort to defer the costs of needed improvements.[12] One of the industry's major reinsurers, Swiss Re, reported in 2006 that the U.S. industry sustained losses four times as high as its overseas counterparts.

In 2013, 143 refineries in the United States processed 17.8 million barrels of crude oil daily, splitting this raw material into gasoline and petrochemicals such as toluene, xylene, and benzene. The OSHA has ended its national emphasis program, citing resource "limitations."[13] On April 2, 2010, an explosion at a Tesoro refinery in Anacortes, Washington, killed seven and on August 6, 2012, a major fire at a Chevron refinery in Richmond, California, sent 15,000 people to hospitals for breathing problems. Both incidents were caused by cracked and corroded pipes attached to equipment that produced volatile liquid and gases.

As for the lessons of the Macondo well explosion, the Oil Spill Commission appointed by President Obama to investigate the causes and the ramifications of the incident was emphatic that although BP was the institution serving as the public face of the explosion and spill, its failures were the industry's failures, and vice versa. The main support for this conclusion is that BP depended so extensively on two of the industry's largest contractors for support – Transocean and Halliburton. The failure of the cement was considered among the most important proximate causes of the well blowout. The three companies are now locked in fantastically complex and expensive litigation to determine who owes how much to whom, a process likely to be the longest-lasting aftermath of the episode. In fact, at the time of the explosion, the rig was run by some 86 Transocean personnel out of a total crew numbering 126, and the BP contingent numbered only 6, although BP engineers "onshore" in Houston played a key role during the last twenty-four mistake-ridden hours.[14]

The Oil Spill Commission was so insistent on avoiding any perception that making BP toe the line would address the problems that it discovered that it

---

[11] Jim Morris & Chris Hamby, *Regulatory Flaws, Repeated Violations Put Oil Refinery Workers at Risk*, CENTER FOR PUBLIC INTEGRITY (Feb. 28, 2011), *available at* http://www.publicinteg rity.org/2011/02/28/2111/regulatory-flaws-repeated-violations-put-oil-refinery-workers-risk.

[12] *Id.*

[13] Greg Hellman, *OSHA Lacks Resources to Commit to Full-time Refinery Emphasis Program*, Occ. Safety & Health Daily (Bloomberg BNA) (Nov. 5, 2010).

[14] Numbers of staff at the Deepwater Horizon from each company.

included the following blunt statement at the very beginning of its report: "The immediate causes of the Macondo well blowout can be traced to a series of identifiable mistakes made by BP, Halliburton, and Transocean that reveal such systematic failures in risk management that they place in doubt the safety culture of the entire industry."[15]

---

[15] National Commission on the BP Deepwater Horizon Oil Spill and Offshore Drilling, Chief Counsel's Report, Macondo: The Gulf Oil Disaster, at vii (2011), *available at* http://permanent.access.gpo.gov/gpo4390/C21462-407CCRforPrint0.pdf.

4

The Workplace

It was typical of them to experience a fire every week, on average. A fire every week is a warning sign that something is critically wrong at the facility.

Mike Sawyer, independent process safety consultant for BP[1]

The question for any company is how good they are at managing *through* two inevitable barriers: the position paradox and the "check the box" mentality. *Texas City is at high risk on these two counts.* Position paradox: The people who have the most influence over the decisions that determine the safety and integrity management of a particular site are almost always the most distanced from those conditions. Unless managed, the result is blindness for the senior-most level of the site as well as those above the site. BP as a corporation has had this blindness and Texas City is no exception.

The Telos Group, in a report written before the explosion[2]

BP on Tuesday placed the lion's share of the blame for the deadly blast at its Texas City refinery at the feet of low- and mid-level workers who it said were lax in following written company procedures during one of the most dangerous times in refinery operations. Had the six operators and one supervisor assigned to the start-up of the refinery's so-called isomerization unit been doing their jobs, the explosion would not have happened ... said Ross Pillari, president of BP Products North America.

Anne Belli and Terri Langford, *Houston Chronicle*, reporting May 18, 2005[3]

---

[1] ABRAHM LUSTGARTEN, RUN TO FAILURE, BP AND THE MAKING OF THE DEEPWATER HORIZON DISASTER 133 (2012). Sawyer worked as a consultant to BP.

[2] TELOS GROUP, BP TEXAS CITY SITE REPORT OF FINDINGS (Jan. 21, 2005), *available at* http://s3.documentcloud.org/documents/5170/the-telos-report.pdf [hereinafter TELOS REPORT]. The quoted passage is from the report's "executive summary" at pgs. 4–5, available at http://www.csb.gov/assets/1/19/Executive_Summary_of_Report_of_Findings.pdf.

[3] Anne Belli & Terri Langford, *BP Blames Staff for Blast*, HOUSTON CHRON., May 18, 2005, at A1.

WHAT HAPPENED: "BANK $150K SAVINGS NOW"

The 52,000 Gallon Geyser

On March 23, 2005, a massive explosion at BP's Texas City refinery killed fifteen people and injured 200, 170 seriously. The blast was so forceful that it damaged houses three-quarters of a mile from the plant. Emergency responders ordered 43,000 people in the neighborhoods surrounding the 1,200 acre site to "shelter in place," meaning that they were directed to go into their homes, seal windows and doors, and remain inside until the all-clear. The incident is considered one of the worst industrial accidents in American history.

The explosion originated in the "isom," one of 30 separate chemical process areas within the plant's gated boundaries. (Isom is short for isomerization, the process by which hydrocarbons are transformed into different substances containing the same atoms in different configurations.) The unit featured a 170-foot "raffinate splitter tower" used to separate petroleum into petrochemicals such as toluene, xylene, and benzene. The tower worked on the principle that when a petroleum mixture containing liquids with different boiling points is heated, some sink to the bottom of the tower still in liquid form, while the others travel to the top in gaseous form. By draining the liquid and suctioning the gas off into different pipes, the components can be stored in forms close to their finished products.

The isom was in start-up at the time of the accident, meaning that it was being put back into service after shutting down for maintenance over a period of several weeks. Start-up is well known in the oil and petrochemical industries as a particularly dangerous phase of operation for any equipment handling volatile and toxic chemicals, requiring punctilious adherence to safety protocols before and during implementation. The hazards were especially acute in this case because the isom was an old piece of equipment, manufactured and installed at the plant in the 1950s. To operate safely, a raffinate splitter tower of this design must never be filled with unfinished petroleum beyond a six to nine foot level. But in this instance, badly trained and unsupervised workers kept pumping flammable liquid hydrocarbons into the tower for over three hours without opening the equipment's outflow valve. Incredibly, the plant's procedures for operating the isom were so flawed that these men were under the impression that they were not allowed to relieve pressure by opening the valve. Worse, they did not realize that by overfilling the tower to a level of 155 feet without draining it simultaneously through the outflow valve, they were in effect making an industrial bomb. In the aftermath of the accident, BP executives had no coherent explanation of why the crew was so clueless about these intolerable risks, although they fired the six lowest level workers, undoubtedly in an effort to drive home the self-serving message that inexplicable human error had caused the blast.

As if to underscore the unfairness of scapegoating these men, independent investigators discovered that because BP had a policy requiring workers involved in shutdown and start-up to work every day until both missions were accomplished, critical crew members had worked twelve-hour shifts for twenty-nine consecutive days. Compounding these fraught working conditions, during the vital few hours leading up to the explosion, a line supervisor left the site to attend to a family emergency and no one was available to replace him.

As the level rose within the isom to the dangerous height of 155 feet, liquid and gas poured out into emergency overflow piping attached to the top of the tower, traveling through the piping across a distance of several hundred feet and into a "blowdown drum" – a large barrel-shaped container with an attached vent stack that opened into the ambient air. As that drum in turn filled to capacity, three pressure relief valves opened for six minutes, discharging a "geyser-like"[4] plume of 52,000 gallons of volatile liquid and gas heavier than the ambient air. The plume drifted inexorably toward the ground. At 1:20 P.M., an idling truck parked against plant rules near the isom unit backfired, producing a spark that ignited the plume, producing a massive and powerful explosion. Most of those killed were working in two trailers located 140 and 126 feet from the isom unit and used for office space, in yet another blatant violation of a long-standing safety rule that such facilities should not be closer than 350 feet from potentially hazardous units at the plant, especially during start-up.

The Trail Back to London

In the aftermath, investigators from the public and private sectors were unstinting in their criticism of the company. Independent reports emphasized the impact of relentless cost-cutting directives from BP's London headquarters, which the Texas City refinery's top management followed despite clear indications that the cuts were producing unacceptable levels of operational risk. For example, the isom, installed five decades earlier, did not have a "flare" (constant flame) at the top of the blowdown drum to burn off emissions before they could ignite at ground level. Flares had been standard equipment on blowdown drums for many years. It turned out that in 1992, OSHA inspectors had cited the plant for failing to have a flare, but had traded away this

4   ANDREW HOPKINS, FAILURE TO LEARN, THE BP TEXAS CITY REFINERY DISASTER (2006).

requirement in a settlement agreement with the Amoco Corporation, which was the owner/operator of the plant. When BP bought Amoco in 1999, its managers had considered retrofitting the drum to incorporate such equipment, which would have cost approximately $2 million, but decided the change was too expensive. They also considered the less expensive alternative of hooking the isom up to a nearby blowdown drum that did have a flare and was located nearby for use with other equipment. Hooking the isom to this existing drum would cost $150,000, but they decided that even this measure was too expensive. An internal company email written at the time said "Capital expenditure is very tight. Bank $150k in savings now."[5]

Among the most damning revelations in the aftermath of the explosion was that senior corporate executives all the way up to the CEO's office in London had received repeated warnings that something was profoundly wrong at the facility but refused to ease their demands that costs be cut. Worried about a series of accidents at the plant, including several fatalities, Texas City plant manager Don Parus commissioned a consulting firm named Telos to conduct a confidential and anonymous survey of employees' concerns about safety. Telos reported that "[w]e have never seen a site where the notion 'I could die today' was so real."[6] Parus tried to make the case against further cuts, taking the drastic step of presenting a PowerPoint containing photographs of workers killed in plant accidents to John Manzoni, the BP Chief Executive for refining, and Michael Hoffman, group vice president for U.S. refining. Manzoni and Hoffman did not yield.[7]

BP hired a blue-ribbon commission headed by former Secretary of State James A. Baker III to evaluate what went wrong. Its 2007 report did not equivocate, concluding that the accident was attributable to a culture that allowed crucial components of the physical plant to "run to failure" and penalized workers for expressing safety concerns.[8]

---

[5] Abrahm Lustgarten, *Furious Growth and Cost Cuts Led to BP Accidents Past and Present*, PROPUBLICA (Oct. 26, 2010), http://www.propublica.org/article/bp-accidents-past-and-present.

[6] TELOS REPORT, *supra* note 2, at 66.

[7] Don Parus, Texas City Plant Manager, PowerPoint Presentation entitled "Texas City is Not a Safe Place to Work," *available at* http://s3.documentcloud.org/documents/11343/don-parus-powerpoint-presentation.pdf; *see also* LOREN C. STEFFY, DROWNING IN OIL: BP AND THE RECKLES PURSUIT OF PROFIT 65 (2011). BP executive John Manzoni's failure to heed Parus's warnings is discussed in *Top BP Execs Blamed for 2005 Texas Blast*, ECON. TIMES, May 4, 2007, http://articles.economictimes.indiatimes.com/2007-05-04/news/28420381_1_texas-city-refinery-john-browne-texas-blast.

[8] REPORT OF THE BP U.S. REFINERIES INDEPENDENT SAFETY REVIEW PANEL 122 (Jan. 2007), *available at* http://www.bp.com/liveassets/bp_internet/globalbp/globalbp_uk_english/SP/STAGING/local_assets/assets/pdfs/Baker_panel_report.pdf [hereinafter BAKER REPORT]; *see also BP Study Blames Managers for 2005 Blast at Texas Refinery*, N.Y. TIMES,

BP also assembled a team of its own senior executives to evaluate management failures at the refinery.[9] Two "confidential" reports[10] prepared "for internal use only" focused on the culpability of five senior executives, including Manzoni, Hoffman, and Parus. BP investigators concluded that Hoffman and Parus, who did not get along, had promoted a "fortress mentality," discouraged underlings from reporting problems, and neglected to supervise or evaluate lower-level managers.[11] After the Texas City explosion, Hoffman resigned and Parus was put on administrative leave. The internal team did their best to exonerate Manzoni by arguing that he had a big portfolio and should not have been expected to focus on "operational" details; he was not disciplined. In a particularly egregious example of the internal team's determination to insulate London executives from blame, its first report insisted that "steers" regarding cost-cutting from London were understood as "orders," papering over the extraordinary pressure London executives exerted on plant managers like Parus.[12] It criticized Hoffman for neglecting to develop "an investment strategy addressing the question of how to manage operational risks inherent at this site against a backdrop of constrained capital for the entire portfolio," as if even such a modest investment proposal could have survived the corporation's relentless cost-cutting requirements.[13]

BP ultimately settled the private lawsuits brought by families of the employees who had died for a total of $2.1 billion. In what has unfortunately become standard practice, the settlement agreements required plaintiffs and their attorneys to keep confidential the internal company documents that were turned over during the litigation. But Eva Rowe, the twenty-two-year-old daughter of two contract employees who died in the blast, courageously held

---

May 3, 2007, http://www.nytimes.com/2007/05/03/business/worldbusiness/03iht-bp.4.5553455. html?_r=o ("A blue-ribbon panel led by a former U.S. secretary of state, James Baker, found a flawed safety culture at all five BP refineries in North America. It said in January that the Texas blast was caused by poor leadership, lack of resources and bad procedures.").

[9] *See BP Study Blames Managers for 2005 Blast at Texas Refinery*, N.Y. TIMES, May 3, 2007, http://www.nytimes.com/2007/05/03/business/worldbusiness/03iht-bp.4.5553455.html?_r=o.

[10] BP produced these documents during the personal injury lawsuit brought by Eva Rowe. I obtained copies of them from Ms. Rowe's attorneys, Brent Coon and Associates. Because the internal team was led by Wilhelm Bonse-Gueking, Group Vice President and Region Head (Europe), these documents are commonly referred to as the "Bonse Reports" and will be given that short form title here. BP Management Accountability Project, Texas City Isomerization Explosion, Final Report (Feb. 2007) [hereinafter Bonse I]; BP Management Accountability Project, Texas City Isomerization Explosion, Supplemental Report (Feb. 2007) [hereinafter Bonse II]. Bonse I evaluated the culpability of all of the senior managers at the Texas City site, as well as Michael Hoffman. Bonse II was focused on the culpability of John Manzoni.

[11] *Id.*

[12] Bonse I at 16.

[13] Bonse I at 10.

out until November 2006 for a settlement that required full disclosure. These documents enabled researchers to examine the internal dynamics at the company to an unprecedented degree and I had access to them when writing this book.[14]

The following, more detailed analysis of the causes of the accident draws on four sources: ProPublica reporter Abrahm Lustgarten's 2012 excellent book *Run to Failure, BP and the Making of the Deepwater Horizon Disaster;*[15] a more technical but equally insightful 2008 book by Professor Andrew Hopkins, *Failure to Learn: The BP Texas City Refinery Disaster;*[16] the U.S. Chemical Safety Board's (CSB) *Investigation Report: Refinery Explosion and Fire;*[17] and internal BP documents provided to me by Rowe's attorneys at Brent Coon and Associates.

No one was ever prosecuted criminally as a result of these events.

Cost-Cutting and Its Ramifications

At the time of the isom explosion, the Texas City refinery was the third largest in the country, producing 11 million gallons of gasoline a day, or about three percent of the country's total consumption. The facility, standing alone, qualified as a Fortune 400 company. Its profit in 2004 was $900 million, a tidy sum even by BP senior management's demanding standards, and a remarkable achievement considering its acute state of disrepair. Yet even this success did not spare the plant from cost-cutting.

Located 45 miles south of Houston, on the coast of the Gulf of Mexico, and built in 1934, the refinery was already well past its heyday when BP bought Amoco in 1999. The physical plant had deteriorated to the point that first-time visitors, even those accustomed to the grit of the refinery business, were taken aback. At first, repelled by these conditions, BP executives considered offloading Texas City and its lurking liability risks to another oil company. But a deal never materialized and Texas City got swept up in upper management's other obsession – cutting costs. Company-wide, BP managers wanted to boost the return on capital from 7 percent in 1999 to 20 percent in 2005. Ultimately, over a period beginning in 1992, when Amoco still ran the plant, until the accident, capital spending was reduced by 84 percent and maintenance was cut by

---

[14] *See* Juan A. Lozano, *BP Settles Last Refinery Blast Suit*, WASH. POST, Nov. 10, 2006, http://www.washingtonpost.com/wp-dyn/content/article/2006/11/10/AR2006111000603_pf.html.

[15] LUSTGARTEN, *supra* note 1.

[16] HOPKINS, *supra* note 4.

[17] U.S. CHEMICAL SAFETY & HAZARD INVESTIGATION BOARD, INVESTIGATION REPORT: REFINERY EXPLOSION AND FIRE 18 (2007), *available at* http://www.csb.gov/assets/1/19/CSBFinalReportBP.pdf.

41 percent. A document obtained by the Rowe attorneys shows the fanaticism of these reductions, with no cut too small to be executed. At Texas City, dozens of maintenance workers were fired to save $1 million, purchases of safety shoes were reduced to save $50,000, and safety awards were cut to save $75,000.

In 2002, Don Parus, a former Amoco executive with two decades of experience in the oil industry, joined the management structure that supervised Texas City and BP's other holdings in the state. In 2004, he became the refinery's "Business Unit Leader" (BUL), a euphemism for plant manager. Stunned by the appearance of the physical plant, he commissioned a study of the depth and severity of maintenance problems, discovering to his further dismay serious reliability issues, including faulty instruments and broken equipment. The report concluded that Texas City needed a major infusion of funding for corrective maintenance. Ultimately, Parus requested $235 million from corporate headquarters in America and London. BP had just experienced three serious fires and explosions at its Grangemouth refinery in Scotland and independent investigators charged that these incidents demonstrated that the company had engaged in over-zealous cost-cutting, given short shrift to risk assessment, and had serious problems with worker training. Parus emphasized that it could not afford similar problems at Texas City.

Some senior executives apparently agreed with Parus and he thought additional funding would be forthcoming. But orders soon came down from London mandating more cuts because Texas City was simply not profitable enough. Why, said senior managers, should Texas City provide 15 percent of refinery profits but consume 18 percent of the corporation's safety budget for that sector? Parus was told to reduce the plant's $300 million operating budget by $65 million. He eventually negotiated the reductions down to $48 million, still a daunting sum considering the large increases in funding that would be necessary to eliminate safety hazards at the plant.

Meanwhile, conditions continued to deteriorate. Accidental spills and fugitive air emissions increased from 399 in 2002 to 607 in 2004. A furnace pipe ruptured in March 2004, causing a fire that cost BP $30 million. Post-incident investigators found that the equipment had not been inspected on schedule the year before and no one had noticed either that omission or the potential for imminent failure. In September 2004, a pipe flange was mistakenly opened by three workers and the pipe burst, killing two of the men and severely burning the third with a mixture of boiling water and steam. Parus asked for the plant's historic fatality record and was once again shocked to discover that 23 men had died in a 30 year period.

Parus decided to take an unusual and, in retrospect, courageous step, traveling in October 2004 to meet with John Manzoni, BP's Chief Executive for Refining and Marketing, a member of CEO Browne's inner circle, and the man who was in charge of the Amoco acquisition. Michael Hoffman, group vice president for U.S. refining, also attended the meeting. Manzoni and Hoffman should have been well aware of conditions at Texas City, which they had visited on several occasions. Parus showed the two executives a five-page PowerPoint with the provocative title page "Texas City is not a safe place to work."[18] It included the news that in 2004 alone, two workers had died and thirty-two were injured. The second and third pages displayed the dead men's pictures, with short biographical details. The fourth listed nine men who had died at the plant over the past decade, concluding that "everyone shown here expected to go home at the start of what turned [*sic*] to be their last day at work."[19]

We will never discover whether Manzoni and Hoffman were too committed to cost-cutting and the larger business strategy it represented or whether they thought that refining was simply a dangerous business and fatalities and serious injuries came with the territory. The two men may simply have had a negative reaction to Parus. He was not Hoffman's choice for plant manager and the two men were known not to get along. Whatever was on their minds, the meeting was a fiasco. Another 25 percent in overhead reductions was demanded in 2005, but the isom exploded before they could be fully implemented. What should be clear, despite their subsequent expressions of shock and concerted efforts to scapegoat Parus for the incident, is that at some point long before the isom exploded, executives like Manzoni and Hoffman had become willfully blind to the probability that people would die because of decisions they were making.

On the afternoon of the explosion, Manzoni was on his way out of town for a vacation with his family when he got an email from a colleague telling him to travel immediately to Texas City. He later reported to this colleague that "[w]e spent the day there – at the cost of a precious day of my leave."[20] Five years later, in a reprise of this reaction, Tony Hayward, who replaced Browne as CEO in 2007, was excoriated by pundits for announcing during the Macondo well blowout and spill that all he wanted was to get his life back.[21] Manzoni managed to escape that kind of backlash after Texas City.

[18] Parus, *supra* note 7.
[19] *Id.*
[20] LUSTGARTEN, *supra* note 1, at 154.
[21] Stanley Reed, *Tony Hayward Gets His Life Back*, N.Y. TIMES, Sept. 1, 2012, http://www.nytimes.com/2012/09/02/business/tony-hayward-former-bp-chief-returns-to-oil.html?_r=0.

During Manzoni's deposition in the personal injury lawsuits brought by the families after the Texas City refinery explosion, he insisted that cost-cutting could not have contributed to the incident:

> I cannot believe they would have cut safety critical items. I cannot believe they would have cut safety critical items, simply because that's not – it simply would – it's not an acceptable thing to do. They would have known that, and the system would have known that.[22]

Because the cases were settled, Parus never had an opportunity to testify regarding the falsity of this blame-shifting claim.

Paper Tigers and Casual Compliance

One of the tragic ironies about the Texas City explosion is that BP had generated a mass of written materials requiring its employees to behave very differently than they did. These written protocols were what I will call "paper tigers," ineffective in influencing practices that had become common at the plant and converged to cause the explosion. Andrew Hopkins, an internationally recognized expert in the deconstruction and critical evaluation of industrial accidents, calls the dissonance between official procedures and actual practice "casual compliance."[23] The most fateful examples of such behavior in the days leading up to the explosion include failure to undertake a safety assessment by technical experts prior to start-up, the operation of motor vehicles within an area where written policies precluded their presence, and the siting of wooden trailers used as office space within 140 feet of the isom unit.

BP's senior "process safety" managers had established a process known as "Pre-Startup Safety Review" (PSSR) that was required prior to reinitiation of operations at any unit like the isom that had been shut down for maintenance. The process required a technical team to verify that the crew conducting the start-up understood all safety protocols and that the equipment needed to implement those protocols was operational. It further mandated that all nonessential personnel be removed from the unit and the area around it. High-level managers, including the plant's operations and process safety chiefs, were required to sign off on each such review. Unfortunately, the

---

[22] Oral Videotaped Deposition of John Manzoni at 71, Miguel Arenaza, Elizabeth Ramon, David G. Crow and Juanita G. Crow, et al. v. BP Products North America Inc., Don Parus, and JE Merits Constructors, Inc., No. 05CV0337-A (Dist. Ct. Galveston Cnty. Tex., Sept. 8, 2006) (copy on file with author).

[23] HOPKINS, *supra* note 4, at 11.

process safety coordinator responsible for the area that included the isom unit was inexplicably unfamiliar with the PSSR requirement and no one else mentioned its applicability. No PSSR was conducted before start-up began.

Possibly because the PSSR was omitted, the start-up crew commenced this hazardous operation despite the fact that several essential pieces of equipment were broken, including a pressure control valve, a "level transmitter" that informed the crew of the height of liquid in the tower, and a "sight glass" used to confirm those levels. All of these problems had been noticed by maintenance crews and work orders requesting repair had been submitted.

The absence of the level transmitter and the opaque sight glass were especially serious problems because, although the tower had an automatic shut-off device designed to prevent liquid levels from rising above 6.5 feet, this equipment was disabled so that operators could fill the tower to levels as high as 9 feet. Their rationale was that if liquid ran down and the bottom of the tower emptied before the process was working properly, other equipment would be damaged. The far more dangerous alternative of manually filling the tower was implemented in 18 start-ups over a five-year period without coming to the attention of process safety experts. But in this instance, crews were literally operating blind because the level transmitter and the sight glass were broken.

According to the CSB report, these omissions were typical of how BP management approached a slew of similar problems. Executives reasoned that in the face of the expenses of regulatory compliance and the urgent need to cut costs, the corporation preferred to rely on its employees rather than hardware improvements, even as it reduced training and thinned employee ranks.

Because refineries include numerous operations that involve volatile liquids and gases and engines produce sparks, vehicle control policies are common. BP's written policy said that during major operations, including shut-down and start-up of production units, vehicle engines should not be left idling "unattended," a term defined as the driver absent from his seat.[24] It further required that site-specific traffic control plans be developed for each such event. Technically, as Hopkins points out, the driver involved in the explosion was not violating the generic policy because he was sitting in his truck when the plume erupted, although it is difficult to imagine a good reason that BP might have had to constrain the applicability of the no-idling policy in this way. Regardless, a specific plan was developed for isom unit start-up and it prohibited any vehicles from parking within a no-access zone around the unit. At the time of the explosion, no fewer than fifty-five vehicles were parked within that zone, in direct violation of this rule.

---

[24] HOPKINS, *supra* note 4, at 36–37.

Hopkins notes that BP executives at the plant and, for that matter, anyone who is part of the U.S. refinery workforce should have been aware of the idling engine hazard because a former Exxon refinery worker, Charlie Morecraft, had given numerous safety talks to industry audiences including several composed of BP Texas City employees. Like BP, Exxon had adopted policies to prevent idling vehicles from being near equipment prone to emit volatile liquids and gases. But Morecraft was gravely injured when he left his truck idling and walked away from it to check a reported gas leak. As he stood near the malfunctioning equipment, he was doused by flammable liquid and, in horror, realized that a vapor cloud was drifting toward his vehicle. As he tried to run to safety, a spark from the engine ignited the cloud and he was engulfed in flame. He was so badly burned that his doctors considered it miraculous that he survived. His rehabilitation took years and was exceedingly painful. After he was back on his feet, he earned his living as a safety consultant and trainer.

Last but not least, Hopkins asks the inevitable question why so many people died in the explosion. Standard precautions during start-up of a unit like the isom unit demand that all unnecessary personnel be removed from the area. The 15 people killed by the explosion had no connection to the operation of the isom. Instead, they worked for a BP contractor and were temporarily located in two trailers that were placed 120 feet and 136 feet from the blowdown drum. The explosion demolished both structures. No one directly involved in the start-up died. To use the chilling term that has become such a popular part of the modern lexicon, the dead were entirely collateral damage.

In 1992, OSHA issued a process safety management standard, which to this day is among the most important rules the agency has ever produced. When Amoco owned the Texas City refinery, this rule was interpreted as requiring the initiation of a risk assessment process before temporary trailers were allowed to remain near a potentially dangerous unit like the isom and this process requirement carried over when BP took over the plant. "Near" was defined as 350 feet. Before making siting decisions, employees were required to complete a forty-page questionnaire entitled the *Facility Siting Screening Workbook*. Inexplicably, the employees who were assigned to complete the questionnaire had never been trained to use this tool and had no experience in evaluating industrial risks. They ignored the 350 feet rule. Instead, they concluded that the most significant risks posed by leaving the trailers so close to the isom had nothing to do with the isom itself but rather focused on the remote possibilities that a nearby oil/water separator would discharge a very small amount of volatile vapor or that a forklift might run into one of the office workers.

But a technician named Joseph Runfola was well aware that the trailers did not belong where they were placed. In a deposition taken by Brent Coon, lawyer for the families of the victims of the explosion, he explained his fruitless efforts to alert management to these issues.[25] Runfola believed that an obvious mistake had been made when the trailers were sited so close to the blowdown drum that had a flare, which was in turn located near the isom, because of the danger of explosions and fires. He said he had spoken with a series of low- to mid-level managers, eventually working his way up to Willie Willis, who was the manager of "West Plant," serving directly under Parus. Willis reported back to Runfola that the arrangement had been subject to a risk assessment that found insignificant problems and that the matter was out of his hands. As a last resort, Runfola went into one of the two trailers and spoke to a handful of men working there. He warned them that they should find out when the start-up was planned because they did not want to be in either trailer during that operation. For reasons that are not clear, the men did not heed this advice.

Safety Culture and the Three Little Pigs

When the isom blew up, twelve of those killed had just returned from a luncheon celebrating their unit's exemplary safety record during the preceding month, during which they had not lost a single "man-hour" of work. They were employed by the contractor JE Merit, a subsidiary of Jacobs Engineering, which was hired by BP to work on "turnaround" throughout the plant. The term means shutting units down so that they can be overhauled, updated, and subjected to routine maintenance. The category of safety success celebrated by the Merit crew was the absence of individual injuries caused by falling debris, slick surfaces, or sharp equipment. BP managers at Texas City were carefully tracking performance with respect to these routine injuries. Yet they had lost sight of a second category – so-called process safety – a term connoting the correct operation of units like the isom in order to avoid industrial accidents on a larger scale. As the Baker report emphasized:

> Process safety in a refinery involves the prevention of leaks, spills, equipment malfunctions, over-pressures, excessive temperatures, corrosion, metal fatigue, and other similar conditions. Process safety programs focus on the design and engineering of facilities, hazard assessments, management of

[25] Oral Videotaped Deposition of Joseph J. Runfola (corrected) at 20–23, Miguel Arenaza, Elizabeth Ramon, David G. Crow and Juanita G. Crow, et al. v. BP Products North America Inc., Don Parus, and JE Merits Constructors, Inc., No. 05CV0337-A (Dist. Ct. Galveston Cnty., Tex. May 22, 2006) (copy on file with author).

change, inspection, testing, and maintenance of equipment, effective alarms, effective process control, procedures, training of personnel, and human factors. The Texas City tragedy in March 2005 was a process safety accident. ... BP mistakenly interpreted improving personal injury rates as an indication of acceptable process safety performance at its U.S. refineries. BP's reliance on this data, combined with an inadequate process safety understanding, created a false sense of confidence that BP was properly addressing process safety risks.[26]

According to the panel, which included several experts in process safety protocols and institutional design, BP did not have any real semblance of a "safety culture" designed to prevent process accidents, not just at Texas City but at its four other U.S. refineries. Of BP's eighteen "group values" set forth for its international operations, only one dealt with health and safety.

The Baker panel focused most of its prestige and expertise writing a report that would push BP to radically overhaul this aspect of its operations. These conclusions should have – but did not – put to rest the strenuous efforts of top executives to discredit Parus, blaming his incompetence for the accident. As we shall see in the section evaluating regulatory failure immediately below, the Baker panel's recommendations fell on deaf ears, even at Texas City, as new management continued business as usual at the plant.

One telling sign of the myopic mind-set regarding costs in BP's executive suite was its approach to risk assessment at plants like Texas City. Among the documents released in response to the settlement with Eva Rowe was a packet of what appear to be PowerPoint slides topped by a piece of paper called "Agenda for the Awareness Course."[27] The first slide, entitled "Cost benefit analysis," is illustrated with pictures of three little piggy banks sitting atop a table showing calculations for what would happen if the house is built of straw, sticks, or brick, and the wolf came to blow them down. The table includes columns presenting numerical estimates for "vulnerability," "expectation value of loss," "Cost of House," and "Cost + Expectation Value." The following slide includes the bullet: "Maximum justifiable spend (MJS) – A piggy considers it's worth $1000 to save its bacon." The next slide states that cost benefit analysis "requires monetary evaluations of societal risks, statistical fatalities avoided, and loss of Brand reputation." The following slide assigns the "Target value for existing

[26] BAKER REPORT, *supra* note 8, at x, xii.
[27] Again, I received these documents from Brent Coon & Associates, the law firm that represented Rowe in her lawsuit against BP. The firm's website is http://www.bcoonlaw.com/. It sponsors a site where some of the documents are available, although I needed a special password to download this one. That site is http://www.texascityexplosion.com. A copy is on file with the author and will be provided on request.

facilities" with respect to the risk that a worker or contract employee would die to be 1/2,000 annually – an unusually high risk level – and for "Non-BP workers within the same industrial complex" to be 1/20,000 annually. Members of the public are assigned a risk tolerance of 1/1,000,000 annually. The final slide declares sternly that "[a]ll Business Unit Leaders and Works General Manages must assure the Group that they are not operating in the zone of intolerability by the end of 2005," presumably by performing a cost benefit analysis that somehow calculates whether starting up the isom – or undertaking any other potentially hazardous task – will endanger these various categories more than the specified amounts.

In an email written in 1999 to other BP managers, Robert Mancini, a chemical engineer who was part of BP's risk management team, wrote, "BP embraced the principle that these costs can be specified for the purposes of cost benefit analysis. Amoco was generally unwilling to take this step. This is more a cultural issue than a technical one, but one that will have to be addressed."[28] There is no evidence that line managers actually performed this kind of bizarre number-crunching on a routine basis. But the company's willingness to entertain this approach and to train at least some of its employees in this methodology suggests that the starting place for executives was risk tolerance, not safety.

Mancini's three little pigs presentation sent the strong signal that top company executives were exclusively focused on cost-cutting and profits. Consistent with his own guidelines, Mancini undertook a "fire and explosion" risk assessment for BP refineries.[29] His "immediate motivation" was to find a "risk basis that could be used to set priorities for performing external process safety audits."[30] He was determined to establish the "expected value" of specific risks in order to figure out how much the company was willing to pay to assess and prevent hazards. His assessment of the monetary value of an accident at the isom unit, spread out over the number of years it would likely take for an accident to happen, was $10,000 annually.

In an even stranger coda on the subject, the British newspaper the *Daily Mail* carried an online article on May 5, 2007, reporting that CEO Browne's former life partner, John Chevalier, said that Browne had confided that BP "coldly calculated the value" of a human life at £10 million, or roughly

[28] Ryan Knutson, *Blast at BP Texas Refinery in '05 Texas Foreshadowed Gulf Disaster*, PRO PUBLICA (July 2, 2010), http://www.propublica.org/article/blast-at-bp-texas-refinery-in-05-foreshadowed-gulf-disaster.

[29] LUSTGARTEN, *supra* note 1, at 165.

[30] *Id.*

$16 million.[31] Browne resigned from BP abruptly when he was discovered to have lied about where he met Chevalier – not exercising in the park, but through an online dating service for gay men. Browne is now the leading business adviser to Britain's coalition government. If the story correctly reported what Chevalier said – and it is difficult to imagine that either the reporter or Chevalier would manufacture such an odd claim – the notion that lives were expendable up to a certain financial point pervaded the company, from the top on down.

Warring Bosses and Skewed Incentives

At the time of the explosion, BP followed a "bottom-up" promotion strategy that relied on the identification of talent in the ranks of lower-level managers and then trained and mentored this cadre as they proceeded upward. According to its own internal report, the corporation further insisted that "accountability must be defined and established between a manager and his or her superior."[32] Finally, according to the Baker Report, BP recognized "the importance of stability in the refinery plant manager position."[33]

Regardless of these euphemistic goals, between 2000 and 2007, the facility had eight different managers. According to the internal management evaluation performed in the wake of the explosion, Parus, the plant manager at the time of the explosion, was promoted to the position over the objections of Hoffman, vice president in charge of U.S. refining. Hoffman in turn had a bad relationship with Manzoni, the top London executive responsible for overseeing BP's worldwide refining. All three men seem to have barely tolerated each other, failing to cooperate and even failing to communicate. This constant churning in the top position at the Texas City refinery and the conflict between the plant manager and the executives responsible for overseeing U.S. refining were significant enough factors in causing the incident that BP's internal evaluation team recommended firing all but Manzoni. The management evaluation team was headed by Wilhelm Bonse-Geuking, who was then Group Vice President and Region Head for Europe, and who now serves as the chairman of the board of directors of Deutsche BP AG, a corporation formed in 2012 by merging BP subsidiaries in Austria, Belgium, the Netherlands, and Poland.

---

[31] £10m: *The Price of a Life to Browne's BP*, Daily Mail Online, May 7, 2005, http://www. dailymail.co.uk/news/article-452989/10m-price-life-Brownes-BP.html.

[32] Bonse I, *supra* note 10, at 4.

[33] Baker Report, *supra* note 8, at 34.

Management problems were exacerbated by the incentive, or bonus, system BP established for the plant. Euphemistically called "variable pay,"[34] it awarded money on the basis of the entire plant's performance. Or, in other words, individual performance did not have any influence on such decisions. The lowest level of workers only received small bonuses, amounting to about six percent of their overall pay. But 40 percent of the compensation of top executives such as Parus depended on bonus decisions. The criteria for determining good performance weighed cost-cutting at 50 percent and safety at 10 percent; even then, safety was interpreted as lowering the personal injury rate. Process safety was not part of the equation. The Baker Report noted that this incentive system may have resulted in pressure on line workers not to report workplace injuries.

Failure to Learn

In his excellent book on the BP Texas City incident, Hopkins examines in detail its causes, from fanatical cost-cutting, to the preoccupation with personal- and the corresponding neglect of process safety, to the willful blindness of top executives regarding the implications for worker safety of their corporate-wide development strategy. He considers all of these problems through the lens of a distinct feature of institutional and individual dysfunction: a chronic "failure to learn" of people who could have prevented the catastrophe. Failure to learn is characterized by systematic resistance to taking any action in response to ample and repeated warnings that severe hazards exist and that they must be eliminated. People may ignore these warnings. Or they may downplay their implications by convincing themselves that the business of refining (or underground mining, deep well drilling, processing peanuts, compounding medicine) is intrinsically dangerous. They may feel powerless when they are not. No one intends for people to die, which is why the criminal law does not consider such behavior to be murder. But at some point that was clearly reached at Texas City, failure to learn becomes gross negligence, or manslaughter in the criminal realm.

Over the ten years preceding March 2005, the crew operating the isom recorded six releases of volatile vapors from the blowdown drum. Four resulted in calling out the firefighting staff and two were serious enough to result in a shutdown of the isom. During the same period, two leaks of flammable liquids from the pipes used to vent pressure from the isom resulted in fires. One was sufficiently serious that it took operators three days to

---

[34] HOPKINS, *supra* note 4, at 83.

extinguish it. Lustgarten's reporting also documents specific warnings sent by middle managers up the line at Texas City. On February 20, 2005, a month before the explosion, a company safety manager wrote in an email: "I truly believe we are on the verge of something bigger happening."[35] Three weeks later, employees responsible for "health, safety, security, and environment" predicted in a new business plan that "[The Texas City site] kills someone in the next 12–18 months."[36]

Hopkins writes:

> [I]nformation about these eight events was not readily available to the [Chemical Safety Board], which found it necessary to sift through a variety of sources in order to reconstruct this history of near misses. It was not a history that was recognised at Texas City; it was not a history from which anything was learned. Had this historical record been assembled and publicised, it would have been clear that it was only a matter of time before one of these incidents culminated in a major accident. Research shows that major accidents are always preceded by warning signs that for one reason or another, are not recognized as such. The warnings of danger in this case could hardly have been stronger.[37]

BP's small cadre of anointed leaders admittedly sat in a different country than the Texas City refinery, and had many management layers between them and the daily operation of the plant. Yet Manzoni was in charge of the team that decided to buy Amoco, and with it the refinery that was among that company's largest assets. He had visited Texas City on several occasions, been informed of the Telos Report, and endured the pleas of Parus to stop cost-cutting and begin greater investment in capital and maintenance. He was undoubtedly aware – or certainly should have been aware – of the three fatalities that had occurred at Texas City the year before the 2005 explosion.

Also worth noting is that BP's huge, 1,730-acre refinery at Grangemouth, Scotland, obviously located much closer to the London mother ship, had experienced three significant safety incidents during May and June 2000, including an uncontrolled release of scalding steam, a serious fire caused by leaking vapor, and a sustained loss of electrical power that resulted in shutdown of large segments of the plant. No one was injured, but the British Health and Safety Executive (HSE) responded by bringing criminal charges against two subsidiaries that were responsible for operating parts of Grangemouth, collecting £1 million in fines because it concluded that BP had "failed to achieve the

---

[35] LUSTGARTEN, *supra* note 1, at 138.
[36] *Id.* at 138–39.
[37] HOPKINS, *supra* note 4, at 61.

operational control and maintenance of process and systems required by law."[38] Specifically, the investigators concluded that BP managers confused personal safety with process safety, did not pay adequate attention to containing leaks of hazardous chemicals, had employed extensive written procedures that were largely ignored, and did not assign personnel with sufficient expertise to work with crews that operated dangerous equipment to prevent accidents. These events, especially the government's stern response, should have alerted top executives in London that refineries worldwide deserved far more determined scrutiny.

Even if you are willing to excuse Manzoni and other residents of the management suite from first-round responsibility at Texas City (and I am not, obviously), continued neglect after the Texas City accident should have triggered the harshest penalties, including criminal prosecutions of individual executives. Instead, the company itself was allowed to plead guilty to felony charges for not having created adequate instructions on the start-up of the isom and for not evacuating the Merit employees from the badly sited trailers, paying $50 million in fines. It agreed to replace blowdown drums throughout the plant with modern units that included flares to burn off escaping gases, at an estimated cost of $250 million. It settled OSHA violations for a record $21 million, only to be caught a few years later ignoring most of the terms of the OSHA consent decree. Given this outcome and continuing violations at the plant, these penalties made barely a dent in BP management's commitment to process safety, personal safety, or environmental compliance.

As Lustgarten notes, when the company issued its annual report a few months after the explosion, one paragraph in five hundred pages mentioned the incident and its main point was to reassure stockholders and prospective investors that settlements of personal injury lawsuits, which ultimately were resolved for $2.1 billion, would not have any impact on its bottom line. And, indeed, its profit attributable to shareholders (excluding interest and tax on operations) was $17 billion in 2004 and $22 billion in 2005.

Meanwhile, during the time between the 2005 explosion and when BP announced in the fall of 2012 that it was selling the Texas City refinery to Marathon Oil Company, the following fatalities occurred at the plant:

---

[38] HEALTH & SAFETY EXECUTIVE & SCOTTISH ENVIRONMENT PROTECTION AGENCY, MAJOR ACCIDENT INVESTIGATION REPORT, BP GRANGEMOUTH SCOTLAND, 29TH MAY–10TH JUNE 2000: A PUBLIC REPORT PREPARED BY THE HSR ON BEHALF OF THE COMPETENT AUTHORITY 9 (2003), *available at* http://www.hse.gov.uk/comah/bpgrange/images/bprgrangemouth.pdf.

- July 22, 2006 – a contractor's employee was killed when he was crushed between a scissor lift and a pipe rack;
- June 5, 2007 – a contractor's employee was electrocuted and died while working on a light circuit in a process area;
- January 14, 2008 – a BP employee died when the top head blew off a pressure vessel; and
- October 9, 2008 – a contract employee died after being struck by a front end loader and pinned on the ground between a guard rail and the bucket of the loader.

REGULATORY FAILURE: THE LITTLE AGENCY THAT CAN'T

Too Little Money, Too Much Jurisdiction

Over the last two decades, OSHA has been so acutely underfunded and so bereft of White House support that it often appears to be an orphan agency. Harsh political reality explains the agency's sharp decline. The federal government's commitment to occupational safety and health was always motivated by the electoral clout of organized labor, which in its heyday, circa 1954, enrolled 28.4 percent of the working population. Total union membership has been on the wane for years. It fell from a high of 21 million in 1979, when the U.S. population was 225 million, to a low of 14.5 million in 2013, when the population stood at 315 million. Public sector workers are unionized at a level of 35.3 percent, but only 6.7 percent of private sector employees belong to unions. The Texas City Refinery did have a union, the United Steelworkers International, which fought constantly, albeit unsuccessfully, with management, regarding maintenance and process safety.

OSHA is dysfunctional because the relationship between its sprawling job description and limited funding is grossly disproportionate. This shortfall sets the agency up to fail at the same time that politicians attack agency officials on a bipartisan basis when their constituents are killed at work. The agency's jurisdiction extends to eight million workplaces that employ 130 million workers. Its entire workforce in FY 2013 was 2,258. OSHA has deputized counterpart agencies in 26 states and two territories to help it carry out workplace safety and health inspections. Together, they fielded just 2,200 inspectors in FY 2013, or one for every 59,000 workers. Even California, the eighth largest economy in the world, has only 170 inspectors, or one for every 109,000 workers. That same year (FY 2013), federal and state OSHA inspectors managed to conduct 39,228 inspections, covering 0.5 percent of workplaces over which they have jurisdiction.

OSHA's authorizing statute allows violators to appeal when they are ordered to fix old equipment or order new equipment to eliminate a safety hazard. Companies about to be cited commonly negotiate for sharp reductions in the penalties they are asked to pay in exchange for their promise that they will eliminate the hazard quickly. Of course, this approach means that companies can, in essence, hold inspectors hostage because the agency's first priority must be abatement, making it difficult if not quite impossible to establish any momentum in deterrent enforcement, which depends on assessing penalties large enough to deter others from similar violations.

For the last several years, OSHA has been relegated to a reactive role, doing its best to appear resolute in the aftermath of well-publicized workplace accidents, especially those that involve loss of life and extensive injury. Although the agency has the authority to issue preventive rules, during the first six years of the Obama administration, it produced a small handful, none of which will have a major impact on workplace safety. Its civil enforcement record is equally anemic, despite concerted efforts by Dr. David Michaels, the Obama administration official who heads the agency. Criminal enforcement has never been a priority for the agency, which has referred only a small handful of cases to the Department of Justice (DOJ) for the last several years. In fairness to the agency, federal prosecutors downplay the importance of such cases because the statute designates even willfully blind behavior that kills a worker – the functional equivalent of a state felony manslaughter charge – as a misdemeanor punishable by six months in jail and a $70,000 fine. Yet other felony charges are available to determined federal prosecutors, and OSHA has never considered working with state prosecutors to encourage criminal investigations of workplace fatalities in the worst cases.

In the years leading up to the Texas City explosion, as cost-cutting took its toll on maintenance, OSHA was barely present at the facility. Between 1985 and 2005, OSHA inspectors conducted a planned visit to the refinery to review process safety management only once, in 1998. Inspectors made unplanned visits several times in response to accidents, complaints (from individual workers or union representatives), or referrals (from local officials such as the police or health inspection agencies), but unplanned inspections are significantly less thorough, especially at a facility the size and complexity of the Texas City refinery. During this twenty-year period, when ten fatalities occurred at the refinery, OSHA proposed $270,255 in penalties, but ultimately settled those cases, collecting $77,860.

The agency did its best under both the Bush II and Obama administrations to throw the book at BP in the wake of the explosion, conducting 17 separate inspections over the six subsequent years. In September 2005, OSHA signed a consent decree with BP requiring payment of $21.3 million in penalties, the largest amount it had ever collected. The agreement required 660 safety improvements.[39] The settlement required BP to hire an independent auditor to evaluate its Process Safety Management program, and to implement all "feasible" recommendations made by the auditor. Feasible is a term of art that is not defined in the agreement, but it generally means that the company will select state of the art technology to prevent process safety accidents, so long as the technology is not unreasonably expensive to buy, install, and implement.

The consent decree, the adverse publicity, and the personal injury lawsuits on behalf of the dead and injured, would appear to have given BP ample incentive to mend its ways, at the very least at Texas City. But in 2009, OSHA returned for a follow-up inspection at the plant, learning that 270 violations from the first consent decree remained unaddressed and discovering 439 new violations.[40] The agency issued 439 citations covering both categories of violations, asking for civil penalties in the unprecedented amount of $87.4 million. BP vowed to fight this second case but ultimately settled for $50.6 million in penalties and more detailed requirements regarding safety and prevention. In August 2010, during the Gulf spill, BP agreed to pay $50 million in penalties to settle these new citations.[41]

On March 3, 2009, in a case developed by the EPA, a federal judge accepted a plea agreement from BP and the DOJ for criminal violations of the Clean Air Act, assessing a $50 million fine and putting the corporation on probation for three years. Victims' families contested the settlement, alleging that its terms were too lenient. Unfortunately, the sum total of all these assessments were so small in comparison to BP's multi-billion-dollar profits that, judging from the Macondo blowout fiasco, they appear to have had the effect of throwing a pea at a battleship as it steams toward the open sea.

The U.S. CSB included a brief evaluation of OSHA's performance in its report on the explosion. It discovered that the agency was able to field only one

[39] See News Release, U.S. Dep't of Labor, OSHA Fines BP Products North America More Than $21 Million Following Texas City Explosion (Sept. 22, 2005), *available at* https://www.osha.gov/pls/oshaweb/owadisp.show_document?p_id=11589&p_table=NEWS_RELEASES. For the actual settlement agreement, see Settlement Agreement, *In re* Inspection of BP Prods., N. Am., http://www.osha.gov/as/oc/BPSettlementAgreementFinalDoc.pdf (last visited Mar. 19, 2014).

[40] See News Release, U.S. Dep't of Labor, U.S. Department of Labor's OSHA Issues Record-Breaking Fines to BP (Oct. 30, 2009), *available at* https://www.osha.gov/pls/oshaweb/owadisp.show_document?p_table=NEWS_RELEASES&p_id=16674.

[41] See Marian Wang, *BP Agrees to Pay $50 Million for Earlier Texas City Problems*, PROPUBLICA, Aug. 12, 2010, http://www.propublica.org/blog/item/bp-agrees-to-pay-50-million-for-earlier-texas-city-problems. *See also* Settlement Agreement, Solis v. BP Prods. N. Am. (2010), *available at* https://www.osha.gov/pls/oshaweb/owadisp.show_document?p_table=CWSA&p_id=2002.

team of inspectors qualified to evaluate high-hazard facility compliance with the agency's process safety management rules. OSHA created a special inspection process for those rules, called a "Program Quality Verification" evaluation, but only managed to evaluate 0.2 percent of the approximately 2,816 high-hazard facilities it had identified as warranting special attention. The average OSHA inspection at a mainstream manufacturing facility takes approximately 24 hours of onsite work to complete, but refineries are sufficiently large and complex to require 2,000 hours of effort. The CSB concluded that "organizational and safety deficiencies exist at all levels of the BP Corporation."[42] When the report was released in March 2007, Chairperson Carolyn Merritt declared bluntly:

> Rules already on the books would likely have prevented the tragedy in Texas City. But if a company is not following those rules, year-in and year-out, it is ultimately the responsibility of the federal government to enforce good safety practices before more lives are lost. OSHA should obtain and dedicate whatever resources are necessary for inspecting and enforcing safety rules at oil and chemical plants. These facilities simply have too many potentially catastrophic hazards to be overlooked.[43]

Merritt could have avoided leaving the impression that she was kicking OSHA when it was down for self-serving reasons had she called on Congress and then-President George W. Bush to increase the agency's funding.

MASSEY ENERGY'S UPPER BIG BRANCH MINE

I'm a realist. The politicians will tell you we're going to do something so this never happens again. You won't hear me say that. Because I believe that the physics of natural law and God trump whatever man tries to do. Whether you get earthquakes underground, whether you get broken floors, whether you get gas inundations, whether you get roof falls, oftentimes they are unavoidable, just as other accidents are in society.

                          Don Blankenship, former CEO, Massey Energy[44]

---

[42] CSB Report, *supra* note 17, at 18.

[43] Press Release, Chemical Safety Board, U.S. Chemical Safety Board Concludes "Organizational and Safety Deficiencies at All Levels of the BP Corporation" Cause March 2005 Texas City Disaster That Killed 15, Injured 180 (Mar. 20, 2007), *available at* http://www.csb.gov/u-s-chem ical-safety-board-concludes-organizational-and-safety-deficiencies-at-all-levels-of-the-bp-corpora tion-caused-march-2005-texas-city-disaster-that-killed-15-injured-180/.

[44] GOVERNOR'S INDEPENDENT INVESTIGATION PANEL, THE APRIL 5, 2010 EXPLOSION: A FAILURE OF BASIC COAL MINE SAFETY PRACTICES 70 (May 2011), *available at* http://s3.documentcloud.org/documents/96334/upperbigbranchreport.pdf [hereinafter McATEER REPORT].

There should never be another UBB [Upper Big Branch]. … For far too long, we've accepted the idea that catastrophic accidents are an inherent risk of being a coal miner. That mindset is unacceptable.

> U.S. Attorney Booth Goodwin, Southern District of West Virginia[45]

If you don't start running coal up there, I'm going to bring the whole crew outside and get rid of every one of you.

> Performance Coal President Chris Blanchard, in response to a report
> that Foreman Edward Jones had stopped production until
> ventilation problems in the UBB mine could be fixed[46]

What Happened: The Explosion That Spread for Miles

An "Entirely Preventable" Disaster

On April 5, 2010, at approximately 3:02 P.M., just as two of three daily, eight-hour shifts were changing places, a massive explosion shook Massey Energy's Upper Big Branch (UBB) mine in Montcoal, West Virginia. The explosion of combustible coal dust spread over two and a half miles in mine shafts 1,000 feet underground. It traveled at speeds up to 1,500 feet/second, packing an overwhelming force of up to 65 pounds/square inch. The explosion roared through underground tunnels, hit walls, reversed direction, and came back again. Twenty-nine miners died and one was seriously injured, translating the acronym UBB into grim shorthand for the worst U.S. mine disaster in four decades.

Veteran rescue experts said they had never seen so much destruction over so great an area, with rail ties twisted like pipe cleaners, and equipment blown to bits. Toxic gas produced by the blast was pervasive, even affecting above-ground rescue teams attempting to bore vent holes into the mine. Recovery of the dead took days because travel to the blast site was dangerous and time-consuming, requiring a slow ride in low-slung "man trips" that traveled on rails from the mine entrance two miles away. The dead were scattered in small

---

[45] Press Release, U.S. Dep't of Justice, Alpha Natural Resources Inc. and Department of Justice Reach $209 Million Agreement Related to Upper Big Branch Mine Explosion (Dec. 6, 2011), *available at* http://www.justice.gov/opa/pr/2011/December/11-ag-1577.html.

[46] MINE SAFETY AND HEALTH ADMINISTRATION, U.S. DEP'T OF LABOR, REPORT OF INVESTIGATION – FATAL UNDERGROUND MINE EXPLOSION 60 (Dec. 6, 2011), *available at* http://www.msha.gov/Fatals/2010/UBB/FTL10c0331noappx.pdf [hereinafter MSHA REPORT]. For the full report (including appendices), visit http://www.msha.gov/Fatals/2010/UBB/FTL10c0331.pdf.

groups, thousands of feet from each other, felled either by the force and heat of the explosion or suffocated by carbon monoxide. One miner's remains were impaled on the ceiling.

UBB never reopened for mining.

In the aftermath, a series of investigations were launched that involved joint interviews with 269 witnesses and review of 88,000 pages of documentary evidence. Technical experts walked through what was left of the mine, conducting extensive testing of burned materials throughout the blast area and examining cracks in the floor and walls to discover sources of explosive methane gas. The only participants omitted from the investigation were 18 senior Massey executives who invoked their Fifth Amendment right against self-incrimination. Extensive reports were produced by (1) Mine Safety and Health Administration (MSHA) regulators;[47] (2) an independent panel of experts appointed by then-West Virginia Governor Joe Manchin (D-WV) (he is now a U.S. senator);[48] (3) the National Institute for Occupational Safety and Health (NIOSH), which was asked to evaluate the MSHA's internal evaluation of the disaster;[49] (4) the West Virginia Office of Miners' Health, Safety, and Training (the MSHA's state counterpart);[50] and (5) the United Mine Workers of America (UMW) (the union that represents miners across the country).[51] Unnamed Massey executives tried to exonerate themselves and the company, issuing their own, undated, and "preliminary" investigative report in 2010, just days before the company was taken over by Alpha Natural Resources in June 2011.[52] Alpha issued a terse press release

---

[47] The agency produced two separate reports: (1) the results of its investigation of the explosion and (2) an "internal review" of its role in the incident. *See* MSHA REPORT, *supra* note 46; MINE SAFETY & HEALTH ADMINISTRATION, U.S. DEP'T OF LABOR, INTERNAL REVIEW OF MSHA's ACTIONS AT THE UPPER BIG BRANCH MINE SOUTH (Mar. 6, 2012), *available at* http://www.msha.gov/PerformanceCoal/UBBInternalReview/UBBInternalReviewReport.pdf.

[48] McATEER REPORT, *supra* note 44.

[49] NATIONAL INSTITUTE FOR OCCUPATIONAL SAFETY & HEALTH, AN INDEPENDENT PANEL ASSESSMENT OF AN INTERNAL REVIEW OF MSHA ENFORCEMENT ACTIONS AT THE UPPER BIG BRANCH MINE SOUTH (Mar. 22, 2012), *available at* http://www.msha.gov/PerformanceCoal/NIOSH/Independent%20Assessment%20Panel%20Report%20w_Errata.pdf [hereinafter NIOSH ASSESSMENT].

[50] WEST VIRGINIA OFFICE OF MINERS' HEALTH, SAFETY & TRAINING, REPORT OF INVESTIGATION INTO THE MINE EXPLOSION AT THE UPPER BIG BRANCH MINE (Feb. 23, 2012), *available at* http://www.wvminesafety.org/PDFs/Performance/FINAL REPORT.pdf.

[51] UNITED MINE WORKERS OF AMERICA, INDUSTRIAL HOMICIDE: REPORT ON THE UPPER BIG BRANCH MINE DISASTER (May 2010), *available at* http://www.umwa.org/files/documents/134334-Upper-Big-Branch.pdf [hereinafter UNITED MINE WORKERS REPORT].

[52] MASSEY ENERGY COMPANY, PRELIMINARY REPORT OF INVESTIGATION UPPER BIG BRANCH MINE EXPLOSION (June 3, 2011), *available at* http://www.eenews.net/assets/2011/06/03/document_pm_01.pdf [hereinafter MASSEY REPORT].

stating that release of the report by Massey Board Chair Admiral Bobby R. Inman was "unauthorized."[53]

The five teams pronounced the tragedy (to use the MSHA's words) "entirely preventable,"[54] and blamed chronic violations of safety rules as the primary causes of the explosion. They concluded that if Massey had complied with the law, the tragedy could have been avoided or would have been far more limited in scope. The reports produced by the governor's independent panel, the union, and the NIOSH also excoriated MSHA regulators who knew about the mine's startling deficiencies but did not use their legal authority effectively to motivate Massey managers to run it safely.

Massey executives accused the MSHA and, by implication, the other panels, of disregarding scientific data and conducting a "deeply flawed accident investigation that has been predicated, in part, upon secrecy, protecting its own self-interest, witness intimidation, obstruction of Performance's investigation, and retaliatory citations."[55] (A Massey subsidiary, Performance Coal, owned and operated the mine and Massey referred to Performance rather than using its own name at every opportunity.) The company's report claimed that the explosion was caused by a massive incursion of highly explosive methane – or perhaps natural gas – that leaked from a crack in the floor of the mine into the area where the men were working. Because mining inevitably produces sparks, and the amount of this freakish leak was so large, the gas ignited, causing a lamentable, but unforeseen and unpreventable, Act of God.

Three Life-Threatening Hazards

All of the independent reports revolved around the three most important and life-threatening hazards that accompany the extraction of coal from underground mines. These hazards are amplified by the development of the "longwall mining" practiced at UBB and many other high-production, modern mines.[56] Mining companies install huge, long, and narrow machines mounted on tracks and positioned parallel to a mine wall, with powerful rotating blades on the side nearest the wall to cut coal. The UBB machine was capable of making 1,000 foot passes along the wall before it

[53] Press Release, Alpha Natural Resources Comments on Unauthorized Release of Preliminary Report on Upper Big Branch Mine (June 3, 2011), *available at* http://alnr.client.shareholder.com/releasedetail.cfm?ReleaseID=582709.

[54] MSHA Report, *supra* note 46, at 2.

[55] Massey Report, *supra* note 52, at 2.

[56] For an excellent description of the process, see Carl Hoffman, *What Can Go Wrong: The Dangers in Longwall Mining*, Popular Mechanics, Apr. 8, 2010, http://www.popularmechanics.com/science/energy/coal-oil-gas/dangers-in-longwall-coal-mining.

reversed and traveled back in the opposite direction. As the blades chewed through the coal, chunks fell onto conveyor belts and were carried out of the mine. A roof was installed over the track to protect miners and the machine from falling rock and other debris. Longwall machines produce only isolated sparking when they move through coal, but when they reach the sandstone that is intermixed with the coal, they can produce "hot streaks" or sustained sparking. To prevent hot streaks from igniting ever-present methane gas, the longwall machine has nozzles designed to spray a steady stream of water when the machinery is cutting a mine wall in order to douse any flames. But seven of the nozzles on UBB's longwall equipment were missing, and others were often blocked by grit contained in the river water used to fill water tanks on the machine.

The buildup of methane, which is a plentiful by-product of extraction, is a pervasive problem in deep mining because the gas is odorless, colorless, and poisonous in concentrated amounts. UBB was well known as a "gassy" mine that produced plentiful methane. Methane is the reason why miners in the nineteenth century brought cages of canaries into shafts. The canaries would drop dead when the lethal gas rose to dangerous levels, alerting the miners to abandon the area. Today, electronic monitors have taken the canaries' place, but they must be in operating condition and miners must pay careful atten-tion – and must be allowed by management to pay careful attention – to the alarms they sound. Monitor maintenance was not a top priority at UBB. Concrete block barriers, removable curtains, and air lock doors scattered throughout the mine were designed to channel methane away from active mining areas, but the curtains and the doors were often taken down or left open to increase the pace of coal production.

Closely related to methane buildup is the urgent need to design and build effective ventilation systems that bring clean air from the surface into the mine. These channels are fed by gigantic fans drawing air from the surface. The MSHA is so concerned about the correct operation of such systems that it requires mining companies to get its approval of the initial design and any subsequent modifications. UBB's ventilation system was inordinately complex because it had been built on the cheap. Instead of semipermanent barriers that provide the best capacity to direct air but are more expensive, Massey had installed many air lock doors and curtains that required constant manipula-tion to maintain appropriate levels of clean air. Miners in a hurry frequently left the doors open or removed the curtains, interfering with their capacity to prevent the infiltration of methane and carbon monoxide (CO). On the day of the explosion, mine tunnels were flooded with water because pumps designed to keep them clear were turned off the previous day, which was Easter Sunday.

When the pumps were turned back on, they malfunctioned. Maintenance crews spent much of the first day shift wading through neck-high water trying to fix them. The flooding further interfered with the flow of available air. Compounding this problem, several witnesses said that UBB's fans seemed to be operating in reverse, sucking fresh air out of the mine rather than pushing it into areas where miners were working.

The final and most important hazard is highly combustible coal dust. The MSHA has strict rules requiring mine operators to constantly suppress this dust by spreading inert gray "rock dust" over all active mining surfaces. Massey's rock dusting crew consisted of three men who were so overburdened with other work that they could only work part-time on this vital task, neglecting rock dusting for days at a time. The mine had two rock dusting machines, but one was inoperable.

"Coal Pays the Bills"

Like the Texas City refinery explosion, the UBB collapse had disturbing precursors that should have prevented this disaster. On January 2, 2006, another explosion at the International Coal Group's Sago mine in Upshur, West Virginia, killed twelve miners and injured one. The incident received extensive publicity. Seventeen days after the Sago mine explosion, a conveyor belt caught fire at Massey Energy's Aracoma mine in Logan County, West Virginia, killing two miners. The second accident was sufficiently small in scope that it might have escaped national media attention, but reporters were still camped around Sago and had little difficulty traveling to Aracoma. They discovered that unlike Sago, where lightning played a role in sparking the methane explosion inside the mine, the Aracoma fire resulted from pure negligence: poor maintenance, bad training, missing safety equipment, and lax pre-shift examinations of potential safety risks. Negative public reaction was exacerbated when lawyers trying a civil case against Massey discovered a 2005 internal memorandum written by CEO Don Blankenship to his "deep mine superintendents":

> If any of you have been asked by your group presidents, your supervisors, engineers, or anyone else to do anything other than run coal (i.e. build overcasts, do construction jobs, or whatever), you need to ignore them and run coal. This memo is necessary only because we seem not to understand that coal pays the bills.[57]

---

[57] Frank Langfitt, *Former Massey Workers Say Blast Wasn't a Surprise*, NPR, Apr. 27, 2010, *available at* http://www.npr.org/templates/story/story.php?storyId=126292007.

Provoked by this and other evidence, the DOJ indicted the company and three of its foremen. Massey ended up pleading guilty to violations of mine safety law and paid what was at the time a record $2.5 million criminal fine. The three foremen received probation.

Sago and Aracoma motivated Congress to pass the Miner Act in June 2006, the first update of mine safety law since 1977. The Act upgraded the rigor of emergency rescue and response procedures and substantially stiffened civil penalties although it left criminal violations of safety rules as misdemeanors.

Scofflaw Underground

The Aracoma criminal case against Massey was extraordinary for its time and was intended not only to shock the company out of its complacency but to get CEO Don Blankenship's very public disdain for safety rules the attention – and condemnation – that regulators thought he deserved. This effort not only was unsuccessful, it seemed to backfire. Blankenship and his management team did absolutely nothing to change their ways, continuing their defiance of federal and state regulators.

Troubled by the perception that the industry was making them look foolish, senior MSHA officials directed their inspectors to become more aggressive regarding enforcement. Citations for violations increased by one-third in number, and began to include the emergency preparedness requirements of the 2006 Miner Act and reflect the higher penalties allowed by the new law. The mining industry was unhappy, and soon developed retaliatory tactics. When companies received citations for significant violations, rather than settling the case by paying a reduced fine and remedying the problem, they appealed the citations to the Federal Mine Safety and Health Review Commission (FMSHRC), the independent agency that tries all of the MSHA's contested cases. The tactic produced a fivefold increase in the number of appeals pending before the FMHSRC. The key advantage of appealing citations was that while they are pending, they did not count toward a finding that a mine operator has engaged in a "pattern of violations" (POV), triggering substantially enhanced enforcement authority for the agency.[58]

On the day that UBB exploded, FMSHRC had a backlog of 18,000 cases, involving $210 million in potential penalties, up from 2,300 in 2005. Ironically, Massey was among the most enthusiastic filers of appeals, challenging 34 percent of its citations in comparison to a national average of 27 percent.

---

[58] 30 U.S.C. § 814(e) (2006).

Citations involving Massey accounted for 11.2 percent of the FMSHRC total and represented $10 million in the penalties sought by MSHA enforcers.

As these numbers indicate, Massey and UBB were becoming a significant drain on MSHA resources. In 2009, MSHA inspectors spent 1,854 hours at UBB, twice the time they spent in 2007. During the first three months of 2010, leading up to the April explosion, MSHA inspectors had already logged 803 hours at the mine. The rise in citations was accompanied by disturbing increases in injury rates: UBB's "Operator Nonfatal Days Lost Rate" increased by 100 percent in 2007–2009, up from 2.41 to 5.81 per 200,000 hours worked; the national average over the same period declined from 4.75 to 4.03.

To their credit, despite Massey's recalcitrance, line inspectors stuck to their guns. The Federal Mine Safety and Health Act authorizes MSHA inspectors to issue "withdrawal orders" requiring the immediate evacuation of work areas if they discover violations serious enough to present a health or safety hazard. (The main health hazard in coal mining is black lung disease; safety hazards are threats like fire, an explosion, or a roof collapse.) Mine operators get one warning and a chance to fix the problem, but if an inspector returns within ninety days to find the same hazard unaddressed, he may issue a withdrawal order.[59] Such orders are effective immediately with limited opportunity to appeal. They are taken quite seriously by the industry because they halt production. Miners may not return to the area of the mine targeted by the order until the problem is fixed. In 2009 and the first three months of 2010, UBB was subject to sixty-one withdrawal orders, a large and, in retrospect, foreboding amount. The most common violations cited by the MSHA involved UBB's most serious and chronic problems: bad ventilation (the subject of 23 percent of citations nationwide) and inadequate coal dusting (24 percent of all citations).

On the fateful day of the explosion, the day shift crew encountered repeated mechanical problems with the longwall, running it along its 1,000 foot track between 7:30 and 11:00 A.M., but then shutting down between 11:00 A.M. and 1:30 P.M. because a piece had fallen out of the equipment. Ventilation was once again a problem, and methane gas was seeping from the mine wall into the area where the men were working.[60] When they started running the machinery again between 2:30 and 3:00 P.M., one of the bits struck sandstone, producing a spark that ignited 3,000 cubic feet of methane mixed with air – the equivalent of a 19-by-20-foot room with an eight-foot ceiling. The resulting

[59] 30 U.S.C. § 814(d) (2006).
[60] To help educate policymakers about the UBB explosion, the MSHA prepared a 13 minute video that visualizes these events. It can be accessed by visiting http://www.msha.gov/stream ing/wvx/UBBAccidentScenario.wvx.

fireball might have killed or severely injured miners in the immediate vicinity of the longwall but would never have caused a massive explosion were it not for the large quantities of coal dust floating in the air. All of the investigative reports except the one written by Massey concluded that central cause of the accident was inadequate rock dusting. As United Mine Workers (UMW) investigators explained:

> The only logical explanation for an explosion to travel seven miles underground is that it had to have been propagated by a continuing supply of highly explosive fuel. The only available fuel supported by the evidence that is sufficient to propagate an explosion of this magnitude is float coal dust.[61]

Aware that this allegation could prove pivotal in subsequent state civil lawsuits for damages and federal criminal prosecutions, a major theme of the report put out by Massey executives is that the explosion was fueled not by coal dust but by seepage of a large quantity of either methane or natural gas from a crack in the floor near the longwall. MSHA and UMW investigators spent considerable time disproving that assumption. In the technocratic language used throughout its 972-page (with appendices) report, the MSHA explained its testing of this hypothesis: "Extraction of sandstone from the floor heave slab's brow fully exposed the crack and confirmed earlier observations that the fracture was rootless, and did not extend farther than 12 inches into the floor."[62] Or, in the plainer English of the UMW report:

> Massey claims that a crack in the floor of the mine was the source of a natural gas inundation that caused the explosion. That claim is simply not supported by the evidence revealed in the investigation. When it was excavated, the "crack" only extended a short way, becoming solid rock again and showing no signs of gas seepage from the underlying coal seam.[63]

As for Massey's negligence regarding rock dusting, in the 15 months preceding the explosion, UBB was cited numerous times every month for coal dust violations. In the aftermath of the explosion, the MSHA conducted extensive forensic work to determine the origin, scope, and force of the explosion, as well as the precise nature of the material that burned. Laboratory analysis of the 1,803 samples of burned material collected by MSHA investigators throughout the mine showed that coal dust was present at very high levels and that incombustible rock dust was present at unacceptably low levels.

---

[61] UNITED MINE WORKERS REPORT, *supra* note 51, at 13.
[62] MSHA REPORT, *supra* note 46, at 377.
[63] UNITED MINE WORKERS REPORT, *supra* note 51, at 13.

Investigators also interviewed miners assigned to a tiny team that had responsibility for compliance with rock dusting requirements. They reported that UBB had two rock dusting machines. One was irretrievably broken and sat in a dusty heap outside the mine, cannibalized for spare parts, while the second was a "track duster" pushed or pulled by motorized equipment that was driven by a miner. The working machine was manufactured in the 1980s and appeared to be far past its useful life. It regularly broke down, forcing the crew to spend hours unplugging clogged hoses and tinkering with machinery so that rock dusting could recommence. Compounding these challenges, the three-man crew assigned to rock dusting was often pulled off that task to do other maintenance work. The upshot was that the crew operated the rock duster at most three times a week for limited periods of time, a period that was way too short, even if they had functional equipment, to rock dust a mine the size of UBB.

Miners Gary Young and Clifton Stover, who were assigned to the rock dusting crew right before the explosion, shared a small notebook where they recorded their activities. Three entries, recorded on March 9, 11, and 23, in light of what happened just weeks later, are chilling: "Had no motor to run duster." "Had no motor again, no ride either." "NO RIDE, NO help, NO spotter. I'll call you today. I'm set up to fail here."

Contemporaneous written records kept by so-called preshift examiners confirm the neglect of rock dusting. Examiners – generally experienced miners who have been on the job for years – are assigned to walk several miles through the mine before production shifts in order to check whether conditions are safe. If they discover hazards, they are supposed to get them fixed. In the month before the explosion, the examiners requested additional, remedial rock dusting for 561 locations, but only 65 responses to those requests were ever logged in the records.

The Massey Way

It's like a jungle, where a jungle is the survival of the fittest; unions, communities, people – everyone is going to have to learn to accept that in the United States, you have a capitalist society, and that capitalism, from a business standpoint, is survival of the most productive.

Don Blankenship, former chief executive officer of Massey Energy[64]

---

[64] Brad Johnson, *Flashback: Don Blankenship Warned West Virginia that He Believes in 'Survival of the Fittest,'* THINKPROGRESS (Apr. 8, 2010), http://thinkprogress.org/green/2010/04/08/174629/blankenship-survival-fittest/. A taped interview with Blankenship that contains this

Much has been made in the media of the pugnacious attitude of Don Blankenship, self-made multimillionaire and coal baron, who began as Massey's CEO in 1992 and was driven out by the company's board of directors a few months after the UBB catastrophe. Born to a single mother with three children who ran a service station in one of West Virginia's most economically desolate areas, Blankenship was admired at a distance by many contemporaries as a self-made man who never forgot his roots and settled where he was born, albeit with two large homes and a garage containing a Bentley and Lamborghini. Blankenship reveled in the attention, declaring proudly during a speech to West Virginia business leaders: "I don't care what people think. At the end of the day, Don Blankenship is going to die with more money than he needs."[65]

Dubbed "the dark lord of coal country" in a post-UBB portrait by *Rolling Stone* reporter Jeff Goodell,[66] Blankenship prided himself on his combative relationship with regulators, liberal Democrats, businessmen who opposed what he perceived as his and Massey's financial interests, and reporters who wrote critical stories about how he ran the company. He never backed down from confrontation, no matter the circumstances. Perhaps the most egregious example of Blankenship's self-absorption is that in the immediate aftermath of the Aracoma fire, with media attention focused on the demands of families of the two dead men for an explanation of the incident, Blankenship would not allow MSHA regulators into the mine, forcing them to obtain a court order to gain access. With the benefit of hindsight, the most troubling aspect of this confrontation, as well as the many other controversies Blankenship engineered, is that none of the many government officials who endured such treatment felt able or ready to respond effectively.

Blankenship was also quite aggressive in the political realm, where he had the temerity to make unprecedented contributions to influence elections for judges assigned to resolve litigation filed against him. The most notable case was brought by Hugh Caperton, owner of a small coal company that Massey tried to buy in the late 1990s. A West Virginia trial court ruled in favor of Caperton, finding that Massey had engaged in fraud, concealment, and tortious interference in contractual relationships and Massey appealed. In the interim, Blankenship successfully engineered the election of Brent Benjamin to the appellate court, giving the jaw-dropping sum of $3.0 million

comment is also available on YouTube. *See* Think Progress, *Survival of the Fittest*, YouTube (uploaded Apr. 8, 2010), http://www.youtube.com/watch?v=S9lBWdK37VM.

[65] *The Kingmaker* (W. Va. Public Television, Nov. 2005), *available at* http://www.annasale.com/work/2009/06/08/the-kingmaker/ (at 1 min.:45 secs.).

[66] Jeff Goodell, *The Dark Lord of Coal Country*, ROLLING STONE, Nov. 29, 2010, http://www.rollingstone.com/politics/news/the-dark-lord-of-coal-country-20101129.

to his campaign. Caperton's attorneys asked Judge Benjamin to recuse himself from the case. He refused.

With the small West Virginia community of influential people abuzz over these developments – many states elect judges, but such races rarely attract such obvious influence peddling – Blankenship pushed on. In January 2008, the *New York Times* published a photograph and highly critical story describing Blankenship's social outings on the Riviera with Elliot Maynard, another judge on the appellate panel assigned to the Caperton case. Three months later, an ABC television crew tried to interview Blankenship for a story about the case scheduled to air on Nightline. Blankenship grabbed the reporter's camera and told him, "If you're going to start taking pictures of me, you're likely to get shot.[67] Caperton asked the appellate court to rehear the case without Maynard and Benjamin. The court still sided with Massey, setting the stage for the trip to the U.S. Supreme Court, which decided that Benjamin's participation had irrevocably tainted the case.[68] (If this story sounds like a John Grisham novel, that's because his 2008 book *The Appeal* tells a story about the influence of political contributions by corporate officials on state judicial elections.)

In the immediate aftermath of the UBB explosion, Blankenship and the company were swamped by adverse publicity as details about the company's chronic history of law violations began to filter out. A surprisingly large group of top-notch reporters from national, regional, and local media converged on the scene. Competing with each other in the best tradition of print journalism, they dug quickly and deeply into Blankenship and Massey's histories. By late April 2010, key details of the conditions that preceded the incident were known.

Despite the bad publicity, Blankenship maintained his defiant, son-of-West-Virginia stance, but it began to wear thin in the broader, more diverse arena occupied by the national media. He blithely dismissed disclosures about the hundreds of pending safety citations by insisting that violations are "a normal part of the mining process"[69] and insisted that accidents, including inundations of natural gas from cracks in a mine's floor, are bound to happen. He hired Robert Luskin, the lawyer who represented Karl Rove in the Valerie Plame affair, and a firm called Public Strategies, Inc., which was headed by

---

[67] Brian Ross & Maddy Sauer, *Coal Boss: If You Take Photos, "You're Liable to Get Shot,"* ABC News, Apr. 3, 2008, http://abcnews.go.com/Blotter/story?id=4582452&page=1.

[68] Caperton v. A.T. Massey Coal Co., 556 U.S. 868 (2008). The case and Blankenship's larger than life profile in West Virginia are described in Laurence Leamer, The Price of Justice: A True Story of Greed and Corruption (2013).

[69] Goodell, *supra* note 66.

former George W. Bush administration communications chief Dan Bartlett, to help him deflect the latest challenge by developing a strategy of resisting government investigators and circling the wagons against a takeover bid.[70] But when Blankenship appeared before a Senate appropriations committee inquiring into the tragedy on May 20, 2010, he was confronted by a clearly irate Senator Robert Byrd, then 92 and in the waning days of his long career. Byrd said:

> I cannot fathom how an American business could practice such disgraceful health and safety policies while at the same time boasting about its commitment to safety of its workers. I can't understand that. The Upper Big Branch mine had an alarming record of withdrawal orders. Now, where on Earth – where was the commensurate effort to improve safety and health? Where was it?[71]

Blankenship left Massey before it was bought by Alpha Natural Resources in 2011, forced out by his own board of directors. His departure was eased by a "golden parachute" package valued at $86 million. Blankenship has started a personal website, named the "American Competitionist,"[72] where he continues to excoriate his enemies.

As provocative and revealing as these episodes appear – and readers should know that I am only scratching the surface here: if you want to learn more, I recommend Laurence Leamer's *The Price of Justice: A True Story of Greed and Corruption* – Blankenship's shenanigans tell only part of the story. To embrace the dark coal lord imagery as the primary reason UBB exploded is to overlook the complexity of what was happening in the mine and, not incidentally, what is probably happening at this very moment in many other mines across the country and around the world. True, Blankenship was widely known as a micromanager and was clearly in control of every aspect of mine operations, earning the resentment of some of the people who served under him. He required foremen to telephone onsite managers every thirty minutes to report

---

[70] The best account of these events appears in Peter A. Galuszka, Thunder on the Mountain: Death at Massey and the Dirty Secrets Behind Big Coal (2012).

[71] *Investing in Mine Safety: Preventing Another Disaster: Hearing before the Subcomm. of the S. Comm. on Appropriations,* 111th Cong., 2d Sess. 30 (2010) (statement of Sen. Robert C. Byrd).

[72] *See* Don Blankenship: American Competitionist, http://www.donblankenship.com/ (last visited Mar. 20, 2014). For the fourth anniversary of the UBB explosion, Blankenship sponsored the release of a documentary of the explosion that pinpoints MSHA as the culprit. *See* Paul M. Barrett & Justin Bachman, *Notorious Former Coal Chief Makes His Case for Vindication,* Bloomberg Bus. Week, Apr. 2, 2014, http://www.businessweek.com/articles/ 2014-04-02/former-massey-ceo-don-blankenship-a-notorious-former-coal-chief-makes-his-case-for-vindication.

production numbers; they passed the information on to him at two-hour intervals. Miners who wanted to stop equipment to address safety concerns were threatened with being fired and mid-level managers were prepared to deliver on the threat. Blankenship hated unions and did everything he could to thwart several UMW efforts to organize UBB. He hired a dozen temporary "contract employees" in an effort to stoke job insecurity among the men in his permanent workforce. All of this behavior rightly bothered many miners. "I felt like I was working for the Gestapo at times," miner Stanley Stewart, a fifteen-year veteran of UBB who was 300 feet underground at the time of the blast, told a House of Representatives panel at a field hearing in West Virginia intent on investigating the explosion. "We did some things right, but were forced to do some things wrong."[73]

But UBB miners earned salaries in the range of $68,000–84,000 depending on experience, an extraordinary amount of money by West Virginia standards where the median household income is $40,000. Massey set up an elaborate system of bonus points to reward individual miners and work teams if they avoided injuries that caused lost work time. The points could be exchanged for luxury goods and miners participated enthusiastically. Employees were also offered lucrative contracts that gave them "enhanced" pay and bonuses for staying with the company. Few read the fine print that required them to pay back all of the extra money if they left the company's employ or were fired for poor performance. Massey brought doctors to the area, funded college scholarships for local children, supported volunteer fire departments and sporting events, and organized Christmas gift-giving for local school children. And when families and their friends came out first to stand vigil and then to mourn the miners lost at UBB, many wore blue jumpsuits with the Massey Energy logo that were copies of the required uniform at the mine.

In their report on the explosion, the independent panel appointed by West Virginia Governor Joe Manchin referred to sociologist Diane Vaughan's theory that the "normalization of deviance" within NASA set the stage for the Challenger disaster.[74] The panel defined the phenomenon correctly as "a gradual process through which unacceptable practices or standards become acceptable."[75] Yet the report also indicates that other miners were not inured to the risk and instead went to work with a sense of dread. The report recounts

[73] Mike Lillis, *Massey Miner: "I Felt Like I Was Working for the Gestapo,"* Washington Independent, May 25, 2010, http://washingtonindependent.com/85650/massey-miner-i-felt-like-i-was-working-for-the-gestapo.

[74] *See* McAteer Report, *supra* note 44, at 97 (referring to Diane Vaughan, The Challenger Launch Decision: Risky Technology, Culture, and Deviance at NASA (1996)).

[75] *Id.*

a conversation between Gary Wayne Quarles, a second-generation miner who died in the explosion and fellow miner Michael Ferrell, who survived to tell the story, on Easter Sunday, the day before the explosion. Quarles told Ferrell that he was "scared to go back to work" because "we ain't got no air" and "you can't see nothing" and that "[e]very day, I just thank God when I get out of that coal mines that I ain't got to be here no more. I just don't want to go back. When I get up in the mornings, I don't want to put my shoes on. I don't want to make myself go to work. I'm just scared to death to go to work because I'm just scared to death something bad is going to happen."[76]

How do we reconcile this miner's strong sense of impending doom with the idea that men (and one woman) went to work every day believing that their working conditions were normal?

The answer lies in the diversity of their circumstances: some miners were young and had never worked at any other mine. To them, black surfaces coated with coal dust seemed par for the course. In contrast, Quarles was 33 when he died, and his father was also a miner. He understood better than the younger men the implications of the hazards he could see around him. Other veteran miners, including Edward (called "Dean") Jones, fifty, a foreman at the mine, tried to improve conditions but were badgered into silence by senior Massey executives. Jones's wife reported to independent panel investigators that in the months leading up to the explosion, her husband came home complaining about poor ventilation. She asked her husband if he had reported the problem and he replied that he had talked about it with mine super-intendents Everett Hager and Gary May, as well as with Chris Blanchard. "He told Chris Blanchard, you know, a dozen times that I know of," Mrs. Jones said. "At one point her husband told her he shut down the section for lack of air, and "Chris Blanchard called the dispatcher and told him to tell Dean if he didn't get the section running in so many minutes he would be fired," she said.[77] The Joneses' teenage son suffers from cystic fibrosis, and quitting his job meant losing health insurance.

As for upper-level managers, the constant withdrawal orders and citations should have informed anyone but the most delusional person that existing maintenance, including rock dusting, was not remotely up to code. Hostility toward MSHA inspectors would have to veer toward the paranoid to justify ignoring everything they said or did, especially when withdrawal orders were costing so many hours of downtime. Top executives were deeply involved in the daily details of the mine. For example, Chris Blanchard, the president of

[76] *Id.* at 14–15.
[77] *Id.* at 59.

Performance Coal, the Massey subsidiary that ran UBB, was a constant presence around the mine and his employees knew him well. Several miners besides Jones reported conversations with him about ventilation problems and the breakdown of rock dusting equipment to investigators. Blanchard appears to have shrugged off these complaints. Instead, he left written notes for foremen to read as they exited the mine after their shifts, chiding them for failing to meet production targets or accomplish other aspects of assigned tasks.

Of course, Blanchard, like everyone else at UBB, was under constant pressure to produce, epitomized by the thirty-minute reports phoned in by foremen and passed on to Blankenship every two hours. To advance within the company clearly meant to resist time-consuming maintenance efforts that impede production. Yet it is hard to imagine that they would have knowingly embraced the risk of a catastrophe like the UBB explosion had they been able to perceive it approaching. Instead, more than the miners themselves, executives suffered from a kind of myopia that prevented them from appreciating the imminence or scope of the hazard.

The U.S. Attorney Climbs the Chain

Booth Goodwin, the U.S. Attorney for West Virginia, has indicted four Massey employees so far, moving upwards in the corporate hierarchy.[78] West Virginia coal country is awash in rumors that Goodwin is intent on going all the way to an indictment of Don Blankenship.[79] As required by ethics and good judgment, Goodwin is playing his cards close to his vest.

The most minor of the four cases involved two felony counts of making false statements to the U.S. government, as opposed to violating the safety requirements imposed by the MSHA, which trigger misdemeanor charges only but were the proximate cause of the twenty-nine miners' deaths. Thomas Harrah, a former UBB mine foreman, was sentenced to ten months in prison after entering a plea agreement before federal District Court Judge Irene Berger on September 22, 2011. Harrah had failed an examination for certification as a foreman but served in that capacity. When confronted with this deception by FBI agents in the aftermath of the explosion, he claimed that company executives had helped him accomplish the false certification. They had not.

---

[78] *See* Ken Ward, Jr., *Former Massey Official Sentenced to 42 Months in Prison*, CHARLESTON GAZETTE, Sept. 10, 2013, http://www.wvgazette.com/News/201309100025? (discussing Goodwin's prosecutions against Thomas Harrah, Hughie Elbert Stover, Gary May, and David C. Hughart).

[79] *Id.*

Next on the list was Hughie Elbert Stover, who headed security at UBB. He was indicted on two counts of making false statements regarding whether he had provided advance notice to men underground that inspectors were traveling down into the mine and one count of document destruction for directing an unnamed subordinate to get rid of evidence relevant to the ongoing civil and criminal investigations of the explosion. Stover adopted the defiant stance patented by Blankenship, went to trial, and was convicted by a jury. Goodwin urged Judge Berger to give Stover the full sentence provided by law – 25 years' imprisonment, even though relevant, but nonbinding, sentencing guidelines recommend 31 to 44 months for this type of violation. Berger stayed within the range of the guidelines, sentencing Stover to a three-year prison term. She explained that providing advance warning is a serious violation because it gives work crews the time to hang curtains, "steal" air, and scatter rock dust before the inspector reaches the work area after a thirty-minute trip down into the mine, thus concealing long-standing violations. But she could not accept Goodwin's argument that this act was a cause of the explosion. She also noted that similar violations had never before been an enforcement priority for the MSHA. Why not is anyone's guess. The element of surprise is vital to regulatory enforcement, especially given the long delay between the inspector's arrival at the mouth of the mine and his arrival at the work site.

The third case charged Gary May, who was hired as a UBB foreman in February 2008 and was promoted to superintendent in 2009, just a few months before the explosion. Superintendents are assigned responsibility for daily troubleshooting; the job is the highest of mid-level management positions. An organizational chart prepared as part of the MSHA investigative report on the explosion[80] lists Chris Blanchard, President of Performance Coal (the Massey subsidiary that ran the mine); Jamie Ferguson, Vice President; and Wayne Persinger, General Manager. Gary May and a second superintendent who worked in a different section of the mine are on the next level. Goodwin charged that because May "exercised control and authority"[81] over the longwall mining section where the explosion began, and because mine safety and health laws were "routinely violated,"[82] he was guilty of a conspiracy to "defraud"[83] the federal government. Specifically, the government alleged – and May ultimately admitted – that

---

[80] MSHA REPORT, *supra* note 43, at 13.

[81] Information at 6, United States v. Gary May, No. 5:12-00050 (S.D. W. Va. Feb. 22, 2012), *available at* http://www.wvgazette.com/static/coal%20tattoo/GaryMayCharges.pdf.

[82] *Id.* at 5.

[83] *Id.* at 7.

he too gave advance notice of impending inspections so that violations could be concealed; directed the falsification of an examination book (again, a method of recording preshift safety checks); and disabled a methane detector so that it would stop shutting off a machine used to cut coal. Judge Berger accepted May's guilty plea and sentenced him to 21 months in prison and a $20,000 fine. He is reportedly cooperating with prosecutors in their investigation of potentially criminal acts by his supervisors.

The fourth defendant is David Hughart, the "highest-ranking mine safety official ever convicted of conspiracy to impede MSHA," according to Goodwin.[84] He received a prison sentence of forty-two months and is also cooperating with prosecutors. Hughart worked for Massey for twenty years in senior executive positions, most recently as the president of the White Buck Coal Company, another Massey subsidiary. He was fired from that position two weeks before the UBB explosion. Hughart was never involved in mining at UBB, but he is reportedly helping Goodwin build his case that Blankenship fostered a scofflaw culture and harassed employees at all levels to put production above any other consideration. The charges against him, which read much like the charges against Gary May, include participation in a conspiracy to promote routine violations of MSHA rules. At his sentencing hearing, Judge Berger asked him whether it was company policy to give advance warnings that inspections were about to occur and, if so, who ordered that the illegal practice be perpetuated. Hughart replied "the chief executive officer," clearly fingering Blankenship.[85] Asked to comment on the surprise allegation, Blankenship's lawyer, William Taylor, responded tartly: "We are not particularly concerned about Mr. Hughart's statement. It is not surprising that people embellish or say untrue things when they are attempting to reduce a possible prison sentence."[86]

In August 2013, shortly before he was sentenced for mine violations, Hughart was arrested for possession of alprazolam, an anti-anxiety medication, and oxycodone. Because Hughart was reportedly fired for failing a random drug test and hiring his son at a high salary, Goodwin will be compelled to salvage his credibility if he takes the stand in criminal trials of other executives.

---

[84] The quote is attributed to U.S. Attorney Goodwin. Howard Berkes, *Former Massey Exec Gets 42 Months in Mine Disaster Case*, NPR (Sept. 10, 2013), *available at* http://www.npr.org/blogs/thetwo-way/2013/09/10/221161240/former-massey-exec-gets-42-months-in-mine-disaster-case.

[85] John Raby & Vicki Smith, *Upper Big Branch Mine Disaster: David Hughart, Former Massey Executive, Implicates Ex-CEO*, HUFFPOST GREEN (Feb. 26, 2013), http://www.huffingtonpost.com/2013/02/28/upper-big-branch-mine-disaster_n_2782183.html.

[86] *Id.*

REGULATORY FAILURE: INSTITUTIONAL CAUTION
BECOMES PARALYSIS

The ability to stand back and take a long look – to see the red flags, to connect the dots – and the ability and willingness to take quick action when necessary distinguishes a regulatory agency which can prevent disaster from one which only reacts.

McAteer Report[87]

The stories written in the immediate aftermath of the UBB explosion were acutely embarrassing for the Obama administration. They revealed Massey's long and successful history of stonewalling regulators, accumulating violations, and avoiding millions of dollars in penalties for years on end. They created the strong impression that the dreadful incident was a direct product of a corporation allowed to run amok. Top leaders at the agency, mortified and on the defensive, assembled an investigative team that examined every aspect of the evidence left by the explosion. Its 972-page, extraordinarily technical report is virtually impenetrable to lay readers, compounding the impression that the agency was so immersed in its lengthy power struggle with Massey that its staff still had not come up for air. As is its custom, the MSHA also conducted an "internal review" of its own conduct, producing a 308-page report analyzing the mistakes its staff made before the explosion and recommending reforms the agency could adopt to improve its performance.

Despite the MSHA's obvious and well-documented institutional agony regarding UBB, political operatives, perhaps at the White House or perhaps in the office of the Department of Labor Secretary Hilda Solis, were unwilling to leave things there. Convinced that an examination of the examiners was warranted, they directed the National Institute of Occupational Safety and Health (NIOSH) to appoint a panel of experts to evaluate the MSHA's internal review. Their relatively brief eighteen-page report is as blunt as it is merciless. In essence, the panel concluded that had the MSHA successfully prosecuted violations regarding methane and rock dusting "it would have lessened the chances of – and possibly could have prevented – the UBB explosion."[88] After three decades studying federal health and safety regulation, I cannot think of any comparable example of a panel of experts convened by the government laying the deaths of people killed by industrial activities so squarely at regulators' feet. The only comparable situation was the opprobrium meted out to managers at the National Aeronautics and Space Administration (NASA) in

---

[87] MCATEER REPORT, *supra* note 44, at 83.
[88] NIOSH ASSESSMENT, *supra* note 46, at ii.

the wake of the Challenger disaster. But in that instance, the operations that caused the deaths were the government's own.

The NIOSH panel seemed especially aggravated by the fact that previous MSHA internal investigations of the Crandall Canyon (2010), Darby (2006), Sago (2006), and Aracoma (2006) mine disasters found the same enforcement deficiencies as the investigation of UBB. "There is a remarkable overlap in the array of enforcement lapses identified," the panel noted drily.[89] Although members of the panel instinctively understood that a failure of will was at the bottom of this persistent institutional failure, its recommendations were relatively mundane. For example, the panel recommended that the agency scale back the responsibilities it assigns to inspectors, including the complex laundry list of requirements it expects them to check, noting that this overload of detail could cause them to lose their capacity to prioritize the worst problems.

A deeper analysis suggests that when inspectors live and work in sparsely populated mine country and end up spending thousands of hours underground, many experience significant internal and external pressure to avoid a constant state of warfare with mine operators, especially ones as aggressively dismissive as Massey. This explanation only goes so far, of course. The temptation to go along to get along obviously did not deter the inspectors who issued 61 withdrawal orders in the 15 months leading up to the explosion.

As it did at Massey, the problem could well lie not with frontline inspectors but rather with the supervisors who reviewed their work at MSHA district offices. Citations were written and issued, but it was this group that never stopped the routine long enough to step back and consider how to put an end to Massey's dangerous scofflaw culture. This failure is a sad comment on how easy it is to get lost in standard practice at any large institution. It also suggests, though, that UBB did not strike MSHA staff as significantly worse than other mines. The implications of that conclusion for coal miner safety are indeed grim to contemplate.

In the aftermath of UBB, the MSHA has adopted some very important changes to its enforcement program, including issuance of a new rule streamlining how it deals with pattern of violation (POV) cases.[90] The Mine Safety and Health Act authorizes the agency to set forth criteria for determining when a mine operator has become a recidivist with a clear track record of ignoring the law.[91] Once it determines that bad practices at a mine have fallen

---

[89] *Id.* at 10.
[90] Pattern of Violations, 78 Fed. Reg. 5056 (final rule Jan. 23, 2013) (to be codified at 30 C.F.R. pt. 104).
[91] 30 U.S.C. § 814(e) (2006).

into such a pattern, the MSHA is empowered to keep issuing withdrawal orders until every single violation posing a risk to health or safety is fixed. Unlike the withdrawal orders mentioned earlier, POV status means that MSHA inspectors are not compelled to give the company a chance to remedy the violation, nor are they limited to ordering evacuation only when they find the exact same violation repeated. Instead, any significant violation can trigger evacuation until fixed. After UBB, the agency changed its interpretation of the statute and now asserts that the agency will not wait until citations have been resolved by the FMSHRC to declare that a company has achieved POV status. This change is especially important because the FMSHRC reported in April 2013 that although it had made some progress, its backlog would remain at 11,000 cases through the end of FY 2014. A coalition of state and national trade associations challenged the new rule in the federal Court of Appeals for the Sixth Circuit, but the court ruled it had no jurisdiction over the matter, letting the rule stand.[92]

Alpha Takes Over

At the end of January 2011, Alpha Natural Resources bought Massey Energy in a deal valued at $8.5 billion. Massey owned and operated 35 underground mines and 12 surface mines in Kentucky, Virginia, and West Virginia, producing 40 million tons of coal annually, making it the largest coal producer in Central Appalachia. The purchase made Alpha the second largest coal producer in the country, with five billion tons of coal reserves.

In December 2011, Alpha signed a deferred prosecution agreement with the Justice Department that was worth $209 million, with the bulk of the money committed to upgrading its mines ($80 million), conducting mine safety research ($48 million), paying restitution to the miners' families ($48 million), and satisfying civil penalties accrued by Massey ($34 million).[93] "Deferred prosecution" means that Alpha did not plead guilty to any crimes and the prospect of deflecting corporate criminal charges was undoubtedly an incentive for the Massey board of directors to approve the takeover.

The jury is still out on whether Alpha will be able to stamp out Massey's culture of neglect, even hostility, toward compliance with safety rules. Alpha

---

[92] The case is National Mining Association v. Mine Safety & Health Administration, No. 13-3324, ___ F.3d. ___ (6th Cir. 2014), *available at* 2014 WL 4067861. See Dylan Lovan, Associated Press, *Federal Mining Rule Beats Challenge*, CHARLESTON GAZETTE & DAILY MAIL, Aug. 20, 2014.

[93] Press Release, U.S. Dep't of Justice, Alpha Natural Resources Inc. and Department of Justice Reach $209 Million Agreement Related to Upper Big Branch Mine Explosion (Dec. 6, 2011), *available at* http://www.justice.gov/opa/pr/2011/December/11-ag-1577.html.

executives have publicized their efforts to reeducate Massey employees regarding the company's "Safety First" program, which they insist is very effective. On the negative side, Alpha hired several top Massey executives, including Chris Adkins, Massey's chief operating officer at the time of the UBB explosion. Adkins, who began work at Massey in 1981 as a very young man, was appointed to help run the Safety First program, a discordant choice given his prominence as the executive in charge of the corporate response to UBB and Aracoma. As troubling, Alpha has vociferously opposed any and all efforts to toughen regulatory requirements or to strengthen the MSHA's authority through legislation. The company resistance is odd, given the $80 million investment in state-of-the-art safety equipment required by its agreement with federal prosecutors. From an economic perspective, Alpha should be intent on persuading the government to impose the same requirements on its competitors so that all operate on the proverbial level playing field. Either Alpha executives are so preoccupied with their conservative, deregulatory ideology that they have lost sight of these competitive dynamics or they do not see these investments as having much significance for the company's bottom line.

As mentioned earlier, U.S. Attorney Booth Goodwin seems intent on bringing criminal charges against individuals as far up in the corporate hierarchy as the evidence will allow. He has gained the cooperation of David Hughart, a senior Massey manager who has stated in open court that Don Blankenship, Massey's CEO, was his "co-conspirator" in perpetuating violations of mine safety rules. Because Congress never passed legislation addressing MSHA's weaknesses as revealed by UBB and because the agency remains chronically underfunded, these prosecutions represent the best hope for real reform in coal country. And there can be little question that such reform is long overdue. Although it may be tempting to write off Massey as an isolated rogue, the checkered history of safety problems throughout the industry contradicts such wishful thinking.

Coal mining remains among the most hazardous industries with an overall fatality rate of 24.8/100,000 workers compared to 4.3/100,000 in private industry as a whole. Nonfatal injury and illness rates for coal mining were 4.4/100 workers, compared to 3.9/100 in private industry as a whole.

The United States possesses the largest coal reserves in the world and historically has been a net exporter. Although the nation has decreased its dependence on coal to produce electricity – the fuel provided 37 percent of power generation in 2012, as compared to 50 percent in 2007 – increased demand by developing countries with lax environmental rules such as China and India has stimulated exports, with amounts exported in 2012 breaking a record set in 1981. As Alpha CEO Kevin Crutchfield bragged to the *Wall Street*

Journal in January 2011, the acquisition of Massey gave his company the "hot commodity" of twenty-five million tons of annual port capacity.[94] These developments suggest that unless U.S. Attorney Goodwin succeeds in imposing individual accountability on former Massey managers, safety culture is unlikely to take root within this dangerous industry.

CONCLUSION

A close reading of the Texas City and UBB investigative findings suggests that such catastrophes will recur, causing preventable loss of life, debilitating injuries, and economic damage, because these corporations – and arguably their industries as a whole – lack the motivation to overcome what internationally recognized safety expert Andrew Hopkins calls the "failure to learn."[95] Although the recent indictments of Massey managers are encouraging, none involve executives at the top level who made the decisions to cut corners on essential safety measures. Time will tell whether federal prosecutors are able to use these cases to develop evidence that justifies higher-level indictments.

---

[94] Kris Maher, *Alpha CEO: Premium for Massey Well Worth It*, WALL ST. J., Jan. 31, 2011, http://online.wsj.com/news/articles/SB10001424052748704653204576112941714152296.

[95] ANTHONY HOPKINS, FAILURE TO LEARN: THE BP TEXAS CITY REFINERY DISASTER (2010).

5

The Environment

BP'S MACONDO WELL

The explosion of the rig was a disaster that resulted from BP's culture of privileging profits over prudence.

Lanny Breuer, Assistant U.S. Attorney, Criminal Division[1]

The immediate causes of the Macondo well blowout can be traced to a series of identifiable mistakes made by BP, Halliburton, and Transocean that reveal such systematic failures in risk management that they place in doubt the safety culture of the entire industry.

National Commission on the BP Deepwater Horizon Oil Spill and Offshore Drilling[2]

[T]he extent to which a company is a good social citizen is less a function of its managers' moral compass than of their competence and perspective on what constitutes a good business model. ... If they develop badly thought-out incentives and enforce them blindly, there will be unintended consequences, something the financial sector has illustrated on a grand scale in recent years.

Tom Bergin, *Spills and Spin: The Inside Story of BP*[3]

---

[1] Press Release, U.S. Dep't of Justice, BP Exploration and Production Inc. Agrees to Plead Guilty to Felony Manslaughter, Environmental Crimes and Obstruction of Congress Surrounding Deepwater Horizon Incident (Nov. 15, 2012), http://www.justice.gov/opa/pr/2012/November/12-ag-1369.html.

[2] NATIONAL COMMISSION ON THE BP DEEPWATER HORIZON OIL SPILL AND OFFSHORE DRILLING, REPORT TO THE PRESIDENT: DEEP WATER – THE GULF OIL DISASTER AND THE FUTURE OF OFFSHORE DRILLING, at vii (Jan. 2011), *available at* http://www.gpo.gov/fdsys/pkg/GPO-OILCOMMISSION/pdf/GPO-OILCOMMISSION.pdf [hereinafter REPORT TO THE PRESIDENT]. *See also* NATIONAL COMMISSION ON THE BP DEEPWATER HORIZON OIL SPILL AND OFFSHORE DRILLING, CHIEF COUNSEL'S REPORT, MACONDO: THE GULF OIL DISASTER (2011), *available at* http://permanent.access.gpo.gov/gpo4390/C21462-407CCRforPrinto.pdf [hereinafter CHIEF COUNSEL'S REPORT].

[3] TOM BERGIN, SPILLS AND SPIN: THE INSIDE STORY OF BP 267 (2011).

After nearly three years and tens of millions of dollars in investigation, the government needs a scapegoat. No one should take any satisfaction in this indictment of an innocent man. This is not justice.

> Shaun Clarke and David Gerger, attorneys for Robert Kaluza,
> BP well site leader[4]

WHAT HAPPENED: CORNER-CUTTING AND THE BIG KICK

The Well from Hell

The gigantic derrick loomed 20 stories above the sea, the centerpiece of a $350 million, 30,000-ton drilling rig named the Deepwater Horizon. Stationed 49 miles offshore in the Gulf of Mexico, it was owned by the largest rig provider in the world, a company called Transocean, and leased by one of the biggest oil companies in the world, BP (formerly British Petroleum) for the princely sum of $1 million/day. Years earlier, BP and its partners, Anadarko Petroleum and Moex USA, had paid the federal government $34 million for oil and gas drilling rights to a nine-square-mile underwater plot named Macondo after the mythical village in the Gabriel García Márquez book *One Hundred Years of Solitude*. In a truly bizarre twist, BP had donated the opportunity to name the well to the United Way, which in turn sold it to a group of Colombians who were fans of the author and named the well to commemorate him.

From the beginning, the well field posed exceptionally difficult geological challenges. BP and Transocean employees on the front line of the project started referring to Macondo as the "nightmare well" or "the well from hell."[5] Drilling began in 2009, but ended abruptly in November when the Marianas, another Transocean rig, managed to sink a hole 4,000 feet below the seabed but was so badly damaged by Hurricane Ida that it had to be hauled away for repairs. BP and Transocean were not ready to try again until more than a year later, in January 2010, when they positioned the Deepwater Horizon directly over the uncompleted well, with the goal of drilling a hole 2.5 miles beneath the surface, which would make Macondo among the deepest in the Gulf or, for that matter, the world.

The schedule for completion of the project called for 51 days of drilling at a cost of $96.2 million. But the drilling lagged six weeks past that deadline, with a cost overrun of $58 million. Finally, on the morning of April 20, 2010, the

---

[4] *BP Workers Being Made Scapegoats with Deepwater Horizon Death Charges, Defense Lawyers Say*, CBS NEWS, Nov. 16, 2012, http://www.cbsnews.com/news/bp-workers-being-made-scapegoats-with-deepwater-horizon-death-charges-defense-lawyers-say/.

[5] REPORT TO THE PRESIDENT, *supra* note 2, at 2.

Transocean crew, in consultation with the onsite BP "company man" and a squadron of BP engineers based in Houston, Texas, prepared to complete the temporary abandonment of the well. This operation would seal the hole with waterproof cement. The Deepwater Horizon would move on to a new drilling job and BP would install a permanent production platform to extract the oil.

The Deepwater Horizon was a state-of-art "semi-submersible platform" with sleeping quarters for 126 crew and several guests. The living space sat atop a gigantic platform housing the derrick, staging areas for heavy drilling equipment and piping, huge pits for recirculated "drilling mud" (more on that critical substance shortly), and a helicopter landing pad to accommodate frequent trips to and from shore. Giant pontoons positioned 130 feet beneath the surface kept the rig afloat, and sophisticated computers and heavy motors maintained the rig's vertical position above a "riser pipe." The pipe itself was made of giant, three-story-high segments that were screwed together and extended thousands of feet into the well.

The plans submitted to the deepwater drilling regulator, the Department of the Interior's Minerals Management Service (MMS), called for drilling the well 19,650 feet deep. But when the well reached a depth of 18,400 feet (5,000 feet from the surface of the Gulf and 13,000 feet below the ocean floor) the drill fractured fragile rock formations at the bottom of the well, risking a blowout. BP and Transocean stopped drilling and spent five days contemplating their next move. Because they had already crossed two layers that appeared to contain significant deposits of oil and gas that would make well production quite lucrative, they decided to stop trying to make it any deeper and instead to prepare for its temporary abandonment.

The most serious hazard on any deepwater rig is a blowout of oil and gas deposits held under enormous pressure within rock formations. Once drilling reaches any significant deposits, "kicks" – or explosive releases – can occur. To equalize the pressure between the drill pipe and those deposits, crews pour drilling mud down the pipe. The mud is – a thick, viscous sludge manufactured of oil, synthetic fluids, polymers, and chemicals that is roughly twice the weight of water. The mud serves the dual purpose of keeping the drill bit relatively cool. Drilling mud is constantly recirculated in a deepwater well. When it reaches the rig, equipment filters out chunks of rock and other debris displaced by the drilling and the mud is then pumped back into the pipe. The influx of mud must be carefully monitored because, if the load in the pipe becomes too heavy, the pipe can sway, running the risk of fracture and kicks.

If a kick occurs and is large enough, it displaces the drilling mud and seawater inside the pipes, traveling at frightening speed to the surface, where it erupts within the rig, catching fire and exploding. To protect the rig and its crew from this dangerous condition, a gigantic piece of equipment known as a "blowout preventer" or BOP was positioned near the bottom of the Macondo well. Weighing in at an impressive 300 tons (roughly 12 garbage trucks) and standing five stories high, it had shearing rams that could close the pipe in the event of an emergency.

The combined factors of the well's depth and fragility and the delays and cost overruns exhausted the onshore and onsite crews. All were feeling tremendous pressure to plug the well and move on. Plans for drilling the well were compiled with meticulous care, over many months, with schematics approved by federal regulators. But the process of accomplishing temporary abandonment was a surprisingly hurried and chaotic affair implemented over a single week. Dozens of men worked – often at cross-purposes – to complete the delicate operation, which involved withdrawing the drill bit, squeezing out huge quantities of drilling mud and seawater from the riser pipe and the area around the well head, and replacing this sodden material with a cement plug that would harden in place to keep the boiling, high-pressure gas and oil in place until the new platform was ready to receive them. Corners were cut, decisions were made in large groups, ostensibly by consensus, self-justifying emails with large attachments were circulated to long lists of recipients, and lines of communication became twisted, then frayed, and finally shorted out.

As Abrahm Lustgarten writes:

> The most delicate part of constructing an oil well, though, isn't drilling a hole in the ground. ... Rather, it is the transition from drilling to producing oil that presents some of the toughest technical challenges, and the greatest risk. The well needs to be stabilized – its construction finished so that it is certifiably leakproof and strong enough to withstand the natural pressures of the earth – and prepared to be shut in.
>
> From the moment they stopped drilling, BP's crews, along with the Transocean and Halliburton contractors working for them, would face a rapid-fire succession of critical decisions that would draw heavily on the judgment and depth of experience of their management. Almost every one of the decisions that team would make would turn out to be wrong.[6]

At 9:45 P.M. on April 20, drilling mud erupted from the wellhead, pouring over the Deepwater Horizon's deck. The huge rig began to shake. The explosion that followed consumed much of the rig in flames as crew tried desperately – and far too late – to trigger the blowout preventer designed to shut the well

---

[6] Abrahm Lustgarten, Run to Failure: BP and the Making of the Deepwater Horizon Disaster 305 (2012).

opening in an emergency. By the time they tried to activate that last line of defense, the piping at the bottom of the well had bent, and the shearing rams could not seal it.

Panicked by flames and smoke, with some seriously injured by flying debris, people jumped 125 feet into the water below while others struggled to lifeboats. When they were rescued by a supply boat mercifully located nearby, eleven men were missing and the gaping hole in the seabed was beginning to pour oil into the Gulf. BP executives and their consultants seemed to be operating in slow motion, as they tried to find a way to stop the spill. A growing group of career regulators, political appointees from several agencies and departments with overlapping authority, and even the President himself circulated at the edge of the dysfunctional little circle of BP experts and executives waving their arms, giving inconsistent advice, and expressing raw, politically expedient outrage. The Deepwater Horizon sank into the sea two days later. The spill continued for 87 more days, until July 15, 2010, pouring 4.9 million barrels – or 210 million gallons – into the Gulf. (By way of reference, the 1989 Exxon Valdez spill in Alaska's Prudhoe Bay spilled an estimated 30 million gallons, albeit much closer to shore.)

Aftermath

In the weeks following the explosion, as the spill remained uncontained, the president summoned BP executives to the White House and managed to extract a commitment that the corporation would pay up to $20 billion to compensate people harmed by the spill throughout the Gulf region. The company began those payouts but has recently had a change of heart, taking out full-page ads in major U.S. newspapers to advance its complaint that it has paid too much in unjustified claims. Lawsuits to apportion liability among the three business partners (BP, Transocean, and Halliburton) will continue for years, although most observers expect BP to be left shouldering the lion's share of costs over the long run. The DOJ and the companies have yet to determine how much the three will pay in so-called "natural resource damages" – a rough and imperfect calculation designed to set damages for the destruction of natural ecosystems in the sea and along the coast.

The EPA managed to convince its federal counterparts at the Department of Defense (DOD) to accept a ban on new government contracts with BP – a remedy known as "debarment" that is called the "nuclear option" by the criminal law bar. The ban lasted for a little over a year, but was lifted in March 2014 when the corporation signed a settlement agreement imposing yet another set of audit and compliance conditions.

BP conducted its own evaluation of the spill, although most knowledgeable observers criticized it as a self-serving document that previewed its legal defense in lawsuits against Transocean and Halliburton. BP's unifying theme was to blame the accident on the other companies. Unlike at Texas City, though, BP did not authorize a rigorous review of its own management failings. Two upper-level executives were fired as a result of the costly incident: Tony Hayward, the CEO whose performance during the Gulf spill crisis was lackluster to say the least, and Andy Inglis, Hayward's number two who served as BP's head of exploration. Hayward is now representing a consortium of wealthy investors looking for new oil deposits in Iraq. Inglis is the chairman and CEO of Kosmos Energy Ltd., a company described by *Bloomberg* as a "10-year-old company with a market value of about $4.4 billion" that is "the oil wildcatter behind one of the biggest West African discoveries in decades."[7] No other top executives lost their jobs.

On November 15, 2012, Attorney General Eric Holder announced a settlement of criminal charges against the company that collected an unprecedented total of $4 billion in fines and other penalties.[8] This huge amount included $525 million to settle charges developed by the Securities and Exchange Commission (SEC) that BP had deliberately misled investors by claiming that the size of the spill was 5,000 barrels/day when the company had developed data indicating that the well was gushing far more than that amount. In February 2013, the DOJ settled a case against Transocean for Clean Water Act violations for $400 million in fines. Federal prosecutors collected $200,000 in criminal penalties from Halliburton for destroying evidence – namely, modeling conducted several weeks after the blowout that showed the safety implications of using 21 as opposed to 6 centralizers. Halliburton, which has close ties to the Republican Party through former CEO and Bush administration Vice President Richard Cheney, also agreed to donate $55 million to the National Fish and Wildlife Foundation.

The Justice Department obtained indictments against BP mid-level managers Robert Kaluza and Donald Vidrine, the well supervisors or "company men" aboard the Deepwater Horizon. In an unusually severe indictment made possible by a federal law dating back to the 1800s, prosecutors charged the two men with manslaughter, or the unintentional killing of their 11 fellow

[7]   Bradley Olson, *Kosmos Hires Former BP Exec Inglis in Billion Barrel Hunt*, BLOOMBERG NEWS, Jan. 13, 2013, http://www.bloomberg.com/news/2014-01-13/kosmos-hires-former-bp-explorer-inglis-in-billion-barrel-hunt.html.

[8]   Azmat Khan, *BP to Pay Record $4.5 Billion for 2010 Gulf Oil Spill*, FRONTLINE (Nov. 15, 2012), http://www.pbs.org/wgbh/pages/frontline/business-economy-financial-crisis/the-spill/bp-to-pay-record-4-5-billion-for-2010-gulf-oil-spill/.

workers.[9] A third man, David Rainey, BP's second in command on the federal taskforce that struggled for three months to close the well, has been charged with lying about the volume of oil that was spilling, a sensitive point because the company claimed at the time that a mere 5,000 barrels/day were spilling from the hole, when 60,000 was the accurate number. All three men pled not guilty and are expected to go to trial. A fourth man, Kurt Mix, a former BP engineer, was charged with obstructing the federal criminal investigation when he deleted text messages and voicemails after the spill began. He was convicted by a jury on one of two charges in December 2013. The Halliburton employee who actually ordered the destruction of evidence, Anthony Badalamenti, was charged individually with one misdemeanor count, and was sentenced to probation, 100 hours of community service, and payment of a $1,000 fine.

Federal prosecutors have said that their investigation is ongoing, leaving open the possibility, if not the likelihood given the many years that have passed, that more senior corporate officials could be charged.

No image better conveys the implications of the disaster than the photograph of President Obama crouching on a Louisiana beach, grimacing at a tar ball he retrieved from the sand. And no episode was more revelatory about the Obama administration's confused energy policy than the outlandish claim by White House energy advisor Carol Browner, a former administrator of the EPA who should have known better, that five months after the well was sealed, the "vast majority" of the spilled oil was "gone."[10] The truth was that federal officials had made the decision to allow BP to disperse the oil with a chemical mixture known as Corexit that had never been tested for toxicity. Some 1.8 million gallons of this mystery mixture broke the oil from a shiny slick into thinner black liquid that was not nearly as visible. The environment paid a heavy price for this expedient. Scientists later concluded that the addition of the dispersant made the oil 52-fold more toxic to representative aquatic life than the crude oil alone. Years later, ecologists still do not have a firm grip on how the spill undermined the complex natural systems in the Gulf.

---

9   *See* Tom Zeller, Jr. & John Rudolf, *BP Oil Spill Settlement Announced, Robert Kaluza and Donald Vidrine Charged With Manslaughter*, HUFFINGTON POST, Nov. 15, 2012, http://www. huffingtonpost.com/2012/11/15/bp-oil-spill_n_2136063.html; Clifford Krauss, *In BP Indictments, U.S. Shifts to Hold Individuals Accountable*, N.Y. TIMES, Nov. 15, 2012, http://www.nytimes. com/2012/11/16/business/energy-environment/in-bp-indictments-us-shifts-to-hold-individuals-accountable.html. However, note that some of the manslaughter charges against Kaluza and Vidrine have been dismissed (as of December 2013). Nate Raymond, *Ex-BP Supervisors Win Dismissal of Some Manslaughter Charges*, REUTERS, Dec. 10, 2013, http://www.reuters.com/ article/2013/12/11/us-bp-spill-idUSBRE9BA01U20131211.

10 Jim Polson & Allison Bennett, *"Vast Majority" of Oil Gone from Gulf, Browner Says*, BLOOMBERG NEWS, Aug. 4, 2010, http://www.bloomberg.com/news/2010-08-04/-vast-major ity-of-oil-gone-from-gulf-of-mexico-u-s-energy-adviser-says.html.

The political backlash against the Obama administration was exacerbated by the fact that just three weeks earlier, on March 31, 2010, the president held a press conference against the backdrop of a Green Hornet fighter jet to announce that in order to end the nation's dependence on foreign oil, he would expand offshore drilling on southern and western coasts. In a clear break with bipartisan policies that limited offshore drilling for 20 years, his administration would expand well-field leasing off the coast of Virginia, in the eastern portion of the Gulf of Mexico near Florida, and in Alaska's Beaufort Sea. "We'll employ new technologies that reduce the impact of oil exploration. We'll protect areas that are vital to tourism, the environment, and our national security. And we'll be guided not by political ideology, but by scientific evidence," he said.[11]

Conservative Republicans soon dubbed the disaster "Obama's Katrina"[12] and progressives urged him to embrace and articulate the importance of the federal government's role in mitigating such disasters.[13] Despite reelection in 2012 by a healthy margin of several million votes, the Obama administration has yet to improve the offshore regulatory framework to the point that blowouts will not recur. Fortunately, the oil industry itself has made significant progress in developing, building, and deploying equipment capable of sealing a blown out well far faster.

As has become the norm, investigators from a variety of organizations converged on the scene. An Oil Spill Commission was appointed by President Obama to analyze the causes of the incident and make broad recommendations regarding how another catastrophe could be prevented. Chaired by former Senator Bob Graham (D-FL) and former EPA Administrator William Reilly, it issued two hard-hitting reports – the first signed by Commission members[14] and the second produced by its General Counsel and his staff.[15] The following analysis relies on these documents; Abrahm Lustgarten's 2012 book *Run to Failure: BP and the Making of the Deepwater Horizon Disaster;*[16] a more technical but equally interesting 2012 book by industrial disaster expert Andrew Hopkins entitled *Disastrous Decisions: The Human and Organisational Causes of the Gulf of Mexico Blowout;*[17] and exemplary

---

[11] Abrahm Lustgarten, Run to Failure: BP and the Making of the Deepwater Horizon Disaster 299 (2012).

[12] Joe Weisenthal, *FLASHBACK:The Gulf Oil Spill is Obama's Katrina*, Business Insider (May 27, 2010), http://www.businessinsider.com/deepwater-horizon-obamas-katrina-2010-4.

[13] Frank Rich, *Obama's Katrina? Maybe Worse*, N.Y. Times, May 29, 2010.

[14] Report to the President, *supra* note 2.

[15] Chief Counsel's Report, *supra* note 2.

[16] Abrahm Lustgarten, Run to Failure, BP and the Making of the Deepwater Horizon Disaster 133 (2012).

[17] Andrew Hopkins, Disastrous Decisions: The Human and Organisational Causes of the Gulf of Mexico Blowout (2012).

reporting by American media. Because criminal charges would be far more productive in deterring future risk taking within the industry if they focus on the behavior that caused the blowout, I also end the story right after it occurred without exploring BP's lengthy efforts to seal the well.

The Frankenstein Effect

As generations of liberal arts undergraduates know only too well, Mary Shelley's 1818 novel *Frankenstein* has spawned a treasure trove of papers on the so-called "Frankenstein effect" – the idea that humans can lose control of technology, creating nightmarish destruction of their natural environment and themselves. In a sense, pressing the envelope of technology in a hectic manner by taking poorly controlled, unacceptable risks is the beginning and end of what happened on April 20, 2010, when the cumulative effects of a series of bad judgments went unchecked by a shockingly dysfunctional management structure.

Everyone aboard the Deepwater Horizon that day and all of the people providing support onshore were well aware that drilling an oil well in very deep water is an extraordinarily hazardous process. Maintaining a balance between pressure in the drilling pipe and pressure rising from the well is a delicate endeavour, depending on the consideration of multiple factors. As much vigilance as drilling the well requires, those circumstances are routine in comparison to the task of temporarily closing the well. Like a syringe submerged in liquid, extricating the drill is like pulling a plunger: it causes liquids at the bottom of the well to rise rapidly, threatening a blow-out. But because the goal of the operation is to suppress the volatile contents of the well, temporary closure requires days of effort, as teams struggle to stabilize the casing that shored up the long column through which the drilling equipment had penetrated, slowly withdrawing that equipment while filling the mouth of the well with specially formulated cement, all in murky depths with unmanned equipment that is difficult to position and read.

Compounding the technical difficulties of the process is the fact that employees working for several companies are integrally involved in decision making regarding temporary abandonment of the well. At Macondo, there were five: BP, the lead investor; Transocean, the owner and operator of the rig; Halliburton, provider of the cement to plug the hole; Sperry Sun, a subsidiary of Halliburton, hired by BP to monitor the use of drilling mud to equalize pressure as the drill bit was withdrawn and the well was sealed; and Schlumberger, a consultant hired to conduct vital tests regarding the condition of the well prior to closing. All of the contractors, including the vast majority of the Transocean employees on the rig, worked for BP and its investment partners and, with one notable exception, appear to have been overly committed to keeping the customer happy. The exception was a man named Jesse Gagliano, who worked for Halliburton onsite and was assigned responsibility for testing the cement to ensure it would harden properly. For reasons that are not entirely clear but will undoubtedly come out in lawsuits to determine the apportionment of damages among the companies, BP managers were so disgusted with Gagliano that they asked Halliburton to withdraw him from the job. Before that move could be accomplished, Gagliano tried to warn them that their temporary abandonment plans were unduly risky. His advice fell on deaf ears.

Of course, none of these onsite workers would knowingly risk their own lives, and employees working onshore, generally white collar professionals, also had ample incentives to prevent a blowout. Rather, the problem was the acute dysfunction in the *ad hoc* process for making decisions. Far too many people participated in different aspects of the challenging process without any single person having both ultimate accountability and full authority to ensure the operation was conducted safely and effectively. Decisions were made by consensus, often using email. In the end, the Oil Spill Commission attributed much of the blame for the disaster to BP, producing a damning chart of nine decisions that "increased risk at Macondo while potentially saving time."[18] It attributed seven to "BP onshore"– namely, the engineers in Houston. The chart is replicated as Figure 5-1, below. It may well serve as an important exhibit when the criminal cases against Robert Kaluza and Donald Vidrine, BP's well site leaders, are tried.

Proximate Causes

Fifty-one days and $58 million over their original drilling plan, with delays costing $1 million/day just in rig rental fees, BP managers pushed so hard to plug the well that their errors began to multiply. Most accounts focus on five decisions that investigators deemed to be the most important causes of the blowout. The risk they created was cumulative.

The Long String
To accomplish temporary abandonment, BP and Transocean needed to insert a last liner – or "production casing" – into the well. They had two options:

---

[18] REPORT TO THE PRESIDENT, *supra* note 2, at 125.

Decision	Was There a Less Risky Alternative Available?	Less Time Than Alternative?	Decision Maker
Not Waiting for More Centralizers of Preferred Design	Yes	Saved Time	BP Onshore
Not Waiting for Foam Stability Test Results and/or Redesigning Slurry	Yes	Saved Time	Halliburton (and Perhaps BP) Onshore
Not Runnning Cement Evaluation Log	Yes	Saved Time	BP Onshore
Using Spacer Made from Combined Lost Circulation Materials to Avoid Disposal Issues	Yes	Saved Time	BP Onshore
Displacing Mud from Riser Before Setting Surface Cement Plug	Yes	Unclear	BP Onshore
Setting Surface Cement Plug 3,000 Feet Below Mud Line in Seawater	Yes	Unclear	BP Onshore (approved by MMS)
Not Installing Additional Physical Barriers During Temporary Abandonment Procedure	Yes	Saved Time	BP Onshore
Not Performing Further Well Integrity Diagnostics in Light of Troubling and Unexplained Negative Pressure Test Results	Yes	Saved Time	BP (and Perhaps Transocean) on Rig
Bypassing Pits and Conducting Other Simultaneous Operations During Displacement	Yes	Saved Time	Transocean (and Perhaps BP) on Rig

FIGURE 5-1: Examples of decisions that increased risk at Macondo while potentially saving time. Source: Oil Spill Commission Report at 246

setting a "long string" or using a "liner and tieback." Both had pros and cons, although the second option was the most commonly used, was more expensive, and, while it had the potential to cause more problems when the well converted to permanent production, it was considered significantly less risky during temporary abandonment. From a safety perspective, the essential difference between the two alternatives was that a long string approach depended exclusively on successfully cementing the bottom of the hole, with only the blowout preventer available to control a kick. In contrast, the liner/tieback option was accomplished lower in the well and involved a second shutoff device that segregated the annulus (empty spaces between the drill pipe and the liner), significantly reducing the risk of blowout.

BP chose the long string, making a successful cement job absolutely essential to plug the well.

Centralizers

BP's plan to close the well called for the gradual removal of all drilling mud and its replacement with much lighter seawater. This process is precarious because the drill shaft may sway, causing drilling mud and cement to mix together and preventing cement from reaching the bottom of the well and setting properly. To prevent this development, deepwell developers use equipment known as "centralizers" to stabilize the shaft.

Halliburton has a proprietary (secret even from customers) model that predicts how many centralizers are necessary to obtain a good cement job using a long string. When BP confirmed its choice of a long string, Halliburton engineer Jesse Gagliano ran the model, concluding that no fewer than 21 centralizers would be needed to ensure that uncontaminated cement reached the well bottom. After significant email traffic, BP engineers made the decision to go with six, primarily because it would have taken an additional ten hours to install the full 21. They ignored further protests from Gagliano that this decision would jeopardize the cement job.

Cement

In consultation with Halliburton, BP managers had decided to use "nitrogen foam cement" – a formula that lightened the cement by adding tiny bubbles of nitrogen gas. The advantage of this lighter cement was that it was less likely to fracture the fragile rock formations around the well, avoiding a surge in pressure, a potential kick, and possibly a blowout. If the initial effort to plug the well with cement did not work, BP engineers reasoned, the crew would need to launch a remedial "squeeze" job that involved making holes in the piping near the bottom of the well, and squeezing reinforcing cement through the holes into the annulus (or space) between the pipe and the well's rock and dirt wall. For the engineers, trying one approach first and then turning to the alternative made commercial sense: they would save millions if the first job worked. No one appears to have considered the possibility that given the unpleasant alternative, the crew would fall into the trap of "confirmation bias" – straining to ratify their initial decision regardless of evidence that it was wrong.

Gagliano asked Halliburton laboratory personnel to conduct initial "pilot tests" on the lighter cement. The results showed that this formula was unstable. Gagliano sent these tests to BP engineers on March 8 as an email attachment. According to the Oil Spill Commission, they did not react. Documents gathered after the disaster showed that Halliburton technicians also tested the lighter formula a second time in February 2010 under somewhat different conditions and it failed even more severely. These results were never reported to BP. A third group of tests were conducted in mid-April, just before crews on the rig started pumping the lighter cement. The first of this series, conducted seven days before the blowout, once again showed the formula was unstable. Halliburton technicians then initiated a third test that was designed to run for 48 hours, beginning it on April 18. But the decision to begin pumping the cement on April 20 was made hours before that second test was completed.

BP managers made one final mistake. They had hired a team employed by the consulting firm Schlumberger to perform testing called a "Cement Bond Log" that was designed to verify that the cement was in place and was holding. The Schlumberger team was ready and waiting on the rig. But for reasons that remain unclear, BP managers decided to send the team home without conducting the test. This decision saved the cost of the test – about $128,000 and about ten hours of time, making it among the most penny-wise and pound-foolish decision in modern corporate history. It's worth noting here that when the Schlumberger team was told at 7:00 A.M. on the day of the blowout that BP had decided not to go through with the test, they were sufficiently concerned about the safety of the rig that they demanded a helicopter immediately. They departed at 11:15 A.M., about ten hours ahead of the disaster. Of all the firms involved in the Macondo blowout, Schlumberger has the best reputation for technical rigor and independence.

As the cement injected in the well deteriorated, the stage was set for a very serious kick.

Pressure Testing

BP's last-minute plan for completing temporary abandonment of the well was distributed to the Transocean crew at an 11:00 A.M. meeting on the fateful day in the form of a seven-step list labeled as an "Ops Note." This plan had undergone four iterations in the nine days leading up to its distribution. "There is no evidence that these changes went through any sort of formal risk assessment or management of change process," the Commission stated flatly.[19] A risk assessment considers how the new plan compares to the original one, while a management of change procedure ensures that everyone involved in the new plan is aware of those revisions. Corporations in high-hazard industries like oil drilling typically require both forms of analysis whenever a major change in design or implementation is made.

Steps one and four of the seven-step protocol called for the performance of a "positive pressure test" and a "negative pressure test" to confirm the well's "integrity," or, in other words, that the casing could withstand deepwell

---

[19] *Id.* at 104.

pressure and that the cement job was not leakingh. The positive pressure test began at noon. It involved closing access to the well itself by shutting one of the blowout preventer's blind shear rams. The men then pumped fluid into the piping up to the closed blowout preventer in order to generate high pressure that would allow them to determine whether the well's walls would hold. The well passed this test.

The negative pressure test involves simulating the lower pressure in the well that would occur when the cement sets and the well is temporarily abandoned. The first step in the test is to bleed off any pressure that had built up in the well down to zero pounds per square inch (psi) in the drill pipe. If no liquids or gases flow up from inside the well and the pressure does not increase within the piping, the test would show that the well was sealed. The Macondo crew accomplished these conditions by putting a large quantity of so-called "spacer fluids" down the pipe. The fluids were supposed to separate oil-based drilling mud from seawater. Once this separation was accomplished and the heavy drilling mud was isolated from the seawater, they could reduce pressure in the pipe. But the crew did not use conventional spacer fluids that were specifically designed to accomplish this result. Instead, the engineers convinced themselves that they could use two batches of material that they had on hand to patch fractures in the rock formations leading to the well. They wanted to reuse these materials because the only alternative was to haul them back to shore and pay to have them disposed of as a hazardous waste.

To make a long story short (the description of this aspect of the Macondo blowout consumes many pages in the Oil Spill Commission's two reports), the negative pressure test on the drill pipe did not work. The test began at 5:00 P.M. The crew was unable to get the pressure below 266 psi and even then, it jumped to 1,262 psi after a short time period. The crew tried two more times to lower the pressure. Each time, the pressure initially fell to 0 psi but soon rose again.

At this point, the *ad hoc* group of men present near the control room accepted a remarkable theory advanced by Jason Anderson, a senior tool-pusher on the rig who had spent ten years on the Deepwater Horizon and had considerable influence with other members of the Transocean drilling crew. Tool-pushers at that level of seniority are typically high school graduates who learn on the job and are valuable because of their extensive experience. They foster a strong culture among themselves akin to military *esprit de corps*. According to Anderson, the rise in pressure – essentially, the failure of the test – could be explained by a phenomenon he had heard about called the "bladder effect." He said that leaking around the rubber rings used to seal the gaps between segments of drill pipe allowed enough pressure to infiltrate the drill pipe and cause a small kick. Because the source of the pressure was infiltration from the leaking rings, high readings did not mean that the well itself was leaking. In the aftermath of the blowout, investigators were unable to find any engineering expert in deepwater drilling willing to acknowledge the validity of this theory, which appears in retrospect to be akin to an urban legend, albeit with catastrophic consequences. Jason Anderson was killed in the explosion, blunting somewhat the retrospective criticism of the theory, although it will undoubtedly feature prominently in the ongoing litigation among the three corporate giants.

In any event, as Anderson explained the bladder effect, a crowd of men gathered to debate its validity and the implications of the failed negative pressure test. The two BP company men on the rig – Robert Kaluza and Donald Vidrine, who would later be indicted for eleven counts of manslaughter – initially expressed skepticism about the theory, but eventually backed down in the face of ridicule by the tool-pushers and their own confusion. Remarkably, neither man thought to consult with engineers in Houston. Vidrine insisted that a second, modified negative pressure test be performed. Again without any reliable technical rationale, the crew decided they would simply switch pipes, conducting the test on the "kill line" rather than the drill pipe. The kill line was a relatively small pipe measuring three inches in diameter that was used to circulate fluids into and out of the well. The negative pressure test on this second pipe showed zero psi for 30 minutes. The crew continued to ignore the fact that the drill pipe itself still measured excessive pressure – 1,400 psi for an extended period of time.

Mud Monitoring

Upon completion of the jerry-rigged negative pressure tests, the crew had one final opportunity to confirm that the well was ready to be closed: monitoring the outflow of drilling mud as it was pumped from the pipes and displaced with seawater. The amount of mud should be the same as the amount BP had sent into the well. If the total volume was less, the shortfall would constitute a serious warning that the well was leaking, the cement job had not worked, and a kick was possible. But, once again, a fatal shortcut was taken. Rather than pumping the mud into huge containers on the surface of the rig's deck where it could be measured, it was pumped overboard into supply vessels moored alongside the Deepwater Horizon. At some point, the pumping was re-directed into the sea. Both practices were a serious departure from routine protocols.

Blowout

Pressure in the drill pipe continued to build, although the crew did not realize the significance of this development until 9:30 P.M. The crew shut off the pumps to investigate. Drill pipe pressure decreased briefly once the pumps were off, but began to climb again. At 9:39 P.M., the pressure suddenly began to fall, in what the Oil Spill Commission said was "in retrospect ... a very bad sign [because] lighter-weight hydrocarbons were now pushing heavy drilling mud out of the way up the casing past the drill pipe."[20] At about 9:40 P.M., mud began to spew on deck. By 9:45 P.M. the mud had reached the top of the derrick as the crew tried desperately and unsuccessfully to close in the well. The first explosion occurred at 9:49 P.M.

The Oil Spill Commission and, especially, its General Counsel's Team chided BP senior managers for failing to establish adequate training programs and for neglecting to write internal protocols that would require risk assessment at every stage of such a dangerous operation. They criticized BP engineers for failing to appreciate the cumulative risk caused by the rush to complete temporary abandonment. They condemned Transocean employees for standing by passively as BP skirted closer and closer to practices never tried before, especially the cost-saving use of the recycled well sealant and the adoption of the strange bladder effect theory. But their sharpest disdain was reserved for BP engineers and well managers, with the General Counsel's Team stating:

> BP engineers certainly recognized some of these risk factors and even tried to address some of them. ... But it does not appear that any one person on BP's team – whether in Houston or on the rig – ever identified all of the risk factors. Nor does it appear that BP ever communicated the above risks to its other contractors, primarily the Transocean rig crew. ... More importantly, there is no indication that BP's team ever reviewed the *combined impact* of these risk factors or tried to assess the overall likelihood that the cement job would succeed, either on their own or in consultation with Halliburton. Rather, BP appeared to treat risk factors as surmountable and then forgettable. ... Reviewing the aggregate effect of risk factors may not even have led BP to change any of its design decisions. But if done properly, it may have led BP engineers to mitigate the overall risk in ways that could have prevented the blowout.[21]

Evacuating the Rig

The two groups of federal officials most heavily implicated in the Macondo blowout – regulators from the Minerals Management Service who were responsible for the safety of drilling operations and Coast Guard officers who bore responsibility for crew safety – undertook their own joint

---

[20] *Id.* at 113.
[21] CHIEF COUNSEL'S REPORT, *supra* note 2, at 103.

investigation of the disaster.[22] The MMS was reorganized out of existence within weeks of the incident and regulators were assigned to the newly formed Bureau of Ocean Energy Management, Regulation, and Enforcement, which was then renamed as the Bureau of Safety, Environment, and Enforcement. Their voluminous 562-page reports are the most detailed, if not the most incisive, accounts of what went on in the several days leading up to the blowout and the 48 hours that followed the rig's eruption in flame. Of the two, the Coast Guard report is the most valuable because it covers ground given relatively short shrift in other reports: how did people get off the rig and why were 11 men left aboard when they might have been alive when the rig was abandoned? The account makes depressing reading.

Incredibly, Transocean had never conducted a single training exercise that simulated a blowout of sufficient severity to require evacuation of the rig. The rig held regular fire drills, but they occurred at the same time and on the same day every week and drilling personnel were excused from these exercises. The crew regarded them as a tedious distraction. The average public elementary school does better.

The direct consequences of these remarkable omissions were that no general alarm sounded immediately after gas detectors went off. No one conducted a head count before all of the available lifeboats and rafts were deployed, leaving open the horrible possibility that they deployed before everyone had a chance to get off the rig. Instead, people not seriously injured by flying debris, burns, or smoke ran helter-skelter – some to lifeboats and some to jump directly into the water. An alarm was eventually sounded, a "May Day" was belatedly phoned into shore, and a delayed effort was made to activate the blowout protector. No one can be certain what would have happened if a better trained crew had taken all three actions as soon as evidence of a kick first emerged.

The lack of training for a blowout evacuation and a casual attitude toward the worst case scenario also meant that serious problems in the lifeboat area were never recognized. The area was not shielded from the heat of a fire that could incinerate the escape vessels. The configuration of the boats and rafts made it very difficult to load a stretcher or even to seat a tall crew worker on board.

---

[22] U.S. Dep't of Interior, Bureau of Ocean Energy Management, Regulation and Enforcement, Report Regarding the Causes of the April 20, 2010 Macondo Well Blowout (2011), *available at* http://www.bsee.gov/uploadedFiles/DWHFINALDOI-VolumeII.pdf; U.S. Coast Guard, Report of Investigation into the Circumstances Surrounding the Explosion, Fire, Sinking and Loss of Eleven Crew Members Aboard the Mobile Offshore Drilling Unit Deepwater Horizon in the Gulf of Mexico, April 20–22, 2010 (2011), *available at* http://permanent.access.gpo.gov/gpo16794/Vol.%201/2_DH%20Volume%201_redacted_3.pdf.

Burdened with people, one raft was successfully lowered into the water, only to remain tied to the rig as occupants tried to paddle away. One man was tossed in the water – he was later retrieved – and, in their panic, the others in the boat almost did not manage to free the raft before debris rained on their heads.

The death toll might well have been much higher but for the great luck that a supply ship named the Damon B. Bankston was located nearby and was able to use fast rescue craft to rescue at least fifteen survivors. No one knew what the death toll was until the survivors assembled aboard that ship and a complete count was taken. The bodies of the eleven killed aboard the Deepwater Horizon were never found because the rig sank within two days of the blowout. One reason for that outcome was that the rig was so badly maintained that several of its supposedly watertight barriers failed, flooding portions of the rig.

The Coast Guard identified several other maintenance problems that exacerbated the blowout, included gas detectors that were either inoperable or had been shut off so that constant sirens did not disturb the sleep of off-shift crew. The Deepwater Horizon was not fitted with adequate blast protection for the crew. Barriers separating the "drill floor" at the bottom of the derrick from living quarters would slow fire but they did not resist explosion. Electrical equipment close to the point where mud and gas erupted from the well was corroded, and investigators speculated that sparks from these sources may have triggered the explosion. When power failed, the crew did not have access to nonelectric (e.g., diesel-powered) extinguishers.

Management Dysfunction

Safety expert Anthony Hopkins attributes the many errors in judgment made aboard the rig to a blatantly dysfunctional management structure. He argues quite persuasively that as disastrous as the Texas City refinery explosion was for the corporation's reputation and bottom line (for want of a few hundred thousand dollars in maintenance costs, 15 workers were killed and BP paid out at least $2 billion in personal injury claims), the corporation's CEO and the senior executives who surrounded him in London never stopped focusing on cost-cutting and downplaying process safety. This fixation at the top was communicated down through the corporation, settling on the shoulders of mid- and low-level (operational) managers like a cold fog.

BP and Transocean executives constantly looked over their shoulders at cost overruns and drilling delays. Their articulated reasons for bad decisions were that the chosen approaches would save time and time is money. On top of the frenzied atmosphere prompted by the Macondo well's delays and the need to get the Deepwater Horizon off to its next job, BP's entire system of financial incentives for its employees made staying on schedule wise and veering off it quite expensive. BP managers monitored the rig's operating costs on a daily basis to see how far they had deviated from the expenditures authorized under the original plan. The company also employed "cost analysts" and "cost engineers" who reported these results up the line to more senior executives. In contrast and perhaps needless to say, the benefits of avoiding a blowout were never quantified. Despite the obvious and extensive evidence to the contrary, no one thought an incident of the magnitude of Macondo was anything but a remote possibility.

To drive home the message that time is money, the executives responsible for oil production in the Gulf benchmarked the pace of production there in comparison to other drilling organizations elsewhere in the world, including both BP and its corporate competitors. Before beginning to drill a well, managers and engineers would meet to "drill the well on paper" – a term of art meaning meetings held to analyze each step in the complicated process. A central goal of this table exercise was to consider the best times achieved by other entities. Of course, drilling in reality often fell behind schedule for a variety of reasons, especially geological complications (for example, fragile rock formations near the well head), but the acceptance of these deviations was always short-circuited by the recrimination that other, better groups had surmounted similar challenges even faster. Hopkins explains that this approach to costs created an "every dollar counts" culture, which degenerated into such pettiness that the chief of drilling operations for the Gulf of Mexico – in itself a multi-billion-dollar business – was twice asked to explain to the executives above him why he was buying coffee for his Houston headquarters that cost $70/month more than another specific brand.[23]

Like many businesses, BP offered managers bonuses based on performance that could amount to as much as 50 percent of their base salaries. One key criterion for determining eligibility for a bonus was speed of drilling, a double-edged sword if ever there was one. When regulators reviewed the performance evaluations of Macondo BP personnel, twelve of thirteen referred to cost-savings as a specific performance measure.

Like their counterparts at the Texas City refinery, on the rare occasion when BP managers in the Gulf did focus on safety, they confused two disparate types of indicators: personal safety (preventing falls on a slippery deck) versus process safety (preventing a kick or blowout). BP and Transocean managers prided themselves that the rig had an exemplary individual safety record. But the managers were haphazard when deploying the most basic techniques

[23] ANDREW HOPKINS, DISASTROUS DECISIONS: THE HUMAN AND ORGANISATIONAL CAUSES OF THE GULF OF MEXICO BLOWOUT 86 (2012).

necessary to ensure process safety. Especially in the last two weeks before the crew attempted to temporarily abandon the well, tools like iterative risk assessments and management of change procedures fell by the wayside.

The neglect of these internal controls in turn produced alarming corner-cutting, with decisions made to short-circuit, circumvent, or misinterpret crucial tests needed to assess well integrity. Onsite and onshore managers took gambles that were not just life-threatening but beyond any margin of what an objective expert would consider reasonable risk. Because these same problems were featured so prominently in the reports issued after Texas City, including an investigation launched by BP itself and chaired by no less prominent a figure than former U.S. Secretary of State James Baker, it is fair to attribute responsibility for their persistence to the two corporations' most senior managers, including CEO John Browne and his successor, Tony Hayward. Surely these people should be held personally accountable for failing to master the implications of the reports, as well as failing to take mitigating action.

Hopkins notes that from the top down, the giant corporation embraced a self-image of intrepid and fearless explorer, attributing its rapid growth and startling profits to that ethos. A fierce commitment to doing "whatever it takes" to achieve the next commercial milestone of corporate success was paramount. Hopkins quotes BP executive Andy Inglis, then head of its exploration and production department, who wrote in 2007:

> BP operate[s] on the frontiers of the energy industry – geographically, technically and in terms if business partnerships. Challenges and risks are our daily bread. ... Companies like BP increasingly work in extreme weather conditions, in increasingly deep water and in complex rock formations. ... There are five key advantages [of being an international oil company]. First, taking major risks; second, assembling large and diversified portfolios; third, building deep intellectual and technical capability; fourth, making best use of global integration; and, finally, forging long-term, mutually beneficial, partnerships ... So, first, risk.[24]

Ironically, Inglis lost his job in the aftermath of the Macondo blowout.

Accountability Diffused

Daily operations on board the Deepwater Horizon were governed by a garbled management structure that was decentralized, multilayered, and diffuse. Figure 5-2, taken from the Oil Spill Commission's General Counsel's Team

---

[24] *Id.* at 15–16 (bracketed additions in original).

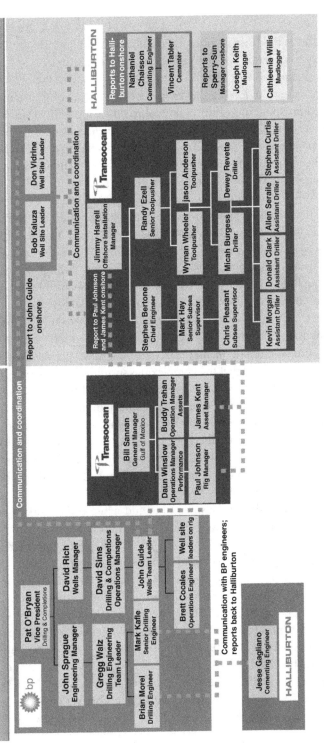

FIGURE 5-2: Organizational Chart for Drilling of the Macondo Well. Source: Oil Spill Commission, General Counsel's Report

report, shows the lines of authority onshore and offshore for the three most active corporate entities: BP, Transocean, and Halliburton.

This organizational chart illustrates the complexity of the chains of command in a multitude of dimensions: onshore versus offshore; corporation versus corporation and, within that realm, customer (BP) versus contractors (Transocean, Halliburton); management versus line workers; and engineers versus operational personnel. It also indicates that the rig did not have a single person in command of all its disparate operations. Hopkins notes that the daily operation of the rig was controlled largely by Transocean tool-pushers, who had no formal training in engineering. Instead, they had worked their way up the organizational hierarchy from the entry-level position of roughneck. For example, the person who advocated the theory of the bladder effect was a senior tool-pusher whose career followed exactly this trajectory and who was a natural leader among the men who manned the drilling controls. Their understanding of the perils of deepwater drilling may well have been excellent, but it was undoubtedly different from the knowledge base of BP's engineers, placed mainly onshore, who had studied the dynamics of the equipment and its potential effects on the geology of the well from a completely different, more theoretical, yet disciplined perspective. To some extent, BP recognized that the complexities surrounding temporary abandonment demanded careful supervision by deepwater drilling experts trained in the engineering alternatives used to accomplish this hazardous operation. But instead of deploying a group of such professionals out to the rig, if not at all the times then at least during the most crucial two weeks when final decisions were implemented, BP kept the engineers in Houston. BP and Transocean's failure to knit the two together laid the seeds for adoption of the bladder effect theory and the final mistakes before the blowout.

Compounding the rift between blue and white collar workers and intercorporate tensions, which were exacerbated by a distance of many miles and the BP engineers' inability to sense what was happening on the rig without filtering by the Transocean crew, the engineering department was hobbled by two additional, inexplicable practices. First, engineers were supervised by well site managers who were responsible primarily for keeping cost overruns in check, as opposed to more senior engineers with enough clout within the corporation to prevail in any important disagreement over the best practices of their profession. BP recognized the problems with this inappropriate command structure and was in the process of creating a more independent engineering department when the rig blew.

Second, the engineers consulted with each other via email, and followed consensus-based decision making. Or, in other words, one engineer would send email to a group of other engineers, often with complex technical documents as attachments, and ask recipients whether anyone had a problem with a proposed solution. In an incident highlighted by Hopkins, several recipients did not respond, much as recipients of any large group email often behave in far less momentous situations. The absence of any individual accountability that is produced by a consensus-based process and intensified by the technology of email and its use to send messages to large groups of people in an instant also means that any decision depends on the composition of the group and inevitable distortions of "group-think." Hopkins writes:

> This de facto practice of collective decision-making paved the way for various psychological processes to take over. The first is the phenomenon of "risky shift." It has been experimentally demonstrated that groups are often more inclined to make risk decisions than individual group members would make when acting alone.... [W]hen decisions are to be made by small groups, there is a presumption that they will be unanimous. There is no logical reason why this should be so. In larger groups, we are happy to accept majority decision-making, but in small groups, the presumption is that everyone will agree. [T]he doubters are in a strong position because they have the power to block consensus. But this in turn means that enormous pressure may be brought to bear on them by other members of the group ...[25]

Once again, these phenomena are illustrated by the crucial juncture when bladder effect was accepted by a group that included Kaluza and Vidrine, who stifled their doubts in the face of teasing by the Transocean crew.

Death in the Sea

As the spill spread throughout the Gulf region, familiar pictures of pelicans coated in crude oil started to appear in the media. BP made the decision to use a detergent-like dispersant called Corexit to break up the oil into more soluble droplets in an effort to prevent oily slicks from reaching Gulf coast beaches just as the summer tourist season was about to start and, not incidentally, avoiding more inflammatory pelican pictures. Some 1.8 million gallons of dispersant were dumped in the water in the effort. Because dispersant had never been used on a spill of this magnitude and Corexit's toxicity had never been tested, the long-term effects of this approach on natural resources were – and are – unknown.

Three central concerns recur in any discussion of the spill's effect on nature, including damage to (1) endangered species such as the brown pelican, northern gannets (a white seabird), and laughing gulls; (2) ecosystems in the deep ocean

---

[25] *Id.* at 47–48.

that support marine life as a whole; and (3) the $40 billion in fishing and tourism that sustains the economy of the Gulf. Unfortunately, funding was not immediately available for independent scientific research. Environmentalists in the Gulf region accused BP of hiring every available expert in the range of a few hundred miles, opportunistically creating conflicts of interest that stymied efforts to get an independent perspective on the spill's ecological implications. Uncertainties about the size of the spill and the adverse effects of using Corexit further frustrated independent work. By the time the money began to flow more freely and experts without ties to BP could be located, the opportunity to establish a comprehensive baseline for pre-spill conditions in the Gulf was lost.

The most prominent scientists now working in the Gulf agree that we will not grasp the full effects of the spill for many years. As part of their settlements with the DOJ, BP and Transocean were compelled to donate billions to this effort. The U.S. Department of the Interior is also in the midst of an effort to quantify the value of natural resources for the purposes of another huge lawsuit that will seek recovery of those sums, which are likely to be in the many billions of dollars, from BP, Transocean, and Halliburton. Unless it is settled, the case will be among the most complex ever staged in an American courtroom because the values underlying such assessments are so poorly established. As just one, first order question, how can we quantify the value of natural systems that human beings do not use unless we can somehow establish that without them, we would not have fish to eat? Or, to put it another way, do oceans have value to us beyond serving as a food source? And, if so, what is that value and how do we quantify it?

Perhaps anticipating this fight, BP's top executives, who in the early days of the spill had dutifully done a kind of "perp walk" into the Oval Office to meet with President Obama, emerging from the meeting with the pledge to pay $20 billion to compensate Gulf residents, have recently done a 180-degree turn in the middle of the road. They now accuse applicants for relief of filing fraudulent claims for funding. The corporation balked when a settlement fund it estimated as being worth approximately $7 billion, looked as if it might climb upwards, approaching $9.6 billion. BP's original lawyers on that case had negotiated a payment scheme that did not require claimants to prove a link between their losses and the spill. After firing that law firm, BP hired a more aggressive team and tried to get out from under the liability, taking full-page ads out in national newspapers like the *Washington Post* and the *New York Times* that ridiculed claimants and having the British government open diplomatic channels to discuss the problem; BP stock is a prominent feature of British pension fund investments. In March 2014, a three-judge panel on the Fifth Circuit Court of Appeals rejected BP's efforts to get out from under this settlement reasoning that the company was well aware of its terms when it signed on and should not be permitted to exercise buyer's remorse.[26]

If BP decides to litigate natural resource damage claims, funds for restoration, as opposed to research, could be unavailable for many years.

BP as Rogue

Led by ExxonMobil, which has its own ragged history of environmental damage, the largest American oil companies have gone to considerable lengths to advance the dual theories that BP is a rogue company and that apart from the Macondo blowout, which was caused by BP's unique brand of corporate recklessness, deepwater drilling in the Gulf is absolutely safe. In testimony before Congress in June 2010, the chairmen of ExxonMobil, Chevron, Shell, and ConocoPhillips portrayed BP as an outlier in the industry and claimed that they do not operate as it does, especially with respect to cutting corners to save time and money. "We would not have drilled the well the way they did," pronounced Rex Tillerson, chief executive of ExxonMobil.[27] The Oil Spill Commission explicitly rejected this conclusion, highlighting the active participation of Transocean and Halliburton in the fiasco of decision making that preceded the blowout as the best evidence that inappropriate risk taking is an industry-wide problem.

The backbone of the claim that BP was a rogue on a reckless mission is the company's admittedly terrible track record with respect to regulatory violations. BP certainly leads the industry with respect to OSHA citations for violations of workplace safety requirements, primarily because of the unusually rigorous inspections it endured after the Texas City refinery explosion in 2005. But other companies have hosted comparably deadly – and avoidable – incidents. In 2010, seven workers were killed at a Tesoro refinery in Washington state. In 2012, a fire at a Chevron refinery located on the San Francisco Bay sent thousands of residents to local hospitals. When the OSHA responded to these episodes by expanding and intensifying its inspections within the refinery sector, an effort that continued until the agency ran out of funding, it concluded that poor maintenance and ineffective safety systems are chronic throughout the industry. A 2010 study done by the private sector group RiskMetrics, which used as indicia fatalities, injuries, spills, and regulatory citations, found that although BP was in the bottom quartile of

---

[26] *In re* Deepwater Horizon, ___ F.3d ___, 2014 WL 841313 (5th Cir. 2014).

[27] John M. Broder, *Oil Executives Break Ranks in Testimony*, N.Y. TIMES, June 16, 2010, http://www.nytimes.com/2010/06/16/business/16oil.html?_r=0.

companies included in the survey, Shell and Chevron joined it there, while ExxonMobil landed in the second-lowest quartile.

As for the industry's track record offshore, a *New York Times/Greenwire* story published in June 2010 reported that an analysis of MMS records demonstrates that BP's performance was comparable to other major oil companies.[28] As for the assessment of civil penalties between 1997 and 2010, Chevron was the worst, at $2.1 million, while Kerr-McGee Corp. and Anadarko Petroleum Corp. (which have merged) came in second at $781,000. BP was third, paying $766,000. In 2009, eight BP workers were injured offshore. But Chevron and Murphy Exploration & Production Co. had nine, ATP Oil & Gas Corp. had four, and ExxonMobil had three. BP was not cited in 2009 for loss of well control, but citations were issued to Stone Energy Corp., Murphy, and LLOG Exploration Offshore Inc. BP had four fires, but Chevron had fifteen, ExxonMobil had fourteen, and Kerr-McGee had two.

In May 2010, the Obama administration issued a moratorium on new exploration projects in the Gulf that lasted until the following October. When the ban was lifted, the administration was attacked from the left by environmentalists, who thought it should have lasted longer, and by oil industry representatives, who fretted that companies would have to comply with more stringent permitting rules. Once the dust settled, the push out to the edge of the envelope of what technology can manage safely once again picked up speed.

One excellent example of the risks at stake in this development is a $3 billion rig called Perdido, a Spanish word that, depending on context, can mean lost, incorrigible, or in trouble. Other rigs share equally unfortunate names, such as Blind Faith, Mad Dog, and Atlantis. Perdido is operated by Royal Dutch Shell in water 9,600 feet deep at a mooring point 200 miles from shore. Supply boats must travel 20 hours to reach it. The Perdido is designed to produce up to 130,000 barrels of oil daily, relying on a complex web of wells that will extend over 30 miles on the ocean floor. Instead of pumping oil to the platform and separating oil from gas and water there, as is done at the vast majority of comparable facilities, engineers designed new separation equipment on the sea floor near the wells, improving efficiency, but making equipment much harder to monitor and repair. Water at those depths wreaks havoc with equipment, especially when hurricanes, which have increased in intensity, sweep through the Gulf. How the Perdido would be evacuated in the event of a severe blowout is unclear.

The *New York Times* reported in the summer of 2010 that more than 20 percent of all 2009 bids in the Gulf were for leases covering water deeper

---

[28] Mike Soraghan, *Industry Claims of "Proven" Technology Went Unchallenged at MMS*, N.Y. Times, June 2, 2010, http://www.nytimes.com/gwire/2010/06/02/02greenwire-industry-claims-of-proven-technology-went-unch-55514.html.

than 6,500 feet.[29] Edward Chow, a former industry executive and fellow at the Center for Strategic and International Studies predicted more bad times: "Our ability to manage risks hasn't caught up with our ability to explore and produce in deep water. The question now is, how are we going to protect against a blowout as well as all of the other associated risks offshore?"[30]

Given these escalating levels of risk, protecting worker safety and the environment depends either on industry self-regulation or on dramatic improvements in federal oversight. Unfortunately, the regulatory failures that were prevalent in the lead-up to that blowout have not been addressed.

REGULATORY FAILURE: A FUNDAMENTAL CONFLICT OF INTEREST

Leasing a Billion Acres

Oil and gas companies the world over are known for a kind of relentless pride of place. When I worked on Capitol Hill for James Florio (D-NJ), a congressman who was sponsoring legislation to prevent leaking from underground storage tanks at gas stations across the country, my far more experienced boss, the subcommittee's staff director, warned that a paper I was producing would have a half-life of 30 seconds. As soon as it was distributed, oil and gas lobbyists would pick it apart. His message was to be ready and, to the furthest reaches of my ability, to make it good. He was right, of course, and although we had the wind at our backs of fervent and popular environmentalism, whether we would make it past this gauntlet and on to the enactment of a good law was by no means a foregone conclusion. We did, but by a whisker, not a nose.

The regulatory failure that made Macondo possible began three decades before the well blew, when Ronald Reagan appointed James Watt the Secretary of the Department of the Interior and Watt founded the MMS. Its overriding purpose was to promote drilling on the Outer Continental Shelf. The Shelf, consisting of all the major coasts of the United States out to about 200 nautical miles from shore, is controlled exclusively by the federal government. Watt vowed to issue one billion acres of leases over five years – an amount covering virtually the entire area. Not wishing too much interference with his salesmanship from environmentalists who were on high alert given President Reagan's outspoken opposition to protective regulation, Watt grabbed oversight authority from the innocuous U.S. Geological

---

[29] Jad Mouawad & Barry Meier, *Risk-Taking Rises to New Levels As Oil Rigs in Gulf Drill Deeper*, N.Y. TIMES, Aug. 30, 2010, http://www.nytimes.com/2010/08/30/business/energy-environment/30deep.html?pagewanted=all&_r=0.

[30] *Id.*

Survey. The result was a captured cadre of regulators, submerged in an institution with the overwhelming purpose of promoting domestic oil production. The stated purpose of expanding offshore drilling was to end the country's dependence on foreign oil, a political imperative that continues to preoccupy U.S. presidents on a bipartisan basis.

Watt never accomplished his goal of leasing a billion acres, stymied by the environmentalists' resistance, and moratoria on drilling off the California, Alaska, and Florida coasts. But the schizophrenic institution he created was a more lasting legacy, as was the indirect effect of these moratoria on drilling in the western Gulf. Like the proverbial cheese in the nursery rhyme, the coast off Louisiana and Mississippi stood alone. Despite its status as home to some of the most productive fishing in the continental United States, the western Gulf was wide open for drilling and overseen by regulators who considered themselves allied with the oil and gas industry.

In the late 1980s and early 1990s, Britain and Norway dramatically strengthened safety regulation in the North Sea in response to disasters like the explosion and fire aboard the Piper Alpha oil rig that claimed 167 lives and cost £1.7 billion in property damage. Regulatory agencies in those countries were separated from government offices that were responsible for fostering private development offshore and allowed to operate independently. They were encouraged to adopt stringent rules that would prevent future disasters. But the U.S. Department of Interior ignored these developments, and MMS regulators still sought approval from oil and gas industry representatives to adopt more stringent requirements.

Meanwhile, all was definitely not well within the conflicted ranks of the MMS. In 2008, stories about the leasing division's wild parties with the oil industry broke in the *New York Times*. A portion of the agency's revenues were provided "in kind": that is, the companies gave the government actual oil and gas and MMS personnel resold these supplies on the open market. Because they were engaged in the same marketing as their fellows in the private sector, MMS employees in the Denver office convinced themselves that they could ignore government ethics rules. They enjoyed extravagant parties with oil industry executives, received lavish gifts, and were perceived as corrupted by these close ties. When confronted, they said they needed to become part of the industry's "marketing culture" in order to successfully sell leases and mineral rights.[31] Even though the regulatory side of the house was not directly involved in the worst of these offenses, it could not help but be influenced by the ethos

---

[31] Charlie Savage, *Sex, Drug Use and Graft Cited in Interior Department*, N.Y. Times, Sept. 11, 2008, at A1.

of keeping the oil and gas industry happy. This story was published around the time that President Obama was elected for his first term, and he was well aware of the need to reform the agency. Unfortunately, the task did not rise to a sufficiently high level on his administration's list of priorities.

As for the substantive regulations that the MMS had put in place to prevent or at least mitigate a blowout, it turned out that all were modeled on guidelines developed by the American Petroleum Institute (API), the largest and by far the most powerful trade association in the oil and gas industry to this day. Although those guidelines included useful requirements, they represented the least common denominator of what the least tolerant API members were willing to accept. The Oil Spill Commission reported that in 1997, one top MMS official explained the prevailing philosophy as follows: "We want to approach our relationship with the offshore industry more as a partner than a policeman. We need to create an atmosphere where the primary concern is to fix the problem, not the blame."[32]

On the rare occasion when federal regulators tried to deviate from industry standards, they were quickly slapped down. In 2003, for example, they tried to develop a rule requiring the reporting of "key risk indicators" but the White House intervened at the behest of the oil companies and killed the proposal.[33] Rather than disclosing all gas leaks, the rule was revised to require reporting only if the leak was serious enough to shut down a major piece of equipment, even though smaller leaks could indicate brewing safety problems. In a similar vein, when oil industry lobbyists contended that blowout preventers were sufficiently reliable that the MMS should cut in half the number of required well integrity tests, regulators backed down, despite the relative ease of conducting the tests and the implications of even minor blowouts. The rule change remained in effect despite third-party studies showing that blowout preventers were experiencing high failure rates because newly developed drilling pipes were more difficult for their shearing rams to cut. Yet another soft spot in the regulatory regime developed when third-party contractors such as Halliburton and Transocean took over many routine functions and the MMS did not change its rules to cover these developments.

Despite a significant increase in drilling activity through the 1990s, the MMS grappled with constant funding shortfalls. In 1990, oil production in the Gulf was 275 million barrels with only 4.4 percent coming from deepwater wells. By 1999, the Gulf produced 567 million barrels, a whopping 80 percent from deep wells. In 1996, the MMS reached the lowest funding level in its

[32] Report to the President, *supra* note 2, at 71–72.
[33] *Id. supra* note at 72.

history, and even though the level of funding rose very gradually after that point, the push offshore into increasingly deep water outstripped its resources by a wide margin.

In 1996, investigative reporter Jim Morris published a major piece of investigative reporting in the *Houston Chronicle*. It revealed that 54 fires, explosions, and blowouts occurred in the Gulf in 1992. By 1995, that number had risen to 98, an increase of 81 percent. He quoted Mike Farley, a U.S. Coast Guard commander stationed in Port Arthur, Texas: "There's a cowboy mentality out there: 'Don't think about it, do it.'"[34] Because the oil industry was booming, new recruits were rushed out to rigs without sufficient training. As troubling, small companies were moving in to take over deteriorating production sites when major companies had abandoned them to move on to more lucrative real estate.

The MMS shares offshore inspection responsibility with the Coast Guard, although the Coast Guard suffers from an even greater funding shortfall. In this dual system, the MMS has authority over the mechanics of production (for example, wellheads, piping, blowout protectors, well integrity tests, etc.), while the Coast Guard checks worker safety procedures and equipment (for example, fire extinguishers and life jackets).

As of the time of Morris's reporting, in December 1996, the number of people each agency had available was pitiful in comparison to the scope of drilling activity in the Gulf: the MMS had 49 inspectors and the Coast Guard fielded 21 to oversee 3,800 platforms and 140 mobile drilling units. In the Coast Guard's busiest zone, a north-south segment of the Gulf with staff deployed from a regional office in Morgan City, Louisiana, three inspectors were expected to oversee 1,700 platforms and 80 mobile units scattered over a 22,000 square mile area. Although the three men were averaging 35 inspections a month, in the process spending 30 hours in helicopters that flew them out to the facilities, the U.S. Department of Transportation Inspector General criticized the Coast Guard for failing to inspect 84 percent of new offshore facilities.[35] The Coast Guard agreed with these findings, probably in the hope that more resources would be forthcoming if it acknowledged that it could not do its job with those on hand. But sufficient funding never materialized.

All of these shortfalls in oversight occurred despite serious accidents in the Gulf and ample opportunities for Congress to improve regulatory oversight.

---

[34] Jim Morris, *Lost at Sea/OFFSHORE RISKS/Safety Concerns Rise with Return of Oil, Gas Boom*, HOUSTON CHRON., Dec. 22, 1996, at A1.

[35] OFFICE OF THE INSPECTOR GENERAL, U.S. DEP'T OF TRANSPORTATION, SEMIANNUAL REPORT TO THE CONGRESS: APRIL 1, 1996–SEPTEMBER 30, 1996 (Oct. 7, 1996), *available at* http://www.oig.dot.gov/sites/dot/files/pdfdocs/sar996.pdf.

For example, in March 1989, an ARCO facility called South Pass Block 60, Platform B, exploded when a worker cut through an 18-inch gas pipeline without checking to see if it was empty. Seven workers were killed and the rig was destroyed.[36] The workers, many of whom were poorly trained, were employed by contractors because ARCO was downsizing, trying to cut costs, and contracting out the responsibility to provide roughnecks for the rigs and platforms. In the aftermath of the South Pass explosion, the Marine Board of the National Research Council (a part of the National Academies of Science, the nation's gold standard for scientific and technical expertise) audited the MMS's performance and concluded that it had inadequate resources, weak regulation, and was having great difficulty keeping up with technological developments in deepwater drilling. But in 1990, prompted by the Exxon Valdez spill, Congress passed the Oil Pollution Act without addressing any of the regulatory deficiencies or resource shortfalls that crippled oversight of a dangerous, rapidly expanding industry.

The MMS limped along through the remainder of the 1990s and into the new millennium. At the time of the Macondo spill, according to an internal investigation compiled for Department of Interior Secretary Kenneth Salazar, it fielded 55 inspectors to cover 3,000 Gulf facilities, a ratio of 1:54, even though the ratio of inspectors was 1:5 in the MMS Pacific region. These small numbers could not possibly manage thorough examinations of rigs such as the Deepwater Horizon. Not only was a team of specialized experts necessary to do a thorough job, inspections of a complex facility take days. MMS engineers complained that they got no ongoing training in the rapidly changing technology that was used on the rigs, and of course did not have time to visit the most dangerous operations with any consistency. As discouraging, when they did manage to inspect a portion of the complex operations on a large rig or platform, and discovered ongoing violations of the rules, the penalties they collected were so small that the cases fell far short of creating the deterrent effect essential for a program where inspections are few and far between. After Macondo, ProPublica reported that oil companies paid an average penalty of $45,000 between 1998 and 2010.[37] The MMS collected total penalties of $20 million during that period, or approximately $1.6 million annually for the entire Outer Continental Shelf.

[36] MINERALS MANAGEMENT SERVICE, U.S. DEP'T OF THE INTERIOR, INVESTIGATION OF MARCH 19, 1989, FIRE SOUTH PASS BLOCK 60 PLATFORM B LEASE OCS-G 1608 (Apr. 1990), *available at* http://www.bsee.gov/Inspection-and-Enforcement/Accidents-and-Incidents/Panel-Investigation-Reports/90-0016-pdf/.

[37] Marian Wang, *Oil Companies Pay a Pittance in Penalties to Offshore Drilling Regulator*, PRO PUBLICA (May 4, 2010), http://www.propublica.org/blog/item/oil-companies-pay-a-pittance-in-penalties-to-offshore-drilling-regulator.

In addition to enforcement of existing rules, the MMS administered a permit program that was supposed to approve the safety aspects of new drilling operations. But its engineers were overwhelmed by applications. A report compiled at the request of Secretary Salazar noted that MMS regional offices tried to respond to requests from the oil industry on a 24/7 basis despite limited funding. During a four-year period between 2005 and 2009, applications increased 71 percent, from 1,246 to 2,136, and each office received as many as 20 after-hours calls each week. Because the MMS could not field enough engineers to process all the applications, its staff reported the unfortunate development of forum shopping:

> [S]ome operators call various district offices to find an engineer who will eventually give approval. For example, during the current drilling suspension, an operator contacted one district office for a special drilling departure, but was told to wait. The operator then contacted another district office and received approval. The operator was eventually told not to drill, but this example illustrates the lack of coordination and standardization among the district offices.[38]

As if to verify this sad state of affairs, reporters discovered that the spill control plan BP had filed with MMS for approval identified walruses, sea otters, and seals as animals that could be affected by the spill. None exist in the Gulf. It turned out that Exxon and Chevron had similar language in their plans, the product of a careless consultant's cut and paste job from documents written for Arctic locations.[39]

After Macondo, the Obama administration split the MMS into two parts, isolating the land-based leasing of mineral, oil, and gas rights from oversight of offshore drilling. Secretary Salazar then separated the offshore portion into two bureaus, one for leasing and the other for regulation. These changes were criticized as inadequate because the regulators still reported to a single boss.[40] Many had urged that the regulators be given complete autonomy from the institution that runs the leasing program, as they are in Britain.

---

[38] U.S. Dep't of the Interior, Outer Continental Shelf Safety Oversight Board Report to Secretary of the Interior Ken Salazar (Sept. 1, 2010), *available at* http://www.doi.gov/news/pressreleases/upload/OCS-Safety-Oversight-Board-Report.pdf. *See also* Report to the President, *supra* note 2, at 74.

[39] Rick Jervis, *BP Response Plan Shows Lack of Readiness*, USA Today, May 18, 2010, at 3A; Stephen Mufson & Juliet Eilperin, *BP's Spill Plan Puts it in Good Company*, Seattle Times, June 16, 2010, at A3.

[40] Michael Jasny, *The Latest MMS Outrage – and Why Salazar's "Restructuring" Plan is Insufficient*, Switchboard: NRDC Staff Council Blog (May 14, 2010), http://switchboard.nrdc.org/blogs/mjasny/the_latest_mms_outrage_and_why.html.

Whether this lack of independence will become a significant impediment to the new regulatory division – called the Bureau of Safety and Environmental Enforcement (BSEE) – is unclear.

What is clear is that the BSEE remains woefully underfunded. In many ways, in fact, it appears at least as impotent as it was on the eve of the blowout because it has issued a slew of new rules but has little hope of enforcing them effectively. In Fiscal Year 2011, the BSEE spent about $145 million, which supported 638 full-time employees (FTEs). The next year, after the full implications of the Macondo blowout were explained by the reports and books cited here, as well as congressional hearings and the media, $197 million was authorized, an increase of 65 additional FTEs. Although the agency's budget materials seem almost deliberately convoluted and opaque, they indicate that somewhere in the vicinity of 60–85 inspectors are now available to visit 3,500 rigs and platforms, many of which are located hundreds of miles offshore and are accessible only by helicopter.[41] For FY 2014, the Obama administration requested a $222 million budget, but it is unlikely to get this amount in final negotiations with House Republicans.

Anticipating that significantly increased funding would be crucial to reinvigorate BSEE regulatory and enforcement programs, the Oil Spill Commission recommended that Congress enact legislation to take the money from the billions of dollars in revenues that the federal government earns offshore. A bill was introduced but it died in a gridlocked and vituperative Congress.[42] Royalties, rents, and bonus payments for offshore extraction of oil and gas collect over $9 billion annually. The BSEE assesses fees to support inspections, but they are tiny compared to this overall largesse. To their credit, Oil Spill Commission members do monitor progress in the Gulf even though its professional staff has disbanded. Annual reports issued in 2012 and 2013 awarded a grade of "D" to the category of "ensuring adequate resources."[43]

---

[41] U.S. Dep't of the Interior, *supra* note 38, at 13.

[42] *See, e.g.,* the Oil Spill Accountability and Environmental Protection Act of 2010, H.R. 5629, 111th Cong. (2010); *see also* the Offshore Drilling Safety Improvement Act, H.R. 5634, 111th Cong. (2010) (subsequently reintroduced in 2011 as H.R. 1520 (112th Cong.)). Even currently, there is pending legislation in Congress seeking to improve the oversight and regulation of offshore drilling; *see* SAFEGUARDS Act of 2013, H.R. 1820, 113th Cong. (2014).

[43] *See* Oil Spill Commission Action, Assessing Progress Three Years Later 2 (2013), *available at* http://oscaction.org/wp-content/uploads/FINAL_OSCA-No2-booklet-Apr-2013_web.pdf; Oil Spill Commission Action, Assessing Progress, Implementing the Recommendations of the National Oil Spill Commission 2 (2012), *available at* http://oscaction.org/wp-content/uploads/OSCA-Assessment-report.pdf.

CONCLUSION

The central justifications for criminal enforcement are punishment and deterrence. It is hard to imagine how much more of a deterrent punch – or, for that matter, punishment – could be meted out to a corporation as large as BP than what the DOJ has already extracted. Four billion dollars in criminal penalties is a staggering amount of money, even in these times of hedge funds and multi-million-dollar executive pay, and the company will end up paying several orders of magnitude more than that amount in cleanup costs, compensation to Gulf residents, natural resource damages, legal fees, and – perhaps most important of all – lost opportunity costs. BP may be coming back, slowly but surely, to its past profit margins, but its competitors have leapt far ahead of it. Exxon's stock price on March 21, 2010, shortly before Macondo, was $67; by the same date in 2014, it was $94. BP's stock price at the same time in 2010 was $48; in 2014, it was $46.

For those who harbor doubts that even such ambitious remedies and devastating market fallout may not be enough to inspire discipline, there may be hope of creating a more powerful incentive if Kaluza and Vidrine are convicted. But prosecutors are likely to have to work overtime to win those cases. The two men seem quite capable of cutting pitiful figures. Both are near retirement – Kaluza will be 64 and Vidrine 67 by the time the trial begins. Given the confusion on the rig in the days leading up to the disaster, multiple corporate and individual players in the melodrama, lack of any coherent policies for preventing such disasters, and weakness of the regulatory requirements that applied to the rig, prosecutors will find it challenging to tell a simple story to the jury, who perhaps could not be blamed for thinking that Vidrine and Kaluza are relatively low-level scapegoats thrown to the wolves by higher-ranking BP executives.

While it would certainly be a good start on achieving the goals I advocate here for the BP case to set a new floor on the severity of criminal penalties in other corporate prosecutions, the added dimension of deterrence offered by individual prosecutions must aim higher than such relatively low-level managers.

6

The Public's Health

I think that the F.D.A. has not been able to catch some of these things as quickly as I expect. ... At bare minimum, we should be able to count on our government keeping our kids safe when they eat peanut butter. That's what Sasha eats for lunch probably three times a week. And, you know, I don't want to have to worry about whether she's going to get sick as a consequence of having her lunch.

President Obama[1]

If someone is convicted of a felony in the criminal justice system, they go to prison and are not allowed to vote. But, if you poison Americans via their food supply what are the consequences? You pay a fine and keep producing? Is this right? Is this what we as Americans want?

Peter Hurley, police officer, Portland, Oregon and father of surviving salmonella-poisoned child[2]

WHAT HAPPENED: THE LARGEST FOOD RECALL IN HISTORY

Team Diarrhea's Discovery

In the fall of 2008, Minnesota public health officials were alarmed by an unusually high number of illnesses and deaths caused by salmonella poisoning. This outbreak of foodborne disease, one of the largest in history,

---

[1] Gardiner Harris, *Product Recall Took Company Approval*, N.Y. TIMES, Feb. 2, 2009, at A13.

[2] Mr. Hurley is the father of Lauren, 5, Jacob, 3, and Alyssa, 8 months. Jacob was sickened by Austin peanut butter crackers in January 2009 but survived. *The Salmonella Outbreak: The Continued Failure to Protect the Food Supply: Hearings Before the Subcomm. on Oversight & Investigations of the H. Comm. on Energy and Commerce*, 111th Cong. 5 (2009) (testimony of Peter K. Hurley), *available at* http://democrats.energycommerce.house.gov/sites/default/files/documents/Testimony-Hurley-OI-Salmonella-Outbreak-2009-2-11.pdf.

ultimately resulted in the deaths of 9 people and sickened 714.[3] Twenty-three percent of those made ill were hospitalized and half of the ill were young children. Medical experts who have studied the incident say that even these high numbers likely underestimate the outbreak's impact because salmonellosis remains a significantly underreported disease. They say that the number of illnesses and deaths could be as much as 16 times more than reported.[4]

Graduate students employed by the Minnesota health department and jokingly referred to as "Team Diarrhea" deployed the tedious and time-consuming "trace-back process," which involves interviewing victims and their families in detail about what they ate in order to discover common foods. Once they established links between what sick people ate, experts at the Centers for Disease Control and Prevention (CDC) undertook sophisticated testing of the suspect food, reporting their results on PulseNet, the national molecular sub-typing network for foodborne contaminants that allows scientists to develop genetic profiles of such bacteria.[5] By January 2009 – many months after Minnesota first noticed excess illness – federal and state government officials determined that the outbreak was caused by a strain of salmonella typhimurium with the same genetic code as samples taken from an unopened jar of King Nut peanut butter found in Connecticut and an unopened package of peanut crackers found in Canada. They eventually determined that the victims had all consumed peanut products supplied to schools, nursing homes, and other institutions by the Peanut Corporation of America (PCA) from its facilities in Blakely, Georgia, and Plainview, Texas. In addition to producing peanut butter marketed under the "King Nut" brand, the company made peanut paste used in a wide variety of products, from cereal to desserts to pet food. Large food producers such as the Kellogg Co. and Nestlé had been PCA customers, as was the federal government, which bought peanut products for schools, the military, and victims qualifying for disaster relief.

Salmonella is a bacteria found in the intestinal tract of animals. It is introduced into the food supply through the spreading of animal waste, either deliberately, when manure is used as a fertilizer, or inadvertently, as in the PCA's case, where a leaking roof allowed rainwater to wash bird and rodent feces into

---

3   Ross Anderson, *How Minnesota Cracked the Peanut Butter Case*, FOOD SAFETY NEWS (Dec. 13, 2010), http://www.foodsafetynews.com/2010/12/bingo-how-minnesota-sleuthed-the-pca-bug/#.Uw OG5oXEFeE.

4   Elizabeth Cavallaro et al., *Salmonella Typhimurium Infections Associated with Peanut Products*, 365 NEW ENGL. J. MED. 601, 607 (2011) (citing CDC estimates).

5   For an excellent description of this detective work, see Cavallaro et al., *supra* note 4. For a shorter summary of Team Diarrhea's work, *see* Ross Anderson, *How Minnesota Cracked the Peanut Butter Case*, FOOD SAFETY NEWS (Dec. 13, 2010), http://www.foodsafetynews.com/2010/12/bingo-how-minnesota-sleuthed-the-pca-bug/#.UwOG5oXEFeE.

the plant. The bacteria are quite persistent. Once peanut products are contaminated, the bacteria can survive during the entire shelf life of peanut products – from 18 to 24 months.

The illness caused by salmonella exposure includes symptoms such as nausea, vomiting, and diarrhea. Healthy adults generally recover within a matter of days. Children, the elderly, and people with compromised immune systems are far more vulnerable to serious debilitation. Salmonella poisoning can spread from the intestines into the bloodstream and cause death in acute cases.

In well-run facilities, salmonella is eliminated by roasting peanuts at temperatures of at least 350°F (180°C). The roaster at the Blakely plant was not heating correctly for critical periods when raw peanuts were processed into peanut butter and peanut paste. In addition, peanuts roasted to eliminate salmonella can be reinfected if the finished product is not stored in sanitary conditions. At Blakely and Plainview, storage areas were used for both finished and presumably sanitized products and contaminated raw peanuts.

Although the FDA lacked legal authority to demand that products containing PCA peanuts be pulled off the shelf – a stunning gap in the law that has since been fixed – the agency persuaded the PCA to recall voluntarily all the shipments it produced in 2007 and 2008.[6] Publicity inspired regulators to broaden the scope of the alert. Before the incident was over, the FDA web site listed some 3,900 products as potentially affected. The site received 28 million hits as consumers logged on to determine whether their kitchen cabinets held potentially dangerous food. People shied away from peanut products throughout this period, and the peanut industry lost an estimated $1 billion.[7] Losses by finished food processors have never been estimated.

On February 21, 2013, Michael Moore, the U.S. Attorney for the Middle District of Georgia unsealed a 76-count indictment against Stewart Parnell, owner and president of PCA; Michael Parnell, his brother and a food broker who worked on behalf of PCA; Samuel Lightsey, operations manager of PCA's Blakely, Georgia plant; and Mary Wilkerson, receptionist, office manager, and quality assurance manager at Blakely.[8] The indictment quite literally threw the

---

[6] Harris, *supra* note 1.

[7] Zach Mallove, *USDA Releases Study on Peanut Industry*, FOOD SAFETY NEWS, Feb. 4, 2010, http://www.foodsafetynews.com/2010/02/usda-releases-study-on-peanut-industry/#.UzWoWPl dV8F.

[8] Brent Kendall & Devlin Barrett, *Four Accused of Salmonella Coverup*, WALL ST. J., Feb. 21, 2013, http://online.wsj.com/news/articles/SB10001424127887324503204578318024027438166? mod=googlenews_wsj&mg=reno64-wsj&url=http%3A%2F%2Fonline.wsj.com%2Farticle% 2FSB10001424127887324503204578318024027438166.html%3Fmod%3Dgooglenews_wsj. See Indictment, United States v. Stewart Parnell at al., No. 1:13-CR-12-WLS, at 7 (M.D. Ga. Feb. 15, 2013), *available at* http://www.justice.gov/iso/opa/resources/6120132211142635o488.pdf.

book at this group: including charges of conspiracy, introduction of adulterated and misbranded food into interstate commerce with the intent to defraud, wire fraud, and obstruction of justice. Lightsey and a fifth PCA employee, Daniel Kilgore, Blakely operations manager from April 2002 through February 2009, pled guilty and testified against the other defendants at trial. On September 19, 2014, the jury convicted the Parnells of multiple felonies, the first such convictions in a food safety case.

Although the indictment is an unprecedented, momentous, and excellent development, it does not include the names of any of the nine people who died as a result of the defendants' grievous malfeasance because the FDA does not have authority to prosecute the charge of manslaughter. Punishing PCA managers for killing consumers could only be achieved by an ambitious state or local prosecutor. Instead, PCA's corporate customers are identified as the primary victims of its federal crimes. So, for example, the indictment focuses on "Customer No. 11" – an unnamed multinational food products company with its principal place of business in Battle Creek, Michigan – almost certainly the Kellogg Co.[9] The PCA was sending the company two to three tanker trucks of peanut paste a week at 44,000 pounds per load. Contrary to Kellogg's specifications that it only wanted products made with American peanuts and that lots it bought had to be tested for salmonella and other common pathogens, 69 percent of PCA's product was made from Mexican or Argentinian – not American – peanuts and 63 percent of it was never tested.

Mice, Roaches, Bird Feathers, and a Leaking Roof

The PCA began and ended as a family-run business. In the mid-1970s, Stewart Parnell and his father, Hugh, began buying peanuts in bulk from growers in Gorman, Texas and reselling the product to candy and ice cream makers. Eventually, they purchased a facility in Gorman where they could roast the nuts, and, within a few years, expanded to a 65,000-square-foot plant with 95 employees and $30 million in yearly sales. In 1994, the Parnells sold the plant, but Stewart Parnell bought it back in 2000. He lived in Virginia and ran the company from a home office in his garage.

David Brooks, a retired buyer of bulk ingredients for a snack company, told the *Washington Post* that the Parnells ran a half-baked operation that paid

---

[9] *See* Indictment, United States v. Stewart Parnell et al., No. 1:13-CR-12-WLS, at 7 (M.D. Ga. Feb. 15, 2013), *available at* http://www.justice.gov/iso/opa/resources/61201322111426350488.pdf.

minimum wage, had a "barebones" front office, and bought the cheapest lots of peanuts they could find. "The old man used to look for distressed situations: Someone over-inventoried or had peanuts from last year they had to move. He would aggressively look for these, making phone calls, hunting people down. Stewart grew up in that and was the same way."[10] Brooks chose not to buy peanuts from the Parnells, explaining that he visited the Gorman plant three times in the mid-1980s but each time gave the plant a "failing grade."

> It was just filthy. Dust was all over the beams, the braces of the building. The roofs leaked, the windows would be open, and birds would fly through the building. ... It was just a time bomb waiting to go off, and everybody in the peanut industry in Georgia, Virginia and Texas – they all knew.[11]

Although the PCA was processing peanuts at nine production facilities throughout the United States in the fall of 2008, the Blakely and Plainview plants were targeted as the sources of the salmonella outbreak, with Blakely producing the lion's share of contaminated peanut butter and paste. The PCA soon shut both plants down. The company filed for bankruptcy on February 13, 2009, and went out of business. In addition to criminal charges, its executives also face civil suits for damages brought by stricken consumers or their families.

When FDA inspectors converged on Blakely, they found a slew of serious safety violations:

- the aforementioned leaking roof, which was a major source of salmonella contamination;
- mold growing on ceilings and walls;
- pervasive rodent infestation with dead mice and "REPs" too numerous to count (the acronym, a particularly pungent example of bureaucratic euphemism, stands for "rodent excretion pellets");
- filthy nut processing receptacles;
- feathers, lint, and dust in the air filtration system;
- a roaster encrusted with peanut meal that had not been calibrated for proper temperature in an unknown period of time and was cleaned once a month rather than weekly, which was the industry standard;
- employees wearing the same clothing to work as they used in the supposedly sanitary peanut processing area; and
- hand-washing facilities required employees to touch a filthy handle to turn the water on and off, negating the sanitary advantages of the washing.

---

[10]   Lyndsey Layton & Nick Miroff, *The Rise and Fall of a Peanut Empire*, WASH. POST, Feb. 2, 2009, at A1.
[11]   *Id.*

Interviews with former employees filled out the picture. Blakely employee David James told the *Chicago Tribune* that he opened a huge peanut "tote"[12] – the industry name for a gigantic plastic bag used to store up to one ton of nuts – only to find baby mice living in it. "It was filthy and nasty all around the place," he said.[13] Terry Jones, a janitor, said that peanut oil was left to soak into the floor of the plant and that the roof constantly leaked into the plant. James Griffin, a cook, said he never ate the peanut butter, despite the availability of free samples, and would not let his children eat it.

Post-outbreak investigations also revealed that in April 2008, Canadian officials had rejected a "filthy and putrid" shipment of chopped peanuts from the PCA because it contained metal shavings.[14] The shipment was returned to Blakely and PCA workers made abortive efforts to "decontaminate" it. FDA inspectors visited the plant to ensure the shipment was destroyed, but for reasons that remain unexplained, did not notice the conditions that caused the Canadian problem and the subsequent salmonella outbreak.

As for the PCA facility in Plainview, Texas, investigators discovered that it had operated for four years without a license from the state. Of course, because officials did not know the plant existed, no inspections occurred before the outbreak. State inspectors added Plainview products to the recall list when they discovered that the plant's air handling system was pulling debris from a crawl space strewn with dead rodents, rodent excrement, and feathers into the areas where peanuts were processed.[15] Emails between Stewart Parnell and plant employees describe an incident where totes of peanut meal from Plainview were air hosed to remove dust and rat excrement and then shipped to a customer.

---

[12] Peanut tote bags are generally made of plastic and hold a ton of the product. They have heavy-duty handles so that they can be lifted on and off conveyance vehicles and emptied in a plant where their contents will be used. *See, e.g., One Ton Tote Bags*, WEIFANG LIFA PLASTIC PACKING CO., LTD., http://lifapack.en.alibaba.com/product/622476416-213685248/one_ton_tote_bags.html (one bag sold by this company costs $2,600 as of December 14, 2013).

[13] Dahleen Glanton, *Inside "Nasty" Peanut Plant: Ex-Employees Say Rodents, Roaches, and Mold Were Commonplace Long Before Salmonella Outbreak*, CHI. TRIB., Feb. 4, 2009, http://articles.chicagotribune.com/2009-02-04/news/0902030962_1_peanut-butter-peanut-corp-american-peanut-council.

[14] Dahleen Glanton, *Peanut Plant Woes Not New, FDA Details Trouble at Firm Tied to Outbreak*, CHI. TRIB., Jan. 31, 2009, at C4.

[15] Plainview is featured far less prominently than Blakely in the federal indictment. But the document identifies one of its past operations managers as an unidentified and unindicted co-conspirator of the named defendants. *Unnamed Plainview PCA Official a Co-conspirator in Peanuts-Salmonella Case, Four Plant Officials Indicted in 2009 Outbreak*, LUBBOCK AVALANCHE-J., Fed. 21, 2013, http://lubbockonline.com/local-news/2013-02-21/unnamed-plainview-pca-official-co-conspirator-peanuts-salmonella-case.

Testing Fraud

Although these disgusting conditions understandably preoccupied FDA inspectors, congressional investigators, and the media, PCA's malfeasance had a second twist that undoubtedly played a crucial role in the decision to prosecute Parnell. Most of the felony charges set forth in the indictment involved economic crimes of fraud based on allegations that managers routinely shipped products accompanied by paperwork that was deliberately falsified. For example, PCA products tested positive for salmonella twelve times in 2007 and 2008, but the company shipped these lots to customers anyway after a retest produced negative results. "'The practice of initially obtaining a positive sample and subsequently of getting a negative results and not having cleaned up the plant is illegal," Michael Rogers, FDA director of the division of field investigation told the *New York Times*.[16]

The defendants also falsified the Certificates of Analysis (COAs) sent to its customers to show that the product had been tested and that coliform and other bacteria were not detected. Most coliforms are not harmful in and of themselves but because they derive from fecal matter, they indicate that the product was not produced in sanitary conditions and that more dangerous organisms may be present, including bacteria, viruses, protozoa, and multicellular parasites. Plant managers went so far as to use test results from previously shipped batches to accompany batches that had not been tested.

The PCA used two independent laboratories – J. Leek Associates (JLA) and Deibel Laboratories – to test its products. Darlene Cowart, a food safety consultant who was the president of JLA, told PCA managers in 2006 that the Blakely plant's roasting process was not working well enough to destroy salmonella:

> Based on our discussions, PCA Blakely does not document the inbound raw material microbial load and does not validate their roasting conditions to confirm temperature levels within the roasting zones. Salmonella is typically destroyed at 240F for 30 minutes. This time and temperature condition is based on even roasting and heating under ideal conditions without variation in moisture contents. Peanuts typically vary in moisture such that much of the roasting is an effort to drive off moisture first and then begin roasting. The roasting process used by PCA should be sufficient to kill most bacteria but

---

[16] Gardiner Harris, *Peanut Product Recall Grows in Salmonella Scare*, N.Y. Times, Jan. 29, 2009, at A15.

without documentation to validate roasting temperatures, a kill step cannot be assumed.[17]

No record has yet been made public that successful steps were taken to remedy any of these problems. Cowart told the *New York Times* that the PCA stopped using her services because managers thought the lab produced too many positive results. Deibel, the lab that became the sole source of PCA testing, ran more than 1,600 tests on Blakely products between 2004 and 2008; approximately six percent showed positive results for salmonella. Deibel technicians became so concerned that PCA products might contaminate other customers' test batches that they ended up quarantining PCA testing in one section of their Chicago facility.

Charles Deibel, the president of Deibel Labs, testified before Congress that, while "[i]t is not unusual for Deibel Labs or for other food testing laboratories to find that samples clients submit do test positive for salmonella and other pathogens … [w]hat is virtually unheard of is for an entity to disregard these results and place potentially contaminated products into the stream of commerce."[18] Deibel and Cowart, also a witness, agreed in response to questioning that re-testing following a positive result, even if subsequent tests were negative for salmonella, should never serve to exonerate that batch of a product. They explained that testing results were often inaccurate because lots of peanut paste could be so large that sampling throughout would be prohibitively expensive. But a positive test on one portion of the lot should be sufficiently reliable to require that the entire lot be destroyed.

REGULATORY FAILURE: THE FDA MISSING IN ACTION AND THE STATES ILL-EQUIPPED AND INEFFECTIVE

The U.S. population spends more than $1 trillion on food annually, nearly half of it outside the home. Foodborne diseases sicken 48 million people (one in every six Americans) every year, cause the hospitalization of 128,000, and the death of 3,000. These numbers understate the problem, likely by orders of magnitude, because records are not collected systematically, symptoms are often mistaken for unrelated illnesses, and people can be seriously ill without being hospitalized. According to FDA number-crunching, the *average* cost

---

[17] Letter from Darlene M. Cowart, Ph.D, President and COO, JLA USA, to Stewart Parnell (Nov. 2, 2006), *available at* http://democrats.energycommerce.house.gov/sites/default/files/documents/Letter-Cowart-Parnell-Salmonella-Peanut-Investigation-Blakely-Georgia-2006-11-2.pdf.

[18] *The Salmonella Outbreak: The Continued Failure to Protect the Food Supply: Hearing Before the H. Comm. on Energy & Comm. Subcomm. on Oversight & Invest.*, 111th Cong. (Feb. 11, 2009) (testimony of Charles Deibel).

per case of foodborne illness is estimated at $1,626, or a total, at the least, of more than $78 billion per year.[19] These numbers include days of work or school missed as well as the costs of medical treatment. Obviously, cases requiring hospitalization or involving death are far more costly. Or, in other words, the economic case for improving the safety of the food supply is quite powerful.

The FDA is responsible for regulating 80 percent of the food we eat, although some experts suggest that this number is low and that the agency is really assigned to police 90 percent of the food supply. Every food other than meat and poultry falls within its jurisdiction. Government agencies and departments like the USDA, the Fish and Wildlife Service, and the EPA share responsibility for eggs, fish, and pesticide residues. The FDA oversees an estimated 82,300 U.S. domestic food producers, of which approximately 22,235 are considered "high risk" and 60,000 are considered "non-high risk." High risk facilities include those that produce foods commonly associated with outbreaks (green leafy vegetables, peanut products, eggs, etc.); have a poor compliance history; or have not been inspected in quite some time. Further complicating the FDA's mission is the rapidly growing importation of certain foods. Some 80 percent of seafood, 50 percent of fresh fruit, and 20 percent of fresh vegetables consumed in the United States are imported.[20] About 200,000 foreign food facilities have filed FDA registrations. But given the highly decentralized structure of food production in developing countries such as China, this figure also underestimates the number of facilities where imported food originates.

In 2011, FDA inspectors were able to visit only 6 percent of domestic food producers and 0.4 percent of foreign facilities.[21] A 2010 report by the agency's Inspector General found that 56 percent of domestic food facilities had not been inspected at all between FY 2004 and FY 2008.[22] To improve this record, the agency estimates that its existing food safety budget of $1 billion would need to be quadrupled. None of this money has ever materialized.

---

[19] FDA, FY 2014 BUDGET REQUEST 5 (2014), *available at* http://www.fda.gov/downloads/AboutFDA/ReportsManualsForms/Reports/BudgetReports/UCM349712.pdf (based on a study by Robert Scharff and estimates from the Centers for Disease Control and Prevention: Robert L. Scharff, *Economic Burden from Health Losses Due to Foodborne Illness in the United States*, 75 J. FOOD PROTECT. 123 (2012)).

[20] FDA, INTERNATIONAL FOOD SAFETY CAPACITY-BUILDING PLAN 1 (2013), *available at* http://www.fda.gov/downloads/Food/FoodSafety/FSMA/UCM341440.pdf

[21] Stephanie Armour et al., *Food Sickens Millions as Company-Paid Checks Find It Safe*, BLOOMBERG (Oct. 11, 2012), http://www.bloomberg.com/news/2012-10-11/food-sickens-millions-as-industry-paid-inspectors-find-it-safe.html.

[22] DANIEL R. LEVINSON, DHHS INSPECTOR GENERAL, FDA INSPECTIONS OF DOMESTIC FOOD FACILITIES, at ii (Apr. 2010), *available at* http://oig.hhs.gov/oei/reports/oei-02-08-00080.pdf.

The FDA contracts out 80 percent of food inspections to state agencies. Contracting out in this context amounts to delegating responsibility and hoping for the best. The job of policing the PCA's Blakely plant was delegated to poorly trained inspectors from the Georgia Department of Agriculture. The FDA had not reviewed the Georgia program in any formal way since 2001 until the onset of the outbreak.

Georgia inspectors visited the PCA plant no less than *nine* times in 2006–2008. According to reporting by the *Atlanta Journal-Constitution*, the average federal inspection takes about a day and a half, but Georgia state inspections took less than two hours. Georgia inspectors tested processed peanuts for salmonella only once, despite widespread news reports in 2007 regarding a comparable outbreak at a ConAgra plant seventy-five miles from Blakely in Sylvester, Georgia. Confined to visual observations, Georgia inspectors noted rust on equipment that could fall into peanut products as they were processed, unlabeled spray bottles throughout the facility, and gaps in warehouse doors big enough for rodents to enter. These problems were labeled "minor violations," and no significant improvements were required.[23]

In Texas, of course, inspections were not an issue because the Plainview plant never registered with the state. Feeling chagrined, Texas officials went looking for other instances of facilities that had failed to register, eventually discovering 355. "[These facilities are] a fraction of the total 24,000 licenses we have in the state," Carrie Wilson, a spokesperson for the state health department, told the *Dallas Morning News*.[24] When the reporter asked how oversight of licensed facilities was conducted, Wilson said that the department had budget authorization for 37 inspectors, but that seven of those positions were unfilled because of a hiring freeze. To do the math, each inspector would have to cover 800 facilities. Either the inspections performed were little more than drive-bys or each facility would only be inspected every several years. In an effort to redeem itself, regulators levied a $14.6 million civil penalty against the PCA, by far the largest it had ever collected.

Large food producers are well aware of marginal effectiveness of federal and state oversight and are appropriately concerned about the potential for bad suppliers to provide tainted products that ruin their brands and impose huge liability costs. To protect themselves, many require suppliers to go through audits that are intended to be more rigorous than state, and even federal,

[23] Gardiner Harris, *Peanut Product Recall Grows in Salmonella Scare*, N.Y. Times, Jan. 29, 2009, at A15.

[24] Sherry Jacobson, *Exclusive: Hundreds of Texas Food Makers Were Unlicensed*, Dallas Morning News, July 18, 2010, *available at* http://www.dallasnews.com/news/state/headlines/20100718-exclusive-hundreds-of-texas-food-makers-were-unlicensed.ece.

inspections. Two of the PCA's largest customers – Kellogg and Nestlé – made such audits a *quid pro quo* for purchasing peanut products from PCA, but with dramatically different results.

Kellogg allowed PCA executives to hire and compensate their own auditor, the American Institute of Baking (AIB). The Kellogg/AIB auditor pronounced Blakely a "superior" facility. Nestlé insisted on sending its own personnel to both the Plainview and Blakely plants. The Nestlé auditors were so appalled by what they found at the two plants that the company stopped doing business with the PCA.

According to independent auditors interviewed by *Bloomberg Markets Magazine*, the institutional affiliation of the client paying the bill makes all the difference. Mansour Samadpour, owner of a lab that does testing for the FDA, said that auditors evaluate a facility using standards selected by their clients. Sometimes, auditors are given a checklist to complete. "If you have a program for adding rat poison to a food, the auditor will ask 'Did you add as much as you intended?' Samadpour said. "Most won't ask, 'Why the hell are we adding rat poison?'"[25] Former auditor Jeffrey Kornacki, who now owns a microbiology consulting company, warned that facility owners often do not let auditors test for bacteria and may even prohibit auditors from entering production areas. Kornacki told the story of auditing a food processor to see if it was complying with its own safety guidelines. He spent a day and a half at the facility and ended up awarding a score of 95 out of 100. "The manager thanked him and then asked a question. 'Can you help me find the source of this salmonella in our plant?' Kornacki says he didn't know there was salmonella at the facility."[26]

One last effort by the federal government to respond to the PCA fiasco deserves an honorable mention here. At the beginning of February, the U.S. Department of Agriculture (USDA) banned PCA from doing any business with the federal government – for example, selling peanut products used to provide school lunches and disaster relief – for one year. USDA spokesperson David Shipley explained: "The actions of P.C.A. indicate that the company lacks business integrity and business honesty, which seriously and directly hinders its ability to do business with the federal government."[27] The company went out of business shortly after this action was taken, but it remains an excellent example of using the power of the purse to strengthen incentives for

---

[25] Armour et al., *supra* note 21.
[26] *Id.*
[27] Michael Falcone, *Peanut Supplier Banned from Federal Business*, N.Y. Times, Feb. 6, 2009, at A18.

food producers – or any other regulated entity – to heed health, safety, and environmental rules.

Missed Opportunity: Congress and the White House Respond with Scant Funding and Weak Rules

In the aftermath of the PCA outbreak, and other harmful incidents involving spinach, jalapeno peppers, cookie dough, and more peanut butter, Congress managed to pass legislation overhauling the FDA's authority over food safety for the first time since 1938. The Food Safety Modernization Act (FSMA)[28] was approved during the lame duck session of the 111th Congress, right before Republicans achieved a majority in the House of Representatives and the prospects for social welfare legislation became nil. The Senate approved the bill by a voice vote and the House voted 215 to 144 in favor. These numbers were made possible not only by a determined Democratic leadership but by the support of a broad coalition of industry and consumer groups – disparate interests that rarely align in such unanimity.

Sadly, what looked like a new day for enforcement of more stringent standards has turned into a jumble of gross underfunding and multiyear delays. Despite ongoing national reporting on the adverse public health effects of contaminated food and a broad social consensus that ensuring its safety belongs on the shortlist of top priority roles for the federal government, a noxious combination of far-right conservatives and a skittish White House have weakened crucial protections and undermined enforcement.

The fight broke out into public view as Congress was in the final throes of voting on the legislation that ultimately became the FSMA when conservative Fox News commentator Glenn Beck declared loudly that the government must get its "hands off our food."[29] Rep. Frank D. Lucas (R-OK) picked up this theme on the House floor: "The federal government will tell our farmers and ranchers how to do something they've been doing since the dawn of mankind. It goes too far in the direction of trying to produce food from a bureaucrat's chair in Washington, D.C."[30] By June 2011, six months after the law was passed, this view had an iron grip on the House of Representatives, where Republicans voted to cut FDA funding for food safety by $87 million, to a total

---

[28] Pub. L. No. 111-353, 124 Stat. 3885, 21 U.S.C. §§ 2201 *et seq.*

[29] *See, e.g.,* Transcript of *Food Safety Bill Has Passed,* GLENNBECK.COM (Nov. 30, 2010), http://www.glennbeck.com/content/articles/article/198/48687/ ("I don't understand how you can have so many people surrounding this president and this administration that believe in horrific things, horrific things. And we give them access to our food supply!").

[30] Lyndsey Layton, *House Approves Food-Safety Bill: Law Would Expand FDA's Power,* WASH. POST, July 31, 2009, at A4.

of $750 million, significantly less than what the agency had received before the new law's extensive new mandates went into effect. Rep. Jack Kingston (R-GA.) declared that the cuts were appropriate because the food supply was "99.99 percent safe":

> "Do we believe that McDonald's and Kentucky Fried Chicken and Safeway and Kraft Food and any brand name that you can think of, that these people aren't concerned about food safety?" Kingston said on the House floor. "The food supply in America is very safe because the private sector self-polices, because they have the highest motivation. They don't want to be sued, they don't want to go broke. They want their customers to be healthy and happy."[31]

The FSMA requires the FDA to write 50 regulations, guidelines, and studies; sets mandatory schedules for its inspections of high hazard production facilities at home and abroad; asks the agency to create partnerships by training state, local, and tribal public health officials; and greatly enhances the FDA's authority to respond to outbreaks, including the power to mandate recalls.[32] To ensure effective implementation, the new law authorized a dramatic increase in the number of FDA staff assigned to work on implementation: 4,000 in fiscal year (FY) 2011, 4,200 in FY 2012, 4,600 in FY 2013, and 5,000 in FY 2014.

Of course, these numbers indicated the level of resources that the House and Senate committees responsible for writing the legislation thought were necessary to implement the program they created. Authorization levels are intended to advise a different group of lawmakers who sit on appropriations committees in both houses how much money to give an agency on an annual basis. Authorizers work to imagine programs without any immediate budget-balancing responsibility, while appropriators are always under intense pressure to weigh one set of expenditures against another. Not surprisingly, then, the two sets of numbers rarely line up, and in almost all cases, appropriations are significantly lower than authorizations. But even in a world of routine downward adjustments in expectations, the difference between the level of resources that the authors of the FSMA thought were necessary and the amounts actually given to the agency is better characterized as a chasm than a gap.

To begin with, it's useful to place the FSMA's authorizing levels in perspective. Although they seem ambitious in relationship to each other – a 1,000 person growth in staff between FY 2011 and FY 2014 – the ultimate number of 5,000 staff responsible for overseeing 80–90 percent of the food supply seems disproportionately low when compared to the 9,000-person staff fielded by the Food Safety and Inspection System (FSIS) of the USDA to oversee the remaining 20 percent. The agency's budget requests fell on deaf ears. In fact, the FDA wrote in a report to Congress in April 2013, modest increases in food safety expenditures awarded during the Obama administration merely returned the funding for the FDA program to the same level of funding as it received before Bush administration budget cuts.

Compounding these serious problems, the Obama administration is far from united in support of the beleaguered regulators. The FSMA instructs the agency to issue a rule that would compel companies like the PCA to write plans that: (1) identify public health hazards in the production of food for human consumption; (2) explain the steps they will take to reduce or eliminate such hazards; (3) monitor their own performance in meeting these requirements; and (4) take steps to correct any problems they discover. The FDA and state officials would then have a tailored set of protective requirements to use during inspections in assessing a production facility's performance. The statute requires the FDA to issue the final rule, called "Preventive Controls for Human Food," no later than July 4, 2012. FDA experts were late in writing a proposed rule, and it did not go over to the White House for mandatory review until November 2011. The proposal languished there for 13 months for two reasons: the Obama administration was loath to allow any potentially controversial regulation to go out in the eight-month period leading up to the 2012 presidential election and White House economists were negotiating with FDA experts over changes that reduced compliance costs by eliminating some of the rule's strongest protections. The *proposed* rule was finally published in the *Federal Register* for public comment in January 2013, 18 months after the statute mandated that the FDA issue the *final* rule.

The proposal immediately ran into a torrent of opposition from the so-called "sustainable agriculture movement" – a loose confederation of organic and small farmers, food co-ops, and farmers' markets that was whipped into a frenzy about its potential impact on their small businesses. Their objections further spooked the White House, which announced in December 2013 that it would re-propose the proposal for public comment over the summer of 2014. The original FDA proposal would have given "small" businesses that employ fewer than 500 people – in other words, the PCA – an additional two years to write plans and come into compliance. Given the opposition to the rule by other small entities, this delayed compliance period may be further extended. Or, in other words, the most plausible scenario is that the FSMA will not have any concrete and binding effect on a mid-sized food producer such as the PCA until over a decade after the outbreak that motivated law reform in the first place.

The gauntlet the FDA was compelled to run within the White House also blunted the proposed rule's effectiveness by eliminating several crucial requirements crafted by FDA experts that arguably would have prevented the PCA outbreak. Dropped on the cutting room floor were requirements that food processors monitor sanitation by swabbing surfaces where food is prepared and do routine tests of finished products to detect pathogens. A requirement that manufacturers such as Kellogg undertake audits of the suppliers that provided them with raw ingredients like peanut paste also fell by the wayside. Using the distorted standard of whether the costs of implementing these basic protections are justified by the value – in dollars – of lives saved and illnesses avoided, OMB economists vetoed them, weakening the final result without blunting industry opposition.

THE NEW ENGLAND COMPOUNDING CENTER

A lot of the blame for the meningitis situation lies at Congress's door. [T]he protections for your cat or dog are stronger than for your wife and children.
Larry D. Sasich, research pharmacist[33]

The Food and Drug Administration has more regulatory authority over a drug factory in China than over a compounding pharmacy in Massachusetts.
Kevin Outterson, Associate Professor, Boston University Law School[34]

WHAT HAPPENED: A "GIANT INCUBATOR" FOR BACTERIA AND FUNGUS

17,676 *Vials*

In the early fall of 2012, people across the country contracted virulent fungal meningitis infections after receiving spinal injections of methylprednisolone, a steroid drug used to relieve back and shoulder pain. Fungal meningitis causes inflammation in the brain or central nervous system; the disease develops one to four weeks after exposure. Difficult to treat, the disease can cause fatal strokes in some patients. Like a slow-moving plague, the illnesses

---

[33] Eric Lichtblau & Sabrina Tavernese, *Friends in Congress Have Helped Drug Compounders Avoid Tighter Rules*, N.Y. TIMES, Nov. 13, 2012, at A16.

[34] Denise Grady et al., *Scant Oversight of Drug Maker in Fatal Meningitis Outbreak*, N.Y. TIMES, Oct. 6, 2012, at A1.

and deaths mounted. By November 2013, 751 people living in 20 states were ill and 64 had died.

Suspicious doctors and hospital officials eventually discovered that the injections had one characteristic in common: all had originated at the New England Compounding Center (NECC) in Framingham, Massachusetts, which had manufactured 17,676 vials of methylprednisolone that were administered to over 14,000 patients.[35] As federal and state inspectors and the media converged on Framingham, the NECC and its sister company, Ameridose, surrendered their pharmacy licenses and soon shut down.[36] Under heavy government pressure, company executives launched recalls of suspected shipments. In December 2012, the NECC filed for Chapter 11 bankruptcy protection; its chief restructuring officer announced that the company wanted to forge a "consensual, comprehensive resolution of claims."[37] At a congressional hearing held in mid-November, Barry Cadden, the company's chief pharmacist, invoked the Fifth Amendment against self-incrimination. No criminal charges had been filed in the case as of when this book went to press.

A Brief History of Compounding

Hospitals and doctors have mixed special drugs – or "compounded" – since the nineteenth century. Historically, drugs were compounded for three reasons: (1) some patients are allergic to components of mass-produced products and need special mixtures that do not include these ingredients; (2) children and the elderly may need doses of medicine not found in standardized products; and (3) when a person is taking a number of medications, mixing them into one dose may help the patient comply with the regimen ordered by her doctor. But in recent years, compounding became far more lucrative and pharmacists began to manufacture and market on a far larger scale popular pain medications, supposedly natural hormone replacement therapies, anti-aging formulas, and veterinary drugs.

The structure of the compounding industry also began to change dramatically. Two decades ago, an estimated 8,200 hospitals made the compounded

---

[35] For a description of this detective work, *see* Carolyn Y. Johnson, *A Deadly Puzzle, and Then a Breakthrough: The Meningitis Outbreak Baffled Doctors Across US Until They Saw Common Cause*, Boston Globe, Oct. 28, 2012, at A1.

[36] For a CDC map and data tables regarding this outbreak, *see* U.S. Centers for Disease Control and Prevention, Multi-State Meningitis Outbreak: A Current Case Count (Oct. 23, 2013), *available at* http://www.cdc.gov/hai/outbreaks/meningitis-map-large. html.

[37] *Compounding Pharmacy Responsible for Meningitis Outbreak Files for Bankruptcy*, 11 Pharmaceutical L. & Industry Rep. (Bloomberg BNA), at 22 (Jan. 4, 2013).

drugs they needed for their patients in-house. But in the early 1990s, hospital administrators began to see the advantages of outsourcing this task. An enterprising pharmacist named Jim Sweeney set up a double-wide trailer in a California hospital's parking lot, and independent compounding was off to the races, growing from a handful of local firms to an estimated 7,500 community-based pharmacies across the country. Within that group, 3,000 make sterile preparations like the steroid drug that caused the NECC outbreak, according to the International Academy of Compounding Pharmacists (IACP), the industry's largest and most influential trade association.[38] The IACP estimates says that compounders sell somewhere between one and three percent of the $300 billion in annual prescription drug sales, providing 40 percent of all intravenous medications used in hospitals, a figure up from 16 percent just a decade ago.[39] However, these figures have never been verified by a neutral source. When congressional overseers asked FDA Commissioner Margaret Hamburg for statistics on the industry, she said that she could not provide them with the information because because compounders are not required to register even their existence with her agency.

The business profiles of independent compounders range from small back rooms at local pharmacies that limit their business to the production of medicine for individual patients to far more ambitious operations like the NECC, which ship large batches of drugs to doctors and clinics across the country. Customers came to the NECC and its counterparts because their prices were cheaper and because drug shortages have made some medications difficult to obtain. For example, the *Washington Post* has reported that the NECC charged $2.00 less per vial for the steroid that caused the outbreak. Compounders routinely stock pre-made supplies of what are known as "workhorse" pain medications, such as fentanyl, midazolam, and propofol, in anticipation that mass-produced supplies provided by large pharmaceutical companies may run out.[40] In one particularly poignant example of unintended consequences, the FDA discovered egregious violations of its regulations establishing good manufacturing practices at several big pharmaceutical plants and took enforcement actions against the companies that operated

[38] International Academy of Compounding Pharmacists, The International Academy of Compounding Pharmacists Responds to Meningitis Outbreak Tied to Compounding Pharmacy (Oct. 4, 2002), *available at* https://ia801009.us.archive.org/14/items/459187-iacp-responds-to-meningitis-outbreak-release/459187-iacp-responds-to-meningitis-outbreak-release.pdf.

[39] *What is Compounding?*, IACP, http://iacprx.org/displaycommon.cfm?an=1&subarticlenbr=1 (last visited Mar. 7, 2014).

[40] David Brown, *Medicine Mixing Stirs up Concerns*, Wash. Post, Oct. 14, 2012, at A1.

them. Some of the factories shut down temporarily to clean up these problems, and drug shortages soon emerged. Compounders were quick to leap into
the breach.[41] Reporting on the economic dynamics of the industry, the *Boston
Globe* quoted an industry spokesman whipping up the troops at a 2002 trade
show in Atlanta. "'Anybody know what the average margin on a compounded
product is?' businessman Mickey Letson, then president of a major compounding supply company, asked [the] group. … 'Seventy-five percent minimum gross profits. Depending on what field you're in it can run into the
thousands of percent.'"[42]

A License to Print Money

The NECC was among the most aggressive of this new breed. Former employees told *60 Minutes* and the *Wall Street Journal* that in 2006, a dramatically
expanded sales team solicited an overwhelming number of orders from hospitals across the country. The company had easily obtained licenses to sell
drugs in as many as 44 states. By 2013, the company had 49 employees. A
former manager who spoke on the condition of anonymity told the *New York
Times*: "It was a license to print money. I've never seen a business grow so fast.
Doug [Conigliaro, an anesthesiologist and one of the owners] was the guy who
was all 'rush, rush, rush. Got to get it done.' There was no question in anyone's
mind that he was the guy in charge."[43]

Another former employee, a quality control technician who also spoke
anonymously to *New York Times* reporters, explained that he once tried to
stop the production line because labels were missing from several vials of
medicine. He was overruled by senior management: "The emphasis was
always on speed, not on doing the job right. One of their favorite phrases was
'This line is worth more than all your lives combined, so don't stop it.'"[44]
Operating as a closely held business, the NECC's owners amassed a small fortune

---

[41] The *New York Times* broke the story about the connection between the shortages and increased
business for compounders. Lest the reader feel any temptation to blame the FDA for short-
sighted enforcement policies, the violations at the larger facilities included "weevils floating in
vials of heparin [and] morphine cartridges containing twice the labeled dose," as well as
"[m]anufacturing plants with rusty tools, mold in production areas and – in one memorable
case – a barrel of urine." Katie Thomas, *Lapses at Big Drug Factories Add to Shortages and
Danger*, N.Y. TIMES, Oct. 18, 2012, at A1.

[42] Liz Kowalcyk & Todd Wallack, *Little Scrutiny as Drug Compounder Expanded, Early Fears
About Tainted Products but no Crackdown*, BOSTON GLOBE, Dec. 9, 2012, at A1.

[43] Abby Goodnough et al., *Spotlight Put on Founders of Drug Firm in Outbreak*, N.Y. TIMES,
Oct. 25, 2012, at A18.

[44] Sabrina Tavernises & Andrew Pollack, *Ex-Workers Cite Safety Concerns at Drug Firm*, N.Y.
TIMES, Oct. 13, 2012, at A1.

as a result of such marketing, withdrawing $16 million before federal and state investigators could freeze the company's assets.

As it turned out, all this haste had a devastating effect on safety and quality control. When the FDA and state inspectors visited the Framingham, Massachusetts, facility following the 2012 outbreak, they discovered rusting equipment caked with green and yellow residue. One-fourth of supposedly sterile steroid vials contained visible "greenish-black foreign matter"; 50 vials were revealed to contain fungus when they were sent for microscopic examination.[45] A leaky boiler near the clean rooms spilled dirty water on the floor. The building that housed the pharmacy was next door to a recycling center operated by one of the NECC's owners. That recycling plant shredded household garbage, filling the air with small particles of debris.

The company maintained two "clean rooms" for the assembly of sterile drug products. Heedlessly cutting corners in defiance of well-known, industry-wide best practices, the air-conditioning in those rooms was shut down between 8:00 p.m. and 5:30 a.m., exacerbating fungal and bacterial growth. Eric Kastango, a consultant who works with compounding pharmacies on quality control, told the *Washington Post*: "This reinforces the fact that this facility was just horrific. The amount of microorganisms in the clean room was out of control."[46] He added that because of improper temperature control, the clean room became a "giant incubator for things to thrive. You never shut down the air conditioning in the clean room."[47] During the first nine months of 2012, routine monitoring by NECC employees of the clean room sterility uncovered mold or bacterial contamination at more than 80 locations. Managers kept the facility operating without taking time for a thorough cleanup.

As investigators came to grips with these conditions and inquired into the company's history of interactions with federal and state regulators, they discovered to their chagrin that the NECC had been cited for violations multiple times since it set up shop in 1998. Just ten months after the company got its Massachusetts state license, regulators discovered that it had mailed mass solicitations containing blank prescription pads to many doctors within its marketing area. That practice is strongly discouraged by the FDA because it has long maintained that compounding pharmacies should produce medications only in response to prescriptions already written for specific individual patients. Yet the blank prescription pad approach became a persistent problem within the industry and the NECC was investigated for similar episodes at least

---

[45] Thomas M. Burton & Jonathan D. Rockoff, *U.S. News: Pharmacy Faulted Further by FDA*, WALL ST. J., Oct. 27, 2012, at A6.
[46] Lena H. Sun, *Officials: Pharmacy Knew About Contamination*, WASH. POST, Oct. 27, 2012, at A2.
[47] *Id.*

five times over the following decade. Yet federal and state regulators were unable to stop the practice.

Starting in 2002 and continuing into 2003, the NECC was also the target of numerous complaints by doctors whose patients were given contaminated drugs, including two patients who were hospitalized with meningitis symptoms. Both the FDA and the Massachusetts Pharmacy Board spent days at the facility on two separate occasions. During the course of these inspections, Barry Cadden, the senior executive on the scene, informed regulators that he had plans to expand his marketing to 50 states, up from the 13 states where he was already licensed to sell compounded drugs. Interstate marketing is also discouraged by the FDA because it provides ample opportunity for violations of the advance prescription rule. Once again, federal and state regulators could not find a way to discourage this expansion.

At the final meeting to review the results of the 2002–2003 investigation, an FDA official named David Elder told company representatives that the NECC's compounding practices, "in particular those relating to sterile products," could have "serious public health consequences" if they "are not improved."[48] Despite the discovery of so many serious problems, Elder said that the FDA was passing the case off to the Massachusetts Pharmacy Board. The FDA's memorandum officially referring the matter to the Board noted ominously: "[We] recommend [that] firm be prohibited from manufacturing until they can demonstrate ability to make product reproducibly and dependably."[49]

The Board did not resolve the case until January 2006 and its final action fell far short of a shutdown. Instead, the Board entered a toothless consent agreement that required the NECC to hire a third-party auditor named Pharmacy Support, Inc. to verify the company's compliance. When auditors visited the facility, they discovered many of the same practices that had so concerned the FDA's Elder three years before, including:

- breaches of sterility requirements, including the absence of written procedures instructing lab personnel to wear proper attire and wash their hands as often as necessary;
- lack of any quality control procedures;
- use of nonsterile solution to sanitize equipment;

---

[48] Health, Education, Labor, and Pensions Committee of the U.S. Senate, The New England Compounding Center and the Meningitis Outbreak of 2012: A Failure to Address Risk to the Public Health 4 (Nov. 15, 2012) (hereinafter HELP Committee Report), *available at* http://www.help.senate.gov/imo/media/doc/11_15_12%20HELP%20Staff%20Report%20on%20Meningitis%20Outbreak.pdf.

[49] *Id.*

- improper calibration procedures for instruments;
- failure to sanitize the floor in a buffer zone adjoining clean rooms for periods as long as three months;
- incorrect assignment of "beyond use" dates to batches of medication;
- holes in gloves used by technicians to handle sterile medications; and
- poor recordkeeping regarding complaints the facility received from its customers.[50]

For reasons that remain unclear, Pharmacy Support, Inc. ignored its own negative findings and instead recommended to the Massachusetts Board of Pharmacy that the NECC be taken off probation. In the aftermath of the 2012 outbreak, investigators made another startling and embarrassing discovery: Ross Caputo, the owner of auditor, Pharmacy Support, Inc., was prosecuted criminally for falsely marketing a sterilizer that could cause blindness and was not approved by the FDA. He received a ten-year prison sentence in September 2006.

Meanwhile, back in Framingham, in September 2004, FDA inspectors were once again called to the NECC in response to complaints that the company had improperly produced Trypan Blue, an injectable dye used in ophthalmic procedures. They discovered that these allegations were correct but this time did not pass the case off to their state counterparts. Instead, two years later, the FDA sent NECC a warning letter, giving the company until January 2007 to respond.[51] Warning letters do not have the force of law unless they are converted into compliance orders, and there is no evidence that the FDA took that step with respect to Trypan Blue.

REGULATORY FAILURE: A LEGAL "NO MAN'S LAND"[52]

Massachusetts Failure

The FDA has long taken the position that primary responsibility for overseeing compounding pharmacies rests with state pharmacy boards that also police

---

[50] *Id.* at 6.

[51] Warning Letter (NEW-06-07W) from Gail T. Costello, Dist. Dir., New England Dist. Office, FDA, to Barry J. Cadden, Dir. of Pharmacy, New England Compounding Center (Dec. 4, 2006), *available at* http://www.fda.gov/ICECI/EnforcementActions/WarningLetters/2006/ucm076196.htm.

[52] Walt Bogdanich & Sabrina Tavernise, *U.S. Concern Over Compounders Predates Outbreak of Meningitis*, N.Y. TIMES, Oct, 23, 2012, at A1 ("Some compounding pharmacies have taken advantage of the legal no-man's land in regulation. The F.D.A. can inspect them and issue warnings, but the agency says states have ultimate jurisdiction.").

their traditional counterparts selling ready-made drugs.[53] The boards are composed of practicing pharmacists who are generally appointed by the governor, with token consumer representation and very limited funding. Board membership can overlap with pharmacists who are in charge of facilities under investigation. Indeed, the IACP, the compounders' leading trade association, has long urged its members to join state boards so that they are in a position to persuade other board members to remain supportive of the industry. In Massachusetts, Sophia Pasedis, a state pharmacy board member appointed in 2004, was a senior vice president at Ameridose. In the wake of the outbreak, state officials urged her to step down but she refused, remaining as a board member until her term expired several weeks later.[54]

As their limited background suggests, state boards specialize in reviewing complaints regarding the professionalism of individual pharmacists and are ill-equipped to regulate manufacturing practices, even on a small scale. Most do not have rules that would prevent the kinds of errors endemic at the NECC. An investigation by Congressman Ed Markey (D-MA) (who has since been elected to the U.S. Senate) found that most state boards do not keep coherent or accessible enforcement records:

This analysis makes clear that state regulators are not, or cannot, perform the same sort of safety-related oversight of compounding pharmacy practices that the FDA has historically undertaken. But it is also clear that absent clear new statutory authority, the FDA's efforts will ultimately be constrained by gaps in regulatory authority and thwarted by an industry that has historically resisted a federal role for the oversight of its activities.[55]

The FDA as Scapegoat

Despite its long-avowed deference to state pharmacy boards as the frstb line of defense against illegal compounding, the FDA's role as chief drug safety watchdog means that the agency has kept a suspicious eye on the compounding industry. FDA staff has watched with growing dismay as compounders

[53] For a good description of the boards and their limitations, *see* William G. Schiffbauer, *Confounded in Compounding Apothecaries: The Critical Need for Confining State Pharmacy Boards to Self-Regulation*, 11 Pharmaceutical L. & Industry Rep. (Bloomberg BNA), at 121 (Jan. 25, 2013).

[54] Aaron Pressman, *Massachusetts Closes Third Pharmacy Since Meningitis Outbreak*, Reuters, Oct. 28, 2012, http://www.reuters.com/article/2012/10/29/us-usa-health-meningitis-closure-id USBRE89R0LR20121029.

[55] Office of Congressman Edward J. Markey, Compounding Pharmacies Compounding Risk (2013), *available at* http://interactive.snm.org/docs/Compounding%20Pharmacies%20-%20Compounding%20Risk%20FINAL_0.pdf.

marketed and shipped products across multiple state lines. As the NECC example shows, the FDA occasionally intervenes in especially troubling cases, generally in response to complaints submitted by patients or medical personnel to its Internet-based center known as "Medwatch."[56] When it does intervene, its long-standing practice is to team up with state inspectors to visit targeted facilities. If serious violations are found, the FDA may pursue the case itself or it may pass it off to state regulators. When the agency keeps a case, it sends a Form 483 – a kind of bad conduct report – to the targeted facility and, if the response is not satisfactory, it may issue a warning letter. Sixty such letters were sent to compounding pharmacies between 2001 and the fall of 2012. Nevertheless, during this same period, the FDA acknowledges that 23 deaths and 83 serious illnesses were connected to unsafe conditions at compounding pharmacies.

As it patrolled the volatile perimeter of compounding, dipping into the fray only in egregious cases, FDA regulators were probably aware that the agency would play the role of scapegoat if anything went seriously wrong. But their efforts to define the parameters for acceptable compounding were hamstrung by crabbed judicial interpretations of the agency's regulatory authority and ferocious industry opposition. In that sense, the NECC was the agency's worst nightmare morphed into reality. To be sure, the Massachusetts board came in for punishing criticism and its staff director was fired soon after the outbreak was traced to Framingham. Deval Patrick, the state's liberal governor, was deeply embarrassed by the board's obvious incompetence and the state legislature soon started to consider a tough compounding law. But these developments were but a sideshow for the punishment the FDA endured, with Commissioner Margaret Hamburg hauled before Congress repeatedly for hours of hostile questioning.

Hamburg tried to explain what had happened by describing her agency's legal travails as it tried to implement prospective guidelines to control the worst practices in the industry. The objective truth is that the FDA was dealt a bad hand by the courts. But because the politicians were too busy posing for the television cameras, few had patience for Hamburg's explanations and a feeding frenzy regarding the agency's incompetence began both on the Op-Ed pages and in congressional hearing rooms. As the *Wall Street Journal* reported with a sneer of disgust, "How these firms escaped closer regulation shows how little happens in Washington absent an emergency."[57] Rep. Timothy Murphy

---

[56] *MedWatch: The FDA Safety Information and Adverse Event Reporting Program*, FDA.GOV, http://www.fda.gov/Safety/MedWatch/default.htm.

[57] Thomas M. Burton et al., *Pharmacies Fought Controls: Industry at the Focus of Meningitis Outbreak Beat Back More Federal Oversight*, WALL ST. J., Oct. 15, 2012, at A6.

(R-PA), chair of the Oversight Subcommittee of the House Energy and Commerce Committee, went so far as to accuse the agency of intentional malfeasance: "Ten years of warning signs, alarm bells, and flashing red lights were deliberately ignored."[58]

Of course, it is a staple of American party politics for the party that does not control the executive branch to find fault with the one that does. But in this case, the FDA was censured on a bipartisan basis. A Democratic staff report compiled for the U.S. Senate Health, Education, Labor, and Pensions Committee concluded that "this crisis should have, and could have been avoided entirely."[59] Piling on to an unusually harsh and unfair extent, the staff even went so far as to suggest that the FDA was more to blame for the meningitis outbreak than NECC executives:

> Given the history of NECC, the fact that the company produced and shipped a contaminated product that has led to 32 deaths and 461 infections to date [November 12, 2012] is not a surprise. The surprise is that they were allowed to continue to engage in drug compounding for over a decade with this record. ... There were a number of authorities and mechanisms for both federal and state regulators to address this issue, but bureaucratic inertia appears to be what allowed a bad actor to repeatedly risk public health.[60]

Had members of Congress and their staff been more patient with the agency, and thought more deeply about what Hamburg was saying about the FDA's legal problems, the outcome of this sad episode might well have been more encouraging. But they did not, instead passing a shockingly weak law that is unlikely to forestall the next compounding industry crisis. More on that discouraging topic will be provided in a moment. First, it's important to take a brief detour into the FDA's legal troubles.

The agency ran into trouble because the statutory framework for its oversight of drugs was established long before compounders started operating across state lines on a large scale. The intricacies of compounding were the farthest thing from Congress' mind as it struggled to devise an effective system for ensuring the safety of mass-produced drugs. The law requires that any entity (think very large pharmaceutical company) wishing to manufacture a new drug must submit an application for FDA approval.[61] Approval of such applications is implemented through a cumbersome process that requires extensive testing to ensure that the formulation is safe for the use (or uses)

[58] Matthew Perrone, *Report Faults FDA for not Closing Mass. Pharmacy*, BOSTON GLOBE, Apr. 17, 2013, at B10.

[59] HELP COMMITTEE REPORT, *supra* note 48, at 11.

[60] *Id.*

[61] 21 U.S.C. § 355 (2012).

specified by the manufacturer. The process takes years and requires hundreds of millions – even billions – of dollars of investment by the corporate applicant. Obviously, this heavy regulatory machinery is ill-suited to the task of making sure that some 7,500 relatively small businesses are safely churning out specialized medications in quantities larger than those needed by individual patients but still far smaller than the typical national pharmaceutical company. Unfortunately, the FDA felt constrained by it.

FDA regulators tried in 1992 to forestall the potentially dangerous expansion of compounding by threatening to prosecute pharmacies for the unauthorized manufacture of new drugs. The agency's "Compliance Policy Guide" said that compounders should only make medications in conjunction with individual prescriptions, although it provided a small amount of wiggle room for them to make batches of drugs in anticipation of receiving prescriptions from doctors with whom it had done business.[62] The Guide warned that the agency would consider enforcement action if compounders used commercial scale manufacturing or testing equipment or compounded regularly available drugs, a practice that it viewed as producing generic copies of drugs manufactured under safer circumstances by large pharmaceutical companies.

This approach ended up trapping the agency in a paradigm that required regulators to sort one group of compounders, those that did not stray very far from the prohibition of manufacturing in bulk, from a second group that routinely marched outside this boundary, selling in bulk without worrying about prescriptions. To maintain a case against the second group, the FDA had to argue that they should have applied for new drug approval even though such procedures were never intended to apply to compounders. The new drug approval process seemed so absurdly inaccessible for small outfits like the NECC that the FDA looked unreasonable or, worse, disingenuous, as if what it really wanted was to put certain compounders out of business. As important, the arbitrary dividing line between the two groups of compounders – the super small and the merely small – has very little to do with safety. To be sure, a super small compounder is likely to kill or injure fewer people than a merely small counterpart. But the FDA and state pharmacy boards should have zero tolerance for dangerous laboratory conditions like those found at the NECC whether the pharmacy makes doses requested by prescription or doses made in anticipation of receiving a prescription someday.

What makes this rigid fealty to the statutory scheme for new drug approval especially disappointing in retrospect is that the FDA has ample authority to take enforcement action against purveyors of "adulterated" drugs, which are

[62] FDA Compliance Policy Guide No. 7132.16 (March 1992).

defined as substances not made in compliance with the agency's rules on good manufacturing practices.[63] Had it focused instead on this authority, the NECC fiasco might well have turned out differently. The shipment of compounded medications contaminated by fungus – or any other deleterious matter – is clearly covered by these provisions. Enforcement against companies like the NECC that sell adulterated drugs has the strong advantage of keeping the focus on safe – that is, sterile – manufacturing practices. The FDA would still face serious practical challenges because compounders are not required to register their existence at the federal level and it does not have the resources to inspect compounders systematically. Nevertheless, had it taken this approach, and worked with receptive states to develop substantive rules for safe manufacture, it would not have spent a decade on the losing side of an increasingly punishing legal battle with the industry.

The Industry Goes to Court

The compounding industry, which is relatively small but unusually well-connected politically, was unhappy with the Compliance Policy Guide. In response to its complaints and the FDA's growing concerns about the expansion of compounding, Congress stepped into the fray, writing a special provision on compounders that became part of the Food and Drug Administration Modernization Act of 1997 (FDAMA).[64] Like the 1992 Compliance Guide, the statute said that compounders should make drugs only in response to individual prescriptions or in limited quantities in the context of an established relationship with a pharmacist, prescriber, or patient. The ingredients of compounded drugs must meet safe manufacturing standards. Compounders must not make copies of commercially available drugs in "inordinate" amounts. The FDA could identify drugs that pose "demonstrable difficulties for compounding," and compounders must refrain from making them. Last but far from least as it turned out, compounders could not advertise. This law had the great advantage of putting the FDA on firm ground legally by relieving it from the necessity of arguing that the new drug approval provisions of the statute somehow applied to compounders that offended guidelines written by unelected civil servants.

Although they had participated actively in the legislative process and even claimed credit for their successes in modifying the legislation, compounders were once again up in arms about the advertising ban and soon raised the

---

[63] 21 U.S.C. § 351 (2012).

[64] Pub. L. No. 105-115, 111 Stat. 2328 (codified at 21 U.S.C. § 353a).

money for a legal challenge. The case reached the Supreme Court in 2002. In a 5–4 decision, the Court overturned the advertising prohibition on the basis that it was an unconstitutional prohibition on compounders' constitutional right to free "commercial" speech.[65] The majority opinion, authored by Justice Sandra Day O'Connor and joined by Justices Antonin Scalia, Anthony Kennedy, David Souter, and Clarence Thomas, reasoned that Congress could have adopted less intrusive remedies that would not have banned all advertising. The dissent was authored by Justice Stephen Breyer and joined by Chief Justice William Rehnquist, John Paul Stevens, and Ruth Bader Ginsburg. They argued that the imperative of protecting public health outweighed these considerations.

Both sides spent considerable time debating the merits of the "direct-to-patient" advertising that was prohibited under FDAMA. The majority accused the dissenters of paternalism for upholding FDA interference with such ads. The dissenters responded that doctors needed protection from insistent patients who, attracted by compounders' claims that they could save big money on their prescriptions, would lobby successfully for that questionable source of supply. In light of what happened later, the justices' preoccupation with this issue was unfortunate, to say the least. More than free speech was at stake and the dissenters' concerns about the adverse effects on public health caused by the unrestricted growth of compounding turned out to be prescient.

By the time of the high court's decision, the FDA was under the firm control of political appointees selected by President George W. Bush who were fundamentally hostile to its regulatory mission. FDA officials under President Bill Clinton strongly supported the FDAMA's compounding section. The Bush administration was less far less enthusiastic. In fact, for reasons that are unclear, the Department of Justice (DOJ) attorneys who were representing the FDA neglected to ask the Supreme Court to "sever" the advertising prohibition from the remainder of the Act in the event that the justices decided to overturn it. If severed, the advertising ban would be null and void but the remainder of the law, including its important restrictions on compounding without individual prescriptions, would remain in effect and enforceable. The failure to request severance was a blatant and inexplicable mistake for any lawyer to make. The destructive result was that the Supreme Court refused to address the matter, leaving a Ninth Circuit Court of Appeals decision invalidating the entire law in effect.[66]

Because the Ninth Circuit only covers Alaska, Arizona, California, Hawaii, Idaho, Montana, Nevada, Oregon, and Washington, the FDA took the intrepid

[65] Thompson v. W. States Med. Ctr., 535 U.S. 357 (2002).
[66] W. States Med. Ctr. v. Shalala, 238 F.3d 1090 (9th Cir. 2001).

position that it still had authority over compounders in the rest of the states. Infuriated, ten compounders returned to court in 2004 seeking a "declaratory judgment" (an advance ruling issued outside the context of a specific enforcement action) that compounded drugs should not be subject to the new drug approval process. In 2008, the Fifth Circuit Court of Appeals rejected their arguments, declaring all the provisions of the 1997 law regarding compounders' to be valid with the sole exception of its advertising ban.[67] This victory left the FDA free to invoke the law anywhere in the Fifth Circuit, which covers Louisiana, Mississippi, and Texas, but its efforts in other states were still hamstrung. The FDA retreated in disarray from its efforts to prescribe industry-wide rules, although it still attempted to bring individual enforcement actions outside the Ninth Circuit in egregious cases.

In 2011, a federal district court judge in Florida rejected the FDA's contention that compounders who market veterinary drugs that are made from ingredients sold in bulk commit a *per se* violation of Food, Drug, and Cosmetics Act.[68] A pharmacy called Franck's Lab made medication containing the wrong dose of a key ingredient, killing 21 horses belonging to the Venezuelan national polo team. The federal government sought to enjoin the pharmacy from continuing to sell all such medications. Judge Timothy Corrigan wrote a lengthy opinion extolling the good done by compounding in the context of treating so-called non-food-producing animals," concluding that Congress could not have intended to authorize the FDA to take such drastic action. In May 2012, less than a year after Judge Corrigan's decision, the Centers for Disease Control and Prevention (CDC) issued an advisory as part of its "Morbidity and Mortality Weekly Report" explaining that 33 cases of fungal endophthalmitis – a serious human eye infection – had been discovered in seven states and had been traced back to contaminated medications compounded by Franck's Lab. The CDC investigators announced grimly that "[c]linicians should be aware of the ongoing investigation and should avoid use of compounded products labeled as sterile from Franck's during this ongoing investigation."[69]

As the agency limped through the Bush administration with steadily decreasing budgets and entered the Obama administration hoping for a reprieve, FDA staff struggled to maintain its grip on the supervision of major pharmaceutical

---

[67] Med. Ctr. Pharmacy v. Mukasey, 536 F.3d 383 (5th Cir. 2008).

[68] United States v. Franck's Lab, Inc., 816 F. Supp. 2d 1209 (M.D. Fla. 2011).

[69] Suber Huang et al., *Notes from the Field: Multistate Outbreak of Postprocedural Fungal Endophthalmitis Associated with a Single Compounding Pharmacy*, 61 Morbidity & Mortality Weekly Rep. 310 (2012), *available at* http://www.cdc.gov/mmwr/preview/mmwrhtml/mm6117a5.htm.

companies and paid scant attention to far smaller compounders. Coping with these intense little outfits that were not registered and that reacted so angrily to any challenge to their practices was just too much trouble for an agency with far more widespread problems to solve. Former Clinton-era FDA deputy commissioner Mary Pendergast reminded the *Washington Post* in October 2012 that the agency barely had sufficient resources to inspect large pharmaceutical plants: "There's a legitimate worry about spreading resources too thinly. They play Whac-a-Mole with compounding. If there's a problem, they whack at it. That's not necessarily an irrational approach when you consider the bigger problems they're dealing with."[70]

Criminal Behavior: The NECC as Rogue or Representative

In the aftermath of the NECC outbreak, the FDA made the wise decision to undertake a "risk-based" audit of compounders. Targets were selected on the basis of warning signs, including serious adverse event reports, historical inspection data, and complaints about product quality.[71] Twenty-eight facilities that met two of these three criteria, or that were associated with a reported death, were placed on the inspection list. Three more were added on the basis of information discovered during the initial round of visits, for a total of 31 in 18 states. The agency used specially trained and experienced federal inspectors, who teamed with their state counterparts in 90 percent of cases. The inspections were quite thorough, including visual observation of the production process; interviews with technicians and management; and review of documents on the firm's operations, standard operating procedures, and products, especially with regard to sterilization and drug stability. Investigators collected samples where appropriate, and also researched episodes where failures had occurred with respect to potency, sterility, and endotoxins. The agency had completed 29 of 31 inspections by April 2013, and it issued a Form 483 (bad conduct report) to 28 of that number. (The lone exception was not manufacturing sterile drugs.) The Form 483 reports are depressing reading. Frequently mentioned are the same universe of problems turned up at the NECC: multiple violations of best practices to preserve sterilization, from gloving to gowns to effective sealing of clean rooms; failure to calibrate equipment; lack of written procedures; inadequate testing of finished

---

[70] Lena H. Sun et al., *Officials: Murky Rules Harmed Meningitis Case*, WASH. POST, Oct. 12, 2012, at A1.

[71] Information about this investigation appears at *Summary: 2013 FDA Pharmacy Inspection Assignment*, FDA (2014), http://www.fda.gov/Drugs/GuidanceComplianceRegulatoryInfor mation/PharmacyCompounding/ucm347722.htm.

products to detect dangerous contamination; poorly trained personnel; and filthy equipment. How the FDA will pursue these multiple violations is not yet clear.

A Bizarre Coda: Congress and Regulatory Volunteerism

Given the growing evidence that the compounding industry harbors a significant number of firms with practices similar to the NECC's and daunting challenges that the FDA and the states still confront in preventing further outbreaks, you might expect that Congress would take the opportunity to pass a new law straightening out confusion over the FDA's legal authority and giving the agency the tools it needs to crack down on the worst actors within this little industry. And, if history was any guide, you would be right. Congress typically passes new, more stringent laws whenever a public health or environmental crisis has emerged until recently when, as we saw in the chapters discussing the Upper Big Branch mine disaster and the Macondo well blowout, it was too polarized to take action. Lack of action is bad, but it pales in comparison to what happened in the wake of the NECC crisis. Congress passed a shockingly weak new law, hailed as a wonderful example of bipartisanship in an era of anything but.[72] A short explanation of the compounding industry's political clout is necessary to understand this outcome.

By Washington standards, the industry's size and resources are small and niggling. The IACP, the industry's leading trade association, has about 2,100 members who managed to spend $1.1 million on lobbying in the past decade. To gauge its political clout simply by its size would be a mistake. As the *New York Times* has reported, "by positioning itself as a more affordable, community-based alternative to huge drug manufacturers, compounders have attracted broad support from politicians [becoming] popular among proponents of hormone therapy to slow aging and advocates for the autistic, who often distrust the traditional pharmaceutical industry."[73] The center of the industry's influence is in Texas, where particularly active firms built alliances with Tom DeLay (R-TX), former House Majority leader, and Rep. Joe Barton (R-TX), outspoken member of the powerful House Energy and Commerce Committee.[74]

The IACP has long taken the position that the FDA does not have any authority over compounders and should not play a role to play in overseeing

---

[72] Drug Quality & Security Act of 2013, Pub. L. No. 113-54, 127 Stat. 587.

[73] Eric Lichtblau & Sabrina Tavernise, *Friends in Congress Have Helped Drug Compounders Avoid Tighter Rules*, N.Y. Times, Nov. 14, 2012, at A16.

[74] *Id.*

their performance. It has advanced this position in every venue possible, from the courts, to Congress, to the media, to the regulatory agencies at the federal, state, and local levels. As an example of the rhetoric that has characterized this positioning, consider the following quotes from a piece of IACP propaganda sent to members in an effort to forestall passage of the FDAMA amendments in 1997.

Alert: compounding crisis
Senators Kennedy, Burr and Roberts have drafted legislation that would give FDA control of compounding and take away patient access to many critical compounding medications. Among key evils, the proposal would:

- Give FDA broad authority over compounding, including the ability to do full inspection of compounding pharmacies [and]
- Severely restrict out-of-state distribution of compounded medicines, including patients who live near borders, those in rural areas and vacationers
- And much more.

We have been working to spread the word about this bill, but many have not read or acted. This is the most critical threat pharmacy compounding has ever faced. The time is now, the day is here. If you value your career, your practice, the hope you bring to the patients you serve, you must act now![75]

Having failed to control the outcome of the 1997 legislative battle, compounders continued the assault on the FDA's jurisdiction in the courts throughout the ensuing 15 years. In 2002, as the FDA prepared to issue a revised compliance guide, the IACP told the agency that "[w]hatever FDA's statutory power over pharmacies may be, IACP believes that FDA has no authority to set national safety standards for pharmacies that are not 'manufacturers.' ... We strongly believe ... that Congress never authorized FDA to act as the National Board of Pharmacy."[76]

---

75 IACP, Compounding in Crisis (2007). The document was released as an attachment to a letter sent to The Honorable Tim Murphy, Chairman of the Energy and Commerce Committee's Subcommittee on Investigations and Oversight by Reps. Henry Waxman, Diana DeGette, John Dingell, and Edward Markey on April 11, 2013, *available at* http://democrats.energycommerce.house.gov/index.php?q=news/democratic-committee-leaders-request-testimony-on-meningitis-outbreak-from-academy-of-compoundi.

76 IASCP Publishes Draft Comments Regarding FDA's Compliance Guide Regarding Compounding Pharmacy (July 30, 2002), *available at* http://democrats.energycommerce.house.gov/sites/default/files/documents/FDA-Compliance-Policy-Guide-for-Compounding-Pharmacy-2002-7-30.pdf.

The IACP did not confine itself to outside advocacy. It also produced advice for its members regarding what to do if FDA inspectors sought access to their facilities:

> FDA investigators generally are not trained to inspect pharmacies, and many investigators do not know that there is this exemption for pharmacies. However, this exemption was upheld by the district court in the *Medical Center Pharmacy v. Gonzalez* case. ... Therefore, if the investigator tries to insist that he or she has a right to inspect the records, you can use this decision to explain that FDA may not inspect your records.[77]

As the NECC crisis erupted, the IACP deployed its members across Capitol Hill, buying just enough time for the crisis to wane and for news stories about additional illnesses and deaths to be relegated to the back pages of both print and electronic media. And so it was not until November 2013 that Congress finally passed, and the president signed into law, the "Drug Quality and Security Act," with Democrats and Republicans both taking victory laps for their bipartisan approach to the problem.[78]

The new law does not require compounders to register with the FDA unless they elect voluntarily to do so, and it does not increase either the civil or the criminal penalties that the agency can impose in the event that a compounder ships tainted drugs to customers. Instead, the law depends on compounders that make sterile drugs without individual prescriptions to volunteer to become official "outsourcers" of compounded drugs. A voluntary choice to participate in the system triggers an obligation to pay user fees to support FDA oversight and subjects the facility to periodic FDA inspections. Sponsors of the legislation rationalize this system on the basis that market forces would drive most compounders to register as hospitals and other customers refused to do business with unregulated firms. The new law declares that the provisions of the 1997 law – except the advertising ban deemed unconstitutional by the Supreme Court – are now in force throughout the country. It does not strengthen the FDA's authority to enter and demand written records from suspect compounders who do not volunteer for such treatment.

Ironically, the public statements by the IACP and the FDA were in general accord regarding the new law's capacity to prevent another outbreak. The IACP was, as usual, in full dudgeon: "If the goal of this legislation is to prevent

---

[77] IACP, FDA Inspection of Pharmacies: What Should You Do? (undated), *available at* http://democrats.energycommerce.house.gov/sites/default/files/documents/Document-IACP-FDA-Sample-Request.pdf (citing Med. Ctr. Pharmacy v. Gonzales, 451 F. Supp. 2d 854 (W.D. Tex. 2006)).

[78] Drug Quality & Security Act, Pub. L. No. 113-54, 127 Stat. 587 (2013) (codified in scattered sections of 21 U.S.C.).

another NECC, which has been stated many times over, then the American public must know that this bill will not accomplish that goal. A voluntary category of outsourcing facilities is not the answer."[79] The FDA characterized the new law as a "step forward, but expressed disappointment that it fell short of giving the agency fuller regulatory power."[80]

Only time will tell whether a market-based approach can improve safety within an industry that has such potential to endanger public health. If anyone sets up a pool to bet on the outcome, though, smart money will stay out of it.

CONCLUSION

The PCA and the NECC stand in stark contrast to the other companies featured in these three chapters because they are so small. BP and Massey Energy created fatal conditions out of a displacement of responsibility within huge, poorly organized, and badly led institutions. The people who produced salmonella-laced peanut butter and fungus-contaminated steroids were intimately familiar with the root causes of those outcomes. The fact that Barry Cadden, Doug Conigliaro, Stewart Parnell, and Samuel Lightsey persisted for years in their drive to push product out the door, despite one safety fiasco after another, provides clear evidence of guilt. The FDA had the legal authority and ample evidence to prosecute all of these individual defendants criminally many years ago, before their recklessness killed people. Yet the extensive record developed in the wake of the two outbreaks bears no sign that this approach was ever considered.

---

[79] *Pharmacies Face Scrutiny*, THE TENNESSEAN, Nov. 19, 2013, at A1.
[80] Sabrina Tavernise, *Bill on Drug Compounding Clear Congress a Year After a Meningitis Outbreak*, N.Y. TIMES, Nov. 18, 2013, at A15.

Part Three

Solutions

JUDGE RAKOFF'S LAMENT

In a short essay that sent shockwaves through the contentious world of prosecutors, judges, defense attorneys, and corporate counsels, federal district court
Judge Jed Rakoff wondered recently why no bank executives have been
prosecuted for causing the 2008 economic meltdown. Rakoff, considered a
maverick by his friends and an iconoclast by his foes, noted that the five-year
statute of limitations (deadline) for such prosecutions would soon arrive.
Careful to acknowledge that he is not privy to all the facts, the judge nevertheless managed to skewer prosecutorial timidity while professing sardonic
bewilderment:

> I have no opinion whether any given top executive had knowledge of the
> dubious nature of the underlying [subprime] mortgages, let alone fraudulent
> intent.
>
> But what I do find surprising is that the Department of Justice should view
> the proving of intent as so difficult in this case. Who, for example, was
> generating the so-called "suspicious activity reports" of mortgage fraud that,
> as mentioned, increased so hugely in the years leading up to the crisis? Why,
> the banks themselves. A top-level banker, one might argue, confronted with
> growing evidence from his own and other banks that mortgage fraud was
> increasing, might have inquired why his bank's mortgage-based securities
> continued to receive AAA ratings. And if, despite these and other reports of

suspicious activity, the executive failed to make such inquiries, might it be because he did not want to know what such inquiries would reveal?

This, of course, is what is known in the law as "willful blindness" or "conscious disregard." It is a well-established basis on which federal prosecutors have asked juries to infer intent, including in cases involving complexities, such as accounting rules, at least as esoteric as those involved in the events leading up to the financial crisis.[1]

Rakoff speculated that the DOJ's phobia about Arthur Andersen or, as it is known colloquially, the notion that some institutions are "too big to jail" plays a large role in the dearth of corporate prosecutions. He argued as I did at the outset of this book that such ill-founded anxiety creates fundamentally different standards for prosecuting the rich and the poor. Yet the concern that some firms are too big to jail, however misguided, does not explain why individual executives involved in subprime fraud have not been charged when their colleagues accused of insider trading have been compelled to trot into court with regularity. This damaging prosecution gap, says Rakoff, is attributable to mismanagement fostered by the Obama administration, which has never made such prosecutions a priority, instead spreading responsibility for them broadly among numerous U.S. Attorneys' offices. None had the expertise to develop the cases, with the notable exception of the elite southern district of New York office headed by Preet Bharara, which was already preoccupied with insider trading and the Madoff case. Consequently, the banking industry largely escaped prosecution and the message was sent that if very bad behavior is widespread among the nation's most prominent financial institutions, it may be pursued with impunity.

Judge Rakoff, a former prosecutor with extensive experience in Wall Street litigation, has been on a mission to expose prosecutorial hypocrisy for quite some time. In November 2011 he was asked to approve a DOJ and Securities and Exchange Commission (SEC) settlement with Citigroup regarding criminal charges of securities fraud. Citigroup, like many Wall Street banks, had sold investors mortgage-backed investments while simultaneously betting its own money against their profitability. Investors lost $700 million and the bank made $160 million. Yet the DOJ and the SEC allowed the company to sign a

---

[1] Jed S. Rakoff, *The Financial Crisis: Why Have no High Level Executives Been Prosecuted?*, N.Y. REV. BOOKS, Jan. 9, 2014, http://www.nybooks.com/articles/archives/2014/jan/09/financial-crisis-why-no-executive-prosecutions/. *See also* Adam Liptak, *Stern Words for Wall Street's Watchdogs, from a Judge*, N.Y. TIMES, Dec. 16, 2013, http://www.nytimes.com/2013/12/17/us/judge-raises-questions-on-the-paltry-effort-to-prosecute-wall-street-executives.html; Louise Story, *Bank of America Opposes Judge's Proposal for an Outside Pay Consultant*, N.Y. TIMES, Feb. 17, 2010, http://www.nytimes.com/2010/02/18/business/18bofa.html.

Deferred Prosecution Agreement that collected $285 million to settle securities fraud charges without requiring the company to either admit or deny any wrongdoing. Such agreements do *not* involve criminal charges, but rather state that such charges may be brought later, if the company acts badly again. Calling the compact "neither fair, nor reasonable, nor adequate, nor in the public interest," the judge refused to approve it, noting that Citigroup was a recidivist that had repeatedly violated SEC rules and therefore did not deserve such kid glove treatment.[2] *New York Times* reporter Edward Wyatt then discovered that banks targeted by SEC enforcement actions over the preceding fifteen-year period (1996–2011) had fifty-one cases of repeat offenses and that Citigroup alone accounted for six of those incidents. Unfortunately, the SEC was successful when it appealed Judge Rakoff's order that the parties prepare for trial to the Second Circuit Court of Appeals, which ratified the settlement, commenting that requiring an admission of guilt "would in most cases undermine any chance for compromise."[3]

THE OBAMA PROSECUTIONS

The stories told in Part II of this book could easily substitute for Wall Street firms' reckless behavior during the financial crisis. Is it any less disturbing to wonder why senior executives at Massey Energy, BP, the Peanut Corporation of America, or the New England Compounding Center have evaded prosecutions despite ample warning that their facilities were likely to kill people? And why doesn't the stomach-turning history of BP's scofflaw attitude regarding health, safety, and environmental laws provoke federal prosecutors to rethink their overweening anxiety about the effect of criminal prosecution on corporate survival? After all, BP was allowed to sign civil agreements and even pled guilty to minor environmental crimes without changing its behavior. Its scofflaw approach suggests that motivating a corporation to change requires the most rigorous criminal enforcement against both the corporation and its most senior managers. When BP's fiasco, the Macondo blowout, dominated the media for four months, the DOJ overcame its squeamishness and hit the giant company with a $4 billion criminal fine that required admissions of guilt regarding serious criminal charges. Even then, BP rose from the ashes, bragged that it is leaner and meaner, escaped debarment, began a campaign to cancel its agreement to pay damages to Gulf residents, and stalked back into the Gulf of Mexico with characteristic swagger. Only

---

[2] Editorial, *The S.E.C.'s Enabling*, N.Y. Times, Nov. 28, 2011, http://www.nytimes.com/2011/11/29/opinion/the-secs-enabling.html?_r=0.

[3] S.E.C. v. Citigroup Global Markets Inc., 673 F.3d 158, 163 (2d Cir. 2012).

time will tell if BP's huge financial losses have reformed its corporate culture, but preparing to go out of business it is not.

The DOJ deserves credit for the efforts it has made over the last three years to develop criminal prosecutions against individual, mid-, and lower-level managers in situations in which workers and consumers died and the environment was decimated. These accomplishments are especially significant given the weak track records of other presidents. Cases brought by U.S. Attorneys in Georgia and West Virginia are encouraging because they required assistant U.S. Attorneys in those offices to grapple with arcane rules and overcome resource shortfalls to indict relatively senior managers in the peanut and Upper Big Branch incidents. Prosecutors have pledged to keep climbing up the corporate ladder regarding Macondo and Upper Big Branch. Yet years have gone by with no further sign of indictments.

Until and unless Goodwin reaches former Massey CEO Don Blankenship, his prosecution of lower-level executives could have a boomerang effect. The other men indicted in the aftermath danced to Blankenship's tune, which is not to excuse them, but rather to urge that to have lasting deterrent effect, accountability must travel to the top. The same lesson can be drawn from the Macondo blowout: the two men prosecuted for the core offense of blowing out the rig are mid-level managers who shared authority with many other actors, including executives from other corporations. Limiting criminal prosecution to them suggests that the strategy of picking a fall guy works. Or, in other words, as trade union experts repeatedly warn, a conservative legal strategy that requires presence at the scene of a disaster to prove *mens rea*, or a guilty mind, means that only low- to mid-level supervisors have anything to fear. This cramped approach destroys the criminal law's capacity to motivate adoption of a safety culture that to be meaningful, must be endorsed, funded, and implemented from the top down.

Plenty of "low hanging fruit" is available for prosecution now, despite statutory gaps in the definition of crime and the severity of available punishment, especially if state and local prosecutors could be persuaded to utilize their authority to prosecute manslaughter and reckless endangerment cases more aggressively. The incidents that I selected for analysis here are among the worst of the worst. But autopsies of similar, less notorious events could fill several more volumes. Their close spacing over the last decade suggests that regulatory failures and corporate corner-cutting mean that many more will occur. The highest levels of corporate hierarchies are aware of these problems and either exacerbate or ignore them.

The following chapters focus on two changes to the existing system: reinterpretation of the constricted rules governing proof of *mens rea* in individual prosecutions and abandonment of Deferred Prosecution Agreements as the default for settlements with corporate defendants. The federal track record over the last five years indicates that the fierce undertow that makes prosecutors hesitate to pursue criminal investigations is largely psychological. A more expansive reading of willful blindness and reckless negligence doctrines is justified under existing law. If the misguided practice of giving large corporations a free pass through the entry of Deferred Prosecution Agreements is abandoned, federal prosecutors will be able to return to their core mission of enforcing the law.

These reforms are all possible under existing law. If Congress could accomplish an overhaul of these policies, the Executive Branch would be far more likely to implement changes rapidly. One unfortunate reality is certain: regulatory agencies and preventive rules are unlikely to experience a comeback any time soon, making it inevitable that prosecutors will have ample opportunity not just to intercede, but to make a real difference.

Establishing *mens rea*, or a guilty mind, is only half the battle and many problems plague the other side of the equation – establishing *actus reus*, or a bad act, generally by statute. The reason why the DOJ has to use wire fraud and false statement provisions to prosecute managers who preside over entirely preventable tragedies is because federal law lags far behind accepted best practices in many industries. The only federal statutes allowing prosecution for manslaughter cover deaths on the Continental Shelf or on land controlled by Native American tribes or the U.S. diplomatic corps. In other contexts – worker safety is a discouraging example – the penalties for criminal violations are so low that the DOJ typically does not bother to pursue the cases.

I set the expansion of the universe of *actus reus* and the strengthening of the criminal penalties aside here for practical, not principled, reasons. For a variety of reasons, federal and state legislatures are polarized; in the midst of strident battles organized on partisan or ideological grounds; swamped by problems they see as far more urgent (for example, budget deficits, rising health care costs, access to education); or heavily influenced by corporate contributions. They are disinclined to pass new laws at all. Even in states where legislatures are active, they hesitate to penalize business for fear that such reforms will chill economic recovery. To change these dynamics, prosecutors must demonstrate that criminal cases can be brought and should be won. The best way to encourage the expansion of criminal prosecutions is to tackle the difficult problem of *mens rea* when corporate executives who control the terms of operations and conditions at industrial plants are not standing at the scene when accidents happen.

7

Institutionalized Recklessness

The guys who built the Pintos had kids in college who were driving that car. Believe me, no one sits down and thinks: "I'm deliberately going to make this car unsafe."

Lee Iacocca, former CEO Chrysler Corporation[1]

For most managers, especially for those who are ambitious, the real meaning of work – the basis of social identity and valued self-image – becomes keeping one's eye on the main chance, maintaining and furthering one's own position and career. This task requires, of course, unrelenting attentiveness to the social intricacies of one's organization.

Robert Jackall, *Moral Mazes: The World of Corporate Managers*[2]

With other violent crimes we tend to seek explanations as to why people turn to violence – and often use terms like deranged, psychotic, drugged, psychopathic, pathological and other concepts from the vocabulary of severe psychiatric disturbances – and also demand severe punishment ... for offenders. Managers, in contrast are ostensibly normal and their decision-making takes place in the board-rooms of companies where well-educated and well-groomed (and arguably "well-balanced") executives debate business decisions on the basis of strategic, marketing, financial and other considerations. ... Presumably no one is fully aware that they are planning death. And yet companies do end up killing and maiming people. Feelings of justice should surely dictate that responsibility will be located at the point where decisions were made, that the corporate

[1] Lee Iacocca, Iacocca: An Autobiography 172 (1986)
[2] Robert Jackall, Moral Mazes: The World of Corporate Managers 202 (1988). Jackall is a sociologist. This book, still highly influential in the study of white collar crime, was based on extensive interviews he did with managers at a small chemical company, a defense contractor, and a public relations firm. Jackall teaches at Williams College; his background is available at http://web.williams.edu/AnthSoc/jackall.php.

officials concerned will be prosecuted, and that they and/or the company
will be heavily punished.

> Maurice Punch, *Suite Violence: Why Managers Murder
> and Corporations Kill*[3]

ACCIDENTS HAPPEN

White collar criminal prosecutions have been forestalled for decades by the
claim that human errors committed by frontline workers are the real cause of
industrial catastrophes. Proponents of this worldview argue that because
people make mistakes, the causes of industrial accidents (critical equipment
failure, explosions, fires, tainted consumer products) and the consequences of
such events (fatalities, injuries, environmental damage, and large economic
loss) are inevitable. They do not acknowledge evidence demonstrating that
institutional dysfunction is at the root of the worst incidents.

As much as they can, senior managers of high-hazard industrial operations
encourage this interpretation of real-world events. For example, in the immediate aftermath of the Texas City refinery explosion, Ross Pillari, president of
BP Products North America, informed the press: "Had the six operators and
one supervisor assigned to the start-up of the refinery's so-called isomerization
unit been doing their jobs, the explosion would not have happened."[4] This
ham-handed effort to blame the bottom rung of the corporate hierarchy was
later contradicted by the special investigative panel chaired by former U.S.
Secretary of State James Baker. Its exhaustive report concluded that neglected
maintenance, inadequate training, corporate incentives to do work quickly,
and acute gaps in supervision not only caused the accident but were problems
at all of BP's American refineries. Later it became clear that these problems
also infected the giant corporation's oil exploration and production practices
in the Gulf and on Alaska's north slope.

These problems are not limited to large companies. The lab workers at the
New England Compounding Center told the owners of the closely held
company that unsanitary conditions in the clean room required urgent
attention. Senior managers responded that "This line is worth more than
all your lives combined, so don't stop it."[5] The line churned out thousands of

---

[3] Maurice Punch, *Suite Violence: Why Managers Murder and Corporations Kill*, 33 CRIME L. &
     SOC. CHANGE 243, 272 (2000). Punch is a prominent sociologist who specializes in the analysis of
     white collar crime. He teaches at the London School of Economics; his background is available at
     http://www.lse.ac.uk/socialPolicy/Researchcentresandgroups/mannheim/Staff/punch.aspx.
[4] Anne Bell, *BP Blames Staff for Deadly Texas City Blast*, HOUSTON CHRON., May 18, 2005.
[5] Sabrina Tavernises & Andrew Pollack, *Ex-Workers Cite Safety Concerns at Drug Firm*, N.Y.
     TIMES, Oct. 13, 2012, at A1.

vials of steroid injections contaminated by fungal meningitis because the siren call of big sales and fast profits overcame sterile laboratory practice for people who knew – and, as important, should have known – better.

A second, closely related argument is that even if an incident springs from institutional failure, high-ranking corporate executives do not have sufficient *mens rea* (guilty mind) to deserve indictment. Admittedly, senior executives make decisions about cost-cutting, determine whether the company emphasizes process safety, exert pressure to do work very quickly, and structure bonus programs to reward cutting corners. But because they are physically removed from the actual scene of the crime (the oil rig during the blowout, the mine when the methane ignited, the isom unit as it overfilled), they are not culpable.

Further undermining the prosecution of white collar crime is a campaign by conservative commentators and white collar defense lawyers who argue that the inordinately complicated and technical prohibitions governing arcane activities like securities stock market trading or the operation of sophisticated manufacturing equipment are ill-suited to criminal prosecution. After all, they say, violations of these convoluted rules are not *malum in se*, or obviously wrong, but instead are *malum prohibitum*, or wrong according to stacks of rulebooks stowed in the back of corporate lawyers' libraries and too esoteric for the average executive to understand.

These constrained readings of the criminal law focus on the proximate cause of the fiasco. No matter how much the stage is set for disaster by managers who take unconscionable risks, critics argue, the determination of causation should walk back only one or two steps to events immediately preceding an explosion. By keeping the viewpoint myopic, institutional failure – however acute – is off the grid and companies and their executives remain free to repeat mistakes over and over again because institutional reform is never forthcoming.

This chapter argues for a more expansive view that traces causation back to the conditions that impose unacceptable risk. Those conditions make it nearly impossible for frontline workers to avoid disaster. The symptoms of institutional dysfunction are straightforward: excessive tolerance of high risk; paper procedures, rules, and guidelines that are ignored; relentless cost-cutting without any evaluation of its implications; senior and mid-level managers who discourage the reporting of bad news; promotion of group think and concomitant erosion of a chain of command; and dearth of individual accountability at the senior executive level.

Assembling the details of five notorious fatal accidents and placing them side-by-side for examination reveals systematic patterns of misbehavior at the highest levels of the corporations that were involved. The narratives also indicate that catastrophes will continue to occur, despite our clear ability to prevent them, because the regulatory system is in so much trouble. Refineries remain among the most hazardous large facilities in America, but are not policed by the OSHA because it cannot afford routine inspections. Explosions and other fatal accidents that could be prevented continue to occur. Coal mining proceeds under the distracted eye of a regulator that cannot even clear its backlog of old cases. Violations for ignoring fundamental safety measures like rock dusting to suppress flammable coal dust continue to mount. Deepwater drilling moves out to the edge of the envelope of available technology, but is overseen by regulators who lack the training or the resources to discern what this risk-loving industry is doing, much less what it is doing wrong. Inspections are rarely a surprise and the penalties collected are an affordable surcharge on daily production. Implementation of the new law designed to forestall the ongoing series of foodborne illness is stalled, largely because House Republicans refuse to fund the program at a reasonable level. They argue that government has grown too big and pledge to reduce its size. The bleak landscape created by underfunding and its inevitable result, regulatory ossification, allows food processors to cut corners on the most basic sanitary practices. In a similar vein, drug compounders manufacture almost half of the injectable medications administered in this country without the benefit of any consistent regulatory oversight at the state or federal level and, as the case of the New England Compounding Center illustrates, relatively small, closely held companies can cause disastrous results for public health. But, Congress recently decided, they may operate without any federal oversight unless they volunteer for it.

These and other incidents noted throughout this book demonstrate that the root causes of severe industrial accidents are not one, two, or even three mistakes made by line workers immediately beforehand. The growing incidence of such accidents over the last decade suggests that more will occur unless proactive enforcement reinstates a baseline of individual accountability in the most troubled industries. By far the most efficient way to accomplish that goal is through criminal enforcement.

Obviously, rebuilding the government's capacity to produce preventive regulation would also help, preventing accidents rather than punishing people. But waiting for that outcome is like waiting for Godot; there are no signs on the horizon that federal institutions have the capacity or will power to rebuild, and the president seems uninterested in the problem. Into this vacuum, criminal enforcement can and should proceed.

I do not argue here for any loosening of constitutional protections with respect to white collar defendants. The privilege against self-incrimination, the protection against illegal search and seizure, and the rights to effective counsel and due process must apply with equal force and substance to the street criminal and the well-heeled white collar defendant. I do advocate the disentanglement of those constitutional privileges and rights from the question of culpability.

THE CAROTID ARTERY OF THE CRIMINAL LAW

Narrow Origins

The emphasis on *mens rea*, or guilty intent, runs like a carotid artery through criminal common law, the Model Penal Code, and federal, state, and local statutes. As criminal law expert Joshua Dressler explains, *mens rea* is constrained by the two central goals of the criminal law: deterrence and retribution. A person who does not intend to cause harm, many argue, will not be deterred by criminal punishment. Instead, hapless actors should be required to provide compensation to injured parties.

As for retribution, as the Supreme Court explained in a 1952 case, convicting a person who unintentionally causes harm makes as much sense as locking up a child who protests "[b]ut I didn't mean to."[6] Dressler writes:

> Crimes are public wrongs. The implication of a guilty verdict is that the convicted party wronged the community as a whole. By convicting a criminal defendant, society denounces the actor; it condemns and stigmatizes him as a wrongdoer. Respect for human dignity suggests, if it does not dictate, that such stigma should not attach, and liberty should not be denied, to one who has acted without a culpable state of mind.[7]

These analyses derived from situations where the commission of the crime had an immediate effect on the victim. Routine assault, theft, and murder cases involve facts that enable juries to decide whether the person who takes the affirmative action intended to cause the consequences that occurred or whether these outcomes were sufficiently surprising – or attenuated – to abnegate bad faith. Most of the time, intent is clear. But some situations are more ambiguous. If I shoot a fellow hunter in the forest and claim the wounding was an accident and that I had no bad intent, the subsequent investigation must consider whether I had a motive to harm that particular person or whether circumstances (poor visibility, the victim's clothing, rainy weather) might vindicate my claim.

For white collar crimes that have long chains of causation and involve ostensibly reputable defendants (people with upper-middle-class status and demonstrated success running things), the question of intent is more complicated. White collar defendants cover their tracks through layers of bureaucracy

---

[6] Morissette v. United States, 342 U.S. 246, 251 (1952).

[7] JOSHUA DRESSLER, UNDERSTANDING CRIMINAL LAW 121 (6th ed. 2012).

that provide multiple opportunities to obscure or avoid knowledge. Executives operate far from the scene of the accident and the social ramifications of holding them criminally culpable are profound. Or, in other words, if top executives are held criminally responsible for admittedly awful incidents in industrial settings far removed from corporate headquarters, does that outcome offend the wispy but valid notion of respect for human dignity?

Overall, the legal profession displays shocking inattention to these issues. Despite the growing debate over the repercussions of white collar crime, the prosecution of street crime continues to dominate the legal system and consumes most of its resources. The legal academy remains similarly preoccupied, with commentary in journal after journal focusing repetitively on due process in drug arrests, the sociology of prison, and the constitutionality of surveillance that uses advanced technology. As relevant as these subjects may be, white collar crime is of at least equal importance to the society as a whole. Three-quarters of a century after sociologist Edwin Sutherland coined the phrase white collar crime in a speech to the American Sociological Association, judges, practicing attorneys, and law professors do not devote much energy to proactive development of the law of white collar crime, as opposed to debating at tedious length whether such prosecutions are a good idea. The legal profession's disinterest in pushing the criminal law's application out to the frontier of high-hazard activities further discredits a fundamentally cautious and tradition-bound profession that seems chronically unable to think outside the box.[8]

The profession's apathy is doubly disturbing because it ignores several promising inroads suggested by judges in hard cases at the state level. For, as it turns out, the evolution of the criminal law is rife with doctrinal hooks that could support a more ambitious infrastructure.

Knowledge versus Recklessness

At its inception long before the Industrial Revolution, *mens rea* was defined as *actual* knowledge by the defendant that he did something wrong. A person who shoots another when not under threat knows that he has committed the forbidden act of murder. Or, as the Supreme Court opined in 1952, the defendant must have "an evil-meaning mind with an evil-doing hand."[9]

---

[8] An exception is the work of David Uhlmann, former head of the DOJ Environment and Natural Resources Crime Section. *See, e.g.,* David M. Uhlmann, *After the Spill: The Gulf of Mexico, Environmental Crime, and the Criminal Law,* 109 MICH. L. REV. 1413 (2011); David M. Uhlmann, *Environmental Crime Comes of Age: The Evolution of Criminal Enforcement in the Environmental Regulatory Scheme,* 1223 UTAH L. REV. (2009).

[9] *Morissette,* at 251.

Someone must set out to do harm, and not just bumble into harmful action inadvertently. Bumblers may be compelled to pay damages in a civil case, or they may lose their license to engage in certain activities, but they won't be sent to jail for causing death or injury, no matter how dreadful. Or, in other words, people don't generally go to jail for mere negligence.

The emphasis on how the behavior looks to outside parties is quite important to keep in mind. Criminal activities are judged by a reasonable person standard, meaning that a jury is asked to determine culpability on the basis of what an average person would have meant or intended in similar circumstances. Conversely, this standard also means that in making their case, prosecutors are not constrained by what a defendant confesses, or even what the defendant admits to knowing, if she takes the stand to give evidence at her own trial. Instead, prosecutors present – and juries consider – objectively provable facts about what happened.

In the postindustrial age, the concept of criminal knowledge branched out in response to social and economic conditions. Most states have adopted the Model Penal Code and it is also quite influential in federal prosecutions. It includes four states of mind that constitute *mens rea* in criminal cases.[10] In descending order from the most culpable mind-set to the least, they include (1) purpose; (2) actual knowledge; (3) recklessness; and (4) negligence.[11] Acting with a clear purpose or with actual (reasonable person) knowledge is typically the foundation for conviction in felony cases. In contrast, a negligent (careless) state of mind is usually treated as a misdemeanor. Cases involving a reckless mind-set are relatively rare and courts have trouble with them, sometimes punishing them as felonies and sometimes dismissing criminal charges on the grounds that the defendant was merely negligent. A defendant in a negligent, or run-of-the-mill careless, frame of mind is never guilty of more than a misdemeanor.

Shooting a person in the face with premeditation is to act with purpose, the most culpable state of mind. Because it is virtually impossible to argue that corporate managers go to work with the conscious intent of killing their employees, harming the public, or destroying the environment, this category is irrelevant to the following discussion. Prosecutors who have the resources to mount a successful case against a well-resourced defendant are reluctant to pursue mere misdemeanor cases involving a negligent state of mind, so they too may be placed to one side. These eliminations leave us with actual knowledge and recklessness as the two most relevant states of mind in potential white collar prosecutions involving industrial accidents.

---

[10]   All are defined in MODEL PENAL CODE § 2.02.
[11]   Kenneth W. Simons, *Rethinking Mental States*, 72 B.U. L. REV. 464, 469–71 (1992).

Actual knowledge means that, to be convicted, a person must have "practically certain knowledge" that she will produce a criminal consequence.[12] The line between conduct displaying purpose and conduct indicating knowledge that harm will almost certainly result can be paper thin in many cases. But these nuances preoccupy judges and the criminal bar. They may also concern juries, although it is difficult to tell exactly what goes on inside their deliberations. Again, knowledge is practically certain not because the defendant admits that it is, but because a reasonable person would know it to be so.

One branch of culpability based on knowledge applies when the defendant contrives his own ignorance by remaining willfully blind to facts that demonstrate he committed a crime. Courts have split on the question whether the defendant must have failed to investigate or whether it is enough for prosecutors to show a reasonable person would have known, although, again, the line between these two states of consciousness can be paper thin. Willful blindness cases that lower the burden of proof required in actual knowledge cases are controversial, and some judges and legal commentators are suspicious of them.

Finally, defendants may be deemed to have a "reckless" state of mind when they "consciously disregard a substantial and unjustifiable risk."[13] The typical cases in the street crime arena involve parents whose children have come to harm, police accused of using excessive force during an arrest, or people who cause a bad accident while drunk or otherwise impaired to the point that the accident was foreseeable. A smattering of cases, both successful and unsuccessful, asserts this mental state in an industrial context and several leading ones are examined further below.

Foreseeable Risk

Appellate courts have struggled with the recklessness doctrine because in many scenarios, something sympathetic about the defendant deters them from ratifying the conviction even when a jury has voted a guilty verdict. A mother whose children are dead because she was reckless has already suffered enough, or so the thinking goes. A policeman who shoots an unarmed suspect because he panics also engenders sympathy. Police have hard and dangerous jobs and, again, accidents happen with remedies available in a civil, not a criminal, context. These interpretations of recklessness, which view it as overly expansive because it imposes criminal culpability for

---

[12] *Id.*
[13] *Id.*

merely negligent behavior, are extraordinarily unfortunate when they are extended to an industrial context. Correctly understood, reckless behavior can cause grave harm for no good reason when any reasonable person would have known better. In the sometimes murky territory that divides practically certain knowledge from conscious disregard lie the foundations for more effective white collar prosecutions.

Reduced to its essentials, recklessness means behaving in a way that triggers a foreseeable, unacceptable risk. As a matter of daily routine, people assume potentially disastrous risk when driving a car in speeding traffic, living in an area subject to earthquakes, jogging on smoggy days, or taking a medicine for the first time. When other people's lives are at stake and the disaster becomes more foreseeable, recklessness can escalate to the point that it triggers liability for money damages in a civil case. From there, such behavior can cross the line to criminal negligence, generally a misdemeanor. In its most extreme version, recklessness becomes the *mens rea* necessary to be convicted of a felony. This last formula has three components:

1. Defendants must be conscious of – or recognize–the risk of their behavior. The more obvious the risk, the easier the proof of criminal culpability.
2. The risk must be substantial, including but not necessarily limited to death, serious injury, or irreparable harm.
3. Acting in the face of a recognized risk must be unjustifiable. Or, in other words, the defendant's motivation for undertaking risky behavior – what criminal law expert Kenneth Simon calls his "desire" – must appear selfish to the point of triviality.[14]

The standard hypothetical that law professors offer their students when explaining the recklessness doctrine involves a car speeding toward an intersection as the light is about to turn. The relationship of factors like how fast the driver is traveling, the speed limit, road and weather conditions, how many pedestrians use the intersection, and whether the driver sees the yellow caution light are considered as a whole in order to determine consciousness of the risk that the car will hit a pedestrian crossing with the light. The same external factors apply to the determination of how substantial the harm is likely to be. But the aspect of the legal test that considers whether the driver is behaving justifiably turns inward, to the reason why he was speeding: a driver rushing a woman in labor to the hospital is considered less culpable than one who is simply late for a dinner reservation or a party.

[14] *Id.* at 478.

Juries and judges have great discretion in considering the facts of specific cases. So, a speeding driver who kills a pedestrian while driving at 80 miles per hour on an icy road may well be found guilty even if she was late for work and about to lose her job for that reason. On the other hand, a driver with a perfect record traveling under the speed limit on a sunny day with a green light may well escape prosecution or conviction if she hits a toddler who darts into traffic after her mother left her unbuckled in her stroller and walked into a store. In the end, perhaps the best understanding of how trial judges and juries evaluate recklessness is that they weigh their compassion for the victim against their reaction to the defendant. Compassion or opprobrium have no part in the three-part test, of course, but this most human of reactions may well be where the rubber hits the road on determining whether to impose criminal punishment. Did the defendant do something heedless and damaging, or did she do something stupid that she later came to regret? Is it possible for a juror to imagine that he might do something equally dumb? How grave was the harm that befell the victim, and how much did she contribute to the reasons the accident occurred?

TOUGH CASES AND MIXED LAW

Because 90 percent of criminal cases end up negotiated out through plea bargains and even when cases go to trial jury verdicts are recorded but not explained, there are a relatively small number of written opinions applying the recklessness provisions of the Model Penal Code. They come from appellate courts that are far removed from the trial courts where judges and juries react intensely to the people involved in the case.

Most appellate recklessness decisions are decided by state courts, although these decisions are relevant to federal cases involving the same standards for *mens rea*. The cases typically deal with street crime, but a smattering of them deal with work-related incidents and many of those were quite high-profile. I have chosen six involving white collar crime and one more correctly characterized as street crime to illustrate the development of this critical doctrine. The decisions indicate how challenging prosecutors find it to win and sustain a conviction against white collar defendants in cases where workers or members of the public die because the manager of an industrial or commercial facility was reckless. Yet they also suggest that such victories are possible and that the trajectory of the law is toward more stringent standards for corporate behavior.

The cases involve difficult questions of *mens rea* that often revolve around the critical question of causation. Again, if the harm is not foreseeable, then a person cannot be deemed to harbor a reckless state of mind. Harm is not foreseeable unless the chain of causation is clear and, preferably, short. The most recent of the six white collar cases illustrates a growing judicial openness to the idea that when a workplace is unsafe, especially as measured by regulatory standards and common practice in the industry, judges will define those conditions as the origin of a chain of causation that can give rise to criminal culpability.

I included one of the most difficult examples of a street crime recklessness case in order to illustrate strong but unstated social judgments that suffuse these decisions. In white collar cases, judges see before them individual defendants who may generate considerable sympathy. They are middle or upper middle class, they are well educated and sincere, and they run plants with advanced technology. Their lives have already been devastated by an accident they did not intend. The question then becomes whether a judge will choose to focus on the defendants' circumstances or the grievous harm visited on those who died or were injured in the accident. My street crime example, which involved two little girls dying in a blazing fire because their mother left a lit candle near their bed and went out, brings the reality of these powerful reactions into sharp relief.

The Nightclub

The Cocoanut Grove was one of Boston's largest and most successful night-clubs; it opened soon after the end of Prohibition and was still going strong in the middle of World War II. On the evening of November 28, 1942, right after Thanksgiving, the club was packed beyond capacity by soldiers on leave, their dates, and other partygoers. Trying to navigate its murky inner reaches in order to turn on an electric light, a teenage bar boy struck a match to see better, re-lit the lamp, and blew out the match without noticing that it had already ignited the dried palm fronds composing the club's décor.[15] As flames rushed through these highly flammable decorations and all the electric lights went out, people panicked and rushed to find an exit. The club had several, including a revolving door that served as its main entrance. But one crucial door was locked, with the key kept in a desk in the club's office, perhaps, the court speculated, to prevent patrons from either entering or leaving without paying. When firemen searched the building, they found two dead bodies in front of the locked door, and a "pile of bodies" about seven feet away.[16] The death toll

---

[15] Commonwealth v. Welansky, 55 N.E.2d 902 (Mass. 1944).
[16] *Id.* at 902.

reached 492, a tragedy so shocking that it prompted the origination of fire codes in Massachusetts and across the country.

The Cocoanut Grove employed about 80 people. Its management was "completely dominated" by one Barnett Welansky, who was hospitalized at the time of the fire with a sudden illness, leaving his brother James in charge.[17] Nevertheless, Barnett Welansky was charged with manslaughter, convicted by a jury, and ultimately sentenced to 15 years in jail. (He was later pardoned by the governor.) The Supreme Judicial Court of Massachusetts upheld that decision, finding that the locked door was part of the normal and routine operation of the nightclub established by Barnett Welansky and followed by James Welansky in his absence. Barnett Welansky testified that he had instructed the head waiter, who died in the fire, to keep the door unlocked at all times, but the jury did not believe him and the appellate court did not disrupt its verdict. Instead, the appellate court found that Barnett Welansky owed a duty of care to his business visitors, and was reckless because he disregarded the obvious consequences of locking the door:

> To convict the defendant of manslaughter, the Commonwealth was not required to prove that he caused the fire by some wanton or reckless conduct. Fire in a place of public resort is an ever-present danger. It was enough to prove that death resulted from his wanton or reckless disregard of the safety of patrons in the event of fire from any cause.[18]

The court was clear that although wanton or reckless conduct "usually ... consists of an affirmative act, like driving an automobile or discharging a firearm, in disregard of probable harmful consequences to another," Barnett Welansky owed a "duty of care for the safety of business visitors invited to premises which [he] controls."[19] In such instances, conduct can mean "intentional failure to take such care in disregard of probable harmful consequences."[20]

The Fireworks Factory

Three decades after the Cocoanut Grove prosecutions, Massachusetts prosecutors indicted Edmund Godin, the president of a fireworks manufacturer, for the death of three workers when an area where fireworks were assembled exploded. The plant included 21 buildings, several of which were used for

---

[17] *Id.* at 902.
[18] *Id.* at 912.
[19] *Id.* at 909.
[20] *Id.*

different stages of pyrotechnic products. The accident occurred in building seven, used to dry completed fireworks and to store the company's product stockpiles. Workers had been on strike for reasons never explained in the opinion and, as a result, an estimated 4,000 to 5,000 fireworks – four to five times as many as usual, were in the building. The evidence submitted at trial indicated that this unusually high quantity of stored product exponentially increased the damage caused by the blast.

Among other legal arguments, the defendant tried to distinguish the Cocoanut Grove case on the basis that the duty a manufacturer owes to its employees is significantly lower than what it owes to the public invited onto its premises to purchase services it has for sale. The court was having none of this suggestion, in the process suggesting that the criminal law embraces different interests than the civil liability system, a crucial distinction because the worker's compensation system generally bars employees from collecting damages from employers in court:

> The Commonwealth has an interest that persons within its territory should not be killed by the wanton and reckless conduct of others. ... The fact that a particular allegation of facts may be nonactionable in tort does not perforce mean the same holds true when those same facts are contained in the material allegations of an indictment for manslaughter. ... An employer whose acts or omissions constitute a disregard for the probable harmful consequences and loss of life as to amount to wanton or reckless conduct is properly charged with manslaughter where a foreseeable death is caused thereby. ... *The State is the offended party where a death is caused by recklessness.* To accept the defendant's arguments here is not only to overlook the fundamentally different purposes of criminal law and tort law but to create a class of persons – employees – as to whom a license to kill by wanton and reckless conduct is given.[21]

The Cyanide Tank

Another, more recent but no less notorious case was the prosecution of Steven O'Neill, Charles Kirschbaum, and Daniel Rodriguez, managers of a Film Recovery, Inc. factory in Elk Grove Village, Illinois.[22] The company's business was to extract silver from used x-ray and photographic film, a process that involved soaking the film in a cyanide/water solution. On the morning of February 10, 1982, a Polish immigrant named Stefan Golab went to stir the solution in one of the tanks with a rake. As he stirred, he was overcome by

---

[21] Commonwealth v. Edmund J. Godin, 371 N.E.2d 438, 442–43 (1977) (emphasis added).
[22] People v. O'Neil, 550 N.E.2d 1090 (Ill. App. Ct. 1990).

fumes that wafted from the dangerous mixture. Feeling dizzy and faint, Golab retreated to the lunchroom, where he went into convulsions, foamed at the mouth, and lost consciousness. He was rushed to the hospital, but was dead on arrival. The indictment charged that the three defendants failed to disclose to Golab that "he was working with substance containing cyanide and failed to advise him about, train him to anticipate, and to provide adequate equipment to protect him from, attendant dangers involved."[23] All three were convicted of both murder and reckless conduct in a "bench trial" where the decision is made by a judge, not a jury.

The appellate court overruled the trial judge because his decision to convict the defendants of both murder, which requires actual knowledge, and reck-lessness, which requires a finding of conscious disregard, was internally incon-sistent. The appellate court tried to unravel the various actions and omissions of the defendants to line them up under the two different, mutually inconsistent theories, but could not: "Because the offenses of murder and reckless conduct require mutually exclusive mental states, and because we conclude the same evidence of the individual defendants' conduct is used to support both offenses and does not establish, separately, each of the requisite mental states, we conclude that the convictions are legally inconsistent."[24] Although the appel-late court remanded for a retrial, the prosecutor did not pursue a second trial.

The cyanide case is well known in the community of sociologists who write about white collar crime, although some do not seem to realize that the convictions were overturned. The grounds for reversal involve the kind of doctrinal distinctions that animate argument among members of the legal tribe. In any event, the prosecutors may not have retried the case because they were convinced that indictment and any time served awaiting trial were sufficient punishment, and the case had already sent an appropriate message of deterrence to companies employing vulnerable workers to handle danger-ous substances. The appellate court opinion certainly does not undercut an effort to prosecute callous bosses under recklessness theory; if anything, it suggests that the doctrine is valid in its own right.

Triangle Shirtwaist Redux

Perhaps no event was more crucial to the birth of organized labor in the United States than the Triangle Shirtwaist fire, which killed 123 women and 23 men, many of whom jumped out of windows at the garment factory where

---

[23] *Id.* at 1093.
[24] *Id.* at 1098.

they worked to escape fire and smoke when it burst into flame on March 25, 1911. Like Cocoanut Grove, the doors were locked, also according to the owners, to prevent petty theft, and people who did not jump died either from smoke inhalation, burns, or being trampled to death as they desperately tried to escape. Most were Italian and Jewish immigrants working for a pittance in the only jobs they could get. The two youngest victims were 14 and the oldest was 43. The owners of the plant, Max Blanck and Isaac Harris, were prosecuted for manslaughter, but a jury of their peers acquitted the two men.

To see how the law has developed, we need only fast forward to 1979, almost seven decades and a dizzying array of social, economic, and political developments away from the Lower East Side in 1911. Sadly, we need not leave New York City. On October 10, 1979, a fire at a warehouse used to store textiles took one life and resulted in the indictment, again for manslaughter, of Zalman Deitsch, the owner of the facility, and fellow managers Joseph Deitsch and Baruch Scher. The Deitsch Textile Corporation was also charged. The six-story warehouse was crammed with bales of cloth, in some places stacked to the ceiling, to the point that only narrow aisles permitted access to stairwells and a freight elevator. Access to the alternative emergency route provided by a fire escape was so obscured that most employees were not even aware of its existence. The warehouse had no sprinkler system and employees had never received instruction regarding what to do in the event of a fire. Fire marshals had not inspected the building because the fire department erroneously listed it as vacant. It took 100 firemen to bring the fire under control, but the textiles provided so much fuel that the fire continued to burn for several days, albeit in a contained condition.

The trial judge assigned to the case dismissed the indictments on the grounds that the defendants' conduct was not a sufficiently direct cause of the employee's death. The appellate court reinstated them because "defendants created conditions in the warehouse which they should have foreseen could result in death in the event of a fire."[25] The appellate decision focused on the defendants' failure to keep escape routes clear, the fact that elevator doors were routinely left open on several floors at once although this practice meant that the elevator could not be moved even if the doors were shut at its departure point, and their failure to maintain a standpipe system that could be used for fire hoses. Significantly, defendants had received citations for the elevator and standpipe systems in the relatively recent past. "We can see no bar to the imposition of criminal liability for deaths caused by a fire upon one who

---

[25] People v. Deitsch, 97 A.D.2d 327, 335 (1983).

maintains what is, in effect, a fire trap, no matter what the cause of the fire," the court observed acerbically.[26]

The Chewing Gum Production Line

The circumstantial evidence in the Deitsch case, including the obvious fire hazard posed by overfilling the warehouse with flammable materials, blocking access to the fire escape, and disabling the elevators, led the court inexorably toward the conclusion that the defendants recklessly ignored a foreseeable and unacceptable risk. In a second case, however, the chain of causation troubled the New York Court of Appeals to the point that in 1980, it upheld a lower court's dismissal of the indictments against Warner-Lambert Company and several of its officers and employees. The defendants were indicted on charges of manslaughter regarding the deaths of six workers on a production line to make Freshen-Up gum, sold in the shape of a square tablet with a jellylike center. To avoid having the gum adhere to the machinery as the outer layer was filled with the inner one, the process used a variety of chemicals and machinery was kept at very low temperatures. In any event, clouds of dust surrounding the machinery and composed primarily of magnesium stearate ignited, causing extensive damage to the building and killing six workers.

The causes of the explosion were never convincingly explained, and this gap bothered the court. If prosecutors could not prove what caused the fire, how could the defendants anticipate the disastrous outcome? The prosecutors argued that what the defendants should have foreseen was that if they did not remove the residual dust, it would one day ignite. But the court remained stymied by proximate causation: "Viewed most favorably to the People, the proof with respect to the actual cause of the explosion is speculative only, and as to at least one of the major hypotheses – that involving oxygen liquefaction – there was no evidence that that process was foreseeable or known to any of the defendants."[27]

The Sewage Tank

Fast forward three more decades (65 years out from the Cocoanut Grove) and a different world presents. The OSHA has had a chance, in its heyday, to write some serious workplace safety standards and one involved the precautions necessary when workers are sent into confined spaces where some dangerous

[26] *Id.* at 336.
[27] People v. Warner-Lambert Company, 51 N.Y.2d 295, 300 (1980).

substance may be present. Unfortunately, the senior managers at the Far West Water & Sewer Co. made no effort to abide by those requirements and the people directly involved in the fatal incident, which resulted in the deaths of two men and severe injuries to a third, knew nothing about them.

Demonstrating her ignorance with tragic results, a supervisor named Connie Charles got it into her head that after a 3,000 tank holding sewage was emptied, renovated, and ready to be refilled, she would fill the tank half-full of sewage and then order an employee to climb inside it to pull a plug blocking a second inflow line. The tank was buried nine feet underground. To gain entry, a person needed to climb down a ladder, through a four-foot-wide manhole cover at the top of the tank. The first man sent on this dangerous mission made it as far as standing on the ladder with half his body inside the tank when he was overcome by the intense fumes of hydrogen sulfide that are produced by raw sewage. He fainted, fell into the tank, and ended up floating face down in the noxious pool. He died, as did another man who went in trying to rescue him, using a rope because the company did not have proper rescue equipment on hand. A third rescuer had to be carried out of the tank and suffered severe injuries. The supervisor responsible for this situation was indicted, as was the sewage treatment company's president.

On appeal, the defendants, who included the sewage treatment company, its president, and chief safety officer, and a company contracted to do the renovation work raised several defenses. The Arizona Court of Appeals rejected them all. Among the court's most important conclusions was that the president of the company, Brent Weidman, and his chief safety officer, Rex Noll, were "high managerial agents" acting "within the scope of their authority" and therefore the corporation and Weidman could be found culpable for manslaughter.[28] Even though neither man was present at the scene, both were seasoned experts in the process of sewage treatment and should have known that confined space and rescue requirements were essential to the safe operation of their business. In fact, six months before the fatal incident, a safety consultant informed them that they needed to get the company in compliance with OSHA standards and order certain pieces of safety equipment. As important, in the immediate aftermath of the accident, Weidman correctly diagnosed the cause of death and Noll acknowledged that safety equipment should have been on site and that the company "should have known better."[29]

[28] State v. Far West Water & Sewer Inc., 228 P.3d 909, 928 (2010).
[29] *Id.* at 927.

On the crucial issue of causation, the court concluded that a "natural and continuous sequence of events stemming from the defendant's act or omission, unbroken by any efficient intervening cause, that produces an injury, in whole or in part, and without which the injury would not have occurred" was sufficient.[30] It traced the origination of the sequence all the way back to the failure to put in place a program implementing OSHA confined space requirements. Or, in other words, "proximate" cause in cases involving blatant violations of regulatory requirements and well-known principles of safe practice within an industry need not be all that proximate provided that such violations set the stage for the disaster.

The Children and the Candle

Finally, there is the disturbing case of Sharan Williams, who was convicted by a jury on two felony counts of injuring a child and sentenced to 15 years in prison because her two children – Precious, eight, and Ujeana, seven – were killed in a house fire at the home of her boyfriend, Herbert Bowden. The Texas Court of Criminal Appeals overturned the conviction on the grounds that Williams was not reckless. Bowden was sentenced to ten years and his appeal was rejected. At first blush, this outcome in an admittedly difficult case seems quite reasonable – 'accidents like house fires happen, and surely this mother has suffered enough already. But then there are the very troubling facts.

Williams and her children lived with her mother, Zula Mae Scott, who regularly cared for the two girls. Occasionally, Williams and the children visited Bowden, who lived in a duplex that had no kitchen, no bathroom, no working utilities (that is, no water, heat, or electricity), and very little furniture. One evening in October 2002, Williams wanted to go out with her friends but her mother had not yet returned home from work. She took the two girls to Bowden's house and put them to bed, leaving a candle burning in an aluminum pie plate close to the mattress edge. Then she left, saying she was going out briefly to buy snacks but failing to return for several hours.

Bowden testified that he left the house once to get a cigarette from a friend down the street. Eventually, he fell asleep on the couch in the living room. At 1:00 a.m., he was awakened by the screams of the children. The bedroom was ablaze. The best guess of the fire marshal was that the candle ignited the bed clothes. Bowden decided he could not reach the girls and ran from the house. A final detail emphasized during the trial was that Scott had warned her daughter about the danger of burning candles at Bowden's house and urged her not to

---

[30] *Id.* at 930 (internal citations omitted).

bring the children there. The jury sat through three days of trial, deliberated for 90 minutes, and returned a guilty verdict.

The Court of Criminal Appeals acknowledged that it was required by Texas law to construe the facts "in the light most favorable to the verdict."[31] This rule applies because appellate judges do not witness the demeanor of witnesses and are unable to ascertain their credibility. Nevertheless, after raking through the trial transcript in an effort to justify its decision to exonerate Williams, the Court of Criminal Appeals concluded that the jury was wrong, analogizing Williams's actions to the behavior of parents who take their children on camping trips in the woods:

> If taking children to spend the night in a structure without utilities is conduct that involves an extreme risk of danger for which one may be subject to criminal prosecution for injury to a child should harm befall that child, the backwoods campers of the world are in serious jeopardy.[32]

Two judges wrote a sharp dissenting opinion:

> This case is not about a family camping trip gone wrong. It's not about a poor family doing the best it could with the little they had. This case is about two little girls who died a horrible death because their mother, for no good reason, took them from a safe home and left them in a place that she knew was a fire hazard. She left them there with a lit candle, telling them she was going to the store to get them snacks and that she would be back, but she didn't come back.[33]

The Upshot

Reasonable people could differ on all of these outcomes, of course, as indicated by the courts' disparate interpretations of what happened. The cases suggest, however, that appellate judges must first orient themselves to the defendants and the victims. All the circumstances at the root of these prosecutions are violent and the victims died – or were injured – in hideous ways. If defendants can portray themselves as clueless and full of remorse they have some chance of winning sympathy from the jury and the judges. On the other hand, provided prosecutors tell a straightforward story about a chain of events, defendants who create obvious hazards for petty and self-serving reasons can find themselves under indictment and even a corporate executive who is not present at the time risks jail.

[31] Williams v. State, 235 S.W.3d 742, 750 (Tex. Crim. App. 2007).
[32] *Id.* at 758.
[33] *Id.* at 770.

In present times, willingness to impose criminal liability is strengthened considerably by the far more extensive safety standards that apply to high-hazard industries. Rock dusting to suppress flammable coal dust, never filling an isom tower past nine feet, measuring drilling mud to detect a kick that would presage a blowout, testing samples for salmonella, maintaining sterility in a clean room – all are obvious and essential rules for safe operation that should be known by line workers and managers far up the corporate chain. When a company has been cited multiple times by regulators for breaking such rules, the case for finding requisite *mens rea* is even stronger.

Despite efforts to cut off any inquiry into the criminal liability of managers who were not standing at the scene of the crime when it occurred, judges in the relatively conservative jurisdiction of Arizona seem quite ready to find that they should foresee a causation chain that begins with the failure to create a safe workplace, with well-trained employees and necessary equipment. Rather than obsessing over the events that occur within a few minutes of a fire or explosion, prosecutors have been successful when they argue that decisions made months or years beforehand should have been foreseen.

The cases show that the greatest potential for revitalizing criminal prosecution of corporate officials in the wake of fatal industrial accidents lies at the state level because federal prosecutors cannot charge manslaughter in most cases. But federal prosecutors have other weapons in their arsenal – including charges involving reckless endangerment and making false statements to the government – if they can only overcome their unjustified squeamishness about climbing the corporate chain.

WILLFULLY BLIND MANAGERS AND EXECUTIVES

The willful blindness doctrine – also called conscious avoidance or contrived ignorance – is located along the continuum somewhere between actual knowledge and recklessness. If prosecutors can persuade judges to explain this idea to juries, they use the so-called "ostrich instruction," which federal appellate Judge Richard Posner explains as follows:

> It is not the purpose of the ostrich instruction to tell the jury that it does not need direct evidence of guilty knowledge to find such knowledge beyond a reasonable doubt. Still less is it to enable conviction of one who merely suspects that he may be involved with wrongdoers. ... The most powerful criticism of the ostrich instruction is, precisely, that its tendency is to allow juries to convict upon a finding of negligence for crimes that require intent. ... The criticism can be deflected by thinking carefully about what it is that real ostriches do (or at least are popularly supposed to do). They do

not just fail to follow through on their suspicions of bad things. They *deliberately* avoid acquiring unpleasant knowledge. The ostrich instruction is designed for cases in which there is evidence that the defendant, knowing or strongly suspecting that he is involved in shady dealings, takes steps to make sure that he does not acquire full of exact knowledge of the nature and extent of those dealings. A deliberate effort to avoid guilty knowledge is all the guilty knowledge the law requires.[34]

The leading case on willful blindness is *United States v. Jewell*, decided in the federal Court of Appeals for the Ninth Circuit *en banc*, meaning that every judge on the court participated in considering the appeal, enhancing its credibility. Defendant Charles Jewell drove a car containing 110 pounds of marijuana worth $6,250 concealed in a secret compartment. He testified that he was unaware the marijuana was in the car because he had not looked in the compartment. Upholding the conviction reached by the lower court, the appellate judges concluded that the jury had heard evidence permitting it to conclude that the defendant "deliberately avoided positive knowledge of the presence of the contraband to avoid responsibility in the event of discovery."[35] The judges continued:

> The substantive justification for the rule is that deliberate ignorance and positive knowledge are equally culpable. The textual justification is that in common understanding one "knows" facts of which he is less than absolutely certain. To act "knowingly," therefore, is not necessarily to act only with positive knowledge, but also to act with an awareness of the *high probability of the existence of the fact in question*. When such awareness is present, "positive" knowledge is not required.[36]

Had the *Jewell* judges left well enough alone, and simply concluded that willful blindness is equivalent to – but not the same as – knowledge for the purposes of determining liability, the doctrine might have had a less difficult time navigating the courts. Their insistence on going beyond that relatively straightforward statement to portray willful blindness as a variety of "high probability" knowledge still confuses application of the doctrine. The gist of the confusion is captured, but unfortunately not resolved, in the *Model Penal Code*, crafted a few years before *Jewell* and embraced by that opinion:

> The rule that wilful blindness is equivalent to knowledge is essential, and is found throughout the criminal law. It is, at the same time, an unstable rule, because judges are apt to forget its very limited scope. A court can properly

---

[34] United States v. Giovannetti, 919 F.2d 1223, 1227–28 (7th Cir. 1990).
[35] United States v. Jewell, 532 F.2d 697, 699 (9th Cir. 1976).
[36] *Id.* at 700 (emphasis added).

find wilful blindness only where it *can almost be said* that the defendant
actually knew. He suspected the fact; he realized its probability; but he
refrained from obtaining the final confirmation because he wanted in the
event to be able to deny knowledge. ... Any wider definition would make the
doctrine of wilful blindness indistinguishable from the civil doctrine of
negligence in not obtaining knowledge.[37]

Or, in other words, probably knowing but pretending not to know is criminal.

Thousands of miles away, three decades earlier, and in a far more serious
situation, a notorious case of willful blindness illustrates the significance of
developing the doctrine beyond secret compartments full of marijuana. In his
essay on the moral and legal questions raised by the doctrine of willful blindness, Professor David Luban explores the "nasty example" of Albert Speer,
whose career in the Third Reich began as Adolf Hitler's official architect.[38]
Speer moved upwards through the Nazi hierarchy, eventually becoming the
minister in charge of armaments. In that capacity, he was responsible for
supervising the use of slave labor at concentration camps and, after the war,
this work landed him in the first tier of defendants prosecuted at Nuremberg.

Speer then pursued the canny strategy of insisting on taking responsibility
for the crimes committed by the Reich. He insisted that he did not have actual
knowledge of the Final Solution, the concerted effort to kill all of the Jews in
the European territory controlled by the Nazis. Speer said that although he
was offered the opportunity to visit Auschwitz, he declined, thus avoiding the
occasion to bear witness to the extermination that his acquaintances must have
described to him often. Despite his lack of knowledge in the most literal
meaning of the term, he did not excuse himself, instead explaining that,
while he had not questioned other high-ranking officials in the regime,
including Hitler, he was "inescapably contaminated morally" because "from
fear of discovering something *which might have made me turn from my course*, I
had closed my eyes."[39] (emphasis added). The upshot of the story is that Speer
was given a 20-year jail term and his counterparts were hanged.

Apart from reminding us of the mystifying potency of an apology in the
aftermath of events that you have worked hard to cause, what are the implications of this episode for the criminal law? We could decide that Speer was
engaged in sophistry and that, whether or not he witnessed the actual implementation of the Final Solution with respect to specific individuals, he knew it
was happening. This approach seems intuitively appropriate in an age

---

[37] MODEL PENAL CODE § 2.02(7) (emphasis added).
[38] David Luban, *Contrived Ignorance*, 87 GEO. L.J. 957, 965 (1999).
[39] *Id.* at 966–67 (quoting ALBERT SPEER, INSIDE THE THIRD REICH: MEMOIRS 375–76
(1970)).

dominated by a 24/7 news cycle and the World Wide Web. But, says Luban, willful blindness construed as knowledge does not hold accountable a corporate executive who sets up an elaborate system for delegating to underlings the official responsibility for the obvious consequences of dangerous decisions.

Alternatively, Luban suggests, we could consider a somewhat different approach and take Speer – or anyone else asserting such an extreme degree of ignorance – at his word. Would Speer have changed course had he actually visited Auschwitz? Or was he splitting hairs in a way that should make little difference to his culpability? Speer may not have witnessed the horror but, even if he had, he would have continued to build armament and pray that his country would win the war. From this perspective, we could say that the law holds the willfully ignorant culpable because we do not believe they would change course, no matter how much they knew.

Of course, this invocation of the Speer case and Luban's insights into its ramifications for modern punishment is not intended to suggest that the upper-level managers at any of the corporations profiled in Part II are the moral equivalent of Albert Speer. Nor am I suggesting that upper-level executives who delegate operational authority to lower-level executives are culpable for anything and everything that goes wrong. Rather, the question becomes how strong the evidence of contrived ignorance must be before the line between innocence and culpability is crossed when very serious harm is the consequence.

The best example of this theory of willful blindness presented in this volume is the behavior of John Manzoni and Michael Hoffman, the top executives at BP who continued to cut costs – or run the plant to failure – after they were told by Don Parus, plant manager at the Texas City refinery, that further erosion of the physical plant, a dearth of supervisors, and inadequate training of line workers would almost certainly cost lives. At that moment, their efforts to distance themselves from the messy problems of drilling for and refining oil collapsed and they chose to proceed without examining the consequences.

How many senior executives who preside over large multinational corporations where disaster is brewing stick their head in the sand? They make themselves blind, willfully, not because they are too busy or are focused on other issues but because they believe that the only way to succeed is to accept the cost of fatal accidents.

THE RESPONSIBLE CORPORATE OFFICER DOCTRINE

The heyday of white collar criminal enforcement with respect to health, safety, and environmental violations was circa 1985–2002, and the vast majority of those cases were brought under federal environmental laws by a special division within the DOJ that was independent of the far more staid criminal division. The environmental statutes made most offenses felonies. Fully understanding that pursuing defendants who were at the low end of the totem pole within a corporate entity would not achieve the deterrent effects they were after, this new breed of lawyers frequently relied upon the "responsible corporate officer" or "responsible relation doctrine" created by the Supreme Court in two cases decided three decades apart for so-called public welfare offenses.

The first case, *United States v. Dotterweich*, decided in 1943 in an opinion written by the renowned Justice Felix Frankfurter, imposed misdemeanor liability on the employees of a small company that shipped misbranded and adulterated drugs in violation of the federal Food Drug and Cosmetics Act, which is administered by the Food and Drug Administration (FDA).[40] Justice Frankfurter explained that people could not protect themselves from "the circumstances of modern industrialism."[41] In order to dispense with the "conventional" – and overly strict – requirement that prosecutors prove actual awareness of wrongdoing, the "responsible corporate officer" doctrine should apply.[42]

In 1975, a second case, also prosecuted by the FDA, upheld a misdemeanor conviction against John Park, the president of a supermarket company that had a food warehouse overrun by rodents. Park claimed that the company was so large, with 36,000 employees and 874 retail outlets, that he delegated maintenance of sanitary conditions at its facilities to other managers. Unimpressed, the Court upheld jury instructions given by the federal district court judge that Park was culpable if he had "a responsible relation to the situation, even though he may not have participated personally."[43] The sanctions provided by the Act impose a "positive duty to seek out and remedy violations when they occur but also, and primarily, a duty to implement measures that will insure that violations will not occur."[44] The requirement that corporate executives exercise "foresight and vigilance" is "demanding," even "onerous," but it is essential to protect the "health and well-being" of the public.[45]

Among the most controversial examples of an environmental case that applied the responsible relation doctrine was the successful felony prosecution of Michael Weitzenhoff and Thomas Mariani, managers of the East Honolulu Community Services Sewage Treatment Plant who were convicted of illegally

---

[40] United States v. Dotterweich, 320 U.S. 277, 280–81 (1943). The doctrine was reiterated in *United States v. Park*. United States v. Park, 421 U.S. 658, 675 (1975).

[41] *Dotterweich*, 320 U.S. at 280.

[42] *Id.* at 281.

[43] *Park*, 421 U.S. at 665 n.9.

[44] *Park*, 421 U.S. at 672.

[45] *Park*, 421 U.S. at 672.

dumping sewage sludge into the ocean.[46] The plant processed four million gallons of "residential wastewater" – what goes down the drains and toilets at a typical home. As part of the process, employees put raw sewage in large tanks, where solid bits of debris would settle to the bottom. This thick wet solid was known as "waste activated sludge" and under the East Honolulu plant's permit to operate, it could not be piped into the ocean like treated wastewater, but had to be hauled away to a plant that had more sophisticated equipment for treating it.

At some point, the East Honolulu plant stopped hauling sludge away and it began to build up in the tanks. Rather than resuming the hauling, Weitzenhoff and Mariani told their employees to pump the excess sludge right into the ocean through the pipe, or "outfall," used for treated wastewater. On 40 occasions between April 1988 and June 1989, an estimated 436,000 pounds of sludge were discharged through the pipe, usually late at night. The Honolulu U.S. Attorney brought charges under the Clean Water Act, which contains a provision making discharges into bodies of water without a permit a felony. Prosecutors introduced general evidence about the public health problems that can be caused by discharges of sewage sludge into ocean waters used for recreation, but did not attempt to prove that the East Honolulu discharges caused severe public health or environmental problems. Instead, as the drafters of the Clean Water Act probably intended, the defendants were prosecuted and convicted because they violated a permit, even though they contended that they read the document to allow sludge discharges when necessary to allow the operation of the plant.

The federal district court trial judge and the federal Court of Appeals for the Ninth Circuit disagreed with the defendants' interpretation of the permit, but ruled it irrelevant because the prosecutor met his burden regarding knowing *mens rea* by proving consciousness of specific conduct, whether or not the defendants correctly understood the legal obligations the permit imposed. Or, in other words, the defendants could be convicted whether or not they knew exactly what the permit said so long as they knew that the sludge was being dumped into the ocean.

Perhaps needless to say, the decision sparked controversy, within the Ninth Circuit and beyond. A majority of Ninth Circuit judges voted not to rehear the case *en banc*. An *en banc* rehearing means that instead of having a decision by a three-judge panel serve as the last word on the subject, the entire group of all the judges who served on the Ninth Circuit would rehear argument and reconsider the three-judge panel's opinion. Rehearings *en banc* are quite rare and generally limited to cases where the lower district courts have

---

[46] United States v. Weitzenhoff, 35 F.3d 1275 (9th Cir. 1993).

rendered conflicting opinions on the same issue; no such circumstance existed in *Weitzenhoff*. Nevertheless, five judges who had voted unsuccessfully to rehear the case wrote a scathing dissent, accusing the three-judge panel that upheld the conviction of broadening the scope of criminal law to cover "innocent" conduct:

> First, [the decision] impairs a fundamental purpose of criminal justice, sorting out the innocent from the guilty before imposing punishment. Second, it does so in the context of the Clean Water Act. This statute has tremendous sweep. Most statutes permit anything except that is prohibited, but this one prohibits all regulated conduct involving waters and wetlands except what is permitted. Much more ordinary, innocent, productive activity is regulated by this law than people not versed in environmental law might imagine.
>
> The harm our mistaken decision may do is not necessarily limited to Clean Water Act cases. Dilution of the traditional requirement of a criminal state of mind, and application of the criminal law to innocent conduct, reduces the moral authority of our system of criminal law. If we use prison to achieve social goals regardless of the moral innocence of those we incarcerate, then imprisonment loses its moral opprobrium and our criminal law becomes morally arbitrary.[47] (internal citations omitted)

Clearly, then, the dissenting judges had big problems with the idea of punishing defendants engaged in a productive activity – treating sewage – under a statute that made behavior a felony whether or not it did grave harm, when the defendants claimed not to know they were doing anything wrong.

On the basis of this case and others like it, defense counsel and conservative commentators have ridiculed the responsible corporate officer (or responsible relation) doctrine. Relatively voluminous commentary condemns the outrageous results of the doctrine when advanced by overweening prosecutors.[48] Critics protest vehemently against the idea that a person can be convicted of crime – whether felony or misdemeanor – when he claims that he was quite confused about what convoluted regulatory laws require and when he is engaged in business that is helpful to society. In fairness to the authors of

---

[47] *Id.* at 1293.

[48] *See, e.g.*, Martin Petrin, *Circumscribing the Prosecutor's Ticket to Tag the Elite – A Critique of the Responsible Corporate Officer Doctrine*, 84 TEMP. L. REV. 283, 296 (2012); Richard J. Lazarus, *Meeting the Demands of Integration in the Evolution of Environmental Law: Reforming Environmental Criminal Law*, 80 GEO. L.J. 2407, 2428–40, 2478–79 (1995); Lisa Ann Harig, *Ignorance is Not Bliss: Responsible Corporate Officers Convicted of Environmental Crimes and the Federal Sentencing Guidelines*, 42 DUKE L.J. 145, 151–55 (1992); Keith A. Onsdorff and James M. Mesnard, *The Responsible Corporate Officer Doctrine in RCRA Criminal Enforcement: What You Don't Know Can Hurt You*, 22 ENVTL. L. REP. 10099, 10100, 10103 (1992).

this extensive literature, courts often appear equally confused. But the result has been that this fundamental misunderstanding of the doctrine has become extraordinarily controversial.

In a well-reasoned and carefully documented piece published in the *Journal of Criminal Law & Criminology*, former DOJ appellate lawyer and now Professor Todd Aagaard argues that despite this confusion, the responsible relation doctrine has nothing to do with diminishing the burden of proof that applies to the *mens rea* element of the prosecution's case. Rather, the doctrine permits the expansion of the scope of potential defendants who are liable for a crime. Providing that prosecutors can prove requisite knowledge on the part of such individuals, they can be culpable even if they stand at a distance when the harm caused by the crime becomes manifest if they had control of the activities that led up to it:

> Criminal enforcement, and in particular prosecuting individuals, can be one of the government's most powerful tools for combating corporate misconduct, but such prosecutions can be tricky. Our intuition may be to hold responsible those upper-level corporate officers and managers who allow illegal conduct to occur on their watch. But criminal liability in our society has historically, and appropriately, been quite circumscribed. ... The predominance of collective action and shared responsibility in business organizations can make it difficult to pin criminal liability on particular individuals acting within such organizations without overstretching criminal law principles. ... The responsible relation doctrine is one way in which such liability may be imposed, and it therefore warrants reexamination. The responsible relation doctrine holds individuals criminally liable for failing to prevent or correct violations that occur within their area of responsibility and control in a business organization.[49]

If only his former colleagues at the DOJ would take this interpretation to heart and consider a different approach to proving *mens rea*.

THE NORMALIZATION OF DEVIANCE

It takes a big, imaginative, and, some would argue, ill-advised step to cross the social and economic divide that separates the life situations of Barnett Welansky (owner of the Cocoanut Grove nightclub), Steven O'Neill (cyanide tank manager), Sharan Williams (mother of two small children who burned to death while she was out), Charles Jewell (transporter of marijuana across the Mexican

---

[49] Todd S. Aagaard, *A Fresh Look at the Responsible Relation Doctrine*, 96 J. Crim. L. & Criminology 1245, 1246 (2006).

border), Albert Speer (Nazi war criminal), Michael Weitzenhoff and Thomas Mariani (sewage treatment plant managers who ordered dumping of sewage sludge in the Pacific Ocean), and Don Parus, plant manager at BP's Texas City refinery. Some would argue that comparing these situations is not remotely appropriate. Speer was a monster and Jewell and Williams were street criminals victimized by their own poverty. Welansky, O'Neill, Weitzenhoff, and Mariani gave the directives that caused the violations but taken together, their businesses would fit in the back lot of one of BP's smallest facilities. BP executives were running a profitable, far-flung business empire of great importance in the world, and they had appropriately delegated responsibility for daily operations to others. To consciously disregard a risk, you have to be aware that it exists. To expect senior executives like Manzoni to be aware of such problems, much less worry about them or be held accountable for them is simply unreasonable.

Again, though, all of these cases have generated ample evidence that senior managers had ample warning of the imminent hazards that ultimately took lives. When Don Parus confronted Manzoni, BP's second in command worldwide, and Hoffman, BP's chief of U.S. refining, weeks before the fatal explosion, he presented a Power Point containing pictures of workers killed at the plant, largely as a result of equipment failure. This message was not new. In internal budget documents, Parus had already documented the need to spend hundreds of millions of dollars to upgrade the plant because it was already in bad shape when BP bought it in 1999 after negotiations headed by Manzoni. Parus had commissioned a consulting firm named the Telos Group to conduct an assessment of safety conditions at the plant. It reported that employees felt unsafe, dreaded showing up for work, and were unable to communicate these legitimate fears to mid-level managers, much less to senior executives with the power to mitigate the risk.

No one was ever prosecuted for Texas City. Were Manzoni and Hoffman conscious of these imminent risks? How about Parus? Or does the blame reside exclusively with the poorly trained frontline workers who operated the isom? Taking the plain meaning of recklessness and responsible relation doctrines as interpreted in the other cases, isn't it at least worth running through the information we have about these catastrophes to see if there is any fit?

And then there is the awkward fact that workers continued to die at the plant in the aftermath of the explosion. Given top executives' direct knowledge of dangerous conditions at that time, shouldn't each subsequent fatality have triggered a criminal recklessness investigation?

Traveling east to West Virginia, we have the case of Don Blankenship's management of the Upper Big Branch mine. Blankenship had levels of management beneath him who worked at the mine daily. But he insisted on receiving reports on its productivity every two hours. Given that level of close – some would say obsessive – monitoring, he must have been aware of the three orders to stop work issued by federal regulators shortly before the methane in the mine ignited. Blankenship was clearly aware of his company's policy of tying up citations for violations of mine safety regulations with constant appeals. Given his level of involvement with each of Massey Energy's subsidiaries, he probably invented the strategy, just as he had communicated to the work force that its priority was to dig coal, and not fret about safety. Blankenship must also have understood the implications of repeated citations for safety issues, such as failure to rock dust in order to suppress flammable coal dust. Had he probed a bit deeper, he would have discovered that the equipment needed to distribute rock dust was broken. The same analysis, minus the abrasive public posturing, applies to other Massey executives, such as Chris Blanchard, president of Performance Coal (the Massey subsidiary that owned the mine).

Macondo, the biggest and most damaging incident, is the hardest to deconstruct using a willful blindness or recklessness theory of *mens rea*. So many people participated in the disorganized, hurried, and technically ill-advised closure of the well that determining who was most active in causing the blowout without access to the witnesses themselves is difficult. In a sense, the tableau, taken as a whole, is a classic case study of the "normalization of deviance" mentioned in Chapter 3. This concept, made famous by Diane Vaughan in her pathbreaking book on the Challenger disaster, connotes the routine use of procedures that should be recognized as extremely hazardous, to the point that such recklessness, or deviance, becomes normal. Pouring drilling mud directly into the ocean so its quantity could not be measured is a prime example of such behavior. Had Deepwater Horizon crew members followed the far safer procedure of pumping the mud into tanks on the rig that were designed for the purpose, and then estimated its volume, they might have realized that too much was missing and that the lower volume was a strong warning that the well was leaking. BP engineers received several warnings against their haphazard decision to install too few centralizers at the well site, some from within their own group. But the pressure to conform was overwhelming, so the group came to a consensus that the deviation was acceptable – a new normal if not a previous one. As for the failure of the cement job, Halliburton employees onshore were dilatory at best, providing delayed test results.

Down in Georgia, Stewart Parnell, CEO of the Peanut Corporation of America, was irritated to discover that peanut paste he was about to ship out to butter contaminated with salmonella. As he awaited a second test, the paste was put on a truck. Parnell could have been charged with manslaughter under state law.

Last but not least is Barry Cadden, chief pharmacist at the New England Compounding Center, who made sterile medicines in an obviously dirty "clean" room. Despite signing settlement agreements with federal and state officials for these conditions, he spent far more energy expanding his business across the country than rectifying these conditions.

CONCLUSION

An identifiable group of disastrous practices is common to the high hazard operations examined here. In most cases, the regulatory system sent repeated, albeit ineffective, signals over many years that the enterprise had severe problems in maintaining process, worker, or consumer safety. Cases were settled or appealed and the underlying cause of the problem was ignored. Lines of authority were blurry. Experts were consulted, but then overridden. Even in the obviously bad situation where more than one company had mutually interdependent roles in a very dangerous operation, no single individual was in charge. Cost-cutting through an internal process that did not consider potential effects on worker or consumer safety combined to magnify the threat to a point that the risk should have been intolerable. In the largest companies, senior and mid-level managers were given significant financial incentives to work fast. No incentives were available to maintain worker safety, public safety, or process integrity. The wrong measure of safety – personal injury as opposed to process – was used to demonstrate the absence of risk. BP repeated this mistake with fatal consequences in Texas City and in the Gulf, over a period separated by several years. No one stopped to reevaluate safety precautions when objective and reliable evidence in the form of numerical measurements by functioning equipment suggested that a worst case scenario was imminent.

The DOJ should incorporate factors such as these in its case selection criteria, as indicia of recklessness and willful blindness that could trigger criminal liability.

8

Deferred Prosecution Agreements

Whether the [DOJ] needs a middle ground between prosecution and decli-
nation [of a case] is far from clear. ... The evolution of the Justice
Department's approach to deferred prosecution and non-prosecution agreements, however, is best described as a policy in search of a rationale.

David Uhlmann, former chief, DOJ Environmental Crimes Section[1]

Corporations suffer a peculiar vulnerability. The rules of criminal liability
allow federal and state prosecutors to unduly punish those corporations that
fall within their crosshairs. But the recent emergency of deferred prosecution
agreements (DPAs) to force major changes in corporate governance should
give pause to even the most ardent populist.

Richard Epstein, Professor, New York University Law School[2]

What has intensified under your watch is a pervasive system of double standards: tough criminal penalties and lifetime stigma for individual street criminals, but second (and third chances) for corporate criminals that promise to
do better in the future. The double standard is all the worse because it
contradicts and undermines the basic purposes of the criminal justice system – deterrence and punishment – for the very actors for whom such
objectives make the most sense. Because corporations coldly calculate costs
and benefits – undertaking careful and detailed risk assessments as a fundamental part of their intentional decision-making process – they are most
likely to be responsive to hard-hitting penalties, not fines easily integrated
and transferred into the "cost of doing business."

Ralph Nader, founder, and Robert Weissman, president, Public Citizen[3]

---

[1] David Uhlmann, *Deferred Prosecution and Non-prosecution Agreements and the Erosion of
Corporate Criminal Liability*, 72 MD. L. REV. 1295, 1315 (2013). Uhlmann is now a professor at
the University of Michigan Law School.
[2] Richard A. Epstein, *The Deferred Prosecution Racket*, WALL ST. J., Nov. 28, 2006, http://online.
wsj.com/news/articles/SB116468395737834160.
[3] Letter from Ralph Nader & Robert Weissman, to Att'y Gen. Alberto Gonzales (June 5, 2006),
available at http://www.multinationalmonitor.org/editorsblog/?p=30.

DIVERSION TECHNIQUE

As documented in the preceding pages, over the past four decades, federal and state track records of prosecuting white collar crimes that threaten public health, worker and consumer safety, and the environment are weak at best and non-existent in the vast majority of instances. With a few notable exceptions – the most prominent are the prosecutions brought by the DOJ Environmental Crimes Section, the FDA's pursuit of off-label drug marketing, and the recent indictments described in Part II of this book – federal agencies and their DOJ lawyers are reluctant to use the legal authority granted to them by Congress. The prosecutions that have made it through the courts are unlikely to provide sufficient deterrence for any company or group of executives with a significant economic interest in breaking the law. For the most part, state prosecutors are missing in action.

During the eight years that George W. Bush was president, the DOJ's lethargy confirmed for many of his critics that his administration was solicitous toward business, although, like most domestic issues, these policies were eclipsed by the September 11 attacks and wars in Iraq and Afghanistan. But when President Obama took office in 2009, expectations were high that the DOJ would pivot 180 degrees, especially given the 2008 financial meltdown and the widespread perception that reckless behavior on Wall Street had not only crashed the country's economy but must involve multiple crimes. President Obama appointed Eric Holder, a career prosecutor and former Deputy Attorney General during the Clinton administration, to serve as Attorney General. The question was whether Holder would revitalize criminal enforcement that had languished under Bush or whether he would allow the DOJ career staff to continue its lethargy. The lethargic approach prevailed. The most salient manifestation of this unfortunate choice is DOJ policies toward corporate settlements of criminal cases.

Holder continued the policy of entering so-called Deferred Prosecution Agreements (or, as they are known in acronym-happy Washington, DPAs) with corporate defendants. Reviled by advocates on both the right and the left ends of the political spectrum, such agreements do not require the defendant corporation to plead guilty to any criminal charge. Instead, the defendant agrees that if it does not abide by the terms of the settlement for a set period of time, the DOJ may then file a criminal case. The DPA includes an admission of "wrongful conduct" and a statement of facts drafted by prosecutors. DPAs are not subject to judicial supervision; if a criminal case has already been filed, the DOJ dismisses it without asking for judicial review. In a second, closely related type of settlement, known as a "non-prosecution agreement," DOJ simply agrees to drop its criminal case in exchange for the company's cooperation in an ongoing investigation, including one to develop the criminal liability of its individual executives. Recent empirical studies have developed useful statistics that conflate results regarding both types of agreements, although the discussion below focuses more on DPAs.

As the above quote from staunch conservative Richard Epstein indicates, the right disdains DPAs because they constitute excessive interference in corporate affairs on the basis of a species of liability that many conservatives object to on principle in any event. If individuals commit bad acts, prosecute them, but don't punish innocent people holding stock in abstract entities formed primarily to accomplish economic development. And, as the quote at the start of this chapter from Ralph Nader and Robert Weissman indicates, the left disdains DPAs because they negate the expressive reasons for corporate criminal liability: they fail to impose the stigma of admitting guilt on institutions that allow the diffusion of accountability for causing grave damage to workers, consumers, the public's health, and the environment.

The phenomenon of using DPAs as a default solution to cases the DOJ considers too hot to handle is a relatively recent development. Before 2001, the DOJ entered into DPAs with potential corporate defendants rarely; a study by Professor Brandon Garrett identified only thirteen DPAs and non-prosecution agreements issued between 1992 and 2001.[4] In 2001, the Bush administration's DOJ started to emphasize this alternative and by 2004–2005, the numbers had increased significantly, averaging thirteen annually, or the same number in each of those years than the previous nine years combined. During the latter part of the Bush administration and the first term of the Obama administration, the numbers accelerated even more. Between 2006 and 2012, the DOJ entered 216 DPAs or non-prosecution agreements, an average of 31 agreements annually. It entered 125 DPAs and non-prosecution agreements during President Obama's first term, just four fewer than the 129 completed during both terms of the Bush administration.

Professor David Uhlmann, also quoted at the beginning of this chapter, points out that the leading enthusiasts for this approach reside in the powerful Criminal Division. Their colleagues in the Antitrust and Environmental Crimes sections, which also have criminal prosecutorial authority, are less enthusiastic and, with some exceptions, U.S. Attorneys have not viewed DPAs and non-prosecution agreements favourably. Between 2004 and 2009, the Criminal Division brought 38 cases against corporations and entered

---

[4] Brandon L. Garrett & Jon Ashley, *Federal Organizational Prosecution Agreements*, University of Virginia School of Law, http://lib.law.virginia.edu/Garrett/prosecution_agreements/ (last visited Apr. 21, 2014).

44 DPAs and non-prosecution agreements, while U.S. Attorneys across the country prosecuted 1,659 corporations and entered 94 DPAs and non-prosecution agreements. Regardless of this obvious internal disagreement, the top political leadership of the DOJ remains committed to deferred prosecution.

Oddly enough, the concept of entering into an agreement that defers prosecution originated in the juvenile justice system, where the diversion of potential defendants away from pleading guilty became popular because it allowed the justice system to attempt rehabilitation before a young person was permanently tarred with a criminal charge. The fact that this policy jumped the tracks to corporate prosecutions is one of the greatest stories about misreading history ever told.

THE ARTHUR ANDERSEN URBAN LEGEND

The period between 1987 and 2002 marked a surge for white collar crime enforcement. Professor Kathleen Brickey has explained this fifteen-year interlude as a product of Watergate, when "the American public learned that making illicit political payments, bribes, and kickbacks; falsifying corporate records; and a host of other questionable and illegal practices had become accepted methods of conducting corporate business in an alarming number of instances."[5] A second explanation is passage of the Sentencing Reform Act of 1984, which established the U.S. Sentencing Commission and federal Sentencing Guidelines that dramatically increased recommended levels of criminal fines that should be assessed against corporations.[6]

Taking full advantage of these developments and a public perception that well-heeled rogues were roaming Wall Street, federal prosecutors began by indicting Wall Street junk bond traders Michael Milken and Ivan Boeske for insider trading, the term connoting the illegal use of confidential information about developments in the corporate world to make money on the stock market. Both pled guilty and each served two years in prison.[7] The high-profile bankruptcies of Enron and Worldcom followed in 2001 and 2002, respectively. Prosecution of Enron's top executives Kenneth Lay and Jeffrey Skilling for securities fraud resulted in conviction; Lay died before he was sentenced and

---

[5] Kathleen F. Brickey, *Corporate Criminal Liability: A Primer for Corporate Counsel*, 40 Bus. Law. 129 (1984).

[6] The Sentencing Reform Act, Pub. L. No. 98-473, 98 Stat. 1987 (1984) (codified at 18 U.S.C. §§ 3551-3673 and 21 U.S.C. §§ 991-998). *See* U.S. Sentencing Commission, http://www.ussc.gov/, for more information about the Sentencing Commission.

[7] *See* James B. Stewart, Den of Thieves (1991).

Skilling is serving a 14-year sentence.[8] Worldcom's chief executive officer Bernard Ebbers was convicted of securities fraud and filing false statements and is serving a 25-year prison term.[9]

Despite these successes, aggressive prosecution of white collar financial fraud petered out by the mid-2000s in direct response to the Supreme Court's decision overturning the conviction of Arthur Andersen, Enron's accounting firm, and the ensuing flood of negative publicity blaming the DOJ for putting the firm out of business.[10] That this criticism was exaggerated, distorted, and unfair made little difference: Andersen's fate became a national symbol of overzealous prosecution and the DOJ retreated in disarray. It has yet to emerge from the defensive crouch it assumed in the aftermath of the Court's opinion.

Ironically, the first set of guidelines for federal prosecutors in deciding when to charge corporations with a crime was written two years before Andersen's demise by none other than the current Attorney General, Eric Holder, who was then serving as the Clinton administration's Deputy Attorney General.[11] This 1999 "Holder Memorandum" was succeeded in 2003 by the "Thompson memo" (Holder's successor was Larry Thompson).[12] The Thompson Memo was replaced by the "McNulty Memo" in 2006 (Paul McNulty was Thompson's successor).[13] The latest document in this series is entitled "Principles of Federal Prosecution of Business Organizations,"[14] which is

[8] *See* John R. Emshwiller, *Power Failure: The Rise and Fall of Enron*, 1 REYNOLDS CT. & MEDIA L.J. 3 (2011).

[9] Carrie Johnson, *Ebbers Gets 25-Year Sentence for Role in WorldCom Fraud*, WASH. POST, July 14, 2005, http://www.washingtonpost.com/wp-dyn/content/article/2005/07/13/AR2005071300 516.html.

[10] Arthur Andersen v. United States, 544 U.S. 696 (2005). For two excellent analyses of these events, *see* Kathleen F. Brickey, *Andersen's Fall from Grace*, 81 WASH. L.Q. 917 (2003), and Gabriel Markoff, *Arthur Andersen and the Myth of the Corporate Death Penalty: Corporate Criminal Convictions in the Twenty-First Century*, 15 U. PA. J. BUS. L. 707 (2013). For an explanation of the contrary view – that Andersen was persecuted out of business by the DOJ, *see* James Kelly, *The Power of an Indictment and the Demise of Arthur Andersen*, 48 S. TEX. L. REV. 509 (2006).

[11] Memorandum from Deputy Attorney General Eric Holder to all component heads and U.S. attorneys, Bringing Criminal Charges Against Corporations (June 16, 1999), *available at* http://www.justice.gov/criminal/fraud/documents/reports/1999/charging-corps.PDF.

[12] Memorandum from Deputy Attorney General Larry Thompson to all component heads and U.S. attorneys, Principles of Federal Prosecution of Business Organizations (Jan. 20, 2003), *available at* http://www.albany.edu/acc/courses/acc695spring2008/thompson%20memo.pdf.

[13] Memorandum from Deputy Attorney General Paul McNulty to all component heads and U.S. attorneys, Principles of Federal Prosecution of Business Organizations (Dec. 12, 2006), *available at* www.justice.gov/dag/speeches/2006/mcnulty_memo.pdf.

[14] These guidelines are now part of the U.S. Attorney's Manual. *See* Title 9, Chapter 9–28.000, U.S. ATTORNEY'S MANUAL, *available at* www.justice.gov/opa/documents/corp-charging-guidelines.pdf (last visited Mar. 19, 2014).

part of the *U.S. Attorney's Manual* and still in effect. All three documents list
several criteria, most of which focus on obvious and reasonable concerns:
(1) "the nature and seriousness of the offense"; (2) "the pervasiveness of wrongdoing within the corporation"; (3) "the corporation's history of similar conduct"; (4) "the corporation's timely and voluntary disclosure of wrongdoing";
(5) "the existence and adequacy of the corporation's pre-existing compliance
program"; (6) "the corporation's remedial actions"; (7) "the adequacy of
the prosecution of individuals"; and (8) "the adequacy of non-criminal
remedies."[15]

But one criterion should be viewed as a far more controversial outlier
because it appears to turn federal prosecutors into economists responsible
not just for enforcing the law but for contemplating the "collateral consequences" of a potential case, requiring that they consider the "disproportionate harm to shareholders, pension holders, employees, and others not
proven personally culpable, as well as impact on the public arising from the
prosecution."[16] Following the DOJ's Supreme Court defeat in the Andersen
case, this factor became a central preoccupation with the DOJ, producing a
sea change in both prosecutorial policy and the gestalt within its fabled Crime
Section. The criterion is of such importance that economic analyses purport-
ing to prove grave dislocation if the DOJ brings criminal charges are now a
standard component of defense attorney presentations to prosecutors. As DOJ
Criminal Section Chief Lanny Breuer acknowledged in a September 2012
New York City Bar Association speech:

> In my conference room, over the years, I have heard sober predictions that a
> company or bank might fail if we indict, that innocent employees could lose
> their jobs, that entire industries may be affected, and even that global markets
> will feel the effects. ... In reaching every charging decision, we must take into
> account the effect of an indictment on innocent employees and shareholders,
> just as we must take into account the nature of the crimes committed and the
> pervasiveness of the misconduct.[17]

Just what catastrophic event happened to push Andersen out of business when
only a year before its demise it employed 85,000 people worldwide (28,000 in
the United States) and generated annual revenues of $9.3 billion, making it
the largest firm delivering professional services in the world? The simple
answer is the spectacular meltdown of Enron, among the two or three most

---

[15] *Id.*

[16] *Id.* at 3.

[17] News Release, Assistant Attorney General Breuer Speaks at the New York City Bar Association
(Sept. 13, 2012), *available at* http://www.justice.gov/criminal/pr/speeches/2012/crm-speech-
1209131.html (including the text of the speech).

reviled corporations in American history. Disclosures that Enron's claimed earnings were based on fraudulent accounting brought the company's stock from a high of $90/share to a value measured in pennies. All of these accounting techniques were approved by Andersen, which had served as Enron's accountant for many years.

Andersen was so enmeshed in Enron's business that it started up its Houston office by hiring forty Enron accountants. From 1989 to 2000, some 89 Andersen accountants left to become Enron employees. But problems went deeper than this rapidly revolving door. Like other Big Five accounting firms, Andersen lost its moral compass during the don't-worry-be-happy 1980s when everyone on Wall Street was getting rich. Its origins as a staid and punctilious audit firm that fired clients who pushed too hard for what the firm regarded as questionable accounting methods eroded as partners rushed to expand its considerably more lucrative consulting business. Andersen long touted four "cornerstones": "produce good service to the client, produce quality audits, manage staff well, and produce profits for the firm."[18] As it entered the 1980s and 1990s, Andersen partners joked that these goals were really "three pebbles and a boulder."[19]

Although it began as an audit firm proud of its independence from clients and rigorous standards in blocking marginal accounting practices, Andersen slowly but surely developed consulting services, beginning in 1950 with the invention and intense marketing of the "Glickiac," an early computer capable of automating clients' bookkeeping.[20] The highly competitive market for consulting services depended on catering to client preferences, and this mindset slowly but surely undermined the firm's vaunted independence. As just one example of the ethical dissonance produced by this mixing of functions, Andersen was paid to manage clients' internal bookkeeping operations at the same time that it conducted annual audits of the same companies – in effect, the firm was auditing its own work. Over time, as consulting profits rose, partner salaries tripled, fueling pressure to keep expanding the consulting side of the firm. Tired of supporting their auditor counterparts, partners who focused on consulting started a multiyear campaign to split the firm in two.

---

[18] Ken Brown & Ianthe Jeanne Dugan, *Arthur Andersen's Fall from Grace is a Sad Tale of Greed and Miscues*, Wall St. J., June 2, 2002, http://online.wsj.com/news/articles/SB1023 40943654200. In addition to reporting by the *New York Times* and the *Wall Street Journal*, the *Chicago Tribune* produced an excellent series on Andersen's history and demise entitled *A Final Accounting*. The four parts of the series – *The Fall of Andersen, Civil War Splits Andersen, Ties to Enron Blinded Andersen*, and *Repeat Offender Gets Stiff Justice* (Sept. 2002), are available at http://www.chicagotribune.com/news/watchdog/chi-andersen,0,865901.special.

[19] *Id.*

[20] *Id.*

In 1989, accounting and consulting were separated into two companies under a single Swiss parent, but the two units continued to engage in some profit-sharing.[21] By 1997, the consulting partners were disgusted and filed an arbitration claim to force a complete split.[22]

Responding to all this pressure, the company's top partner, Steve Samek, pressured auditing partners to conform to what he called the "2X" strategy: on an annual basis, they should produce twice as much in revenues in work outside their area of practice.[23] So, for example, if an auditing partner billed $2 million for checking a company's books, she should sell an additional $4 million in nonaudit services, such as tax advice and technology development. Despite these heroic efforts, the consulting side of Andersen won its arbitration in 2000, achieving the right to form a separate firm under a new name without profit-sharing.[24]

News of Enron's financial distress first dominated the nightly news on October 16, 2001, when the company issued a press release announcing a $618 million net loss for the third quarter.[25] The Securities and Exchange Commission (SEC) wasted no time, notifying Enron the next day that it had opened an inquiry into the company's problems, specifically its use of "off-book special purpose entities" (shell companies) to hide losses from shareholders and investors.[26] At the Houston office, Andersen's Enron team was in constant touch with its clients, and immediately understood that government investigators would soon be knocking at Andersen's door.

On October 23, Houston employees began a frantic effort to shred documents and dump emails that would reveal the worst of the accounting practices at the root of Enron's emerging downfall.[27] The shredding, in supposed compliance with the company's "document retention policy," was conducted in its Houston office, but senior partners at Chicago headquarters were aware it was occurring, and documents located there and at Andersen offices in London and Portland were also destroyed. Over a period lasting only a couple of weeks, tons of paper were destroyed and thousands of emails were purged from company

---

[21] *Id.*

[22] *Id.*

[23] *Id.*

[24] *Id.*

[25] *See* News Release, Enron Corp., Enron Reports Recurring Third Quarter Earnings of $0.43 Per Diluted Share; Reports Non-Recurring Charges of $1.01 Billion After-Tax; Reaffirms Recurring Earnings Estimates of $1.80 for 2001 and $2.15 for 2002; and Expands Financial Reporting (Oct. 16, 2001), *available at* http://picker.uchicago.edu/Enron/EarningsRelease%2810-16-01%29.pdf.

[26] Indictment, United States v. Arthur Andersen LLP, CRH-02-121, at 3 (S.D. Tex. Mar. 7, 2002), *available at* http://www.nysscpa.org/enron/andersenindictment.pdf [hereinafter Andersen Indictment].

[27] *Id.* at 5–7.

computers. The shredding campaign stopped only when the SEC sent Andersen a subpoena for documents on November 8, 2001.[28]

Recovering perspective when they received the subpoena, senior executives consulted with outside counsel and dramatically reversed course. First, they decided to voluntarily disclose the shredding to the SEC and the DOJ; the notification was made on January 4, 2002, and immediately made the news.[29] Of course, the next step was to explain what had happened to federal prosecutors, and at this juncture, Andersen executives made some surprising mistakes. Rather than develop a single, coherent narrative, they veered off in two contradictory directions.

Some claimed that the shredding was a benign effort to clean up the files in accordance with the firm's document retention policy. The policy, which had been in place for a few years, said that once an audit of a client's books was complete, only final copies of the documents – not any drafts or other interim work product – should be retained. Unfortunately, the company had never followed the policy, in part because it had no staff assigned to shred paperwork on an ongoing basis. This reality made the destruction of the Enron paperwork seem very suspicious. Other managers claimed that only a small group of rogue employees in the Houston office had authorized the shredding under the direction of David Duncan, the head of Andersen's large Enron team. Duncan was fired and soon started cooperating with federal prosecutors, further compounding Arthur Andersen's troubles.[30]

Once news of the shredding went public, Andersen clients started leaving the firm in droves, concerned about compromising their publicly held companies' reputations by associating not just with Enron's accountants but with a firm that had behaved in such a guilty and frantic manner. Of course, Andersen's competitors stood ready, willing, and able to harvest this windfall. As the client exodus grew, competitors turned around and started hiring entire practice groups from Andersen. In fact, although an empirical study was never done, it seems likely that few of the firm's professional staff remained out of work for very long. Its nonprofessional staff may have had a more difficult time finding alternative employment.

---

[28] *Id.*

[29] *Destruction of Enron-Related Documents by Andersen Personnel: Hearing Before the House Subcomm. on Oversight and Investigations of the Comm. on Energy and Commerce*, 107th Cong. 16 (2002) (statements of C. E. Andrews, Managing Partner, Global Audit Practice, Andersen LLP, and Dorsey L. Baskin Jr., Managing Director, Professional Standards Group, Andersen, LLP).

[30] Richard A. Oppel Jr. & Kurt Eichenwald, *Enron's Collapse: The Overview; Arthur Andersen Fires an Executive for Enron Orders*, N.Y. TIMES, Jan. 16, 2002, http://www.nytimes.com/2002/01/16/business/enron-s-collapse-overview-arthur-andersen-fires-executive-for-enron-orders.html.

In March 2002, after efforts to negotiate a settlement collapsed, DOJ prosecutors indicted Andersen on a single count of obstruction of justice.[31] The indictment – or rather, the two sides' failure to reach a settlement – came as a shock to observers, especially reporters covering the story who had been told the two sides were close to a deal.[32] The breakdown was provoked by Andersen's adamant refusal to admit criminal culpability. Instead, it wanted an agreement that allowed it to pay its fine with the government deferring a decision about prosecuting the firm.

Andersen's reluctance to plead guilty, even to a charge of obstructing justice – as opposed to providing illegal accounting advice – was motivated by more than mere arrogance. Under SEC rules, a company admitting to a felony would be barred from providing services to American clients, although the agency could waive this prohibition. Andersen's dilemma was amplified by the fact that prosecutors and SEC enforcement staff refused to promise that the SEC would grant the company's waiver. As is often the case in such heated and intractable struggles, DOJ prosecutors believed they were in a tight corner. Andersen had become enmeshed in accounting scandals several times in the years running up to Enron's demise, becoming the target of private investor lawsuits, state enforcement actions, and settlements with the SEC.[33] DOJ Crimes Section Chief Michael Chertoff and his staff viewed the company as an unrepentant recidivist that would continue its sharp practices until and unless it was forced to sign a criminal settlement. Andersen further aggravated the DOJ prosecutors by demanding a speedy trial – a ploy designed to short-circuit the time the government had to investigate its case – and mounting a publicity campaign that featured Andersen employees literally marching on DOJ offices across the country to demand that it back down in order to save their jobs.[34]

---

[31] *See* Andersen Indictment, *supra* note 26.
[32] Compelling coverage of these events was provided by Kurt Eichenwald of the *New York Times*. *See* Kurt Eichenwald, *Andersen Misread Depths of Government's Anger*, N.Y. TIMES, Mar. 18, 2002, http://www.nytimes.com/2002/03/18/business/andersen-misread-depths-of-the-government-s-anger.html; Kurt Eichenwald, *Enron's Many Strands: The Investigation; S.E.C. Had Sought $500 Million in Failed Talks with Andersen*, N.Y. TIMES, Mar. 20, 2002, http://www.nytimes.com/2002/03/20/business/enron-s-many-strands-investigation-sec-had-sought-500-million-failed-talks-with.html.
[33] Professor Brickey describes these episodes and lists twenty-three separate legal proceedings in her article *supra* note 10, at 947–50.
[34] Kristen Hays, *Andersen Pleads Not Guilty and Hopes for a Speedy Trial*, DESERET NEWS, Mar. 20, 2002, http://www.deseretnews.com/article/902697/Andersen-pleads-not-guilty-and-hopes-for-a-speedy-trial.html?pg=all; John Schwartz, *Arthur Andersen Employees Circle the Wagons*, N.Y. TIMES, Mar. 22, 2002, http://www.nytimes.com/2002/03/22/business/arthur-andersen-employees-circle-the-wagons.html.

The DOJ won at trial and again when Andersen appealed its conviction to the Fifth Circuit Court of Appeals.[35] Four years later, however, with the company all but gone, the Supreme Court entered the smoldering battlefield and reversed the conviction on a technical point of law. The Court's opinion, written by Chief Justice William Rehnquist, objected to the deletion of a single, albeit important, word from the jury instructions given by the federal district court judge who presided over the case.[36] Although it is true that the jury deliberated for many days before reaching a verdict, and had to be pointedly urged by the judge to redouble its efforts to decide the case, the possibility that the single word would have reversed the outcome of case is, to say the least, unclear.

A correct understanding of this sequence of events demonstrates that Andersen was bleeding clients several weeks before the indictment was made public. The indictment certainly accelerated these departures, but Andersen's reputation had already suffered a devastating blow. Regardless, it is the revisionist history that counts, and conservative commentators have been pleased to provide it. They characterize the Andersen indictment as the sole trigger of the company's demise and have managed to create a widespread belief, even among career DOJ prosecutors who should know better, that unacceptable collateral damage is inevitable when a large, multinational corporation is indicted and tried. Confirmation of the mainstream status of this supposed "Andersen Effect" was confirmed by no less authoritative source than the nation's auditor, the Government Accountability Office (GAO), which wrote in 2009 that "the failure of the accounting firm Arthur Andersen, and the associated loss of thousands of jobs following the indictment and conviction for obstruction of justice … has been offered as a prime example of the potentially harmful effects of criminally prosecuting a company."[37]

---

[35] United States v. Arthur Andersen, LLP, 374 F.3d 281 (5th Cir. 2004).

[36] Arthur Andersen v. United States, 544 U.S. 696 (2005). The statute at issue made it a crime to "knowingly corruptly persuade" another person to obstruct justice. 18 U.S.C. § 1512(b). (This language has since been changed.) Andersen attorneys urged the trial judge to instruct the jury that it must conclude that Andersen "knowingly and dishonestly, with specific intent to subvert or undermine the integrity" of a proceeding. 544 U.S. at 705. Prosecutors insisted that the word "dishonestly" be dropped and the word "impede" be inserted and the trial judge agreed, instructing the jury that it should convict if it found that Andersen intended to "subvert, undermine, or impede" governmental fact-finding. Id.

[37] U.S. Gov't Accounability Office, GAO-10-110, Corporate Crime: DOJ Has Taken Steps to Better Track Its Use of Deferred and Non-Prosecution Agreements, but Should Evaluate Effectiveness 1 (2009), available at http://www.gao.gov/assets/300/299781.pdf.

THE MYTH OF THE CORPORATE DEATH PENALTY

Recently, Gabriel Markoff, an honors graduate of the University of Texas Law School and a law clerk to federal district court judge Gregg Costa, published an incisive analysis entitled *Arthur Andersen and the Myth of the Corporate Death Penalty: Corporate Criminal Convictions in the Twenty-First Century*.[38] Markoff actually went to the trouble of conducting an empirical analysis of the validity of the so-called Andersen effect or, as opponents of white collar criminal enforcement have labeled it, the corporate death penalty. He found that no publicly traded corporation failed as a result of a criminal conviction during the years 2001–2010. Markoff notes that 90 percent of corporations plead guilty rather than going through a criminal trial unless they can wheedle (my word, not his) prosecutors into giving them DPAs. Among the group of 54 corporations that he studied, 37 are still active, 12 merged with or were acquired by another company, and five failed, although clearly for reasons that have nothing to do with their criminal pleas (for example, three of the five went out of business more than three years after the pleas were lodged). Fines assessed ranged from "diminutive $20,000 environmental fine on XTO Energy to an enormous $1.615 billion total penalty on Eli Lilly for distributing and advertising misbranded pharmaceuticals."[39] And, although it was not included in his database, Markoff notes that BP's guilty plea and $4.5 billion fine did not affect either its stock or its profits, which stood at $27.6 billion at the end of 2012.[40]

Having debunked the DOJ's exaggerated and counterproductive preoccupation with the Andersen effect, Markoff reviews the heated arguments made from the left and right ends of the political spectrum regarding whether they are ever appropriate. He acknowledges that from the perspective of conservatives, the DOJ is abusing its power by forcing multinational corporations to sign expensive agreements that extort remedial action otherwise not required by law.[41] Commentators at the opposite end of the ideological spectrum, such as the authors of the *New York Times* editorial quoted earlier, are concerned that DPAs represent sweetheart deals that allow profitable companies to pay fines that become a cost of doing business without acknowledging culpability.

---

[38] Gabriel Markoff, *Arthur Andersen and the Myth of the Corporate Death Penalty: Corporate Criminal Convictions in the Twenty-First Century*, 15 U. PA. J. BUS. L. 797 (2013).

[39] *Id.* at 826.

[40] *Id.* at 833.

[41] *See, e.g.*, Richard Epstein, *The Deferred Prosecution Racket*, WALL ST. J., Nov. 28, 2006. Never a victim of relying on understatement when overstatement will do, Epstein wrote that DPAs "often read like the confessions of a Stalinist purge trial, as battered corporations recant their past sins and submit to punishments wildly in excess of any underlying offense."

He suggests that both points of view are based on a false premise: that all corporations are situated similarly with respect to the implications of the criminal sanction. Andersen was vulnerable because pleading guilty to a felony – in the absence of a waiver from the SEC that may or may not have materialized – might have made it ineligible to practice accounting even if it had managed to retain its clients. Or, as Markoff puts it, Andersen's core business model was dependent on the outcome of a settlement with the government. For most other companies – and, again, BP is a prime example, pleading guilty or being convicted will have no comparable effects.

THE TRAVAILS OF ERIC HOLDER

Federal prosecutors' ambivalence about using criminal sanction has become so obvious that the DOJ and the SEC have endured sustained criticism in the media and on Capitol Hill for their lenient stance toward "too big to fail" companies in the wake of the 2008 meltdown on Wall Street. In a 2011 column entitled "Why the SEC Won't Hunt Big Dogs," ProPublica's Jesse Eisinger called for "Old Testament justice":

> After years of lengthy investigations into collateralized debt obligations, the mortgage securities at the heart of the financial crisis, the only individuals the SEC has brought civil actions against [are] half a dozen small-timers. ... No major investment banker has been brought up on criminal charges stemming from the financial crisis. ... So the SEC has the wrong approach.
> This is a matter of will and leadership. Its chairwoman, Mary L. Schapiro, while deserving credit for pushing investigations of structured investments, is sending the signal that she does not want to lose. Her agency is meekly willing to get token settlements when the situation calls for Old Testament justice.[42]

At a hearing held in August 2012, Senator Jack Reed (D-RI), chairman of a subcommittee that oversees securities regulation, said: "A lot of people on the street, they're wondering how a company can commit serious violations of securities laws and yet no individuals seem to be involved and no individual responsibility was assessed."[43] And on January 29, 2013, Senators Sherrod Brown (D-OH) and Charles Grassley (R-IA) sent a letter to Attorney General Eric Holder demanding information on whether prosecutors had "designated certain institutions whose failure could jeopardize the stability of

---

[42] Jesse Eisinger, *Why the SEC Won't Hunt Big Dogs*, THE TRADE: PROPUBLICA (Oct. 26, 2011), http://www.propublica.org/thetrade/item/why-the-sec-wont-hunt-big-dogs.

[43] Michael S. Schmidt & Edward Wyatt, *Fraud Cases Often Spare Individuals*, N.Y. TIMES, Aug. 7, 2012, at B1.

financial markets and are thus, 'too big to jail'?"[44] The two senators added: "Our markets will only function efficiently if participants believe that all laws will be enforced consistently, and that violators will be punished to the fullest extent of the law. There should not be one set of rules that apply to Wall Street and another set for the rest of us."[45]

Holder finally came within firing range of his congressional critics when he testified before the Senate Judiciary Committee in March 2013.[46] The topic of the day was a DOJ memo justifying drone strikes that may kill American citizens. But softness on white collar crime ran a close second, with senators grilling Holder about the DOJ's decision in December 2012 to enter into a $1.9 billion DPA with HSBC, the world's third-largest publicly held bank. HSBC stood accused of laundering money for violent international drug cartels in Mexico and Colombia and conducting banking business in violation of U.S. sanctions for clients in Burma, Cuba, Iran, Libya, and Sudan. The senators expressed astonishment that HSBC had qualified for such lenient treatment.

The *American Banker* posted a transcript on its website of the following exchange during the hearing between Holder and Senator Grassley (R-IA):

> **Sen. Chuck Grassley, R-Iowa**: In the case of bank prosecution. I'm concerned we have a mentality of "too big to jail" in the financial sector, spreading from fraud cases to terrorist financing to money laundering cases. I would cite HSBC.
>
> I think we are on a slippery slope and that's background for this question. I don't have recollection of DOJ prosecuting any high-profile financial criminal convictions in either companies or individuals.
>
> Assistant Attorney General Breuer said that one reason that DOJ has not sought these prosecutions is because it reaches out to "experts" to see what effect the prosecution will have on the financial markets. On Jan. 29, Sen. [Sherrod] Brown and I requested details on who these so-called "experts" are. So far we have not received any information. Maybe you're going to but why have we not yet been provided the names of experts the DOJ consults as we requested on Jan. 29? We continue to find out why we aren't having these high-profile cases ...

---

[44] Press Release, Sens. Brown, Grassley Press Justice Department on "Too Big to Jail" (Jan 29, 2013), http://www.brown.senate.gov/newsroom/press/release/sens-brown-grassley-press-justice-department-on-too-big-to-jail.

[45] *Id.*

[46] *Oversight of the U.S. Department of Justice: Hearing Before the S. Comm. on the Judiciary*, 113th Cong. (Mar. 6, 2013) (transcript of testimony of Att'y Gen. Eric Holder), *available at* http://www.americanbanker.com/issues/178_45/transcript-attorney-general-eric-holder-on-too-big-to-jail-1057295-1.html.

Attorney General Eric Holder: We will endeavor to answer your letter, Senator. We did not, as I understand it, endeavor to obtain experts outside of the government in making determinations with regard to HSBC.

Just putting that aside for a minute though, the concern that you have raised is one that I, frankly, share. I'm not talking about HSBC here, that would be inappropriate. *But I am concerned that the size of some of these institutions becomes so large that it does become difficult for us to prosecute them when we are hit with indications that if we do prosecute – if we do bring a criminal charge – it will have a negative impact on the national economy, perhaps even the world economy.* I think that is a function of the fact that some of these institutions have become too large.

Again, I'm not talking about HSBC, this is more of a general comment. I think it has an inhibiting influence, impact on our ability to bring resolutions that I think would be more appropriate. I think that's something that we – you all [Congress] – need to consider. The concern that you raised is actually one that I share.

Grassley: Do you believe that the investment bankers that were repackaging bad mortgages that were AAA-rated are guilty of fraud or is it a case of just not being aggressive or effective enough to prove that they did something fraudulent and criminal?

Holder: We looked at those kinds of cases. I think we have been appropriately aggressive, these are not always easy cases to make. When you look at these cases, you see that things were done "wrong" then the question is whether or not they were illegal. And I think the people in our criminal division ... I think have been as aggressive as they could be, brought cases where we think we could have brought them. I know that in some instances that has not been a satisfying answer to people, but we have been as aggressive as we could have been.[47]

Holder's decision to allow HSBC to take this path away from a guilty plea provoked the *New York Times* to editorialize:

> It is a dark day for the rule of law. Federal and state authorities have chosen not to indict HSBC, the London-based bank, on charges of vast and prolonged money laundering, for fear that criminal prosecution would topple the bank and, in the process, endanger the financial system. They also have not charged any top HSBC banker in the case, though it boggles the mind that a bank could launder money as HSBC did without anyone in a position of authority making culpable decisions.
>
> Clearly, the government has bought into the notion that too big to fail is too big to jail. When prosecutors choose not to prosecute to the full extent of the

47 *Transcript: Attorney General Eric Holder on "Too Big to Jail,"* THE AMERICAN BANKER (Mar. 6, 2013) (emphasis added), http://www.americanbanker.com/issues/178_45/transcript-attorney-general-eric-holder-on-too-big-to-jail-1057295-1.html.

law in a case as egregious as this, the law itself is diminished. The deterrence
that comes from the threat of criminal prosecution is weakened, if not lost.[48]

As for Holder's assertion that the DOJ has been as aggressive at it could have
been, pursuing any worthwhile case involving crimes on Wall Street, it's
worth noting here that in a survey of 250 Wall Street professionals (including
traders, portfolio managers, investment bankers, hedge fund professionals,
financial analysts, investment advisors, asset managers and stock brokers),
29 percent of respondents said that "rules may have to be broken in order to be
successful"; 24 percent said it was "likely that staff in their company have
engaged in illegal or unethical activity in order to be successful"; and 52 percent predicted that "their competitors have engaged in unethical or illegal
activity to gain an edge" in the market.[49] The survey was conducted by
Labaton Sucharow, LLP, a law firm that describes itself as "exclusively
focused on protecting and advocating for SEC whistleblowers."[50] The questions used in the survey were not made public by the firm. Nevertheless, the
numbers of respondents predicting widespread noncompliance are high
enough not only to confirm the widespread public perception that Wall
Street is awash in illegal trading[51] but to validate Senator Grassley's growing
exasperation with the DOJ's timidity.

Two months later, testifying before the House Judiciary Committee, Holder
tried, in Washington-speak, to "walk back" his remarks, "Let me be very, very,
very clear. Banks are not too big to jail. If we find a bank or a financial
institution that has done something wrong, if we can prove it beyond a
reasonable doubt, those cases will be brought."[52]

[48] Editorial, *Too Big to Indict*, N.Y. Times, Dec. 11, 2012, http://www.nytimes.com/2012/12/12/opinion/hsbc-too-big-to-indict.html?_r=0.

[49] Labaton, Sucharow, LLP, Wall Street in Crisis: A Perfect Storm Looming, Labaton Sucharow's U.S. Financial Services Industry Survey 4 (July 2013), *available at* https://s3.amazonaws.com/s3.documentcloud.org/documents/726869/wall-street-in-crisis-a-perfect-storm-looming.pdf.

[50] *Id.* at 2.

[51] *See, e.g.*, Regina A. Corso, *Large Majority of Americans Favor Tougher Regulation of Wall Street*, Harris Polls (May 10, 2012), http://www.harrisinteractive.com/NewsRoom/HarrisPolls/tabid/447/ctl/ReadCustom%20Default/mid/1508/ArticleId/1018/Default.aspx. The poll reported that by an "overwhelming" majority of 82% to 15%, respondents believe recent events have shown that "Wall Street should be subject to tougher regulation." The poll included 1,016 adults surveyed by telephone between April 10 and 17, 2012. It further said that 55 percent believe that Wall Street activities benefit the country, while 42 percent think they harm the country. "Seven in ten U.S. adults (70%) believe most people on Wall Street would be willing to break the law if they believed they could make a lot of money and get away with it."

[52] Mark Gongkoff, *Eric Holder: Actually I Mean to Say No Banks Are Too Big to Jail*, Huffington Post (May 15, 2013), http://www.huffingtonpost.com/2013/05/15/eric-holder-too-big-to-jail_n_3280694.html.

THE ALPHA ENERGY AND TOYOTA DEFERRALS

In December 2011, U.S. Attorney Booth Goodwin signed a $209 million DPA with executives from Alpha Natural Resources that resolved potential criminal charges against Massey Energy regarding the Upper Big Branch mine collapse. Alpha was Massey's white knight, buying the troubled company about a year before the deal was done. It may seem fair at first blush not to tag the new parent with criminal charges for the activities of its errant child, assuming Alpha has clean hands and an exemplary track record. But on March 6, 2014, the DOJ announced that it had reached another civil agreement with Alpha to resolve a case involving 6,289 violations of the Clean Water Act. Seventy-nine of Alpha's active mines and 25 of its processing plants had illegally discharged highly toxic pollutants into rivers and streams in five states over a seven-year period (2006–2013). The civil penalties assessed in the case were a paltry $27.5 million, with the company also obligated to pay $200 million to fix broken wastewater treatment equipment throughout its far-flung systems. Or, in other words, a very big company that let its pollution control equipment run to failure on a massive scale will now have the opportunity to upgrade it without paying penalties remotely equal to the money it made by investing the funds needed for maintenance in more lucrative investment opportunities. Can the right hand of the government (charged with vindicating the deaths of those 29 miners) really be so ignorant of what the left hand (charged with tracking water pollution violations) is doing? Or is the message that smart corporations should take the risk of ignoring compliance because they will be forgiven by the government when they are caught?

Then in March 2014, Toyota Motor Co. won a DPA with the DOJ to settle charges that it had lied repeatedly to the government and delayed recalling models afflicted with so-called "sticky pedal" and "entrapped floor mat" defects that caused them to accelerate out of control. Hundreds of tort cases for damages are pending across the country on behalf of people injured or killed in crashes when their cars suddenly achieved speeds as high as 100 miles per hour. To quote from the DOJ press release on the settlement:

> A 911 emergency call made from the out-of-control vehicle, which was speeding at over 100 miles per hour, reported, "We're in a Lexus … and we're going north on 125 and our accelerator is stuck … there's no brakes … we're approaching the intersection. … Hold on … hold on and pray … pray." The call ended with the sound of a crash that killed everyone in the vehicle.[53]

---

[53] Press Release, U.S. Dep't of Justice, Justice Department Annoucnes Criminal Charge Against Toyota Motor Corporation and Deferred Prosecution Agreement with $1.2 Billion Financial Penalty (Mar. 19, 2014), *available at* http://www.justice.gov/opa/pr/2014/March/14-ag-286.html.

The agreement was widely misrepresented in the press as a criminal settlement, with the *New York Times* reporting that "[a] $1.2 billion criminal penalty, the largest ever for a carmaker in the United States, was imposed."[54] The reporters' confusion gave Attorney General Holder an unchallenged opportunity to scold Toyota for its "shameful" behavior.[55] He said nothing about pursuing cases against individual executives. In fact, the agreement stipulates that if Toyota acknowledges the criminal "information" filed by the government in court, which contains a single charge of wire fraud, and the company behaves itself for three years, the DOJ will dismiss the charge without prosecution.

A Statement of Facts produced by the DOJ revealed that Toyota repeatedly lied to regulators about the nature and scope of the sudden acceleration problem. The company failed to disclose that car models with the same defects were omitted from the recall it negotiated with the National Highway Traffic Safety Administration (NHTSA). It verbally instructed its employees that it was cancelling a design change on cars coming off the line because implementing such remedies would be read as admitting responsibility for the defect that it was ultimately forced to acknowledge. In fact, the Statement of Facts notes in paragraph 4, on its very first page, that an unnamed Toyota executive exclaimed at the end of a meeting between the company and "its regulator" (NHTSA): "Idiots! Someone will go to jail if lies are repeatedly told. I can't support this."[56]

THE EXPRESSIVE PURPOSE OF THE CRIMINAL LAW

As mentioned earlier, the accelerating trend toward making DPAs and non-prosecution agreements a central weapon in the arsenal of at least some federal prosecutors has come under sustained fire from commentators who span the full political spectrum. They raise seven objections: (1) abridgement of corporate "rights" and, closely related, the exercise of corrupt cronyism in the selection of monitors and remedies; (2) lack of judicial oversight that could avoid this abuse and corruption; (3) lack of transparency that shrouds the status of corporate compliance in secrecy; (4) lack of expertise among prosecutors to ascertain compliance with the terms of DPAs and resources to take action if

---

[54] Bill Vlasic & Matt Apuzzo, *Toyota Is Fined $1.2 Billion for Concealing Safety Defects*, N.Y. TIMES, Mar. 19, 2014, http://www.nytimes.com/2014/03/20/business/toyota-reaches-1-2-billion-settlement-in-criminal-inquiry.html?_r=0.

[55] *Id.*

[56] Statement of Facts, United States v. Toyota Motor Corp., http://www.justice.gov/opa/docu ments/toyota-stmt-facts.pdf (last visited Apr. 21, 2014).

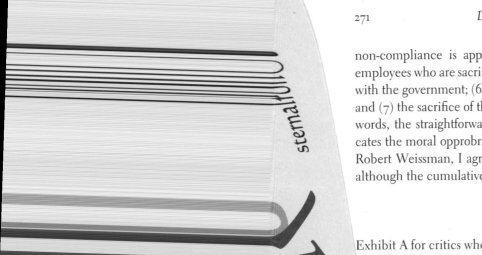

non-compliance is apparent; (5) adverse impact on individual corporate employees who are sacrificed when corporate defendants agree to "cooperate" with the government; (6) disparate treatment of small versus large businesses; and (7) the sacrifice of the expressive purpose of the criminal law or, in other words, the straightforward public punishment of bad actors that communicates the moral opprobrium of the society as a whole. Like Ralph Nader and Robert Weissman, I agree that the final problem is by far the most serious, although the cumulative impact of the others may be equally damaging.

Cronyism

Exhibit A for critics who charge that DPAs provide opportunities for strong-arming potential corporate defendants is the objectionable behavior of New Jersey Governor Chris Christie when he served as the U.S. Attorney for the state. Christie's office negotiated seven DPAs, one for each year he was in office. An agreement with Bristol-Myers Squibb required the company to fund a chair in business ethics at Christie's alma mater, Seton Hall Law School. Another required Zimmer Holdings to hire former Attorney General John Ashcroft, Christie's old boss and a close political ally, to serve as a monitor of its compliance with the agreement. The 18-month contract was worth up to $52 million, including $750,000 in monthly fees and reimbursement for expenses expected to total $100,000–250,000/month. Several other such agreements negotiated by Christie's staff hired other, less prominent Republican political figures in comparable positions, although the Ashcroft contract was the highest profile. One of those situations, which involved the hiring of former federal prosecutor David Kelley, was criticized as a payoff because when he was a prosecutor, Kelley had dropped a criminal case against Christie's brother.

At a hearing called in 2009 by the House Judiciary Committee to investigate the use of DPAs, Christie testified that all of the seven agreements were negotiated with a single goal of achieving "results of justice for the public."[57] One Democrat described the pressure companies felt to accept the prosecutor's choice of a monitor as "an offer you can't refuse," an obvious reference to *The Godfather*, the famous film about the Mafia, and Christie responded that he interpreted the remark as a slur on his Italian American lineage.[58] Then, before the committee chair ended the hearing, in what the *New York Times* reported as "politically charged bedlam," Christie and his staff stood up and

[57] David Kocieniewski, *In Testy Exchange in Congress, Christie Defends His Record as a Prosecutor*, N.Y. Times, June 26, 2009, http://www.nytimes.com/2009/06/26/nyregion/26christie.html.
[58] *Id.*

marched out of the hearing, declaring that the governor needed to attend to "pressing business" in New Jersey.[59]

Lack of Judicial Oversight

In a 2009 survey of twelve federal district and magistrate judges who presided over cases ultimately settled by DPA, the Government Accountability Office (GAO) found that none were involved in supervising either the negotiation or the implementation of such agreements. Critics of the process contend that judicial supervision would have prevented the abuse that occurred during Christie's tenure. Prosecutors and company representatives who favor DPAs told GAO that the "disadvantages to greater judicial involvement – such as the lack of time and resources available to judges and concerns about separation of powers and constitutionality of increased judicial involvement" outweighed "the advantages of involvement – such as the court's ability to act as an independent arbiter of disputes, increased transparency in the DPA process, and decreased perceptions of favoritism in selecting the monitor."[60]

Secret Compliance

Perhaps because federal judges are not involved, transparency has become a significant problem in the implementation of DPAs and non-prosecution agreements. For example, one year after U.S. Attorney Booth Goodwin entered a DPA with Alpha to settle criminal charges related to the Upper Big Branch mine collapse, the corporation filed its first compliance report. *West Virginia Gazette* reporter Ken Ward and a group of family members of miners killed in the incident asked to see a copy of the report, but Goodwin refused, apparently because Alpha had claimed it included confidential business information. The interest of every one of the 11,000 miners who now work for Alpha in the progress it is making to absorb the troubled Massey operation should be obvious but Goodwin, in an unusual display of public insensitivity, remained steadfast. In his widely read blog the *Coal Tattoo*, Ward explained that Goodwin's press release announcing receipt of the Alpha report bragged that the "reportable incident rate, a statistic measuring overall accidents, fell from 5.74 in the quarter just after Alpha assumed control to 3.86 in the quarter

---

[59] *Id.*

[60] U.S. Gov't Accountability Office, GAO-10-110, Corporate Crime, DOJ Has Taken Steps to Better Track Its Use of Deferred and Non-prosecution Agreements, but Should Evaluate Effectiveness, at Highlights Page (2009), *available at* http://www.gao.gov/products/GAO-10-110.

after the Agreement, a decline of 32.8%."[61] Unfortunately, these sta[...]
ignore more important realities about Alpha's behavior under the Agreen[...]

> Not mentioned [in the press release] were other recent incidents, such a[...]
> serious citations following the death of a worker at an Alpha contract mine in[...]
> Virginia, the deaths this year of two Alpha miners in West Virginia ... ,
> personal citations issued to five Alpha mine managers following one of
> those West Virginia deaths, or the conveyor belt incident at Alpha's Road
> Fork No. 51 Mine which – while downplayed by state investigators and the
> company – troubled federal inspectors enough that MSHA launched *the*
> *largest inspection sweep of a single company in agency history.*[62]

The Competence Gap

Although it is undoubtedly true that Goodwin and his lead attorney on the
Massey case, Steve Ruby, have learned a good deal about the mining industry
from their cases, it is hard to imagine that they have either the expertise or the
time to conduct the monitoring necessary to ensure that Alpha lives up to the
terms of its agreement. The U.S. Attorney's office is responsible for the full
panoply of federal enforcement throughout the state and, like most of his
counterparts across the country, spends a significant amount of its time
prosecuting drug offenses. The office carries a full caseload and does not
have a staff of inspectors who can visit Alpha facilities to verify the information
presented in the corporation's compliance report. Goodwin and Ruby also
have a substantial incentive to declare victory after a settlement of the size and
scope of their deal with Alpha.

The Price of Cooperation

A major condition commonly included in DPA and non-prosecution agreements is that the defendant corporation must agree to future "cooperation"
with the government. What this euphemism means as a practical matter is that
corporations are obligated to help the government build cases against their
individual executives. With one group of executives in effect encouraged to
document the malfeasance of another, protection of individual rights against
self-incrimination can be quickly compromised.

---

[61] Ken Ward, *Goodwin Praises Alpha for "Great Strides" Addressing Problems it Inherited from*
Massey Energy, COAL TATTOO (June 15, 2012), http://blogs.wvgazette.com/coaltattoo/2012/06/
18/goodwin-praises-alpha-for-great-strides-addressing-systemic-problems-it-inherited-from-mas
sey-energy/.

[62] *Id.* (emphasis added)

Disparate Treatment

Professor Brandon Garrett reports that small firms are far more likely to sign traditional criminal settlements than large ones.[63] This conclusion makes logical sense. If a leading motivation for adoption of such agreements is really the fear of putting a company out of business, this purely economic concern is exacerbated the larger the company and would motivate more strenuous prosecutorial efforts to craft a DPA. But the disparate treatment makes little if any sense from the perspective of what a criminal justice system is supposed to accomplish – namely fitting the punishment to the magnitude and severity of the crime.

CONCLUSION

Delayed and incomplete prosecutions substantially undermine the deterrent effect of the criminal law. These outcomes are weakened to an intolerable extent by DPAs. As troubling, the DOJ's strong and fundamentally misguided preference for this kind of agreement in corporate criminal cases has the effect of further distorting its policies. Corporations are guilty of crimes because they stand in a position of responsibility – in legalese, *respondeat superior* – for the acts of their individual employees. If a group of employees commits crimes, and the crimes benefit the corporation, it is liable. Yet if the DOJ is so phobic about charging corporations with crimes because it fears they will go out of business, it seems reasonable to wonder how aggressive it will be in charging individuals, especially those higher up in the corporate hierarchy.

In fact, DPAs allow the DOJ to collect enormous sums of money from large corporations that seem not to mind forking over these amounts as a cost of doing business, but resist acknowledging culpability for the harm they have caused. DOJ policymakers would respond that such agreements include corporate reforms that accomplish momentous changes in the way the companies think about compliance. This goal, of course, is synonymous with the mission of a regulatory system that is full of alarming holes. Is it a desirable state of affairs for career criminal prosecutors, even if they are working closely with regulatory experts, to purport to reform large corporations one by one? And when they do undertake such overhauls, can we be confident that prosecutors have the wherewithal to make the terms of the agreement stick?

---

[63] For his findings, *see* Brandon Garrett, *Structural Reform Prosecution*, 93 VA. L. REV. 853 (2007).

One unacknowledged consequence of the DOJ's preoccupation with this approach deserves emphasis: that is, its impact on the mind-set of the prosecutors. What are the implications of all those economists filing into DOJ conference rooms attempting to convince prosecutors that they have the power – thumbs up or thumbs down – to decide if a multi-billion-dollar corporation lives or dies, regardless of what they believe about their criminal culpability *per se*? For a moment, consider the answer to that question in the context of charging individuals with street crimes. Prosecutors must retain the discretion to decide whether to charge such defendants because they may not have adequate evidence or because they lack the resources to see the case through. For precisely these reasons, a bedrock principle of American and English jurisprudence is that decisions not to prosecute are immune from judicial review.[64] When prosecutors make these choices, though, they operate on a binary axis. Either they believe the person is guilty or innocent and they think they do – or do not – have the evidence to prove it. They do not contemplate whether, if defendants are guilty and prosecutors can prove cases against them, defendants should have opportunities to explain what the unforeseen consequences for the larger society might be if they are sent to jail.

When prosecutors become confused about their role in society, in their own minds and for public consumption or when they consult with economists who claim they are able to predict whether a criminal conviction will drive a giant firm out of business, they morph into policymakers determining the future rather than police ensuring consequences for the past. Conservatives are right to be discomfited, although they are wrong about the power dynamic. Many corporate counsel are undoubtedly laughing all the way back to the bank.

---

[64] *See, e.g.,* Heckler v. Chaney, 470 U.S. 821 (1985) (holding that there is presumption of unreviewability of decisions of agencies not to undertake enforcement action, and stating that "[t]his Court has recognized on several occasions over many years that an agency's decision not to prosecute or enforce, whether through civil or criminal process, is a decision generally committed to an agency's absolute discretion. This recognition of the existence of discretion is attributable in no small part to the general unsuitability for judicial review of agency decisions to refuse enforcement.") (citations omitted).

Index